This Great Allegory

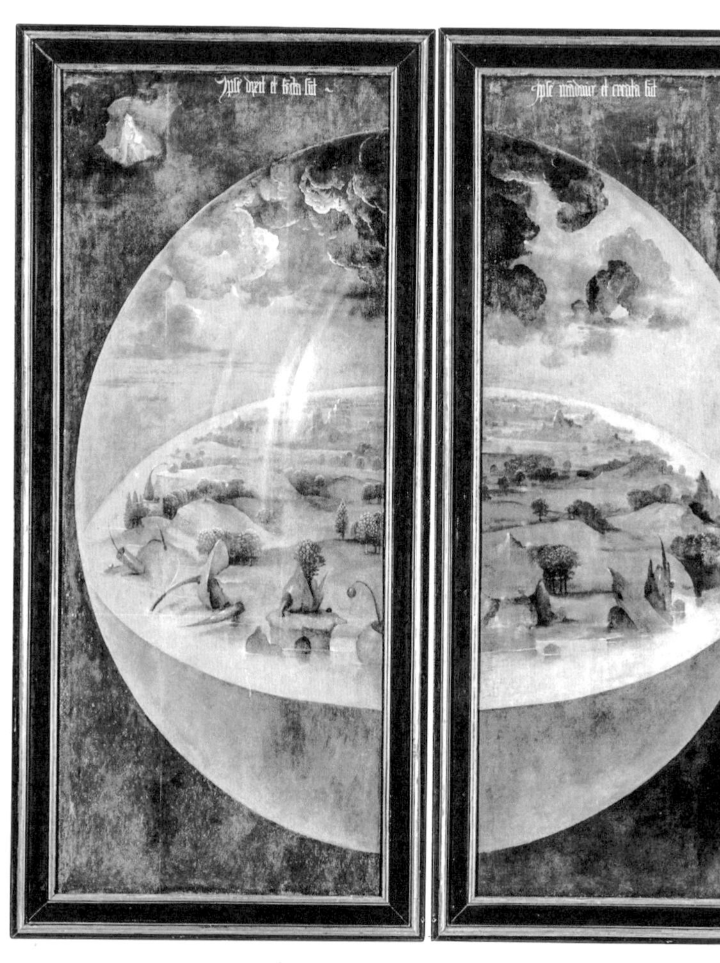

Hieronymus Bosch, *The Creation of the World*, late fifteenth century

This Great Allegory

On World-Decay and World-Opening in the Work of Art

Gerhard Richter

THE MIT PRESS

Cambridge, Massachusetts · London, England

Introduction: The Work of Art and the Notion of World

On November 17, 1851, shortly after the publication of *Moby-Dick*, Herman Melville writes in a letter to his friend Nathaniel Hawthorne: "Ever since Adam, who has got the meaning of this great allegory—the world?"[1] At stake in this rhetorical question is not only the status of any possible meaning of the world (how could one possibly understand it?), but also the idea of the world as such, the world *as* world. Having completed his deeply allegorical novel about the notion of a world and about the relation or nonrelation among different worlds—a novel that seems to ask at every turn what it means to inhabit any one world—Melville appears to know less and less what "world" means the more he thinks and writes about it. What is the meaning of "world"? What is *a* world? What is *the* world? If the meaning of "world" emerges as elusive—appearing only in its withdrawal while perpetually calling itself into question—such elusiveness is not a recent invention. According to Melville's understanding, the world's resistance to meaning, along with the fleeting nature of what it signifies, can be traced all the way back to Adam, the first man. The world is indeed an *ur*-question whose legacy has been handed down to every heir of Adam and thus to everyone who has a father: "Ever since Adam, who has got the meaning of this great allegory—the world?"

It is striking that Melville deems the world a "great allegory," for it is by no means self-evident that any one particular rhetorical figure could more appropriately designate the world than another. Still, the world here is neither a symbol nor a synecdoche, neither a metonymy nor a parable, neither metaphor nor simile. It is, precisely, an allegory, for reasons that Melville does not make explicit. Allegory derives from the Greek *allegorein*, meaning to speak otherwise, to say something differently. If the world is an allegory, perhaps it is because it never simply speaks in self-identical terms, nor yields to a referential pull. To the extent that the world speaks to us at all, it addresses us *differently*, seeming to say one thing while saying something else. The world, in turn, demands that we address it differently as well, that is, with a capacity for speaking, reading, and interpreting *otherwise*. This is especially the case with regard to the so-called experiences we have and create in the world, since our experiences—especially those we consider significant or decisive at any one moment—have a way of not remaining what they are, as their meanings seem to shift over the span of our lifetime. What will have meant one thing in the experience of our world—perhaps a moment of great joy or sorrow, a blossoming relationship or its painful termination, a life-path taken or refused—turns out to mean something that we were incapable of understanding before. We can therefore only approach the world and our experience of it through the movement of allegory and its deferral of meaning. Given that the world presents itself to us in the mode of allegory, we are called upon to read it incessantly, compelled to interpret it always one more time, scrutinizing its apparently uncontainable dissemination of signification with ever-renewed attention and critical vigilance.

Pondering who "ever since Adam" has been able to accomplish the task, Melville asks, "who has got the meaning of this great allegory—the world?" Does his rhetorical question imply that there have, in fact, been human beings who have succeeded in "getting" the meaning of the world as allegory? If so, we would need to read his question literally, in order to provide specific answers to the question posed by the "who." Or ought we rather read the question rhetorically, as if its "who" were designed to elicit no response, no certain human being nor proper name at all, but rather merely "no one"? According to what measuring stick might we ascertain whether Melville's question is to be taken literally or figuratively? One could even go one step further and wonder whether the question irreducibly insists on both its literal and figurative dimensions. If that were the case, how would this simultaneity inflect the ways in which we approach the idea of "world"—and the notion of human beings "ever since Adam" attempting to relate to this world? Would we, like Adam and his partner Eve, be expelled from our world, pushed into another realm whose radically different parameters we must spend a lifetime attempting to understand?

If Melville wonders "who has got the meaning of this great allegory—the world," what precisely does "getting" mean? Does it pertain exclusively to a mode of understanding (as in "I get it"), that is, a hermeneutic problem to be solved by means of astute analysis? In that case, "getting" would designate a mode of conceptual grasping, the way that one grasps a concept, as the German word for concept, *Begriff*—which refers to "what is grasped," or, literally, that which is be-grasped (*be-griffen*) in the form of comprehension—makes palpable. But the "getting" in "who has got the meaning of this great allegory—the world" also resonates on a different level. "To get" here may also imply the idea of a possession, the way one comes to claim ownership over something that one has acquired. Melville's question could then be read as pertaining to the status of possession, ownership, or proprietorship with regard to the meaning of the world. Yet who or what could claim such ownership? Who or what "has got" the world's meaning as a matter of possession, and who could thus claim to be in a position in which freely to reign over this allegedly achieved and possessed knowledge—the way, perhaps, one acquires, and subsequently enjoys sovereign jurisdiction over, a piece of land? Perhaps the meaning of the world, that is, the "meaning of this great allegory," resists ownership, refusing to play its part as a tool in the service of this or that form of instrumental reason.

If the concept of world and its possible meanings are to be negotiated on the allegorical level, then Melville's rhetorical question also implies that they are best confronted within, and through, the work of art. Melville himself, of course, engaged with the problem of worlds and their meaning through the literary and poetic acts that constitute his remarkable oeuvre, and it is hardly an accident that his question pertaining to the meaning of the world and its allegorical inscriptions imposes itself on him in the immediate aftermath of publishing his great novel. Nor is it a coincidence that Melville's question is addressed, if only rhetorically, to another writer, Hawthorne, whose poetic preoccupations display a certain hospitality, perhaps even spectral kinship, toward Melville's reflections on world. It is as though Melville, in addressing his fellow writer, wished implicitly to add yet another layer of meaning onto the question of "who has got the meaning of this great allegory the world?" by implying that the "who" is the artist who confronts the allegories of the world and its meanings in the realm of the aesthetic. Perhaps, then, it is the writer and, by extension, the artist more generally—who, in and through his aesthetic production, can most effectively engage the allegory of world and the modes of reading and interpretation that it elicits. In that case, the question as to what a world is, what it means, and what it calls forth may best be negotiated in relation to the artwork. Viewed from this perspective, the work of art, literary or otherwise, is not a mere repository of achieved meaning, a catalog of stable knowledge, or an archive of self-identical insights about the world, but rather the very site of *poiesis* upon which some of the most vexing and abiding questions with regard to our understanding and experience of world *as* world are brought to the fore.

It is fitting to begin with Melville as we launch our exploration of world in relation to the work of art because, as the pages of this book wish to suggest, it is precisely in and through the work of art that seminal elements of the thinking of world as world are negotiated in the most essential and moving ways. This book, then, concerns the notion of world in relation to, and as an effect of, the work of art, broadly conceived as an aesthetic object or as an aesthetic performance that self-reflexively thematizes its own form. At stake is the relationship between two different kinds of world: the world in which an artwork was first created and which, over time, has perished or decayed beyond hermeneutic accessibility and interpretive understanding; and the world that is projected by the artwork itself, in other words, the world that comes into being as the function of a certain *poiesis*, the act of making or creating through which the artwork sets up a singular and irreducibly unique world. The multiple relations between these two worlds are examined here in a number of seminal thinkers (among them Karl Marx, Martin Heidegger, Maurice Blanchot, Georges Bataille, Emmanuel Levinas, Theodor W. Adorno, Walter Benjamin, and Jacques Derrida), and in various—sometimes competing—modes of aesthetic production, including poetry, painting, music, film, literature, and photography.

Our investigation will focus on how individual works, each in its own idiomatic way, meditate on their relation to the aesthetically mediated idea of world—both *a* world and *the* world, that is, world *as* world. Each work that comes into view here addresses, from a singular and ever-shifting perspective, its own incessant stagings of world as world. This is the case even when a work does not contain an image of the world in a classical sense, that is, when it does not explicitly depict the worldness of the world in the way in which, for instance, Hieronymus Bosch's oil painting *The Creation of the World* portrays it in the late fifteenth century. Bosch's Early Netherlandish grisaille painting, now in the collection of the Museo Nacional del Prado in Madrid, which forms the exterior panel wings of his triptych *The Garden of Earthly Delights*, becomes visible when the wings are closed. The painting depicts the transitional time in which a nascent, almost translucent world is slowly forming, quite possibly on the third day of creation, when land, sea, and plants are brought into worldly existence. Here, an aesthetically mediated world literally and figuratively emerges onto a subsequent world (the one that unfolds on the inside of the triptych) in which the ecstasies of human life, but also its dark underbelly of suffering, are fully on display. In much the same way as the biblical narrative of the creation of the world gives rise to the complex scenes of life depicted in the inner triptych, the physical and intellectual act of opening up an aesthetically constructed world invites the viewer to contemplate the nuanced and irreducible complexity of human life as it comes to pass in the world as world. A triple world-allegory is at work here, even as the Renaissance world out of which Bosch's painting arose has vanished for good. The allegorical depiction of the world embedded in the biblical creation story opens onto the allegorical scenes of human life and its conditions staged on the inside of the triptych in a manner that is itself allegorical by way of the figurativity that is germane to a work of art. Through its triple allegory, Bosch's painting thus evokes an immediate aesthetic engagement with the worldness of world that other artworks seem to approach in a more partial or indirect manner. Whether engaging the idea of world-decay and world-opening from an aesthetic perspective such as Bosch's that appears more referential and direct, or casting a more ancillary light on the two worlds, the works that are the focus of this study challenge us, each in its unique aesthetic way, to revisit the question of what we mean by "world"—and its attendant dialectic of decay and opening in the artistic artifact—always one more time.

From its prehistory, the concept of world has designated a meaningfully structured totality that is determinably separate from other spheres and that implicitly or explicitly provides the contextual framework for experiencing and negotiating that which is. Both the English word "world" and the German *Welt* are akin to the Gothic *wer-alt*, which means "human age" or "human seed or sowing," which in turn translates the Greek *aeon* (αἰών) as well as the Latin *mundus*.[2] While Greek originally had no special word to designate what later came to be referred to as "world," in the fifth century BCE the term *kósmos* began to designate the wholeness of both universe and world.[3] "In classical Greece," as Sean Gaston points out, "*kósmos* had a number of varied meanings, including ornament or decoration, but was broadly defined as an ordering or arrangement that referred at times to the universe and at other times to the world." In effect, the Greek term designates "an *ordered whole* or a world that is ordered and contained by the universe," as becomes evident, for instance, in Plato's *Gorgias*.[4] While the philosophical, theological, and political notion of world is of prime concern for Western thought from Plato and Aristotle all the way to Kant, Schelling, Hegel, Schopenhauer, Nietzsche, Marx, Husserl, Arendt, and beyond, it suffuses the work of no other modern thinker quite as relentlessly and as persistently as that of Heidegger. "World" (*Welt*) is a central issue as early as his magnum opus *Being and Time* (1927), traverses a number of his mid-period texts and lecture courses, including, prominently, "The Origin of the Work of Art," and plays a decisive role in his later investigations of the question concerning technology, the role of humanism in the history of metaphysics, the relation between building, thinking, and dwelling, and the place and path of art, poetry, and sculpture in elucidating the ontological difference (that is, the difference between *das Sein* and *das Seiende*, Being as such and beings as they occur and come to pass). *Welt*, world, does not mean one single thing in Heidegger's variegated corpus, even as the concept traverses that corpus at every turn. Rather, world comes to designate a number of interrelated concerns that are illuminated each time in a unique, differently modulated manner. It is as if "world" in Heidegger deserves to take its place next to the other major terms that preoccupy his work in its entirety, and that his thinking will have taught us forever to hear and think differently and in sheer infinite permutations: Being, time, and death.

6

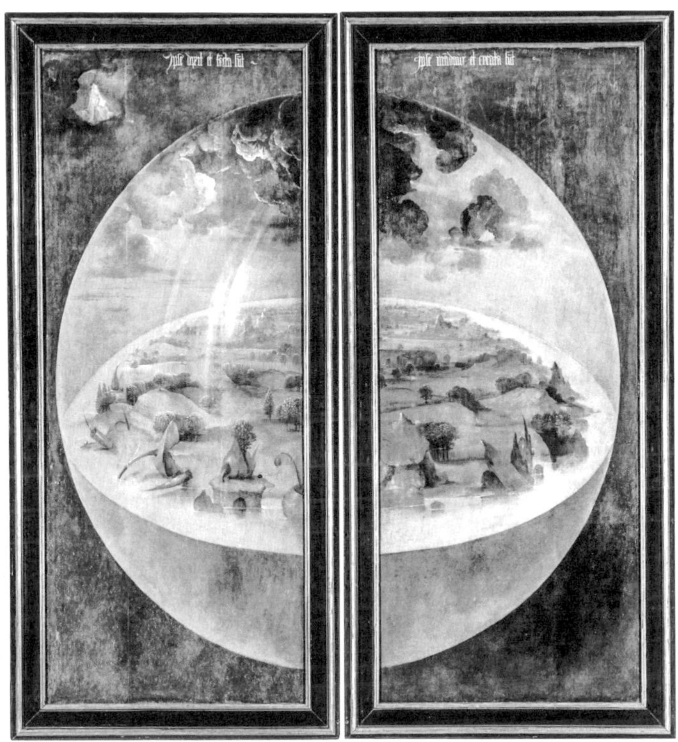

Hieronymus Bosch, *The Creation of the World*, oil painting, late fifteenth century, Museo Nacional del Prado, Madrid.

Heidegger's 1929–1930 Freiburg lecture course, *The Fundamental Concepts of Metaphysics: World, Finitude, Solitude* (*Grundbegriffe der Metaphysik. Welt, Endlichkeit, Einsamkeit*), devotes itself to the patient, ruminative explication of the three concepts indicated in its subtitle, along the way focusing on related issues such as the history of metaphysics, the disclosive properties of boredom, the human-animal distinction, as well as the link between metaphysical thought and the precepts of experimental biology. Early on in the course, he frames his inquiry into the problem of world by quoting the German romantic poet Novalis. Heidegger says:

Philosophy—an ultimate pronouncement and interlocution on the part of man that constantly permeates him in his entirety. Yet what is man, that he philosophizes in the ground of his essence, and what is this philosophizing? What are we in this? Where do we want to go? Did we once just stumble into the universe by chance? Novalis on one occasion says in a fragment: "Philosophy is really homesickness, an urge to be at home everywhere." A strange definition, romantic of course. Homesickness— does such a thing still exist today at all? Has it not become an incomprehensible word, even in everyday life? Has not contemporary city man, the ape of civilization, long since eradicated homesickness? And homesickness as the very determination of philosophy! But, above all, what sort of witness are we presenting here with regard to philosophy? Novalis—merely a poet, after all, and hardly a scholarly philosopher. Does not Aristotle say in his *Metaphysics*: πολλὰ ψεύδονται ἀοιδοί: Poets tell many a lie?

Yet without provoking an argument over the authority and significance of this witness, let us merely recall that art—which includes poetry too—is the sister of philosophy and that all science is perhaps only a servant with respect to philosophy.

Let us remain with the issue and ask: What is all this talk about philosophy as homesickness? Novalis himself elucidates: "an urge to be everywhere at home." Philosophy can only be such an urge if we who philosophize are *not* at

home everywhere. What is demanded by this urge? To be
at home everywhere—what does that mean? Not merely
here or there, nor even simply in every place, in all places
taken together one after the other. Rather, to be at home
everywhere means to be at once and at all times within the
whole. We name this "within the whole" and its character of
wholeness the *world*. We are, and to the extent that we are, we
are always waiting for something. We are always called upon
by something as a whole. This "as a whole" is the world.

We are asking: *What is that—world?* [*Wir fragen*: Was ist
das—Welt?][5]

By approaching the question of world as the question of philosophical thought as such, and taking recourse to Novalis, a poet
associated with German romanticism, Heidegger links the concept
of world to a concern with being at home and with finding oneself
homeless, with the longing for a localizable place that may forever
remain out of reach. There is, then, a question of a Dasein, a being
in the world that opens itself to its ownmost possibility and thus
relates to dwelling "within the whole," even the wholeness of the
whole as such. Indeed, it is precisely the wholeness of the whole,
the nature of the whole *as* whole, that can be named "world." For
Heidegger, the human being is always waiting for something; he is
the one who waits—and the one who waits, precisely, for the whole
as world, and for the world as the whole. To wait here designates
not a passive act, no mere submission to the duration and elapsing
of time; it is, rather, an active waiting, an ontological form of waiting, in which what is awaited is the whole and the experience of
the whole, which is to say, the world. The human being is waiting
to receive the call of the whole, the whole of the world as world. To
the extent that what the human being is called upon to await is the
whole as such, which is to say the world, it is through an interrogation of this call that an inquiry into the concept of world must
proceed. This is precisely the framework in which the question
that will never leave Heidegger can begin to be articulated: What
is that—world? *Was ist das—Welt?*

In beginning to formulate this question, Heidegger enters a dialogue with Novalis, a writer rather than a philosopher. Suspending

the suspicion with which philosophical discourse has, ever since its ancient Greek foundation, viewed a poet's words, he brings philosophy and poetry, logic and rhetoric, into relation. Refusing to erase the difference between philosophy and poetry, even when he focuses his thinking on poetic texts by such writers as Novalis, Hölderlin, Schiller, Rilke, Stefan George, Trakl, Celan, and others, Heidegger insists that the relationship between the philosophical and the poetic can only yield a fruitful harvest if and when their difference is affirmed in the experience of thought itself—that is, in Heidegger's view, precisely when the two become visible as "sisters." When it comes to the concept of world, then, we cannot do without Novalis and his poetic insistence on thinking philosophy itself as a homesickness or a desire to be at home everywhere—which is to say, in the wholeness of the whole that one might call world.

Over the span of the lecture course, Heidegger patiently investigates the concept of world from a variety of shifting angles, sometimes addressing it directly, at other times shedding indirect light on it, as when his main focus is on such questions as duration, boredom, or solitude. It is as if Heidegger were continually preparing thought for the experience of world, rather than determining once and for all what world is. One might say that this perpetual preparation does not constitute a mere failure to deliver a finished thought-product so much as it stages, and affirms in its staging, the fundamentally preparatory nature of all genuine thinking, which is not concerned with "forcibly bringing about a transformation of our Dasein or effecting it in any sense, but only ever preparing it—which is all that philosophy can do."[6] For Heidegger, such preparatory thinking also must come to terms with the idea of a world-forming impulse as it works its way through Dasein, in which the world in its essence emerges as a certain "prevailing" (*Walten*). It is through such investigations of Dasein's efforts at world-formation that the "phenomenon of world" exhibits itself in terms of a "world as manifestness of beings as such as a whole" (terms that, at the end of the lecture course, implicitly return to Novalis's concern with which the course began).[7] Among other things, what this emphasis on Dasein's world-formation reveals is that "the philosophical tradition unknowingly treats—under the title of λόγος, of ratio, of reason—what we are seeking to unfold as the problem of world." Adding a genealogical dimension to this conceptual dissimulation of world, Heidegger remarks that up to "the present day, the problem has remained unrecognizable for us in its disguises, because these titles and what is dealt with under them have long since been taken as extrinsic questions, and can be freed from their concealment only with difficulty." By the same token, we "will learn from history only if we first awaken it and keep it so. The fact that we are incapable of learning anything from history anymore says only that we ourselves have become ahistorical. No period has known such an influx of tradition, and none has been so poor in genuine tradition. Λόγος, ratio, reason, spirit—all these titles are disguises for the problem of world."[8] To confront the thinking of world, then, what is needed is to strip away all the historical guises that have obscured our view onto it—not in a gesture of ahistorical erasure, but rather in a manner that carefully learns precisely from the history of that which is being undone. One might say that this gesture of laying bare a thinking of world through its disaggregation from such concepts as λόγος, ratio, reason, and spirit, which have structured the history of metaphysics in a profound and fateful way, performs the movement of *Abbau* or *Destruktion* (as a careful de-structuring) that *Being and Time* had identified as a prime task for thinking vis-à-vis metaphysics itself.

If what Heidegger calls the unfolding of the problem of world is to be fruitful, it must occasion a certain awakening. He speaks of the necessity of "awakening a fundamental attunement of our Dasein, which is to say, in each case transforming the humanity of us human beings into the Da-sein in ourselves," in a gesture of thought that exposes the precise contours of the problem of world.[9] It is the world-forming dimensions of Dasein as it opens onto Being through an openness toward that casts the thinking of world into sharp relief. This thinking of world cannot be separated from a consideration of its modes of prevailing, and this prevailing is of an originary or primordial nature, whose apprehension and experience we must always already have awaited in order to be receptive to it. "All observation," Heidegger avers, "of whatever kind must remain eternally distant from what *world* is, insofar as its essence resides in what we call the prevailing of world, a prevailing that is more originary than all those beings that press themselves upon us." It is through our fundamental attunement and through our active waiting-for that we relate to the occurrence of this prevailing of world as world. For Heidegger, the "philosophizing entry and return of man into the Dasein in him can only ever be prepared, never effected. Awakening is a matter for each individual human being, not a matter of his or her good will or skillfulness, but of his or her destiny, whatever falls or does not fall to him or her. Everything that contingently falls upon us, however, only falls and falls due to us if we have waited for it and are able to wait. Only whoever honors a mystery gains the strength to wait."[10] To wait in an active manner with regard to our apprehension of the prevailing of world also means to be open to the fundamental mystery that this world is. Being capable of opening up to the prevailing of world as world means being capable of waiting attentively, and preparing diligently, for the thought of this occurrence.

An especially relevant territory of thought for the preparatory waiting in thought for the occurrence of world as prevailing is the ontological distinction itself. When Heidegger differentiates between Being and beings, *das Sein* and *das Seiende*, the "difficulty does not lie in first determining the *kind* of distinction" that is made, but rather in the fact that "we are already unsure and at a loss to begin with" precisely "when we wish merely to attain the field or *dimension* in which to make the distinction." This is so because "this dimension is not to be found among beings," as "Being is not some being among others" and we consequently "do not know where to accommodate it." What is more, according to Heidegger, "if the two are fundamentally different, then nevertheless they are still *related to one another in this distinction*: the bridge between the two is the 'and.' Thus this distinction as a whole is in essence a *completely obscure distinction*." Yet it is precisely this very obscurity that gives rise to the possibility of a disclosure, as long as a thinking prepares itself for the reception of this obscurity. "Only if we endure this obscurity [*Nur wenn wir dieses Dunkel aushalten*]," Heidegger thus argues, "will we become sensitive to what is problematic, and thereby reach a position from which we can develop the central problem inherent in this distinction and thus comprehend *the problem of world* [*wodurch wir das* Weltproblem *begreifen*]."[11]

How we relate in our thinking to the "and" that in turn relates the thought of Being to that of beings in the ontological difference is of primary significance if we wish to learn how to read the problem of world as such. From Heidegger's perspective, world cannot be thought without a patient and sustained meditation on what still relates Being and beings in a world in which the two are at odds with each other, and in which one can be explained neither in the absence of the other nor by means of the other. It is as if to think world means learning to respect and honor, in a thinking manner, the obscurity that names the relation between Being and beings, that is, to allow this obscurity of world to prevail—to let it be. This letting the world be may be thought as one of the ways in which Dasein is capable of actively honoring the sense in which, as Heidegger will say in such later texts from the mid-1930s as *Introduction to Metaphysics* and "The Origin of the Work of Art," "*die Welt weltet*," "the world worlds"—meaning that the world is never merely some objective and already formed space out there that stands before us but rather that it names the realm in which we find ourselves, from birth to death, confronting the openness of Being in the finitude of our Dasein.

Heidegger's engagement with the idea of world here also deserves to be read in relation to his remarks, in *Being and Time*, concerning the problem of what in the metaphysical tradition of philosophy is called "die Außenwelt," or the external world. In the course of section 43 of *Being and Time*, devoted to "Dasein, Worldhood, and Reality [*Dasein, Weltlichkeit und Realität*]," Heidegger references Kant's observation that final proof for the existence of a so-called external world is still missing. Quoting Kant from the preface to the second edition of the *Critique of Pure Reason*, Heidegger points out: "Kant calls it 'a scandal of philosophy and of human reason in general' [*einen Skandal der Philosophie und all gemeinen Menschenvernunft*] that there is still no cogent proof for the 'Dasein of Things outside of us' which will do away with any skepticism. He proposes such a proof himself."[12] To remedy the situation, philosophical thought would have to concern itself first and foremost with proving the existence of a so-called external world. But Heidegger parts ways with Kant, turning his attention to a different philosophical scandal instead.

The "scandal of philosophy" is not that this proof has yet to be given [*bislang noch aussteht*], but that *such proofs are attempted again and again* [*darin, daß solche Beweise immer wieder erwartet und versucht werden*]. Such expectations, aims, and demands arise from an ontologically inadequate way of starting with *something* of such a character that independently *of it* and "outside" *of it* a "world" is to be proved as present-at-hand. It is not that the proofs are inadequate, but that the kind of Being of the entity which does the proving and makes requests for proofs has *not been made definite enough*. This is why a demonstration that two things which are present-at-hand are necessarily present-at-hand together [*Nachweis des notwendigen Zusammenvorhandenseins zweier Vorhandener*], can give rise to the illusion that something has been proved, or even can be proved, about Dasein as Being-in-the-World. If Dasein is understood correctly, it defies such proofs, because, in its Being, it already *is* what subsequent proofs deem necessary to demonstrate for it [*weil es in seinem Sein je schon ist, was nachkommende Beweise ihm erst anzudemonstrieren für notwendig halten*].[13]

Unlike Kant, Heidegger views Dasein as a being-in-the-world that is presupposed by the modes of its dwelling—always already and precisely—within a putative world. Kant aims to remedy a certain psychological idealism that demands the existence of an external world whose objects, by virtue of a demand that is unacceptable to Kant, must be accepted on faith alone; whereas Heidegger's path of thinking leads him to engage with a world that no longer is required to assuage the demands of philosophical skepticism. Instead, he affirms, throughout *Being and Time* as well as later reflections, Dasein's persistent sense of a world in withdrawal, a perishing world that refuses to yield simply to calculative or mathematical modes of explanation and logical manipulation. If the scandal of philosophy, in Heidegger's view, is the ceaseless metaphysical demand for world-transparency in the form of an ontically secured presence, his thinking, by contrast, locates Dasein within a world that is always already in withdrawal and decay. It is this perpetual retreat of world that renders it not only a locus of ontological *Sorge*, that is, of abiding care and concern, but also one of enduring *Unheimlichkeit*, or uncanniness, a place in which Dasein is never comfortably at home. In this opaque world, the Dasein that dwells within it is called upon to confront its own ontological *Angst*, its mood and mode of anxiety and unsettledness. Engaging with this world of *Angst*, rather than futilely attempting to furnish this or that proof of the so-called external world as such, is precisely the comportment of thought that Heidegger's sense of "world" demands. And the work of art, especially for the later Heidegger, is the prime space in which this anxious and nontransparent relation to the world can be negotiated.

*

In the final seminar before his death, given in 2002–2003 and entitled, like the first part of the seminar held the year before, *The Beast and the Sovereign*, Derrida turns his attention to two books that revolve around the concept of world, Daniel Defoe's 1719 novel *Robinson Crusoe* and Heidegger's lecture course *The Fundamental Concepts of Metaphysics*. Commenting on these two documents at length over a period of four months, the seminar interweaves the two unlikely textual companions in far-reaching meditations that gather a number of the core concerns that had preoccupied the late phase of Derrida's thinking in particular. Among other themes, the seminar challenges Heidegger's ontological distinctions between human and nonhuman animals (issues that Derrida also had taken up in such other late texts as *The Animal That Therefore I Am*); it examines questions of sovereignty in relation to issues of animality; it turns its attention to Heidegger's conception of prevailing and violence (*Walten* and *Gewalt*); and it examines the relationship between the idea of an end of the world and ethical and political questions, especially as these made themselves felt, even imposed themselves, through the politics of the day, particularly in the wake of 9/11 and the subsequent acts of war and violence. But perhaps above anything else, Derrida focuses in his final seminar on questions pertaining to "world" and its thinkability, engaging in an infinite dialogue with Heidegger's own preoccupation with world. In a remark from the first session, held on

December 11, 2002, the fundamental orientation or disposition
of Derrida's reading of Heidegger's notion of world and worlding
strikingly comes to the fore. There, he suggests that "neither animals of different species, nor humans of different cultures, nor any
animal or human individual inhabit the same world as another,
however close and similar these living individuals may be," so
that the "difference between one world and another will remain
always unbridgeable." This is so, Derrida explains, "because the
community of the world is always constructed, simulated by a set
of stabilizing apparatuses, more or less stable ... and never natural, language in the broad sense, codes of traces being designed,
among all living beings, to construct a unity of the world that is
always deconstructible, nowhere and never given in nature."[14] And
he continues:

> Between my world, the "my world," what I call "my world"—
> and there is no other for me, as any other world is part of
> it—between my world and any other world there is first the
> space and the time of an infinite difference, an interruption
> that is incommensurable with all attempts to make a pas-
> sage, a bridge, an isthmus, all attempts at communication,
> translation, trope, and transfer that the desire for a world
> or the want of a world, the being wanting a world will try to
> pose, impose, propose, stabilize. There is no world, there are
> only islands.[15]

Whereas for Heidegger the notion of world tends to be the realm
of a gathering, a space in which an encounter with the wholeness
of the whole first becomes thinkable, for Derrida such gathering
and wholeness are foreclosed owing to the irreducible difference
that traverses, each time a being refers to or has an experience
related to, what each being calls "my world." There is no unity, no
shared regularity to this world, even as it is stabilized or propped
up as world by various epistemic, cultural, ideological, political,
or religious functions. While those who insist on having or inhabiting a world will work to construct or support such worldness,
world is irreducibly in deconstruction, at odds with itself, revolv-
ing around its own singularities and modes of difference, so that

there is a fundamental gulf among the living beings who can be said to inhabit something like a world. If for Derrida there is no world, only islands—as if we were all Robinsons stranded on some faraway island—this is because the absolute alterity that forever separates us from others—the other others, to whom we are nevertheless related, but only by being an other ourselves—cordons off what we call our world from those of others. There is no shared world, no gathering into a wholeness, but ultimately only the solitude of the island. Like Robinson, we must learn to live on this island, to make our war and peace with it, to carry it and to allow ourselves to be carried by it.

In the seminar session, Derrida adds a remark that ties his reflections on worlds and islands to a German-language poet to whose poetry he returns on multiple occasions and in a variety of thematic contexts throughout his oeuvre, Paul Celan. Celan, whose work also was of significance to Heidegger and whose poetry in turn is suffused by his own studies of Heidegger, functions in Derrida's seminar as something of a counterpart to Heidegger's invocation of Novalis in the 1929–1930 lecture course. While Novalis in his poetic understanding of philosophy emphasizes homesickness and the unfulfillable desire to be at home everywhere—that is, one might say, in the world, and anywhere and everywhere within that world—Celan fastens upon a world that has perished. As Derrida remarks in connection with Celan's poem "Große, glühende Wölbung" from the collection *Atemwende*: "This is one of the thousand directions in which I would be <tempted> to interpret the last line of a short and great poem by Celan: 'Die Welt ist fort, ich muß dich tragen,' a poem of mourning or birth." On the one hand, a mourning is called into presence, because the world has perished; on the other hand, a birth is insinuated through the figure of a self carrying or bearing the other within. In Celan's poem, "the world has gone, the world has gone away, the world is far off, the world is lost, there is no world any more (to sustain us or ground [*fonder*] the two of us like a ground [*sol*]), I must carry you (either in me as in mourning, or else in me as in birth, for *tragen* is also said of the mother carrying a child, in her arms or in her womb)." Here, "we are *weltlos*, I can only carry you, I am the only one who can and must carry you, etc.; but are we *weltlos*, without world, as Heidegger says of the stone and the material thing that they are *weltlos*?—clearly not. So how are we to think the absence of the world, the non-world?"[16] If Derrida here returns, in his final seminar, to Celan's line "Die Welt ist fort, ich muß dich tragen"—a line to which he had already devoted extensive commentary in previous works, including, among others, *The Work of Mourning*, "Rams: Uninterrupted Dialogue—Between Two Infinities, the Poem," and *Rogues: Two Essays on Reason*—it is not merely with something like an intuition of his own imminent passing, of his own world perishing, but it is also to reaffirm the difficulty and continued significance of one of the fundamental questions that preoccupy him in so much of his later work: What does it mean to inhabit a world if we must contend with the possibility that there is no world, that the world is, as in Celan's poem, forever and irretrievably "*fort*"?

In "Rams," his extended meditation on Celan's line, Derrida underscores the sense in which inhabiting a world with an other means to be alone in the world, as if living on an island under an open and unfathomable sky. He writes:

> No world can any longer support us, serve as mediation, as ground, as earth, as foundation or as alibi. Perhaps there is no longer anything but the abyssal altitude of a sky. I am alone in the world right where there is no longer any world. Or again: I am alone in the world as soon as I owe myself to you, as soon as you depend on me, as soon as I bear, and must assume, head to head or face to face, without third, mediator, or go-between, without earthly or worldly ground, the responsibility for which I must respond in front of you for you. I am alone with you, alone to you alone; we are alone; this declaration is also an engagement.[17]

Being alone in the world means being alone with the other; that is, being alone in a world means inhabiting a world that is not merely given and shared. With respect to Celan's evocative yet enigmatic line, Derrida inquires not only into the cognition of world without a world, a world that has absented itself; he also directs our attention to the pressing ethico-political responsibilities that a perished world places upon us with regard to the other. Even when the world is gone, we are not worldless—far from it, as Heidegger always will insist—and it is precisely the world in withdrawal or retreat, the world as something perishable and perishing, that calls upon us to carry or bear the other. Because the world is gone, the other must rely only on me to carry and bear him, to hold him and to shelter him, to stand in for a world that cannot sustain him. If the world is gone and I must carry you—"Die Welt ist fort, ich muß dich tragen"—this does not mean merely that I now come to stand in for the world, to serve as a substitute for a perished world. It means, rather, that the world is gone for me, just as it is for you, and that what we share, if we share anything at all, is not a world but only an absence. This absence is so fundamental that it cannot even be thought as a distant presence. In this radical absence of world, in the realm of this non-world, the space of absence that we share, I am called upon to carry and to bear you, to devote my care and attention to you, to be your worldless keeper across the abyss of alterity. The infinite alterity that forever separates us is thereby not overcome. If there is no world but only islands, still we cannot link these islands through bridges or ferries or other modes of connection and translation. And yet, precisely in the unconnectability of our islands, which exist in the absence of a unifying, gathering world, I must carry and bear you, most likely without quite knowing how. Here, the act of *tragen* itself constitutes the affirmation of an obligation that unfolds on the far side of world-comprehension and the transparent disclosure of a world saturated with meaning.

If Celan's line "Die Welt ist fort, ich muß Dich tragen" runs like a red thread through Derrida's engagement with Heidegger and Defoe in the course of his seminar, it emerges one more time in the tenth session—the final session of Derrida's final seminar—on March 26, 2003. There, Celan's words are modulated slightly differently by the analysis, this time with respect to its implied *as-if* structure, the requirement of a hypothetical world-projection. Derrida avers that "it seems to be *as if* we were behaving *as if* we were inhabiting the same world and speaking of the same thing and speaking the same language, when in fact we well know—at the point where the phantasm precisely comes up against its limit—that this is not true at all."[18] From this perspective, "if *Die Welt ist fort*, if we think we must carry the other, carry you, *ich muß dich tragen*," the imperative and its implications demand to be understood also in the light of this *as if* and the hypothetical modality that this *as if* imposes on our relation to (an absent) world. When understood through the logic of the *as if* structure, what emerges is an infinitely distant or absent world that requires its modes of bearing the other to carry the day. As Derrida argues,

> where there is no world, where the world is not here or there, but *fort*, infinitely distant over there, … what I must do, with you and carrying you, is make it that there be precisely a world, just a world, if not a just world, or to do things so as to make *as if* there were just a world, and to make the world come to the world, to make as if—for you, to give it to you, to bear it toward you, destined for you, to address it to you—I made the world come into the world, as though there ought to be a world where presently there is none, to make the gift or present of this *as if* come up poetically, which is the only thing that—during the finite time of such an impossible voyage between two non-shores where nothing happens— the only thing that can make it possible that I can live and have and let you live, enjoy or have you enjoy, to carry you for a few moments without anything happening and leaving a trace in the world, that belongs to the world, without a trace left or retained in the world that is going away, that will go away—which, before even going to go away, is going going away, leaving no trace, a world that has forever been going to leave and has just left, going away with no trace, the trace becoming trace only by being able to erase itself.[19]

If Derrida takes up Celan's lines over and over again, it is because he wishes to articulate the ways in which the concept of world is inflected by notions of mourning and melancholia, finitude, the absence or death of the other, survival, and responsibility. In and through the absence or death of the other, my relation to the world first becomes what it is. Indeed, to the extent that the other who is addressed in this line embodies the world for me—not just *a* specific, singular world, but *the* world as such, world as world—his death or absence signifies the end of the world. The end of the world, in other words, is predicated upon the finitude and mortality of the other, whom I must carry, bear, and mourn. The uneasy survival of the one who carries or bears the mortal other names two forms of mourning: the mourning that pertains to the other and his death—even in advance of his actual or empirical death—and the mourning that confronts the loss of world. With respect to this world-loss, at the end of the world, "the *ich muß* dich *tragen* addresses itself as much to the other as—reversing the direction of the apostrophe—to me, to the poet, to the signatory, or even to the poem itself or to the I who, carrying the other in itself, becomes the other at the moment that *Die Welt ist fort.*" In the double address that is directed both at the other and the self in the moment of the world's decay, we become fully mindful of "that end of the world that every death is."[20] The one who lives on, if there is one, is always the melancholy survivor of the end of the world. When seen from the perspective of the end of the world and the injunction to carry the other in the world's absence, the *Da* of Da-sein—the there of being-there—is always also a particular kind of *Fort*-sein, a mode of being gone.

Rather than follow Derrida's meditations on world-loss, death, survival, and responsibility along the most direct lines, we are particularly interested, for the purposes of the present study, in a seemingly minor addition that he makes to the text as he delivers it to his seminar. In the lengthy quotation cited above, following the statement "I made the world come into the world," Derrida, when reading this text aloud, verbally added the word "poetically," as his editors inform us in a footnote. This part of the long sentence thus states: "I made the world come into the world poetically, as though there ought to be a world where presently there is none." This adverb spontaneously added by Derrida, "poetically," is repeated a few words later, when the text reads "to make the gift or present of this *as if* come up poetically, which is the only thing that … can make it possible that I can live and have or let you live." Two "poetically" in short succession, then, with one having been supplemented for emphasis in the seminar session; two acts of poetic creation circulating through a world that is gone and now demands a special kind of comportment. What made Derrida insert this word when he delivered the text? What may have caused him to father it or place it into the world, *in die Welt zu setzen*, as one says in idiomatic German? What caused this *poiesis* of the poetical? It is interesting to note that he does not explicitly develop the notion of the poetic here or in what follows in this last session of his final seminar. Rather, he keeps the *poiesis* of the redoubled adverb "poetically" suspended in the realm of the apodictic and the allusive, implicitly calling upon us to inquire into the implications of its workings.

To create a world poetically implies, first of all, that the world, whatever and wherever it may be, still stands in need of making. This particular *as if* mode of the world demands an act of *poiesis*, in which the worldness of the world must first be brought into presence. One cannot act as though the world already existed, fully formed, ready, and waiting to be inhabited by beings. On the contrary, as Michael Naas aptly puts it, to "make the gift or present of this *as if* poetically would mean ... to live and act without the assumption that there *is* a world, without passing off a performative for a constative in order to sustain the phantasm of the world and our blind confidence in it." Rather, it "would be to make the world performatively—teleopoietically perhaps—from out of the void" or "to allow the world to be made, since this *poiesis* obviously could not be a performance or activity like any other." In other words, "this *poiesis* would be a making *as if* that leaves within the world a trace of the end or loss of the world," so that we are confronted with "a world made *ex nihilo*, as it were, in the knowledge now that the world is and will remain far away."[21] If the world created through *poiesis* not only works to create a world but also to inscribe within itself the traces of its own finitude, it is because this poetic act remains mindful of the fragility and abyssal lack that it can never overcome—neither through a sheer act of sovereign willpower or by means of the workings of a stable, self-identical consciousness that supposedly rules over the act of poetic creation. This irreducibly self-reflexive performativity of poetic world-creating will not turn a blind eye to its own lack, its proper inability to manufacture a world as a stable, transparent, and shareable entity, even as it sets out to project a world through *poiesis*.

Yet the creative act of production named by *poiesis*, which always carries into existence something that did not exist—or did not exist in this particular form—before, suggests a further dimension, one that pertains more particularly to the work of art. After all, *poiesis* also names the kind of formal aesthetic manufacturing that yields an artwork, placing it in or as a world. In the chapters that follow, this sense of *poiesis* as the poetic act associated with the work of art shall stand in the foreground. We wish to suggest that Derrida's insistence that "I made the world come into world poetically, as though there ought to be a world where presently there is none" and his suggestion that this form of aesthetic creation is a form of making "the gift or present of this *as if* come up poetically" serve as an ever-expanding source of illumination with respect to the kind of world-negotiating that occurs in a work of art. Especially in what we call older or historical works of art, for which the world in which they were created has long decayed or fallen away, the weight of the other kind of world—the world that they themselves create poetically—makes itself felt. If the gift of the *as if* that attaches to *poiesis* comes forcefully to the fore in this poetic act, it is because the work of art is called upon to negotiate the tension between world-decay (the falling-away of its world) and world-creation (the manner in which, through the poetic act, it sets up its own—irreducibly singular and unique—world).[22]

The poietic force of world-creating or world-opening is perhaps not unrelated to the thinking of a nascent world, a world that is structured by the idea of birth. In the course of commenting on Arendt's understanding of Kant's conception of judgment, Rodolphe Gasché reflects on the relation between Arendtian natality (itself a reworking of her teacher Heidegger's thinking of *Gebürtigkeit*) and world in terms of the one being born, the newcomer:

> Newcomers are born into a world that already exists, but, as strangers to this world and as beginners, they also bring with them a new world, which did not exist before, a world that they donate to the world and that is a correlate of their natality. Natality is the promise of a new world made from scratch, made all over again, a world created *as if* for the first time. With this newly donated world, the relative durability bestowed on the world through work is reshaped, and, in the same flourish, the world's ground in the pre-worldly

activities of labor and work is both reworked and recast. Through his or her words and deeds, judgments, and actions, the newcomer brings this new world into an appearance, which in turn is judged by others. ... The idea of exemplarity that guides judgment is that of a world that is new and, as a result, other and singular. It is always the first appearance of a world within the world, claiming not only to be novel, as far as world is concerned, but also to be an originary or first donation of a world, of, more precisely, a this-worldly world.[23]

If the newcomer, in being created and born, offers a new world, even donates a world, to what extent might one conceive of the artwork as one of the many figures of such a newcomer? If the artwork, not unlike the newcomer-being (whom we might call a kind of onto-newbie) that brings a new world into appearance, is born into a world while also being the origin of a world, in what sense does the *poiesis* performed through the work of art also demand to be thought in terms of a world donation? What the work of art shares with the newcomer who is born to donate a world is an opening up of an entirely new world, a world made new and *as if* for the very first time. One might even say that, as far as the work of art is concerned, this *as if* is one of the names of aesthetic semblance or appearance itself, what in the German tradition is called *Schein*. It is this *Schein* that, by being born with and through the work of art, donates a world to the world.

Yet what sustains our reflections on the aesthetic *Schein* of the world in the work of art is not the idea that the world as world does not exist. That notion has recently been advanced on the ground that the world itself is the one thing or idea that can never simply be *found* in a world and therefore cannot appear in a so-called field of sense.[24] By the same token, our investigation is not in principle animated by an attempt to reaffirm the potentialities of a certain worldlessness as one of the undercurrents of modern thought.[25] Nor do our forays into the world as it emerges in the artwork necessarily presuppose that the end of the world already has come to pass and that therefore the idea of world can putatively no longer serve as the primary framework for interpreting events and phenomena in the wake of global catastrophe.[26] Rather, the

24

two worlds that are negotiated in and by the work of art call for a particular kind of attentiveness and aesthetic vigilance with regard to the intertwined gestures of world-giving and world-undoing.

If the world in which the artwork, for lack of a better term, originated, and the world to which it gives rise through its act of poetic construction, each make their unique demands, their meaning and their signification cannot be exhausted. These two worlds would rather have to be thought along the lines of what Jean-Luc Nancy suggests when he imagines "the world as being pres-ent of being," in other words, when he proposes the idea "that the world is the origin, and that the worldliness of the world, qua absolute existential condition, exhausts its finite sense—exhausts it, that is, opens it infinitely. *Mundus patet*."[27] It is through this finite sense of world as world that its worldliness is also disclosed, opened, and exposed to an infinite reading, a reading that will always exceed, even as it falls short of, a finite sense. The finitude of sense itself is opened onto the multiplicity and uncontainability of the worldliness of the world. If this radical excess of (merely) finite sense can come into presence at all, it does so with respect to the world(s) of the work of art, where sense itself becomes exposed as a matter of sustained inquiry, ceaseless probing, and vigilant questioning.

In the chapters that follow, this exposure of sense is scrutinized in a variety of contexts and in relation to diverse artworks and conceptual registers. Each chapter represents a particular foray into thinking the connection between the ways in which a world is both foreclosed and constructed through the idiomatic signature of a work of art and the interminable acts of reading and interpretation that the work elicits. The first chapter reconstructs the logic and significance of Heidegger's elucidation of world-decay and world-opening in relation to the artwork, especially as it comes to pass in his "Origin of the Work of Art." It then examines this conception with regard to an unusual archive: the poems by Hölderlin that Heidegger himself chose to be read at his own funeral. Here, the relationship between world-decay and world-construction emerges as urgent in the poetic work especially when interpreted in light of the nothingness of the nothing that Heidegger addresses in his inaugural lecture, "What Is Metaphysics?" The second chapter takes up the relation between the artwork, its precarious worlds, and the question of world-decay by turning to exemplary works of prehistoric art. In the unusually well-preserved cave paintings of Lascaux and Chauvet-Pont-d'Arc, a multitude of aesthetic mediations give rise to particularly enigmatic forms of human being. A reexamination of the trenchant commentaries on this "birth of art" by Bataille and Blanchot, together with the more recent filmic interpretation by Werner Herzog in *Cave of Forgotten Dreams*, allows us to espy in these earliest known aesthetic forms created by humans a kind of spectral world-relation, even a "worlding" in which, through the artwork, our very relatedness to a world is at stake.

The specific nature of the work, its "workness," is the subject of chapter 3. Through a reading of Levinas's reflections on the notion of work as a kind of transcendence-toward, the chapter shows how the world-construction that is offered by the work prepares the self for a time that does not include this self. By creating a dialogue between Levinas and a moment in the poetry of Paul Celan, one nevertheless encounters a world that is stepping toward the self, even as this world remains enigmatic and resists our hermeneutic efforts at translating it into forms of presence and availability. Chapter 4 extends this discussion by asking how the double movement of world-decay and world-constitution that suffuses the artwork must be modulated when one considers that genealogical questions of legacy, tradition, and inheritance play a crucial role in this double movement. By scrutinizing a little-known yet highly suggestive text by Adorno on the question of inheriting music, this chapter suggests that the figure of the musical "subcutaneous"—a term that Adorno borrows from Arnold Schönberg—provides us with an especially fruitful way of approaching the question of inheritance as it pertains to the relation between world-decay and world-opening in the work of art. Chapter 5 then remains in Adorno's orbit in order to interrogate the world-disclosive properties of the color gray, which is conventionally denigrated in both art and conceptual inquiry as dreary, melancholy, and merely abstract, yet secretly emerges as harboring certain liberatory potentialities.

The sixth chapter moves the focus of our attention from the acoustic to the visual—from music to photography. It inquires into the problem of how the world that the artwork sets up would need to be rethought when the very world that it newly opens up is itself suffused by a relentless decay. In order to pursue this question, the chapter places Benjaminian reflections on the image into dialogue with the American photographer Andrew Moore's remarkable archive of images that explicitly thematize a world in decline, a world of loss and ruins that is nevertheless grounded in an abiding resilience. The seventh chapter leaves behind the artistic realms of previous chapters—poetry, painting, film, music, literature, and photography—in order to focus on another significant mode through which a work sets up a world: the narrative act of accounting for one's own origins in autobiographical or confessional discourse. Here, the act of a work's world-creation moves through the refractory idea of selfhood as such, and the self encounters the limits of its own narratability, even as it strives to interrogate how, in the Nietzschean sense, it became what it is, made vivid in a series of trenchant confessional texts by Derrida, Botho Strauß, and Didier Eribon. The eighth chapter examines the question of aesthetic world-construction and world-decay in relation to the work of mourning. Here, the work of mourning emerges as a world of mourning through a close examination of texts by Nietzsche, Kafka, and Derrida. Of particular concern in this context are Kafka's "The Hunter Gracchus"—the story of a man who died a long time ago but is inexplicably still alive—and Derrida's recently published seminar from 1975–1976, entitled *Life Death*, which troubles the metaphysical binary distinction of life and death. The ninth and final chapter returns to Marx's famous eleventh thesis in his "Theses on Feuerbach" in order to investigate the political and conceptual ways in which the ideas of world-decay and world-construction relate to the notion of a world that stands in need of interpretation *and* transformation on the far side of the supposed oppositional pair of thinking and doing.

In the course of our analyses, it will also behoove us always to respect the specificity of the medium and the genre to which the various aesthetic and intellectual productions belong. That is to say, while a diverse and varied range of media and genres is considered in the chapters that follow—including lyric poetry, cave painting, music, film, photography, the confessional discourse of the memoir, and even posthumous "theses" that are difficult to classify—our individual readings must always also be guided by a consideration of the conceptual constraints and singular interpretive demands imposed by each genre and medium. While they all memorably participate—each in its own, singular way—in the double movement of world-decay and world-construction, any reading of this double movement in a work will do well to attend to the irreducible particularities of interpretation that inhabit each individual genre and medium. But a consideration of such genre- and medium-specific particularities can hardly be adjudicated in the abstract, devoid of examples and contexts, but rather demands to be negotiated in the course of each particular act of reading and each singular encounter with the world(s) that arise and decay within that specific work.

The process of world-retreat and world-decay that is operative in the work of art hosts an abiding and irreducibly charged relationship to the historical. Every instance of world-decay as it comes to pass in an artwork is specific to its own historical time, its particular historically shaped episteme. In other words, the kind of world that decays into oblivion in a particular work of art is each time a singular and specific world, a world that existed in this unique way only for a relatively short period of time—for instance, the world of pre-Socratics such as Heraclitus and Anaximander in sixth- and fifth-century BCE Greece; the medieval world of 1248 in which the Gothic cathedral of Cologne was begun under the architectural direction of Meister Gerhard; the world of nineteenth-century St. Petersburg which furnishes the setting for Fyodor Dostoevsky's 1864 short masterpiece novel *Notes from Underground*; or, in the twentieth century, the context of World War II and the gruesome 1937 Nazi bombing of the Basque town of Guernica, which prompted Picasso to create the well-known oil-on-canvas painting that bears the name of that devastated town. Yet while each time the historical world that withdraws is unique, singular, and irreplaceable, all these worlds are also connected to each other on a subterranean level of shared structural decay. These historical worlds, while forever separated from each other in their temporal distance and epistemic singularity, are also related to one another in the very decay to which each is subjected. It is as if they were both separated and connected at the same time, much like the colon in a book title that both separates and connects the two parts of its title. The historical, epochal, and temporal context of the world that is at stake in a particular instance of decay is therefore always singular while at the same time inscribed in a larger movement of historicity that cuts across discrete historical moments, as a movement of change that itself cannot change. No world-decay can ever be arrested or prevented. For all its historical singularity and specificity, the work of art itself always also opens onto this double historicity of world-decay.

As the work of art emerges from a perishing world in order to set up a world of its own, it makes a particular and abiding demand: that it be read and interpreted, even as its own meaning resides in the singular ways in which it both calls for and resists such efforts. The interminability of interpretation that the work of art elicits is predicated upon both the decay of the world out of which it emerged and the artistically created world that arises out of the artwork. Both worlds resist transparent access; both disrupt any kind of hermeneutic closure and the putative triumph of achieved understanding. The particular historical, formal, and epistemological ways in which a former world withdraws cannot be understood without perpetual interpretation and ongoing reflection, even as the new world which an artwork opens up according to its own singular terms cannot be understood without ceaseless unfolding, judicious engagement, and patient acts of reading. Just as Blanchot evokes the idea of an infinite conversation, one might say that the kind of infinite conversation one enters with the decaying and emerging worlds of these works in turn elicits an incessant interpretation. The interminability of world-interpretation within the work of art is therefore always a double one. It is as though we were prevailed upon to revisit, time and time again, Nietzsche's insight in *The Gay Science*: "The world, rather, has become 'infinite' to us once again: insofar as we cannot refute the possibility that it includes *infinite interpretations within itself*. Once again we are seized by the great shudder."[28] To interpret the world, and to interpret it "once again," always also means to think along with, and to experience, this shudder. Every genuine work of art knows this—and lets us know that it knows—in its own, each-time-unique way, as we shall see in the following chapters.

The Work of Art between World-Decay and World-Opening (Heidegger, Hölderlin)

work of art belongs to a world. It may appear at first as though one had not yet said much about a work of art when one advances this proposition. A work of art belongs to a world: what could this mean? Does not everything that is belong to a world, lest it be otherworldly or even worldless? Has not the history of metaphysics long told us that the world is the space where one encounters phenomena through sense perception, whereas noumena are posited objects outside of the world of human perception? What, then, could be gained from insisting on the relation between a phenomenon such as the work of art and a world? And yet, upon further reflection, much follows from the idea that a work of art belongs to a world. After all, a work of art does not necessarily belong simply to *the* world, even when we encounter it in the space of something we call the world, but rather to *a* world, a specific world that is unique to it—a world that both gave birth to it and that it, in turn, has opened up.

But how does a work of art belong to a world? It does not belong to a world in the sense in which one may simply happen to find it there, alongside many other objects and phenomena. In other words, the work of art belongs to a world in a manner that is in each case particular and idiomatic to it, a manner that is not shared in the same way by other phenomena that also may inhabit this world, such as stones, tools, or furniture. In what way, then, does the work of art *belong to* a world? How does it *relate* to a world? And is the world to which an artwork belongs *its* world?

The ways in which a work of art relates to a world cannot be thought in isolation from the truth claims that an artwork makes—claims that can be thought of as the cognitive surplus of a work that exceeds the mere pleasure the work may cause us or the specific emotion it may make us feel. When seen from this perspective, the work of art is not merely, and not exclusively, the sensuous appearance of an otherwise abstract idea, as in the Hegelian view of the aesthetic. To the extent that something essential reveals itself in the work of art—something that exceeds its aesthetic form even while being contained within it—that revelation also transcends the work's thingly character, its material existence in this or that world. To forge a relation with what a work of art may reveal on an essential level—its import or substance—we must consider the manifold ways in which the artwork is embedded in the world of its own time. When reading a play by Shakespeare, for example, one may develop a double perspective on the formal, aesthetic, political, and cultural work that the play performs in relation to the time of its own world—the heterogeneous Renaissance world from which it stems—as well as our own world, in the here and now of its reading.

To achieve this double perspective upon the artwork and its two worlds—the world of its own production and the world in which it is received in any given moment of aesthetic engagement— the most common admonition is to perform a historicizing gesture. Exactly what such a historicization of a work of art and its lost world should entail, however, has been a matter of debate. How should one, for instance, relate to certain questions as one encounters them when engaging with older or even ancient artworks whose worlds have irretrievably perished? These issues may pertain to past worlds informed by distant ideological formations, political convictions, historically and culturally remote forms of subjectivity and affectivity; they may even relate to artistic depictions or viewpoints that are highly refined and aesthetically accomplished on a formal level but are offensive to today's sensibilities and currently accepted attitudes, such as, for example, the tacit or explicit glorification of this or that absolutist ruler in European courtly art, elements of aestheticized racism in the history of painting, the perpetuation of the cult of Venus and her sexualization by the decidedly male gaze of a Titian, the apparent aestheticization of rape in the Flemish baroque paintings of Peter Paul Rubens, or even the transfigurative celebration of militarism, war, and violence that one encounters in Homer's *Iliad* or the *Chanson de Roland*, among many others.[1] Whatever the case, and however one wishes to position oneself vis-à-vis the provocations that emanate from older works of art, it will not suffice to act as though the fact that the world out of which these older works arose has perished were of no consequence whatsoever for how one relates to them today; nor will it suffice to assume a quasi-consumerist relation to such older forms of aesthetic expression by downplaying or even ignoring the enormous distance that separates us from their world. After all, a false sense of immediacy, transparency, availability, and understanding only works to occlude what is most central—and, in most cases, most "other" or alien—in such artworks. Such a misguided appropriation cannot even be masked by what was once fashionable, in the world of art and literature, under the heading of postmodern pastiche. There, the styles, fashions, and aesthetic sensibilities of the past were forced into wildly heterogeneous constellations in which the works of previous historical times appeared only as supposedly ironic cultural citations.

The historical drive and genealogical pathos of the historicizing gesture perhaps have been most memorably condensed in the first sentence of Fredric Jameson's *The Political Unconscious: Narrative as a Socially Symbolic Act* (1981): "Always historicize!" There, what is called "the one absolute and we may even say 'transhistorical' imperative of all dialectical thought" will emerge "unsurprisingly" as "the moral" of such a historicizing method. Such an approach to the historicization of works "turns on the dynamics

35

of interpretation and presupposes" that "we never really confront a text immediately, in all its freshness as a thing-in-itself." On the contrary, "texts come before us as the always-already read" so that "we apprehend them through sedimented layers of previous interpretations, or—if the text is brand-new—through the sedimented reading habits and categories developed by those inherited interpretive traditions."[2] To be sure, it is certainly feasible and, indeed, necessary for a critical practice to engage with the ways in which the inherited sedimentations of previous interpretations of a work modulate our own interpretations of this work as we encounter it today. And yet the limits of this particular exhortation to historicize gradually come into view when we learn that, based on this methodological premise, "our object of study is less the text itself than the interpretations through which we attempt to confront and to appropriate it," so that interpretation itself is here interpreted as signifying "an essentially allegorical act" in the sense that it allegedly "consists in rewriting a given text in terms of a particular interpretive master code."[3] According to the logic of such an approach to a work, what a historically oriented method would propel the critic to engage with is not so much the particularity of a work of art in relation to a world—that is, the idiomatic and singular ways in which it is inscribed in, and yet remains distinct from, a world—but rather the various political uses toward which the interpretations of its supposed substance or import have been vectorized. Here, the critical emphasis in truth shifts from an engagement with the work's disclosure of an essential idea or mode of being to a "rewriting" of it according to so-called codes that are alien to the work itself. What is here named an allegorical act tacitly becomes a reinscription of what is essential and idiomatic to a work of art within the various translations into other discourses and assumptions—mostly ideological—to which it has been subjected over time. But this mode of historicizing runs the risk of relinquishing from the start the necessarily singular manner of a work's being-in-the-world (as opposed to its unavoidable translations, appropriations, and reinscriptions) that allows the dynamic relation between the work and a world to come into focus. If the canonical injunction "Always historicize!" therefore appears not quite sufficient—at least not in its present form and not according to its inherited protocols of reading or nonreading—to explore the mysterious and refractory relation between work and world, a differently modulated perspective on the genealogical and historical dimension of this relation is needed. To investigate the enigmatic relation between work and world, historicization itself stands in need of being historicized differently, so that another history, which is to say another form of historicity, is allowed to emerge.

A further perspective on what one might call the historical irretrievability or lostness of a work's world is opened up when the reader, critic, or scholar acknowledges a certain desire in relation to that very irretrievability—the desire to communicate with the lost voices of the dead that nevertheless appear to communicate, even if only in a spectral way, through the very works that survive them. As the Shakespeare scholar Stephen Greenblatt—prominent exponent of a critical practice that in the U.S. academy of the late twentieth century sailed under the banner of "new historicism"—memorably puts it at the beginning of his *Shakespearean Negotiations*: "I began with the desire to speak with the dead." For the scholar of literature, as perhaps also for the scholar who engages primarily with other forms of art, and especially with historically distant works, such "desire is a familiar, if unvoiced, motive" that is "organized, professionalized, buried beneath thick layers." As Greenblatt confesses: "If I never believed that the dead could hear me, and if I knew that the dead could not speak, I was nonetheless certain that I could re-create a conversation with them." In this spectral conversation, it "was true that I could hear only my own voice, but my own voice was the voice of the dead, for the dead had continued to leave textual traces of themselves, and those traces made themselves heard in the voices of the living." Concerning those who study literature, as well as other historical forms of art, one might say that they "tend to find more intensity in simulations—in the formal, self-conscious miming of life—than in any of the other textual traces left by the dead, for simulations are undertaken in full awareness of the absence of the life they contrive to represent." Greenblatt himself "found the most satisfying intensity of all in Shakespeare."[4] If this desire to communicate with the dead through extant works whose world has fallen away is inexorably intertwined with the movement and logic of inheritance—through which we receive our ideas, language, customs, attitudes, institutions, preferences, in short the basic framework of our being-in-the-world from a long-gone elsewhere that reaches into our own world with a ghostly grasp—it also can never restore to a work a world that has perished for good. To investigate the relation between work and world is only partially aided by relying on a desire—a mere desire, one might say—to speak with the dead. Work and world, while they can never operate simply on the outside, or along the margins, of a realm of desire, relate to each other in such a way as to exceed, structurally as well as historically, the psychological orientation or subjective comportment that characterizes the world of the one who receives a work—be it a reader, a scholar, a listener, or the observer of a painting, sculpture, or work of architecture. While one ought to concede that an imagined conversation with an absent or dead other *can never not* exist, the modes of historicization that this absence postulates with regard to thinking the relation between work and world need to be calibrated in more essential, albeit perhaps more circuitous, terms.

*

In the section "The Work and Truth [*Das Werk und die Wahrheit*]" of his "The Origin of the Work of Art," Heidegger considers the ways in which the particular kind of truth that comes to pass in the work of art—its idiomatic and singular modes of unconcealment— tend to be occluded when works are merely hanging on display "in collections and exhibitions" as "objects of the art industry," rather than as works in and of themselves, that is, in accordance with what and how they are, and how they dwell in the world. Here, the essence of the work of art as a form of unconcealment becomes overshadowed by the mechanisms through which art objects are "made available for public and private art appreciation" and various "agencies assume the care and maintenance of works," while "connoisseurs and critics busy themselves with them," "art dealers supply the market," and "art-historical study" turns the works into objects of academic inquiry. For Heidegger, the question arises whether "in all this busy activity" we even "encounter the work

38

itself."[5] The movement by which these works of art have been torn out of their original context and inserted into an external network of discourses, practices, and attitudes traces the distance that the works take from their inscription in the particular world, and the experience of that particular world, to which they intimately belong and in conversation with which they signify their own idiosyncratic being-in-the-world. The relation that the "art industry" forges to the works, even when its modes of operation are "exercised in every way for the sake of works themselves," can only ever reach the "object-being [*Gegenstandsein*]" of the works, never their "work-being [*Werksein*]."[6] In other words, while the ways of relating to the works that is particular to the art industry fortifies—Marx might even say reifies—the thingliness of their thingly character, these ways of relating miss what is most essential about them, which is to say, not their *Gegenstandsein* but their particular way of being a work, their *Werksein*, which expresses itself in each genuine work of art in singular and irreducibly idiomatic ways.

Yet the particular mode of decontextualization that may befall a work of art when it becomes a mere object of the art industry and its world of exhibition, business, and busyness has been prepared for by the movement that must eventually tear any work of art out of its original context in order to reinscribe it in a realm that is of necessity foreign to it. This mechanism becomes especially striking when one encounters older works of art, that is, works that belong to a world that has long passed or decayed. As Heidegger reminds us in a rarely remarked-upon passage, one that does not pivot on his much-debated engagement with Van Gogh's painting *Peasant Shoes* that occupies such a central role in his reflections, but that rather turns to works of sculpture and drama as well as architecture to advance its argument:

> The Aegina sculptures in the Munich collection, Sophocles' *Antigone* in the best critical edition are, as the works they are, torn out of their native sphere. However high their quality and power of impression, however good their state of preservation, however certain their interpretation, placing them in a collection has withdrawn them from their own world. But even when we make an effort to cancel or avoid

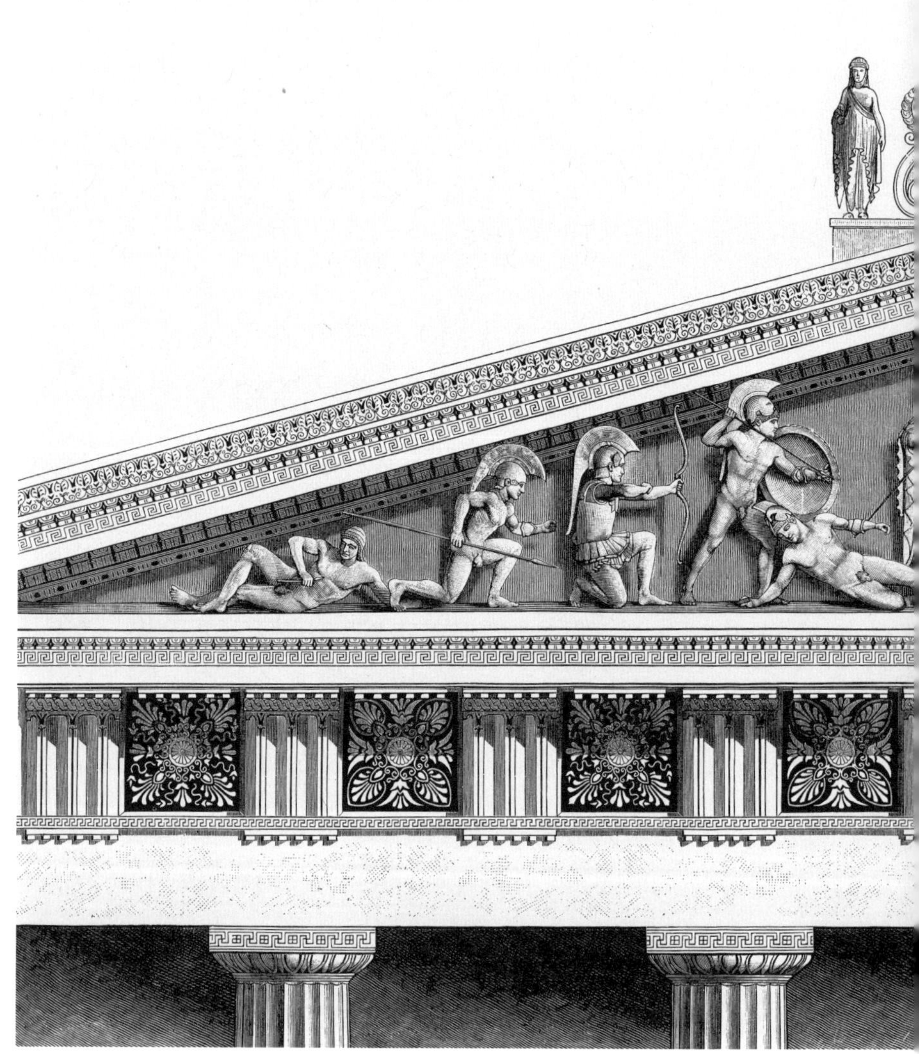

Temple of Aphaia, Greek island of Aegina; reconstruction of the western pediment.
(Falkensteinfoto / Alamy Stock Photo)

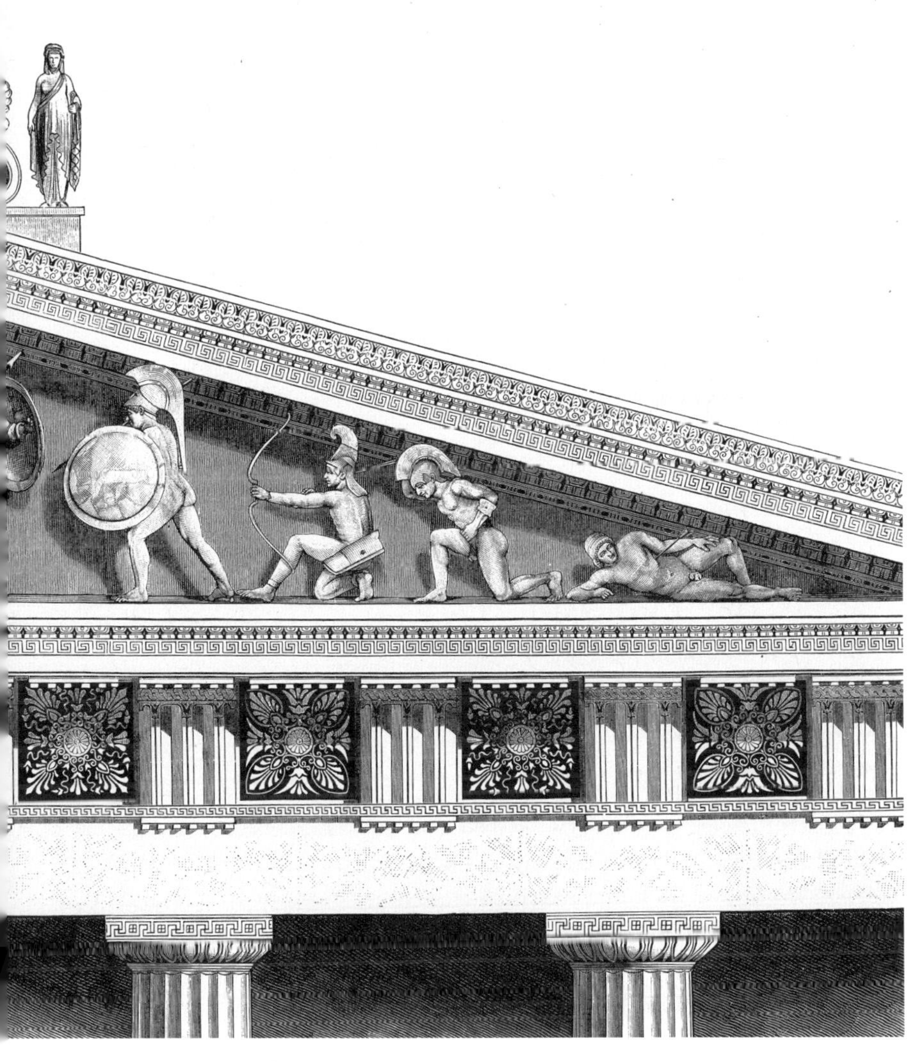

such displacement of works—when, for instance, we visit the temple in Paestum at its own site or the Bamberg cathedral on its own square—the world of the work that stands there has perished [*die Welt der vorhandenen Werke ist zerfallen*].[7]

And he continues to specify, in relation to these works of sculpture, drama, and architecture, the refractory operations of this world-perishing:

> World-withdrawal [*Weltentzug*] and world-decay [*Weltzerfall*] can never be undone [*sind nie mehr rückgängig zu machen*]. The works are no longer the works they were. It is they themselves, to be sure, that we encounter there, but they themselves are gone by [*aber sie selbst sind die Gewesenen*]. As bygone works [*Als die Gewesenen*] they stand over against us in the realm of tradition and conservation. Henceforth they remain merely such objects. Their standing before us [*Entgegenstehen*] is still indeed a consequence of, but no longer the same as, their former self-subsistence [*Insichstehen*]. The self-subsistence has fled from them. ...
>
> However, does the work still remain a work if it stands outside all relations? Is it not essential for the work to stand in relations [*in Bezügen steht*]? Yes, of course—except that it remains to ask in what relations it stands.[8]

The questions to which Heidegger's reflections give rise are manifold and nuanced, yet they all circle around the problem of how to read, in the emphatic sense of the word, a work whose world has fallen away, that is, a work we encounter without having access to the world to which and in which it belongs.[9] This work demands to be interpreted, deciphered, and understood in the here and now, that is, from the perspective of the world of another in relation to its *own* world, a world that has perished for good and that is no longer ours. If certain traces of it continue to reach into our own world at all, they are present to us only in a highly mediated, elusive, even spectral form. If the happening of truth toward which Heidegger thinks in relation to the work of art is inexorably bound to the world in which the work originated and from which its truth claims spring forth, it is because the work finds in that world its most essential determination *as* work. In other words: In the world in which it came to pass, the work showed itself both *as* work and as a work that stands in a particular relation to that in which it is embedded.

It is perhaps no accident that Heidegger chooses as his examples of works torn out of their world the wondrous pedimental Greek marble figures depicting the wars between Greeks and Trojans that belonged to the Temple of Aphaia on Aegina, which date from about 500 to 480 BCE and were acquired by the Munich Glyptothek in the early nineteenth century; and Sophocles' tragedy *Antigone* from about 441 BCE. No matter how well studied and restored the Greek marble figurines and their staging of violent conflict between Troy and Greece, no matter how studiously interpreted and historically glossed Sophocles' play, their worlds have decayed and fallen away for good, never to be resurrected. When we encounter the intricacies of ancient works of art, regardless of how much their intrinsic beauty and rigor may speak to us, we tend to feel a certain bewilderment, the kind we also feel when we encounter ancient or at least "older" works of poetry and philosophy. We wonder: In what kind of world would the concerns that are at the heart of this work make sense? What precisely is Sophocles—or, for that matter, Plato or Aristotle—worried about that makes them think and write in the way they do? With what kind of world does their work engage? What kind of a world has perished that once surrounded the Greek temple at Paestum, or, taking up Heidegger's more recent example, how is it possible to relate in an essential manner to the magisterial Bamberg cathedral in Germany, founded about a thousand years ago (in 1002), at a time when the world from which it arose has perished forever? How, for instance, does one relate from the vantage of today's world to a world in which the dominant styles that provide the Bamberg cathedral with its most prominent architectural features—late Romanesque and early Gothic—intermingle in such an intricate aesthetic dance?

The stakes in pursuing such a line of questioning cannot be reduced to the more familiar-sounding demand for art-historical study, scholarly reconstruction, or empirical historical inquiry, as necessary as these may be. After all, such intellectual activities can never restore, much less revive, a world that has perished. What is lost as world can never be saved, that is, retrieved in the here and now as a mode of former presence. Even if we manage to provide what is commonly called the historical context of an older work of art—say, the myriad concrete references to particular (and largely forgotten) nineteenth-century phenomena and ideas that travel through a poem by Wordsworth or Heine, or the geopolitical situation in which Beethoven, who was exquisitely attuned to the politics of his time, composed his late symphonies—such contextualizations do not constitute a recreation, much less a reinstatement, of the perished world from which they stem. To be sure, establishing various con-texts—literally "with-texts" that signify along with, and in dynamically shifting relation to, the particular text or work under consideration—can be a way of both emphasizing and analyzing the singularity of a work by way of comparison and strategic connection. Yet such retroactive contextualization, such belated remobilizing of the "with-ness" of a work, is not capable of reversing the entropic movement of world-decay in favor of a reclaimed presence that would retrieve the rich fullness of a lost world. The essential question, rather, touches upon the enigma of the relation between a work of art and the world out of which it arose when seen from a position for which that world has decayed and fallen out of sight. The very work-being of the work gives rise to an inquiry into the site where a work of art belongs, and, in this belonging, precisely how it engages with that to which it relates. Heidegger therefore asks: "Where does a work belong? The work belongs, as work, uniquely within the realm that is opened up by itself. For the work-being of the work occurs essentially and only in such opening up."[10] Insofar as a genuine work questions where, precisely, it belongs—that is, to the extent that what makes the artwork an artwork is inseparable from the intensity and determination with which it poses the very question of its belonging anywhere at all, a belonging that cannot simply be assumed as a given—this question returns the artwork to itself, to the work *as* work. For if the work belongs to the sphere that it itself opens up, its character as work, its work-being or *Werksein*, names the essential relation and self-relation that the work performs. One

44

might even say that it is precisely because of the work's double belonging—both to the world, decaying or already perished, in which it originated and to the realm opened up *as* a realm only by the work itself—that the question of how to relate to its multiply retreating spheres is first cast into sharp relief.

On the one hand, world-decay and world-withdrawal inflect the work in decisive ways by causing the world in which the work was created to retreat and thus obscuring the multiple relations the work had once entertained with that world; on the other hand, it is this same world-decay and world-withdrawal that make it possible for another world to become visible: the very world that the work itself creates. *As* a work, as work-being, the work opens a world, that is, it *sets up (aufstellen)*. But this setting-up differs in decisive ways from the manner in which an artwork is exhibited in a traditional institutional framework. "When a work is brought into a collection or placed in an exhibition," Heidegger suggests, "we also say that it is 'set up' [*sagt man auch, es werde aufgestellt*]. But this setting up differs essentially from setting up in the sense of erecting a building, raising a statue, presenting a tragedy at a holy festival."[11] The manner in which the work performs its particular *Aufstellen*, how it sets up a world, is inseparable from the ways in which it keeps an openness open, indeed, from the "dignity and splendor" of that which first can be called world at all. The work "demands" a particular kind of "setting up" that "consecrates and praises" because "it itself, in its own work-being, is something that sets up." Therefore, to ask "What does the work, as work, set up?" is to elicit the response that, "towering up within itself, the work opens up a *world* and keeps it abidingly in force [*In-sich-aufragend eröffnet das Werk eine Welt und hält diese im waltenden Verbleib*]."[12] When viewed from this perspective, it is no longer the world that gives rise to and shelters a work—as was the case for the world that has vanished—rather, it is the work that gives rise to and shelters a world. This world is *its* world, the world of the work, the world to which only it, as a work in its work-being, could have given rise. The work nourishes and sustains this world, safeguarding it from the permanent threat of perishing. It is in this sense that to "be a work means to set up a world [*Werksein heißt: eine Welt aufstellen*]."[13] The world-creating essence of a work can only come fully into view when the world in which the work first emerged is in retreat and decay.

The question arises, then, as to how the vanished world and the world that is set up by the work differ from one another. One may think of the vanished world of the work in terms of its concrete contents, contemporary events, fashions, political formations, social practices, historical specificities, cultural preoccupations, and the like. What one might call the *realia* of a world change over time as they are gradually replaced by new and different *realia* that conspire to consign their predecessors to inevitable oblivion. It is precisely because of this process of world-decay that what we call historical-critical editions of older literary works even exist, in which, among other things, historical and cultural references that would have been immediately understood by inhabitants of the perished world in which the work was created must be explained by knowledgeable scholars and editors to modern readers for whom these references remain obscure. Yet what does it mean for a work to "set up" its own world, the kind that only the work can sustain and safeguard? Such a world differs from the other kind of world, the perished world of *realia*, in significant ways:

> The world is not the mere collection of the countable or uncountable, familiar and unfamiliar things that are at hand. But neither is it a merely imagined framework added by our representation to the sum of such given things. The world worlds [*Die Welt weltet*], and is more fully in being than the tangible and perceptible realm in which we believe ourselves to be at home. World is never an object that stands before us and can be seen. World is the ever-nonobjective to which we are subject as long as the paths of birth and death, blessing and curse keep us transported into Being. Wherever those utterly essential decisions of our history are made, are taken up and abandoned by us, go unrecognized and are rediscovered by new inquiry, there the world worlds.[14]

To say that the world worlds is an attempt to indicate that, whatever else it may do, its primary commitment is to an open region within itself; and it is the work that "holds open the open region of the world [*hält das Offene der Welt offen*]."¹⁵ The work allows the world to hold open the openness of the open as such. If, in our quotidian life, we find ourselves inscribed in a sphere of the concrete and tangible, a sphere we sometimes call our world, the artwork sets up, and then holds into the open, a different kind of world, one in which the world no longer encounters us as a mere object facing our way but rather as a vastness that connects us to what is essential in the experience of Being. To the extent that this openness includes the paths of life and death as well as blessing and curse, it touches upon what is most essential in our experience of being-in-the-world, sending us on a quest for an authentic thinking of Being as Being. Such thinking, facilitated by the very world opened up by the work, unfolds on the far side of the precepts of traditional metaphysics in its calculative, technoscientific framework of measuring and its presumption of self-presence and self-identity that would underlie a sovereign, stable, undivided, and ultimately triumphant consciousness.

If world, in the emphatic sense opened up by the work, is never merely an object of the phenomenal world, an object that "stands before us" as something that can be seen, it should be thought as something that we are held into, something in which we find ourselves. This world that cannot simply be seen is the world of our Dasein, our being-there, as it fleetingly communes with certain aspects of Being as such. The world that is opened by the work and upon which the work opens up is the realm of our being-immersed, or immersedness, in a kind of essential opening. To the extent that whatever is encountered there does not stand over against us as a perceivable object, the world that is opened up by the work shines a light on our modes of dwelling in the world. Here we dwell in a particular way within the sphere of the world set up by a particular work; we experience, and reflect upon, our being-in-the-world in a thinking, reflective manner that cannot be reduced to propositional statements and truth-claims supported by conventional modalities of calculation and scientific models of what counts as proof.

Because the truth of the world as it is set up by a work comes to pass as *aletheia*—the Greek word that is traditionally translated as "truth" but that Heidegger prefers to render more capaciously as "unconcealment" as a way of setting it apart from the narrower, calculative Latin concept of truth as *veritas*—only when the work no longer merely belongs to the lost world in which it was created, one may say that there is a certain untimeliness at play in this conception of work and world. If the artwork is capable of revealing an essential truth in its unconcealment, and if this act of disclosure comes about only within the sphere of a world opened up by the artwork itself rather than in the realm of the perished world in which the work once was fashioned, the work and its most essential effects are imbued with an untimeliness. This untimeliness is a ruptured time that is neither added to the work in the course of its reception nor merely added on to it among a number of other identifiable characteristics. One may argue, rather, that for Heidegger this untimeliness is lodged at the heart of the work and its relation to its two worlds. It is something essential, pertaining to the *Wesen* of the work itself.

In his lecture course *Introduction to Metaphysics* from 1935, the same year he first delivered the "Work of Art" essay as a public lecture in Freiburg, Heidegger remarks on the relationship between genuine philosophical thinking and the question of untimeliness. There, he argues that all "essential questioning in philosophy necessarily remains untimely [*bleibt notwendig unzeitgemäß*]" because "philosophy either projects far beyond its own time or else binds its time back to this time's earlier and *inceptive* past. Philosophizing always remains a kind of knowing that does not allow itself to be made timely but, on the contrary, imposes its measure on the times." Therefore, he argues, philosophy "is essentially untimely because it is one of those few things whose fate it remains never to be able to find a direct resonance in their own time, and never to be permitted to find such a resonance." In those cases in which philosophy does find resonance in its own time, that is, "whenever a philosophy becomes fashion, either there is no actual philosophy or else philosophy is misinterpreted and, according to some intentions alien to it, misused for the needs of the day."[16] If Heidegger here implicitly takes up Nietzsche's privileged trope of untimeliness and the untimely, developed in *Untimely Meditations* and elsewhere, it is because the essential kind of thinking has a potentially transformative significance, to the extent that it is at odds with the prevailing episteme of its world, that is, the world in which it was created. It may be regarded by the contemporaries inhabiting its world as having come either too early or too late, that is, as being out of step with the demands and preoccupations of the world into which it is given. Genuine philosophical thinking, according to this model, is out of time, belated and too early all at once, its significance unrecognizable to its own world.

Something similar could now be argued with respect to the work of art. In the same way that genuine philosophical thought can only occur, if it occurs at all, in a time that is not its own, what is essential in the artwork, its essential unconcealment, comes to pass only in the time of a world that is not the world in which it was created but only the particular world that the work has set up, generated out of itself. The setting-forth that artworks effect through their unconcealment of something essential with regard to Being necessarily occurs in an "untimely" way because the time of the world in whose setting they were made has decayed for good, and the particular time of the world that they themselves have set up—the world that the artworks have created according to their own principles—is not "normal" or historical time at all. That time, rather, deserves to be thought as an aesthetic time, a time that is germane to, and produced as an effect of, the work of art. This aesthetic time, proper to the artwork and its ownmost generation of—as well as meditations on—time, can never coincide with the historical time of the world in which the work was created. In this sense, one might say that the artwork, like genuine philosophical thought, is at bottom untimely, demanding to be interpreted within the framework of the untimeliness that is inseparable from what and how it is in its essence. In the world brought forth by the work, the proper time of the artwork is the time of the other.

To say that the work of art both originates in a world (the one that is in perpetual decay) and simultaneously is the origin of a world (the one that it sets up) is to think the very idea of an origin—both as it relates to artworks and their worlds and as it relates to the thinking of origins more generally. Yet, one might ask, can the ways in which the artwork is rooted in the origin of a decaying world while simultaneously serving as the origin of its own world ever be fully conceptualized? What would it mean to search for origins as primordial ground when it comes to the realm of works and worlds? Is such a thinking of origin not itself already fissured by a primal crack or leap (forever encoded in the German word for origin, *Ur-sprung*), and does our consideration of works and (their) worlds not also become affected by such a fissuring, such a withdrawal from stable signification? In this regard, it can be no coincidence that Blanchot, in "The Work and the Errant Word," remarks: "The central point of the work of art is the work as origin, the point which cannot be reached, yet the only one which is worth reaching."[17] For the purposes of the present context, one might gloss this apodictic reflection by considering how the idea of the artwork as origin inflects our manner of attempting to approach the world that it has set up. But just as the world as origin of the artwork cannot be reached because that world has withdrawn into oblivion, the world that finds its origin in the artwork cannot simply be accessed in a straightforward, unproblematic manner that would yield to our hermeneutic advances. In one's engagement with a particular work, one cannot not attempt to reach the world as set up by the work of art as origin (which, if Blanchot is right, is the only sphere "worth reaching"), because that originary space also resists being made transparent through interpretation, leaving the reader, viewer, or commentator of a work in a state of hermeneutic despair. Perhaps it is precisely through the each-time-idiosyncratic and self-reflexive ways in which a particular work-as-origin sets up a world and bars full entrance to that world that one's encounter with the origins of a work and its relation to its two originary worlds are set forth. To explore a work's modes of relating to its worlds—the historical world that has decayed and the world that has become the subject of the work's particular movements of *Aufstellen*—always also is to inquire into the particular aesthetic experience of not ever being capable of reaching either origin or, by extension, the respective subsequent world once and for all.

*

One particular way of inquiring into the refractory relation between work and world consists in considering the mechanisms and premises that are at play when a work that is associated with a historical time that has long since perished sets up its own world in a singular manner that is self-consciously brought to bear on and in yet another world: the world of its reader and the vanished world of this reader when he eventually meets his own finitude. Such is the circumstance, although not widely known or considered, that obtained at Heidegger's funeral on May 28, 1976 in his hometown of Meßkirch, two days after his death in nearby Freiburg. (If I may be permitted an autobiographical parenthesis as to how I first became aware of this unusual circumstance: In 2007, I participated in an intimate multiday seminar in Meßkirch devoted to a line-by-line critical reading of Heidegger's essay "Die Frage nach der Technik" ["The Question Concerning Technology"], jointly organized by the Heidegger-Archive and the City of Meßkirch. Also in attendance happened to be Heidegger's older son, the late Jörg Heidegger, who, as an engineer, had a particular interest in the topic and shared his recollections of the discussions that he had had with his father about this text. During one of the session breaks, I embarked on the short walk to Heidegger's grave at the Meßkirch cemetery. As I contemplated Heidegger's burial site at the largely unfrequented cemetery, two elderly women approached the grave and engaged me in conversation. The two Meßkirch residents volunteered that they had attended Heidegger's funeral in 1976, as it was their custom to attend all funerals in their small town. They recalled, however, something different, even strange, about Heidegger's burial. They recollected that at his service, the usual reading of biblical passages was replaced by the recitation of verses of poetry, the specifics of which they could not quite remember thirty years after the fact. My curiosity was piqued, and I decided to delve more deeply into the matter.)[18]

As it turned out, in preparation for his own burial ceremony Heidegger had selected a number of verses by Hölderlin, which, according to his wishes, were read aloud at the open grave by his younger son, Hermann Heidegger. The work of Hölderlin had, of course, been one of the seminal touchstones in his ontological probings of Being, a constant interlocutor and archive of reflection along Heidegger's winding path of thinking. As late as his 1966 conversation with the German magazine *Der Spiegel*—which, by mutual agreement, was initially held back and only published subsequent to his death ten years later—Heidegger confirmed the centrality of the poet's work to his own philosophical project. "My thought," he reminds readers there, "stands in an unavoidable relationship to the poetry of Hölderlin [*Mein Denken steht in einem unumgänglichen Bezug zur Dichtung Hölderlins*]. Yet I do not take Hölderlin to be just any poet whose work the literary historians take as a subject next to many others. For me, Hölderlin is the poet who points to the future, who awaits the god—and who can thus not simply remain an object of Hölderlin research in literary-historical presentations."[19] The town of Meßkirch later gathered and made available a slender booklet, available for a while through the town's mayor's office, in which the brief funeral speeches as well as the specific Hölderlin verses that Heidegger had selected are preserved.[20] The five passages were to be read in a special order, also as requested by Heidegger: lines 55 through 62 of the fourth stanza of "Brod und Wein"; the first and second stanzas of "An die Deutschen"; lines 1 through 13 of "Versöhnender, der du nimmergeglaubt ..."; lines 1 through 3 of "Die Titanen"; and lines 41 through 46 of the third stanza of "Brod und Wein."

How do works and worlds intersect in this scenario? The world of these poetic works—Hölderlin's world of the eighteenth and nineteenth centuries—has irretrievably vanished. The vanishing of Hölderlin's world is prefigured and at the same time contained in another vanishing: the disappearance of the poet's former world as he fell into madness. Deemed "incurable" by his doctors, halfway through his life a mental illness largely confined him to a room in his care-givers' tower in Tübingen. The world that Hölderlin's works set up, however, continues to resonate for the readers of another historical world who would venture into it, among them those with an eye for how these works help philosophical thought to formulate the question of Being. Yet the world of those readers also perishes when they meet their own finitude, and their departure works, in a certain sense, to foreclose the readerly paths through the world that Hölderlin's work has opened up. And yet, facing the prospect of his own world disappearing—and, with it, the privileged place that the world created by Hölderlin's works plays in it—Heidegger selects and archives, while still inhabiting his own world yet already in light of his own funeral, certain aspects of the world of Hölderlin's works so that they may reverberate in relation to the anticipated vanishing of Heidegger's world in finitude.

When considered from this perspective, it is perhaps not insignificant that Heidegger chose Hermann Heidegger to be the one to read these verses at his open grave, as it is through his son—and, in particular, the voice of the son—that the worlds opened up by the works of both Hölderlin and Heidegger, now intertwined in finitude, are vectorized, in and as language, toward a futurity. This futurity in turn may be open to receiving, even after the concrete worlds of Hölderlin and Heidegger have decayed, the potentialities in relation to an activity of world-creating that their now imbricated poetic and philosophical works continue to set up. As worlds both vanish and open up on multiple levels and in more than one direction, the works that these worlds sponsored as well as the works that sponsored particular worlds become a sphere of reflection that is inherited and transmitted by those who remain behind and those who are yet to come, even if many years, perhaps millennia, in the future. From the perspective of those who inherit poetic and philosophical works, after the world comes the world—though the world will have been transformed by every act of creation and every death, every setting up and every foreclosure that will have come to pass in its orbit.

It is worthy of note that Heidegger himself once had his readings of a selection of ten Hölderlin poems recorded in a professional studio, and these audio recordings were made available by his publisher as a vinyl LP with the title "Martin Heidegger liest Hölderlin."[21] Undoubtedly his family had listened to these recordings, perhaps together with Heidegger. If Heidegger now wishes to have his son read the selected Hölderlin verses at the open grave, asking him in advance to speak in his stead, that is, to pronounce Hölderlin's words when neither the poet nor the philosopher are capable of ever doing so again, Heidegger confirms that it is the other who speaks. This other, who in the present case is the son—but a son, one should recall, only among other things and among other others—receives the word and the work from the elsewhere of what is the voice of his father, who in turns speaks through his son and through his own, poetico-ontological forebear, Hölderlin.

For Heidegger to speak at his own funeral means to speak not in his own voice but through the voice of his son; yet the voice of the son, speaking simultaneously for, to, and about the deceased father—that is, speaking as him in his stead while also addressing him who lies there, and revealing and performing something essential concerning his intellectual commitments to those other others who are also in attendance at the scene—is the voice of yet another other, namely Hölderlin. More precisely still, since lyric poetry requires that one distinguish between the voice of the author and the voice of the lyrical I—that is, between an authorial voice and the voice that is constructed by the author in an artistic way to speak in the poem—it is the created voice fashioned by and in a work of art that in turn is affiliated with the proper name Hölderlin. Heidegger, while dead, thus speaks at his own grave through a double voice that is both his and not his at the same time, namely, that of the long-deceased poet and that of the son who will survive him, representing him in his absence. Heidegger here stages a rhetorical scenario in which he, through the double voice of the other, speaks in the form of a prosopopeia: the voice of an absent or dead speaker, the voice from beyond the grave. Through this multiply overdetermined prosopopeia, works and worlds interpenetrate at Heidegger's open grave, giving themselves over to the experience of finitude and mourning while simultaneously handing themselves down, through the voice or voices of the other, into other worlds and other works.

It is striking that Heidegger selected five relatively short passages from four Hölderlin poems (with one poem, "Brod und Wein," serving as the source of two separate selections, which bookend, as it were, this small archive), rather than choosing a single poem to be read in its entirety. The philosopher here follows his long-held tendency, with some exceptions, to focus on certain stanzas, verses, and lines in Hölderlin's work that he considers especially illuminating, rather than providing a full account of poems in their entirety, that is, in the way that a classically trained philologist or a literary historian might approach them. For instance, in his lecture "Hölderlin and the Essence of Poetry" (from 1936, the year in which the first—that is, 1935—version of "The Origin of the Work of Art" and its elucidation of works and worlds was revised and expanded), Heidegger chooses five brief lines from Hölderlin's poetry—what he there calls "five guiding phrases"—to elucidate the relation between Hölderlin's work and the very essence of poetry (in the broad sense of densely literary writing, *Dichtung*). It is in the lecture on Hölderlin, too, that Heidegger feels compelled to justify his choice of this poet's work, as if to foreshadow and thus in a sense to explain in advance his later affirmation of that choice in relation to his own funeral, almost exactly 40 years later. Giving voice to an imaginary objection or complaint, Heidegger asks: "Why choose Hölderlin's work in order to show the essence of poetry? Why not Homer or Sophocles, why not Vergil or Dante, why not Shakespeare or Goethe? After all, the essence of poetry also has been realized in the works of these poets, indeed even more richly than in Hölderlin's creation, which broke off so early and so abruptly." And he responds to this imaginary objection: "That may be. And yet Hölderlin, and he alone, is chosen. But can one ever glean the general essence of poetry from the work of a single poet?"[22] Conceding that it would be a mistake to wish to deduce a general concept of poetry from the work of a single author without comparative study of a wide variety of poems and different forms of poetry, Heidegger cautions that such a mistake would only interfere with one's project "as long as we understand 'the essence of poetry' to mean that which is gathered together in a universal concept and is then applicable in equal fashion to all poetry." Yet in Heidegger's conception, such an understanding of essence is to be avoided. After all, "Hölderlin's poetry has not been chosen because his work, as one among many, realizes the universal essence of poetry but rather for the sole reason that Hölderlin's poetry is sustained by the poetic vocation of putting the essence of poetry itself into poetry. For us, Hölderlin is in a preeminent sense the *poet's poet*. For that reason, he forces the decision."[23] Perhaps one might say that it is precisely because Hölderlin's verse, from Heidegger's vantage point, is not concerned with providing universal concepts of the poetic that could be applied subsequently to all manner of lyric poetry but rather concerns itself with staging, within poetry, what is essential in the poetic as such, that certain of his verses may be taken out of their immediate context for the purpose of essential reflection. In other words, perhaps what is essential in Hölderlin's poetry shows itself—or, better, unconceals itself—in the singular moments of certain lines and passages freed of their immediate framing, just as the essence of poetry does not gather the entirety of the poetic and of poetic works under a general master concept but rather reveals itself only fleetingly, sporadically, and in a fragmentary way at certain moments in a work, when something essential, something pertaining to the *Wesen* or essence of the poetic, momentarily flashes up. To be sure, a rich contextualization and broad critical awareness of a poetic text and its many intra- and intertextual allusions and cross-references are essential to the work of literary criticism, as is a broad familiarity with the archive of a poet's corpus, its place in literary history, and its resonances within the cultural, historical, and political epistemes in which the work is embedded. No scholar could in all earnestness deny this. And yet, when considered under the aegis of Heidegger's argument, it becomes possible to appreciate how the reader who is capable of reading a single passage or even a single line of an essential poet *well* perhaps understands more about the essence of that poet and his poetry than someone who reads each of a poet's poems in their entirety, then proceeds to read the entire volume in which a particular poem is collected, all the volumes in that poet's collected works, every theoretical writing by the same poet, all the related literature of the period in the poet's own and adjacent cultures, the poetic production of the entire epoch, each of the most important works of world literature since Greek antiquity, and so on. Even if such an ambitious program of reading were feasible, such a reader may well end up "knowing" practically everything but perhaps understanding less about the essence of poetry or a particular kind of poetic thinking such as Hölderlin's than the reader who spends his time and critical energy on only one Hölderlinian passage or even lingers with a single line, in no rush to move on.

One might ask at this point how Heidegger's method of isolating particular lines from Hölderlin's verses in order to comment upon their essence (or, in the case of his funeral, to have them read aloud) relates to the question of world—the world to which Hölderlin's works once belonged and the world to which they themselves give rise through their particular modes of *Aufstellen*. How does

56

the selection of a particular passage or aspect of a work affect the experience of world as it is constructed by the work? Does one only gain partial access to the world opened up by a specific work, or is the entirety of the world as set up by the work still contained within its individual elements? And in particular passages? Single lines? Certain phrases? Lone words? Insofar as Heidegger's relation to the particular world that is opened up by works signed by the proper name Hölderlin proceeds through an engagement with individual passages and lines, these questions must reverberate in any engagement with that relation. And while Heidegger does not explicitly say whether a philosophical engagement with part of a poem can only yield partial recourse to a partial world opened up through its *Aufstellen*, he appears to be convinced that, however one may conceptualize this problematic, something essential about the world as set up by the artwork is unconcealed when one engages with its particular features or elements. It is, at a minimum, as if the experience of a world were encoded in miniature in certain of the work's fragments—some essence, substance, or import contained in its manifold and singular shards rather than in the supposed apperception of a work's (mere) totality.

By confronting Hölderlin's lines of poetry in this particular constellation, Heidegger engages with at least six worlds, or six ideas of world and work, all standing in complex relation to one another: the historical world in which Hölderlin's work arose; the decay of the world in which Hölderlin's work arose; the specific world opened up by Hölderlin's work itself; the possible retreat of the specific world opened up by Hölderlin's work; Heidegger's world, that is, the world in which his thinking engages so abidingly with Hölderlin's work; and the decay or closure of Heidegger's world as it is manifested in his finitude and his own funeral for which he prepares by selecting these particular passages. Without succumbing to the intentional fallacy—that is, reducing the singular movements of a literary work of art to speculation about the author's supposed intention rather than focusing on the rhetorical operations of the text itself, which always exceed any model of intentionality and authorial control—one cannot help but wonder what made Heidegger choose these particular passages from the Hölderlinian archive of verse for his own funeral. More broadly, one wonders what makes anyone select a certain verse over any other when planning one's own funeral, assuming one is afforded, by the circumstances of one's death, the opportunity to make such a selection, and assuming that one has the capability, inclination, and resources to be involved in any aspect of one's anticipated burial ceremony. What criteria would be appropriate or fortuitous in the selection of passages from a poetic corpus, and how would the multiple relations between the ideas of world and work be negotiated in these selections? How does the one who anticipates his own finitude, that is, his own passing and his being mourned in the company of others, address himself to those who will grieve at his grave by offering them a carefully chosen interplay of work, world, and word as it is staged in the voice of a poet long dead? Did Heidegger imagine the eventual reaction of his mourners when choosing these particular Hölderlinian lines—knowing that he would no longer be there to observe their reactions, with only his lifeless body present as a silent "witness"—or were the selections made solely with respect to something essential that they reveal about the essence of poetry and its relation to a thinking and prob- ing form of Dasein? We shall never know Heidegger's specific rea- soning in this regard. We can only turn our attention to some of the Hölderlinian lines themselves.

It will be impossible, in the context of our present concerns, to consider the entirety of the verses Heidegger chose to be read at his funeral. Instead, we will focus on certain lines to the exclusion of others, making selections from the selections, as it were. In the fifth and final passage, verses 41–46 of the third stanza of the poem "Brod und Wein"—quotations from which, we recall, both open and close Heidegger's small archive of Hölderlinian passages— certain preoccupations that traverse both Hölderlin's and Heideg- ger's work emerge with a particular lyric force. Hölderlin's elegy, first composed between 1800 and 1801 and later revised, follows a triadic composition, its nine stanzas subdivided into three groups of three, and each of the latter three, in turn, organized into three distichs, that is, strophic units of two lines of verse. Imbricated with Christian imagery of sacramental wine and bread is a per- sistent reflection on pre-Christian antiquity, embodied by the Greek deity Dionysus, the god of wine, ecstasy, festivity, theater, and ritual frenzy. The lyrical voice that speaks in verses 41–46 by addressing an other—that is, by orienting its apophantic discourse toward the ear of an other who presumably can receive it—exhorts:

> So komm! daß wir das Offene schauen,
> Daß ein Eigenes wir suchen, so weit es auch ist.
> Fest bleibt Eins; es sei um Mittag oder es gehe
> Bis in die Mitternacht, immer besteht ein Maas,
> Allen gemein, doch jeglichem auch ist eignes beschieden,
> Dahin gehet und kommt jeder, wohin er es kann.[24]

In the English rendition or interpretation prepared by Michael Hamburger, these lines read:

> Let us go, then! Off to see open spaces,
> Where we may seek what is ours, distant, remote though it be!
> One thing is sure even now: at noon or just before midnight,
> Whether it's early or late, always a measure exists,
> Common to all, though his own to each one is also allotted,
> Each of us makes for the place, reaches the place that he can.[25]

It will be impossible to gloss the vast network of allusions, references, and significations that are densely encoded in virtually every word of Hölderlin's six lines here, an undertaking that would require several volumes of commentary. And much could be said about the English translation of these lines as well, if space allowed. In the context of our specific concerns with the relation between the ideas of work and world, it is of particular note that the lyrical voice emphatically appeals to an other ("So komm!") to join in a communal "we" ("wir") to look for—or into—the open ("das Offene"). The openness of the open ("das Offene schauen") as such is here kept open by the world that a work opens up. For Heidegger, the open is central with respect to the kind of world an artwork sets up and with respect to the primordial thinking of Being that an encounter with the open affords to a Dasein. For Hölderlin, too, the open assumes a central function. Not only is it the desired destination for a shared gaze into something that is unsaturated and thus full of potentiality, but it also appears more than once in his corpus. For instance, in addition to its appearance in "Brod und Wein" it also occurs in his 1800 elegy fragment "Das Gasthaus," where it is modulated in a slightly different version as "Komm! ins Offene, Freund!"[26] In that earlier elegy, the open, which opens the poem in the first words of its opening line, stands as the opening of an opening at the text's very opening—albeit this time as a destination to move toward, rather than as a realm to behold as in "Brod und Wein." In both cases, however, it is the open that the poetic address evokes—the realm that keeps possibilities alive as possibilities, without promising certainties of any kind.

By the same token, it is this openness of the open that, according to the lyrical I, allows for a particular search to take place: the search for what is properly one's own ("ein Eigenes"), including one's own world. For what is one's own, what properly constitutes the characteristics of a self, is not to be found merely and already in that self. Rather, what is most proper to a self must be searched and discovered elsewhere, in the realm of an other, an open and unsaturated realm that may very well be in the far-off distance ("so weit es auch ist"). To understand what is properly one's ownmost, one must look *elsewhere*. This line, verse 42 of "Brod und Wein," convenes with an urgent thought that Hölderlin expresses in a letter to Böhlendorf dated December 4, 1801. There, Hölderlin wonders to what extent modernity must become heir to the refractory heritage of ancient Greece in order to recognize what is its own— yet without ever being able to understand that heritage fully. In so doing, Hölderlin raises the question as to whether what one considers one's own must first be negotiated in relation to what has long passed and become an object of transmission. "But what is one's own [*Aber das Eigene*]," he writes, "must be learned fully as well as what is foreign [*muß so gut gelernt seyn, wie das Fremde*]," because "the *free* use of *what is one's own* is the most difficult [*der freie* Gebrauch des *Eigenen* das schwerste ist]."[27] Only through what is other, foreign, or strange—*das Fremde*—does that which is one's own—*das Eigene*—become visible as what it always already was: something that is one's own but that lives only in and through the foreign. *Das Eigene* can only come into its own through the foreignness that silently already inhabits it. The openness of the open names the realm in which one encounters what is one's own in and through the otherness of the foreign, the strangeness that will always already have inhabited the self.

The question of an "Eigenes," the proper or ownmost, also inflects the remainder of these lines as their central poetic and conceptual concern. If the lyrical I pronounces that "one thing remains certain" ("Fest bleibt Eins") in this open-ended search for the ownmost within the sphere of the open, it is because both during the day and during the night—both noon and midnight, "Mittag" and "Mitternacht"—there exists for every Dasein a shared destiny with all others (a common "Maas" or measure) and, at the same time, a unique and singular path. In other words, the two temporal realms on which the entire elegy pivots—the various relations of day and night in both concrete and abstract manifestations—here are brought to bear on the relation between the shared destiny of those who experience being-in-the-world and the irreducible singularity that each Dasein will encounter on its way, that is, the "Eigenes" that only a particular being is capable of experiencing. After all, "immer besteht ein Maas," there always exists a measure that is "Allen gemein," or common to all, yet the commonness of this shared destiny—Heidegger, for his part, might point first and foremost to our shared finitude, our being-toward-death—is pierced by the bestowal of something unique and individual ("eigenes beschieden").

It is noteworthy that the phrase "ein Eigenes"—that which is one's ownmost and which belongs properly to oneself—is the phrase that is replaced in the "Zweite Fassung," or second version, of Hölderlin's "Brod und Wein" with another word: "Lebendiges." In this second version, the line reads "Daß Lebendiges wir suchen, so weit es auch ist."[28] While all the other words of this passage remain unchanged between the first and the second version of the poem, "ein Eigenes" becomes "Lebendiges," something lively, living, or alive. What could have prompted Hölderlin to perform this substitution of one word for another? Or is this less of a substitution than it at first appears—and more of an affirmation, even intensification? It is as if the reflection on the "Eigenes," the ownmost, were precisely the most lively, living element of what is one's own. What is one's own, or thought to be one's own, is precisely what is most alive, so that whenever we search, in the open, for something we can call our "Eigenes," we are in fact looking for a "Lebendiges" that names life itself, for that which is irreducibly living and vital in us, that which makes us who we are and something other than dead. As an experienced intensity of that which is most alive and living (its or our) life, "Lebendiges" reaches across both versions of the poem to connect with "Eigenes" in a substantive way, taking the latter's place yet perpetuating and affirming what is most significant and urgent—most vital—about it. Having been struck out, erased, canceled, "Eigenes" lives on—that is, survives—in the affirmation of the vital life of "Lebendiges."[29]

But what can be said specifically by the poetic work of this ownmost singularity that is embedded within the destiny of a common measure? The elegy suggests that this ownmost, as that which is proper to an individual Dasein in its contemplation of Being (Hölderlin's *Seyn*) as such, is imbricated with the experience of a path or way. Cutting through the openness of the open, this path or way simultaneously leads *toward* something and *from* something, in a manner that is always still to be determined each time a seeking and wondering Dasein ventures to enter upon it. There is thus a perpetual coming and going ("gehet und kommt") on this path through the openness of the open, a movement that is shared by all through the experience of a common measure and yet each time also irreducibly unique and singular. On the path through the openness of the open every Dasein moves toward its unknown ownmost—a Dasein's particular "Dahin," its pull toward a "there" or a "thereto"—in a manner that is germane to its own constitution and particular capabilities. The "Dahin," which opens the final verse of this passage, line 46, self-consciously encrypts a double valence pertaining to these capabilities. On the one hand, "Dahin" and the verb that immediately follows it, "gehet," can be read as articulating the direction of a walking movement, as in "going *there*" (rather than to someplace else). On this level, "Dahin" signifies one possibility of venue-choice among others, as it works to specify the site to which the motion will eventually lead. But, on another level, it is possible to hear "Dahin gehet" in a slightly shifted accentuation, one that stresses the second syllable, "Da'hin gehet," instead of the first. Placing the emphasis on the second syllable would denote a form of "dahingehen," which, in addition

62

to movement toward a site, means, among other things, to decay, to vanish, even to die. In that case, the twin possibilities of moving toward a site that is properly one's own and of meeting one's death are no longer simply opposed. Either way, with respect to the openness of the open, every Dasein's "Dahin" leads it toward the only place this particular Dasein is capable of reaching ("Dahin gehet und kommt jeder, wohin er es kann"). No one can reach a realm that he is incapable of attaining based on his ownmost destiny, that is, without his having-been-sent on a singular path toward that unique destination and realm of experience.

One way of glossing this thought further is to underscore its tacit affirmation of the idea of the human being's capability of dying in the emphatic Heideggerian sense. The human being does not just perish but rather, through its lifelong experience of meditating on Being, human finitude, and being-toward-death, is able to relate to death as death, even as its own death must remain, strictly speaking, unthinkable to it. This common measure or "Maas" on a shared path of Dasein is intertwined with another kind of "being able to" or "being capable of" reaching a realm ("wohin er es kann"). This is the unique realm of a life—for instance, the life of a poet, a musician, a painter, a sculptor, or a thinker, but also the life of a potter, a stonemason, or a master baker, defined as they are by the masterful virtuosity of their handicraft. What the poem sets forth here is the image of a world in which Dasein engages with the call of Being in an essential manner. This Dasein is both mindful of the possibilities opened up precisely by its very finitude and hospitable to the manifold ways in which it may first devise and then travel along singular paths through the openness of the open in order to come to terms with what constitutes its ownmost capability, its very "sent-ness" along a unique trajectory.

Hölderlin's emphasis on capability, on the ability to move in a certain direction or to advance, by means of a unique capacity, with respect to a prospective goal, finds its echo in Heidegger's emphasis on ability and on a certain form of self-enabling capacity (*Vermögen*), which he discusses in various parts of his oeuvre. For instance, in his 1947 "Letter on Humanism," a response to an inquiry by his French colleague Jean Beaufret, Heidegger emphasizes that thinking belongs to a realm that precisely "enables thinking to be a thinking. The element is what properly enables: it is the enabling [*das Vermögen*]. It embraces thinking and so brings it into its essence."[30] The essence of thinking is predicated upon the following idea: "Thinking *is*—this says: Being has fatefully embraced its essence. To embrace a 'thing' or a 'person' in its essence means to love it, to favor it. Thought in a more original way such favoring [*Mögen*] means to bestow essence as a gift." Such "enabling [*Vermögen*] is what is properly possible [*das 'Mögliche'*]."[31] And a few years later, in "What Calls for Thinking?," Heidegger takes up this discourse of an enabling capability when he writes that "we are capable of doing only what we are inclined to do [*wir vermögen nur das, was wir mögen*]. And again, we truly incline toward something [*mögen wiederum wahrhaft nur Jenes*] only when it in turn inclines toward us, toward our essential being [*was seinerseits uns selber und zwar uns in unserem Wesen mag*], by appealing to our essential being as what holds us there."[32] If we are held by that which holds our being into the world through what favors us, what likes us, what inclines toward us, this is so because that favoring and liking is sustained only by our own liking of, and inclination toward, it. We are truly capable of something to the extent that we like and favor it, even love it, in a most essential way and to the extent that it requites our love by liking and favoring us back. To be a genuine poet, one must love and embrace poetry in an essential manner, and poetry has to love one in return. If poetry does not love us back, we cannot truly be poets. If we do not love and embrace the game of soccer in its most essential being, and if soccer does not favor and love us back by inclining toward us, connecting with our being in a fundamental way that transcends the intensity and scope of favor that the sport normally bestows, we cannot be a Franz Beckenbauer, whose extraordinary skill Heidegger greatly admired.[33] In the world set up by Hölderlin's line 46, the coming and going into what is one's ownmost is enabled by a particular kind of skill, a capacity for movement toward what one is able to move toward in an essential way ("wohin er kann"). The final word of that line, the third-person singular verb "kann," thus denotes an ontological capacity that regulates what the human being is capable of reaching and also requires of the human being that this capacity be first understood and then actualized. This potentiality intertwines the essential dimensions of the relation among *mögen*, *Vermögen*, and the *Möglichkeit* to which these give rise. *Können*, the infinitive form of "kann," names what a Dasein and the world that its works set up are able to accomplish when they relate emphatically to the call of Being.

In considering the relation between world and work, Heidegger depends on Hölderlin even in death. The philosopher is convinced that "art is the creative preserving of truth in the work" and that it *"is a becoming and happening of truth"* to the extent that "the opening up of the open region, and the clearing of beings, happens only when the openness that makes its advent in thrownness [*Geworfenheit*] is projected."[34] Among the arts, it is poetry (*Dichtung*) that, from the vantage of Heidegger's thinking, enjoys a privileged position vis-à-vis the world that art constructs as the realm in which truth takes place. As he emphasizes: "*All art*, as the letting happen of the advent of the truth of beings, is as such, *in essence*, *poetry* [Alle Kunst *ist als Geschehenlassen der Ankunft der Wahrheit des Seienden als eines solchen* im Wesen Dichtung]." He continues: "The essence of art, on which both the artwork and the artist depend, is the setting-itself-into-work of truth. It is due to art's poetic essence that, in the midst of beings, art breaks open an open place, in whose openness everything is other than usual."[35] The locution "what is other than usual," one might say, is one of the names of the particular world that art opens up according to its own unique terms. If and when such an opening up of the open occurs within a work so that truth is set forth in and through the world that the artwork holds open, then all art is a kind of poetry.

If Heidegger cannot imagine thinking without Hölderlin's poetry—or, for that matter, dying and being buried without it—it is because this work stages the opening of world and truth in a primordial way that is germane to any genuine engagement with Being. For Heidegger, the poetic worlds that are set forth by Hölderlin's works affirm the idea that poetry, understood in this technical sense, "is not an aimless imagining of whimsicalities [*kein schweifendes Besinnen des Beliebigen*] and not a flight of mere notions and fancies into the realm of unreal" but rather constitutes an urgent form of "unconcealment" in "the open region [*das Offene*] which poetry lets happen, and indeed in such a way that only now, in the midst of beings, the open region [*das Offene*] brings beings to shine and ring out [*zum Leuchten und Klingen bringt*]."[36] What Heidegger shares with Hölderlin is the insight that it is ultimately in and through language that the openness of the open—as revealed by the artwork—reaches into our Dasein as it forges its relation to a thinking of Being, time, and finitude. After all, it is "language alone" that works to bring "beings as beings into the open for the first time," and where "there is no language," by extension, "there is also no openness of beings, and consequently no openness of nonbeing and of the empty."[37] From the perspective afforded by this insight, "language itself is poetry in the essential sense,"[38] and Hölderlin's works give birth to a world, even and especially in death, that is hospitable to this essential insight. One might say that the world set up by Hölderlin's poetic work provides shelter for the disclosive potentiality, even the unconcealment, that is promised by letting language be language, that is, not by thinking, reading, writing, and speaking language as a means of communication, as scientific discourse or technical calculation, but by letting language *be*—by dwelling in *language as language*.

*

If Heidegger's relation to Hölderlin's verse is mediated by the connection between work and world as they come to pass in and as language, one might say that the poetic world that is evoked at Heidegger's funeral enacts the essential bond between thinking and the experience of nothingness and the nothing. The world, as it emerges in Hölderlin's verse and as it opens onto the scene of Heidegger's burial ceremony, provides the very setting in which the nothing can be thought as such. In his 1929 inaugural lecture at the University of Freiburg, "What Is Metaphysics?," Heidegger develops the idea that "the nothing is more original than the 'not' and negation [*das Nichts ist ursprünglicher als das Nicht und die Verneinung*]."[39] While for the institutionalized sciences the nothing can hardly be more than "an outrage and a phantasm," and while "science wants to know nothing of the nothing" so that we "know" the "nothing" only "in that we wish to know nothing about it [*indem wir von ihm, dem Nichts, nichts wissen wollen*]," ontological reflection espies in the thinking of the nothing something essential about our being-in-the-world.[40] The nothing, to which we relate most fully and most essentially in intensely felt moments of anxiety, dread, boredom, and the experience of world-decay, is not a form of nihilism. On the contrary, the nothing gives rise to a thinking of a special kind. The habitual modes of thinking, in which we are "always essentially thinking about something," must be unlearned and relearned when it comes to the nothing. The thinking of something "must act in a way contrary to its own essence when it thinks of the nothing."[41] The nothing evokes a "wholly repelling gesture toward beings that are in retreat as a whole, which is the action of the nothing that oppresses Dasein in anxiety" so that "the essence of the nothing" is at bottom "nihilation [*das Nichten*]." As such, it is "neither an annihilation of being nor does it spring from a negation. Nihilation will not submit to calculation in terms of annihilation and negation. The nothing itself nihilates [*Das Nicht selbst nichtet*, literally 'The nothing itself nothings']."[42] On the far side of our everyday knowledge, the nothing performs its work of world-nihilation. In this movement, "the nothing is the origin of negation, not vice versa [*Das Nichts ist der Ursprung der Verneinung, nicht umgekehrt*]."[43] In other words, the nothing is how and what it is not because something has been negated, as in an act of merely destructive nihilism. Rather, there can only be something like negation because of the ontologically prior and more essential existence of the nothing as nothingness.

To the extent that the nothing is not merely dismissed—in the way that, for instance, "science would like to dismiss the nothing with a lordly wave of the hand"[44]—the nothing retains a world-disclosive dimension for us. In fact, one might even say that "Da-sein means: being held out into the nothing."[45] If, from Heidegger's vantage point, "human existence can relate to beings only if it holds itself out into the nothing," this is because the "question of the nothing puts us, the questioners, in question."[46] An essential engagement with the question of the nothing, and with the kind of questioning that the nothing as nothing demands, points us toward the fundamental possibilities of our ownmost Dasein. Engaging with the question of the nothing, the nothingness of the nothing that is not a function of a prior negation but rather presents our most essential opportunity for engaging with an anxious world in decay, leads us to ask, in our thinking and being in the world, Leibniz's fundamental question taken up by Heidegger at various turns in his intellectual trajectory: "Why are there beings at all, and why not rather nothing? [*Warum ist überhaupt Seiendes und nicht vielmehr Nichts?*]"[47]

The question of *das Nichts*, the nothing, thought in this particular way, sheds new light on the relation between world and work not only as they instantiate themselves in Heidegger's thinking but also as they are staged at the scene of Heidegger's funeral. Their interrelated manifestations of world emerge and perish at the open grave in relation to the world set up by Hölderlin's poetic work. The multiple forms of world-decay that come to pass at the burial ceremony elicit a primordial relation to the way in which the "nothing nothings," that is, to the manner in which a primordial experience of nothingness affirms the kind of questioning worthy of the uncanny experience of being in the world—along with the prospect of departing from it irrevocably. Works and worlds, verses and voices, concepts and words all commune in the chorus of nihilation that is performed by the powerful nothingness of the nothing *as* nothing. Yet this movement of world-*Nichten*, if it is to become, even for a fleeting moment, the object of careful attentiveness and a Dasein's projection of ontological possibility, can hardly make do without perpetual dialogue with the singular world of the poetic work through which our inescapable decay attains significance. If it is indeed the nothing itself that holds us into our life while dangling us over the abyss of our existence, it is the aesthetic world set up by the work of art in which this primordial holding and dangling find their most essential stage and framework for reflection.

Of Cave Worlds and the Birth of the Artwork in Painting and Film (Blanchot, Bataille, Werner Herzog)

The conceptual question concerning the relation among a work of art, its worlds, and the experience of world-decay is cast into particularly sharp relief when one considers instances of prehistoric art. The world to which these artworks belong has long perished, sometimes by tens of thousands of years, and the world that they, as aesthetic constructions, in turn set up tends to resist hermeneutic decoding and interpretive explication, even as the aesthetic world constantly invites, even demands, such elucidation. The irreducible sense of belatedness, deferral, and non-synchronicity that attends the engagement with such prehistoric art and its worlds touches upon something essential that traverses all works of art, along with the world from which they arose and the world—each time singular and unique to a particular work—to which they give birth. Any understanding of such artworks, along with any comprehension of the world out of which they were created and the aesthetic world they call into presence, cannot be based solely on a calculating reconstruction, a historical and conceptual restitution of something that has been occluded but is, in principle, available to interpretive retrieval in the form of an excavation of a more or less stable meaning. On the contrary, to engage with prehistoric works of art means to engage with a world that is perpetually in retreat and with forms of signification that will forever refuse to coalesce into the solid form of an achieved interpretation that would delimit the movement of its excessive significations. For instance, when confronting the variegated animal and nature paintings that in their multitude constitute the remarkable early archive of art found in the decorated caves of Lascaux, near the village of Montignac in the southwest of France, one is struck not only by the beauty and depth of reflection that inheres in these works dating back some 17 millennia, but also by the resistance to any interpretive stabilization of meaning that these enigmatic creations from the world of the Upper Paleolithic and Mesolithic period embody.

This resistance to, or retreat from, stable meaning is deeply encoded in the very fascination that the world of the Lascaux caves exerts on our own world. It is as if our own world were receiving a scrambled message from a long-decayed world of alterity in a way that nevertheless preserves the beauty and aesthetic accomplishment of the dead world in a haunting manner. As Bataille puts it in his pivotal 1955 study *La peinture préhistorique: Lascaux ou la naissance de l'art*, it is as if we had "added very little to the inheritance left us by our predecessors; nothing supports the contention that we are greater than they. 'Lascaux Man' *created, and created out of nothing, this world of art in which communication between individual minds begins.*" He adds that the prehistoric artist of Lascaux "communicates with the distant posterity today's mankind represents for him" in that "he speaks to us through the paintings" which have remained "unaltered after that seemingly interminable space of time." Yet what "preys upon us and transfixes us is the vision, present before our very eyes, of all that is most remote," and we find ourselves confronted "by an inhuman strangeness," even an "animality" that is "nonetheless for us the first sign, the blind unthinking sign and yet the living intimate sign, of *our* presence in the real world."[1] If Bataille is right that the world of the prehistoric artworks at Lascaux and their marvels gives rise to another experience of world—namely our own—how does this giving-presence come about? In what sense does the work of art inscribed in a former world, long decayed, sponsor an experience of world tens of thousands of years in the future? What is this inheritance of a world inside another world as it comes to pass in a work of art?

The idea of a world that has decayed out of existence for good but that, through the aesthetically mediated injunctions to interpret that pulsate through its ancient works of art, continues to resonate is one of the most abiding questions invoked by our experience of the Lascaux paintings. If the Lascaux paintings appear "at first to lie at the furthest possible remove from our contemporary selves," as Bataille concedes, and if "our first reaction to Lascaux is obscure, half mute, only half intelligible," this is so because "the night of time through which it comes is pierced by no more than uncertain glimmers of faint light."[2] These uncertain glimmers of a faint light radiate, one might say, out of a lost world that remains enigmatic. As Bataille suggests, we "know next to nothing of the men who left behind only these elusive shadows, framed within almost nothing, unprovided with any explanatory background." And if we "know only that these shadows are beautiful to look at, to our eyes quite as beautiful as our galleries' finest paintings," we are nevertheless conscious of the radical difference in world and world-legibility that opens up between the Lascaux paintings and those exhibited in our art galleries and museums.[3] After all, when it comes to the latter, "we at least know something: dates, names of the painters, the subject," perhaps even "the intention behind the work. We are familiar with the customs and ways of life they are related to" or "we may read chronicles of the times in which they were produced."[4] In other words, these artworks are "not at all, as are these at Lascaux, the issue of a world about which our information is confined to the knowledge that there were few resources in those days, that man was limited to hunting wild beasts and picking wild berries." And for all that we do know about their world, the paintings "are only the more unintelligible," so that we find ourselves "left painfully in suspense by this incomparable beauty and the sympathy it awakens in us."[5] What, then, are we to make of this sympathy awakened by the beauty of a lost

73

world and its art? If, as the French archaeologist Henri Breuil once memorably suggested, Lascaux deserves to be thought of as the "Sistine Chapel of prehistory," how can its elusive and refractory world be grasped? How are we to read the multiple worlds and their incommensurate temporalities that open onto each other and illuminate one another in such enigmatic ways, as if through the glimmer of a dark light?

When Blanchot, in his meditation "The Birth of Art" (later included as the lead essay in his 1971 *L'amité*) engages with the art of the Lascaux Cave complex by way of his close friend Bataille's book dedicated to it, he locates the experience of the cave, rediscovered by accident in 1940, in a moment of aesthetic astonishment that is shaped in singular ways. For him, "Lascaux fills us with a feeling of wonder: this subterranean beauty; the chance that preserved and revealed it; the breadth and scope of the paintings, which are not in the form of vestiges or furtive adornment but as a commanding presence."[6] As Blanchot reminds us, we encounter there a "space almost intentionally devoted to the brilliance and marvel of painted things, whose first spectators must have experienced, as we do, and with as much naïve astonishment, the wondrous revelation."[7] If Lascaux is the proper name of a "place from which art shines forth and whose radiance is that of a first ray— first and yet complete," this experience gives rise to the "thought that at Lascaux we are present at the real birth of art and that at its birth art is revealed to be such that it can change infinitely and can ceaselessly renew itself, but cannot improve—this is what surprises us, what seduces us and pleases us."[8] Such is, according to this line of thought, what we "seem to expect of art: that, from birth, it should assert itself, and that it should be, each time it asserts itself, its perpetual birth."[9] From Blanchot's vantage point, which communes with that of Bataille, one might say that the prehistoric artworks at Lascaux give birth, in the worlds they create, to the idea of art understood as a kind of birthing, that is, they give birth to birth itself.

If Blanchot concedes that this "thought is an illusion," he adds that "it is also true."[10] In other words, the thinking that would be required to confront the birth of art must be capacious enough to accommodate illusion and truth at the same time without

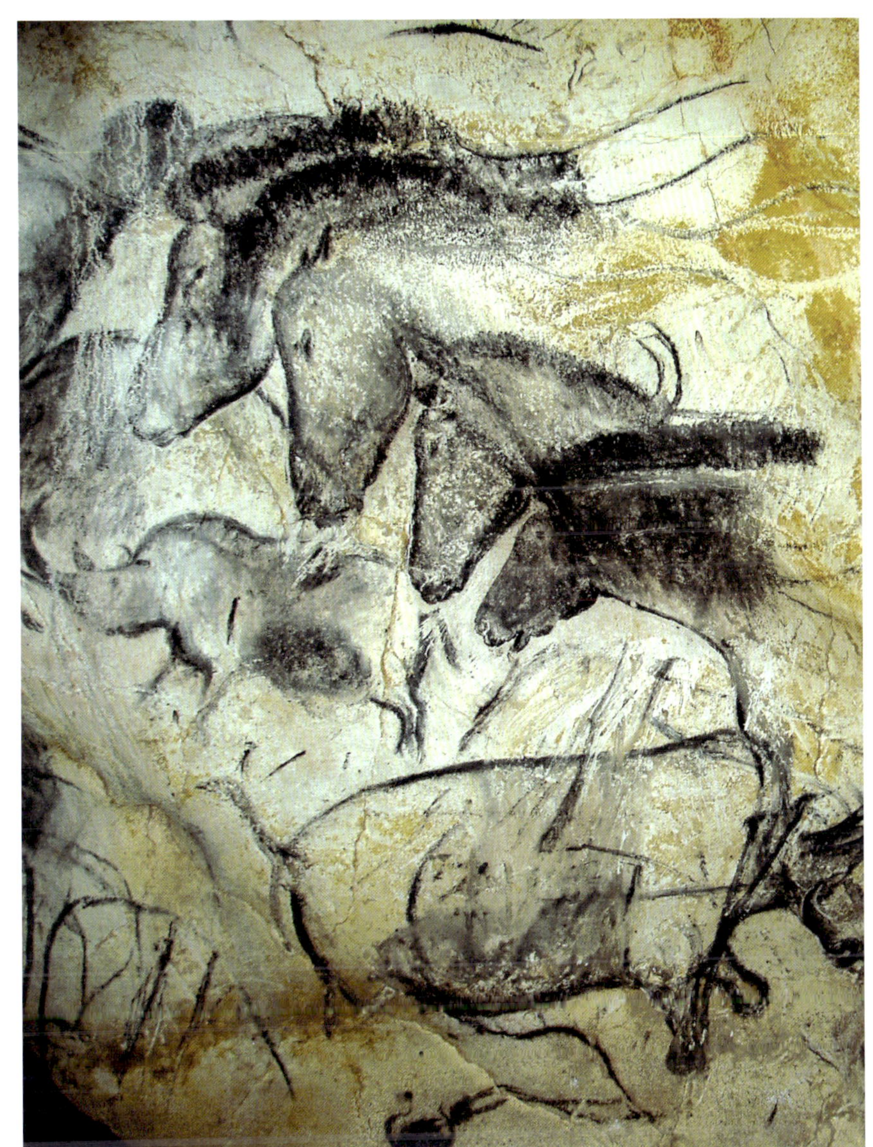

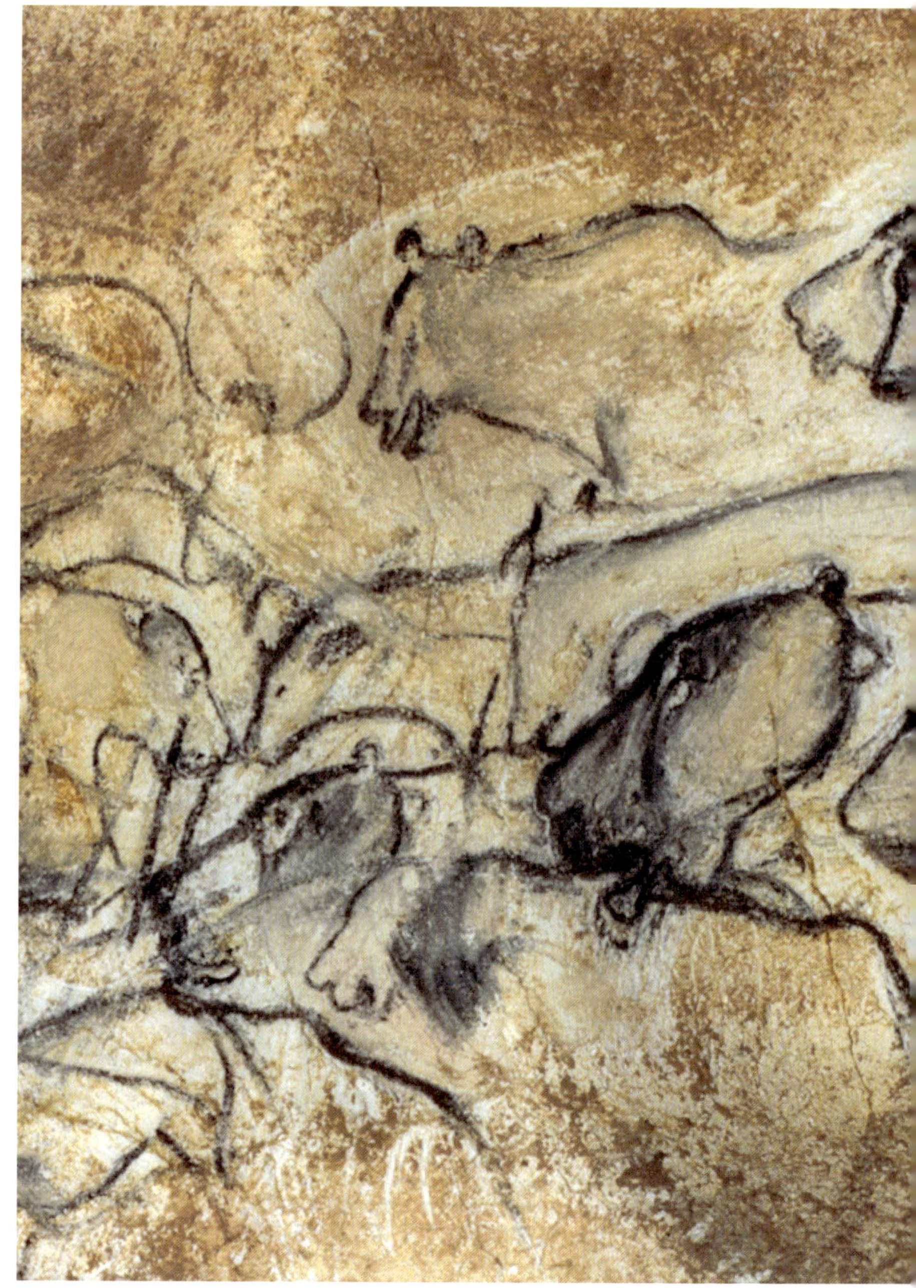

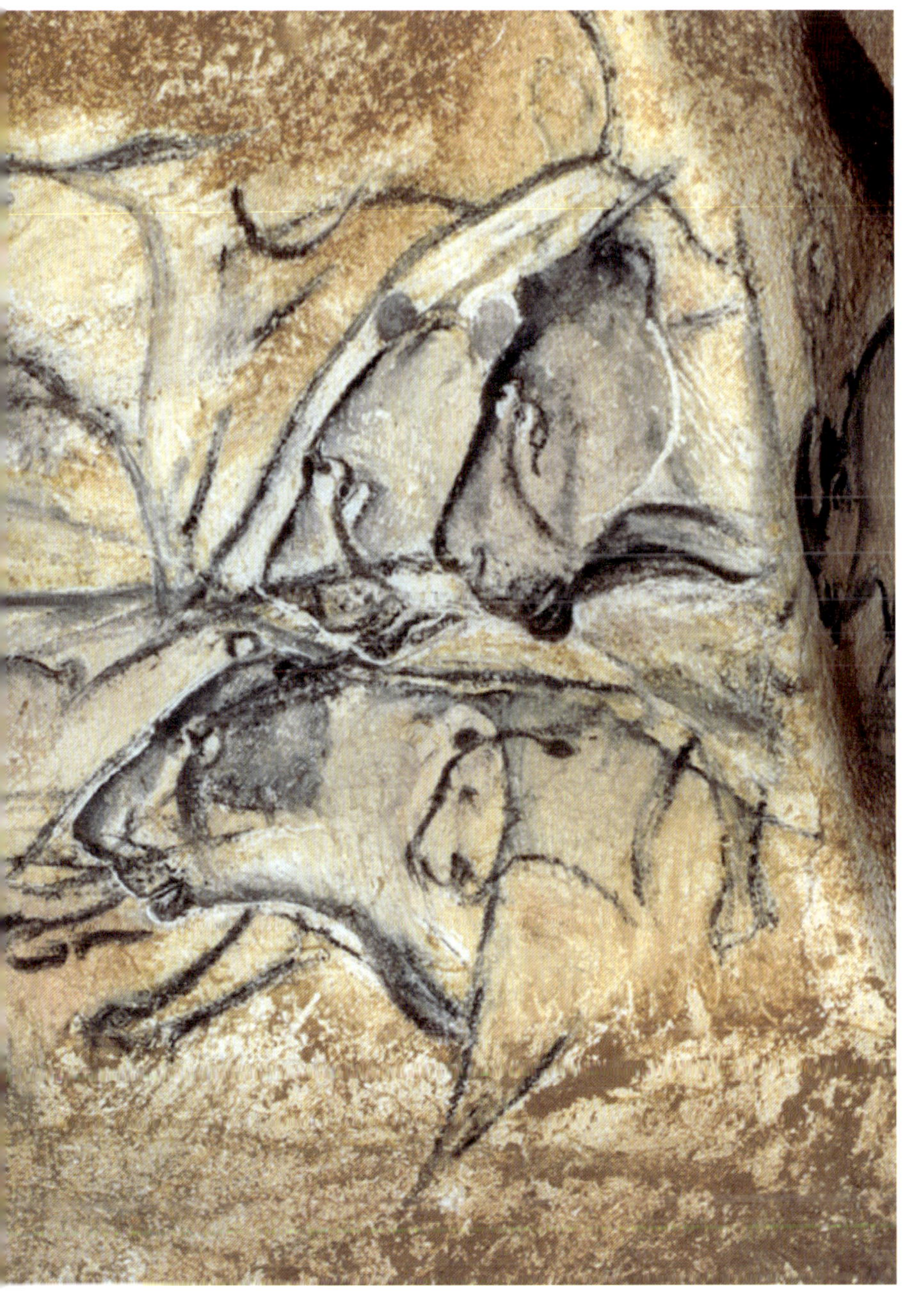

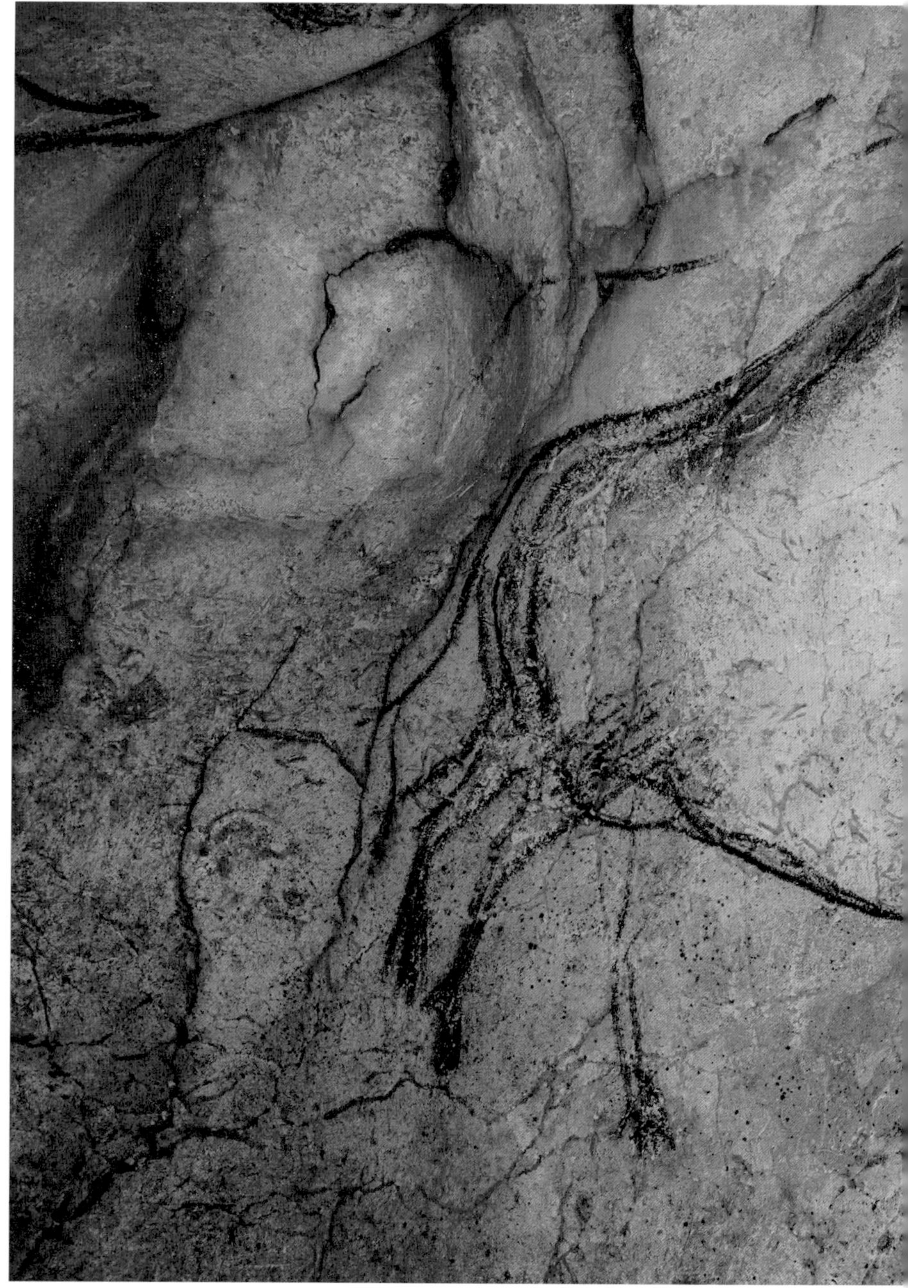

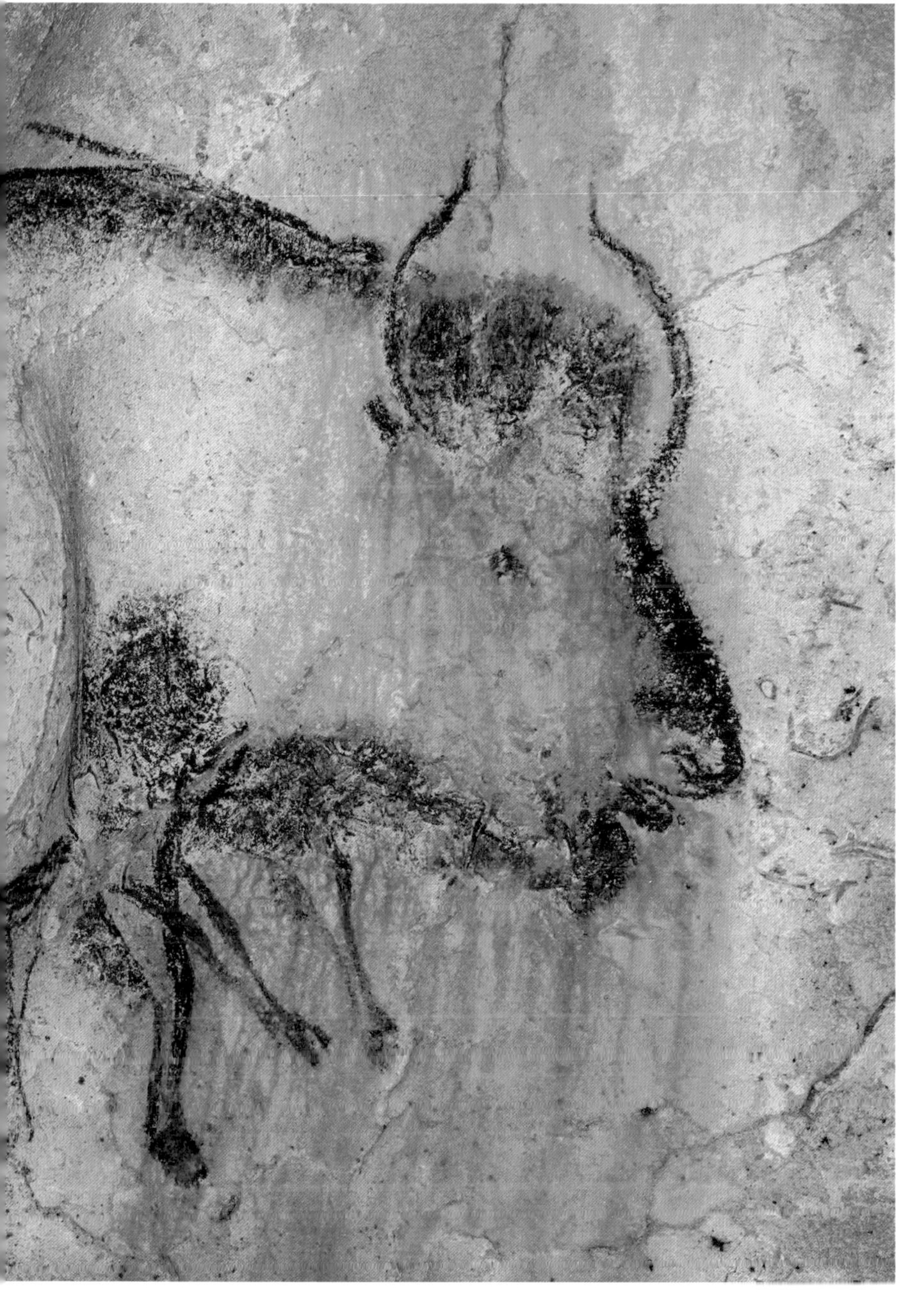

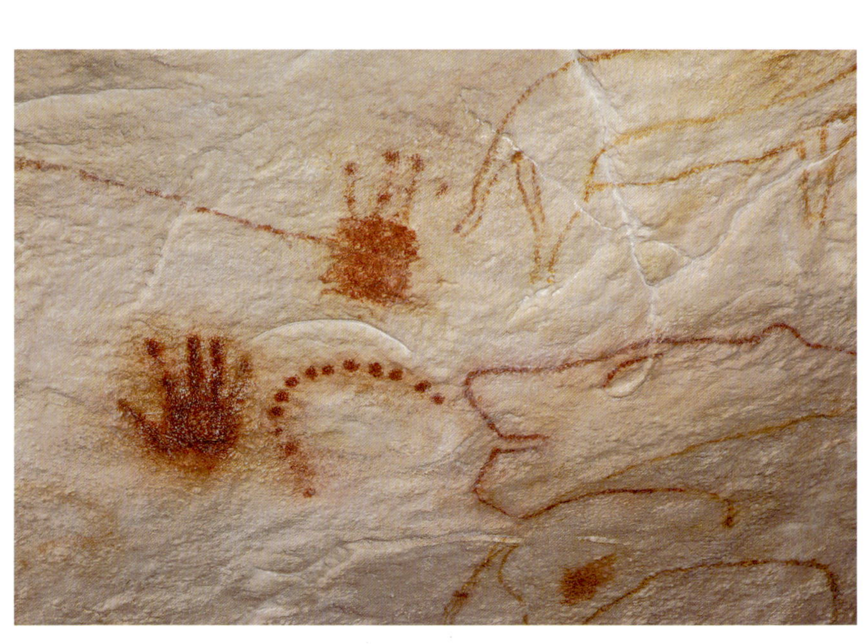

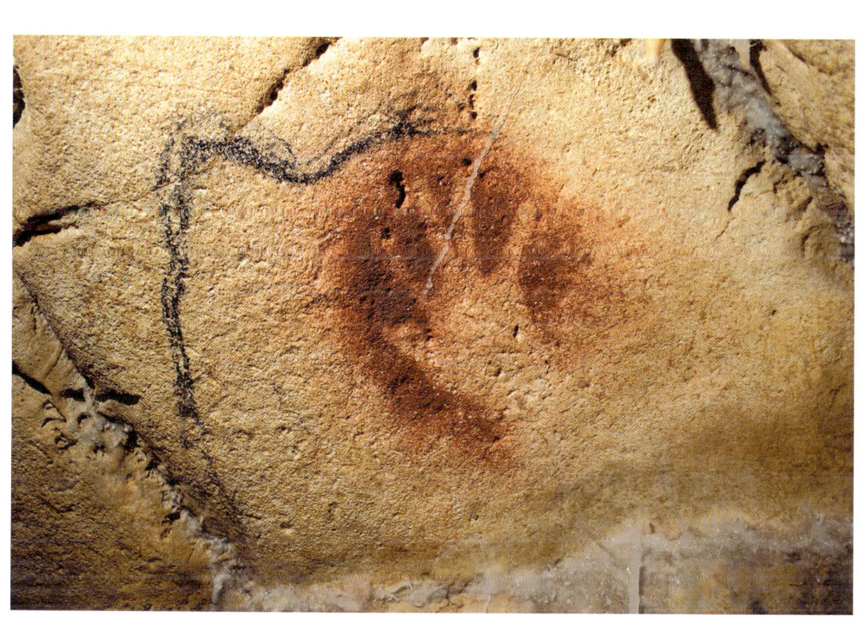

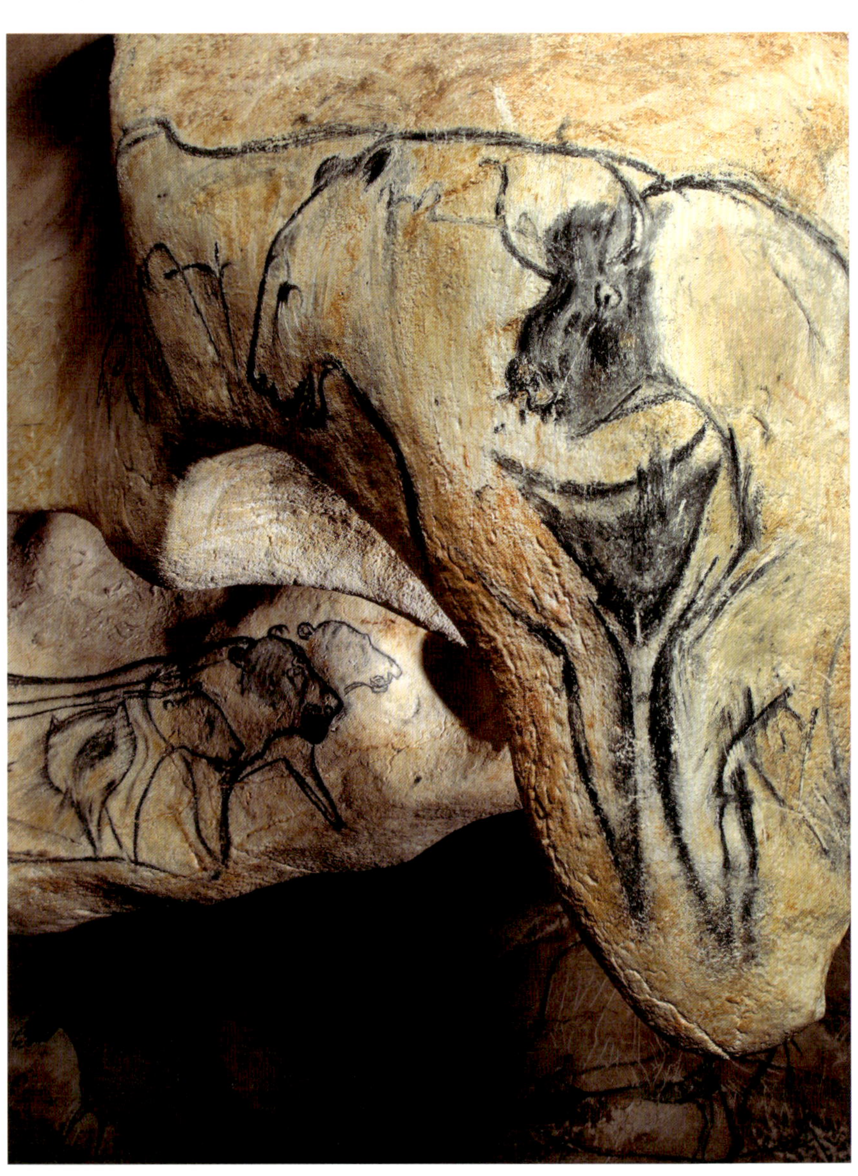

collapsing under the tension created by these two seemingly incompatible designations. It is, one might say, a true illusion. While the thought of the work of art asserting its perpetual birth across time and worlds may be illusory, it also is true insofar as it "directs and propels our admiring search," facilitating and framing our encounter with the work of art in singular ways that otherwise would not have been available to us. After all, it is in marking its own perpetual birth across worlds and their temporalities that the work of art discloses something essential about our relation to it and to the worlds that belong uniquely and idiomatically to it. As Blanchot avers, this thought

> reveals to us in a perceptible manner the extraordinary intrigue that art pursues with us and with time. Lascaux should be both what is most ancient and a thing of today; these paintings should come to us from a world with which we have nothing in common, the barest outline of which we cannot even suspect, yet they should nonetheless make us, regardless of questions and problems, enter into an intimate space of knowledge. This surprise accompanies all works of past ages, but in the Valley of the Vézère, where, in addition, we are aware that the age is one in which man is just beginning to appear, the surprise surprises us still more, while confirming our faith in art, in that power of art that is so close to us everywhere, all the more so that it escapes us.[11]

When they come into focus from this perspective, the prehistoric artworks of Lascaux straddle both temporality and the idea of a world in a bold way. They create the impression, through their aesthetically projected artifice, that they belong to a time and a world that could not be more removed, more ancient, more alien, while at the same time laying claim to a certain contemporancity with our own world, reaching into it with a spectral grasp from beyond time immemorial. As such, these works retain their absolute alterity while prodding us into an engagement with them within the horizon of our own world and its time. These works of art resist us through the unbridgeable otherness that makes them what they are, the rhythms and hues of their ever-so-distant sensibilities and preoccupations, while at the same time marking something intimate and attractive, even a form of knowledge that beckons us. One might say that what emerges at Lascaux with particular force is something essential that all older and ancient works of art silently share—each in its own singular way—but that is deeply inscribed into this prehistoric foundational scene. After all, the world in which these early works of art come to pass—that is, in which they are born and in which they, in turn, give birth to a unique world of their own—also appears to be the age in which the human being is on the brink of emerging onto the world scene, so that, from a certain perspective, the symbolic birth of art can hardly be thought in separation from the birth of what we call the human. At the scene of Lascaux, and within the multiply layered framework of its symbolic registers, more than one world comes into appearance, even as the terms and logic of this coming-into-appearance remain the object of persistent wonderment and questioning.

This wonderment and questioning—which one might say also calls to mind the moment of fundamental amazement, *thaumazein*, that gives birth to philosophical reflection in Plato's dialogue *Theaetetus*—belong to a critical comportment that preserves the dignity of the artwork upon which it reflects by honoring its irreducible alterity, indeed its very resistance to meaning. This is why Blanchot emphasizes, in the context of Bataille's meditation on the world of Lascaux, how "it does not do violence to the figures it nonetheless tears from the earth: it endeavors to shed light on them according to the brightness that emanates from them, a brightness that is always clearer than anything that explanations can offer us in order to clarify them."[12] The multiple ways in which these artworks defy interpretation pertain, among other things, to the structure of unknown magical rites as well as to what could be termed a "mysterious relation—a relation of interest, of conspiracy, of complicity, and even of friendship—between the human hunters and the flourishing of the animal kingdom."[13] To the extent that the multiple relations staged by these prehistoric artworks remain open-ended, at once under- and overdetermined, they elicit an act of interpretation that they always also resist. Without interpretation, the works must remain enigmatic; yet the hermeneutic labor required to make sense of them is unlikely to be rewarded with the stability of an achieved insight into their aesthetic functioning and their world. What arises, therefore, from these elicited yet deflected interpretations is "a world that is heavy, dark, complicated, and distant. Yet if the world of Lascaux is thus a world of obscure savagery, of mysterious rites and inaccessible customs, what strikes us, on the contrary, in the paintings of Lascaux is how natural they are, how joyful and, under cover of darkness, how prodigiously clear."[14] One might even say that, when pondered from a certain perspective, "there is nothing archaic about them" and that "they are less archaic even than the first forms of Greek art, and there is nothing that could be more dissimilar to them than the contoured, overburdened, and fascinating art of primitives today."[15] The resistance to meaning and interpretation that is lodged at the heart of these prehistoric artworks is anchored not merely in their historical distance; their meaning is not refractory merely due to their archaic remoteness from the time and epistemic framework of today's observer. Rather, the resistance to meaning and interpretation that these artworks generate is predicated precisely upon their aesthetic refutation of a mere archaism. If the double gesture with which these works both demand and resist meaning and interpretation were merely based in their archaism, it would be possible to imagine that they were fully transparent and present to themselves in their own time, thousands of years ago. But what if this were a fallacy? What if these artworks were already something of a hermeneutic provocation in their own world and in their own time? In that case, no historical reconstruction and no hermeneutic decoding could retroactively impose meaning on them. This inability to impose retroactive closure on the aesthetic play that an artwork performs is one of the reasons why one might find in these works something both dark and joyful, eternally obscure yet blessed with the illumination of an uncommon clarity. As such, these prehistoric artworks can be conceptualized as prime instantiations of "a communication at a distance and yet immediate that art brings with it, and of which art would be the perceptible affirmation, the evidence that no particular meaning can attain or exhaust."[16] They even communicate, one might add, the very fact *that* they communicate at a distance and *that* their meaning remains inexhaustible.

In a later text, the archive of fragments entitled *L'écriture du désastre*, Blanchot includes a one-sentence fragment, italicized: "*Keep watch over absent meaning* [*Veiller sur le sens absent*]."[17] In this apodictic injunction to safeguard (*veiller sur*) an absence, it is not the fullness or presence of a meaning that is to be cared for. The implied threat is not that of the imminent loss of meaning but rather the threat of a premature and misguided imposition of a meaning, in a manner that would stand to lose the benefits of (a) meaning's absence. Not to keep watch over absent meaning would mean to risk losing the loss—the loss of loss. Relating to the absence of meaning in a radically responsible manner entails safeguarding its very absence, affirming its loss as loss, rather than hopelessly seeking to undo the loss or absence by importing this or that meaning in order to fill a void. Keeping watch over absent meaning is to affirm the dignity and irreducibility of the experience of an absence, including the absence of meaning and the meaning of absence. One might say that this reflection bears in potent ways on our relation to the artwork at the Lascaux cave. Perhaps to do justice to their enigmatic nature and to the irretrievability of their long-perished world, one must affirm, even safeguard, their lacking and unreconstructable meaning. To keep watch over these works of art, to be their proper viewer, steward, and caretaker, means to keep watch over their absent meaning.

It should be noted, too, that in its English rendition, Blanchot's apodictic injunction—"*Keep watch over absent meaning*"—self-consciously omits both a definite and an indefinite article. Here, the translation makes explicit and available, owing to idiomatic necessity, a structure of reflection that is not fully audible as such in the original (which idiomatically gives us the definite article, "le sens") but nevertheless touches its spirit in decisive ways. In the English version, what is to be guarded is not, strictly speaking, "the absent meaning" or even "an absence," but rather absent meaning as such. In other words, it is possible to understand this sentence as a call for watchfulness not merely with regard to this or that absent meaning—a meaning that pertains to a specific situation or sign to be read, a meaning that *in principle* exists in some elsewhere, but happens not to be present *for us*—but rather also with regard to the idea of meaning and its absence as such. Relating to the particular situation of an absent meaning as one experiences it when confronting a certain sign would then also mean relating to the very concept of an absent meaning. In that case, what is to be kept watch over in relation to the absent meaning of something is the notion of absence as such. Is it possible, then, to hear within the injunction to safeguard the absent meaning of the artworks in the Lascaux caves the broader injunction to affirm the value and potentiality of the very idea of a meaning that we encounter only as an absence?

If these artworks at Lascaux and the worlds that they create remain inaccessible to any meaning achieved by hermeneutic interpretation yet at the same time persist in a joyfully nonhermetic state, it is, to evoke one of Blanchot's phrasings, because they dwell in an "inexplicable simplicity."[18] The world of art found at Lascaux therefore has a way of "disorienting us," but "by its nearness and by all that renders it immediately readable to us," it is "mysterious as art but not an art of mystery nor of distance."[19] A different kind of unreadability obtains in these works, one that is not the binary other to readability. The inexplicable simplicity that the viewer encounters in these artworks is of a different order. It is pellucid in its obscurity, yet refractory in its apparent availability. These artworks project a world that remains mysterious precisely to the extent that what is said and thought about it appears transparent and straightforward. If one were to come across a statement such as "He does not have time because he spends his days creating little frog statues," such an utterance might well cause hermeneutic consternation. Its plain declarative form conveys a supposedly simple state of affairs; yet its content remains entirely strange and enigmatic. There tends to be a tenacious kernel of residual obscurity even in the most transparent of statements (and states of affair).

One way of conceptualizing the (figurative) birth of art in the world of its prehistoric setting is to think this art in relation to how it mobilizes, affirms, even celebrates the imbrication of the obscure and the transparent that are idiomatic to its aesthetic form in decisive ways. As Blanchot suggests, we may think of such work as "art that thus comes to our encounter from the depths of millennia, in the lightness of what is manifest, with the movement of the herd in motion, the movement of the life of passage animating all of the figures."[20] With respect to this movement, "we think we touch, through an illusion that is even stronger than theories, the only happiness of artistic activity: the celebration of the happy discovery of art. Art is present here as its own celebration."[21] While the artwork is not present to itself in the sense of any self-identity, any stable meaning, it is present as its own affirmation. Art attends its own inception and birth in the framework of a celebration that is not dependent on arresting this or that meaning. The world of this art nevertheless is one of disclosure, bringing-forth, and setting-into-work—all with a lightness and aesthetic simplicity that respects its enigmatic character. The aestheticized movement of animals, whether in a herd or individually, along with the vistas upon distant scenes of long-decayed worlds, both provoke and preserve an experience of double world-disclosure: a world that has fallen away many millennia ago and an aesthetic world of presentation that continues to be set up—that is, created and projected—by the artworks themselves, even after so much historical time has lapsed.

To mark the advent of art in this manner also is to consider the advent of the human being as a kind of tool-user, a being committed to producing work in a world for which such technical instrumentality designates a departure. In this world, the early human emerges as a worker who, through his art, innovates and progresses, stepping out of the world of nature and into the world of culture and *techné*. The attendant experience of such a stepping-out is inscribed in the very traces of the artworks that adorn the Lascaux caves, even as the precise content of this experience eludes reconstruction today. It is no accident, therefore, that Blanchot invites us to consider the passage from the world of nature via the artwork to what he terms "a place apart," a site marked by its separation from the previous episteme of the world in which the works were created:

> We are of course ignorant of the "feeling" experienced by
> that worker, when, by means of prodigious innovations,
> he began to occupy a place apart and to separate himself
> from other living species. We are tempted to attribute to

him some movement of pride, of power, of disquieting
cruelty that is nonetheless superb. Perhaps such was indeed
the case. However, everything seems to indicate that man
retained a memory of distress and horror of his first steps
into humanity. Everything forces us to think that latent man
always felt himself infinitely weak in everything that made
him powerful, either because he sensed the essential lack—
which alone enabled him to become something completely
other—or because, in becoming other, he experienced as a
mistake everything that led him to fail what we call nature.
This void separating him and the natural community is,
it seems, what revealed destruction and death to him, but
he also learned, not without pain or misgiving, to use this
void: to make use of and deepen his weakness in order to
become stronger. The prohibitions, which Georges Bataille
assumes man used to draw a circle around human possibility
from the very beginning—sexual prohibitions, prohibitions
about death, and murder—are there as barriers preventing
the being who goes beyond himself from coming back, in
order to force him to continue along the dangerous, doubtful
path, a dead end more or less, and thus to protect all forms
of activity that are tedious and against nature, and that have
taken their final form in work and through work.[22]

While exiting from the world of nature into another world—a place
apart—by means of artisanal work and the tool-based creation of
complex works of art is an experience of empowerment and liberation, what attaches to such exiting is also a primal anxiety, a residual discomfort caused by becoming other. If the self-conscious
creation of artworks is the engine of a kind of self-transformation,
even a form of self-othering, such othering is beset by a doubt or
insecurity pertaining to the new world and one's place in it. To the
extent that early man's artful steps into humanity "retained a memory of distress and horror," such memory cannot but be encrypted
in the very art that early man produced. What, one might ask,
constitutes this memory? What accounts for the sense of weakness
that suffuses even the experience of triumph that attends transgression into the otherness of another world? Following the line

of argumentation that Blanchot opens up, it is precisely the latent memory of an essential weakness, even lack, that characterized his previous being-in-the-world—in other words, precisely the state of affairs that first propelled him to move into otherness through the act of aesthetic world-creation—that continues to haunt the early human. It is as if at any given moment, the human could relapse into its previous world, relinquishing the hard-won fruits of its own self-othering in the newly created world. The essential lack that propelled the human to engage in aesthetic world-making cannot simply be filled or erased: it continues to accompany the human as a constitutive feature that makes it what, who, and how it is in the world.

By the same token, the doubt and fragility that continue to accompany the self-othered human may owe their persistence to a suspicion that the world of nature has been inadmissibly betrayed, a transgression for which there might still be a high price to pay. Feeling ashamed for having turned his back on nature in favor of a more technical and aestheticized world, the early human continues to engage in his newly found artistic creation in the nagging consciousness of its futility. To the extent that the abyss separating the early man who creates art from the previously inhabited world of nature is, among other things, also a marker of death and destruction, this knowledge makes itself felt in the art. The work of art produced within this framework thus not only finds its condition of possibility in the separating abyss, but also takes as its very subject the momentous and quite possibly traumatic first steps into humanity. One might say that what obtains in the emerging consciousness of the early human, as well as in the artworks produced by this human, is the dialectic according to which any movement into culture remains suffused with the knowledge of a certain barbarous act of violence that precipitated the movement out of the world of nature into the radical otherness of the "place apart," the new world opened by art and technics. When seen from this perspective, it becomes possible to espy in the very tension of this movement the dialectic of progress and regression that Benjamin memorably formulates in his theses "On the Concept of History": "There is no document of culture which is not at the same time a document of barbarism."[23] Did the prehistoric artists working in the Lascaux cave already entertain an essential relation to the experience of this dialectic?

It is tempting to imagine that those taking their first steps into the world of humanity were at least inchoately cognizant of the inaugurating dialectic of culture and barbarism, progress and regression, triumph and doubt lodged at the heart of their artistic work. Even if their art was not in fact the very first art in a historical sense—as Blanchot rightly suggests, "we know, and we feel, that this art, beginning here, had already begun a long time before"[24]— the artworks at Lascaux speak directly to the very idea of a birth of art and the idea of a world in which art exists. If the caverns at Lascaux are "unique" but "not alone," that is, "first" but not "the very first," this is because for "thousands of years man had been sculpting, engraving, drawing, coloring, and scribbling; sometimes he even represented a human face, as in the figure of Bassempouy."[25] However one wishes to situate the birth of art in the setting of historical time, there can be no doubt as to the significance of the world that the earliest artworks open up, even if art has always already begun. It is through these works that our own idea of world is called into presence in an encompassing and emphatic sense, all the more so as that world, along with those beings inhabiting it, remains enigmatic even to this day. As Blanchot puts it:

> Art would thus provide us with our only authentic date of birth: a date that is rather recent and necessarily indeterminate, even though the paintings of Lascaux seem to bring it still closer to us by the feeling of proximity with which they seduce us. Yet is it truly a feeling of proximity? Rather of presence, or, more precisely, of apparition. Before these works are erased from the history of painting by the ruthless movement that brought them to light of day, it is perhaps necessary to specify ... the impression they give of appearing, of being there only momentarily, drawn by the moment and for the moment, figures not nocturnal but rendered visible by the instantaneous opening up of the night.[26]

According to the figurative sense developed in this line of thought, the advent of art as aesthetic practice emerges as the dawn of a particular form of being-in-the-world: a humanity that is conscious of its own stepping-into-the-world as an exit from a previous world. In this newly created world, the world that is set up in and through the work of art, the human's being-in-the-world ceases to be a self-evident given but rather becomes an abiding question mark. In the wake of the birth of the human through the advent of art, essential questions pertaining to what it means to be human, how to conceive of inhabiting a world in this or that way, and how to relate to finitude are cast into sharp relief as the guiding framework of experience.

If the works at Lascaux are both the traces and the archives of such questions, their apparent proximity, mediated by an "inexplicable simplicity," conveys the experience of a nearness that nevertheless remains irreducibly distant. It is not by chance that Blanchot prefers to speak of a presence not in the sense of a given fullness or the essence of an ontological availability, but rather an elusive and fleeting presence that evokes something haunting and uncanny. The artworks at Lascaux address us like apparitions, specters of unfinished historical business, ghosts of distant former beings whispering to us in hushed and scrambled voices across the abyss of millennia. To appreciate the ways in which these works, in their very visibility as aesthetic forms, simultaneously perform an "opening up of the night" is to be receptive to their spectral communication. The distant figures populating the world of these works touch us like a haunting chant beckoning us to commune with them while at the same time withdrawing from stable signification and legibility. To read the works, to follow the rays of the world-illumination that they sponsor, always also means to accept their invitation to step into the opening of the night that is uniquely theirs.

At this point, the question could be raised as to what kind of origin is embodied by art that is conceived in the sense developed here. If art can neither have nor be a simple origin, it is nevertheless imbricated with the *idea* of an origin, that is, with the retrievability of a certain primordial caesura that worked to open up a world.[27] To the extent that origin is always a retroactive invention, the belated assignment of a meaning that was never present to begin with, a conceptual prosthetic that enables a narrative of

unfolding after the fact, it gives rise to a promise: the promise of a
sheer beginning, of a beginning *as* beginning. It is from this perspective that Blanchot avers:

> Art is intimately associated with the origin, which is itself
> always brought back to the non-origin; art explores, asserts,
> gives rise to—through a contact that shatters all acquired
> form—what is essentially before; what is, without yet being.
> And at the same time it is ahead of all that has been, it is
> the promise kept in advance, the youth of what is always
> beginning and only beginning. Nothing can prove that art
> began at the same time as man; on the contrary, everything
> indicates that there was a significant lapse in time. However,
> the first great moments of art suggest that man has contact
> with his own beginning—is the initial affirmation of himself,
> the expression of his own novelty   only when, by the means
> and methods of art, he enters into communication with
> the force, brilliance, and joyful mastery of a power that is
> essentially the power of beginning, which is also to say, of a
> beginning-again that is always prior. At Lascaux, art is not
> beginning, nor is man beginning. But it is at Lascaux, in its
> vast and narrow cave, along its populated walls, in space that
> seems never to have been an ordinary dwelling place, that art
> no doubt for the first time reached the plenitude of initiative
> and thus opened to man a unique abode with himself and
> with the marvel, behind which he had necessarily to remove
> and efface himself in order to discover himself: the majesty
> of the great bulls, the dark fury of the bison, the grace of
> the little horses, the dreamy sprightliness of the stags, even
> the ridiculousness of the large jumping cows. As we know,
> man is represented—and then merely by certain schematic
> features—only in the scene at the bottom of the well:
> there he lies, stretched out between a charging bison and
> a rhinoceros that is turned the other way. Is he dead? Is he
> asleep? ... Will he come to, come back to life?[28]

Art in the sense in which it arises out of the Lascaux cave is thus
struck with a certain uncircumventable untimeliness. It names an

essential anteriority, a beforeness that cannot be reduced to a mere former presence. But it is also at the same time always already ahead of itself, outpacing itself, reaching ahead into an unnamed futurity in which it marks a perpetual youth. If this youth can, as Blanchot suggests, be thought in terms of the structure of a promise—one that is to be fulfilled and reaffirmed in an undated time to come—it is because it names the very notion of beginning, the beginning of beginning as such, the beginning that will always begin one more time. Much like Heidegger's thought of *der Anfang* or *der andere Anfang*, the beginning toward which Blanchot here wishes to think attempts to capture the other-directedness of a thinking that is committed to an absolute futurity, a time and a world still to come in which the very act of beginning will begin again—and again. While such a beginning-again is always also a previous beginning, a beginning that will in fact have begun even before it begins and before it begins again, what begins in this beginning is the promise of entering, through the artwork, an essential relation to the world that it sets up and into the openness of the open.

To affirm the futurity of an openness through the artworks at Lascaux in this way is to conceive of time itself as having a future. Such an affirmation is not self-evident nor can it be taken for granted. In a letter to Bataille from 1958 or 1959—only a few years after Bataille's book on the caves appeared—Blanchot confides to his friend that he has been struck by a certain "silence between me and myself, as well as a difficult period of waiting, accepting a time without a future."[29] What does it mean to accept a time without a future? What is affirmed in such an acceptance? What kind of time does not have a future? Blanchot does not say explicitly. A time without future is a time folded back upon itself; it figures simultaneously as the absolute present of experience, in which the nowness of a temporal point comes to pass as such, while also serving as the horizon against which thought demands to be measured at any given moment. Although time cannot be arrested, there is an experience of time that is divorced from any futurity, that is, from the to-come structure of what it is not (yet). It marks a relationship to finitude in such a way as to hold open only the *hic et nunc* of lived experience. Is it possible to locate a tension between Blanchot's experience of a futureless time, as manifest by his consenting to a time without a future, and the futurity that is affirmed by the openness of the prehistoric artworks and the worlds they open up? Does our fascination with the images at Lascaux lie partly in the ways in which they silently refuse to consent to a time without a future, even as they seem to disappear into the distant depths of millennia? Beckoning from a time before time, the artworks disrupt futureless time by reaching into a series of remote worlds and eras that are not their own and of which their prehistoric creators could not have dreamed.

Among all the striking images of a world of deer and bulls, cows and bison, horses and stags, what image of the human being emerges? What kind of world does the human being set up through the work of art? Is the aesthetically conscious human being merely a witness to this world, or does the human fully belong to it? Is the human's head diverted from the world and its inhabitants (as depicted in the scene at the bottom of the well), or does the human being seek an active part in a community populated with others—and other world-makers? To dwell in such a world is to expose oneself to the radical fragility and transitoriness of being-in-the-world, the experience of not knowing how to relate to the world in which one is situated at any given time. The prehistoric artworks at Lascaux provide an image of how art gives rise to perpetual reflection—even an infinite conversation, as Blanchot might say—on these questions as they conspire to yield a world that makes and unmakes us.[30]

The world that arises out of the Lascaux art cave places the human being "in touch with everything he has ceased to be, also allows him never to be simply himself," as Blanchot aptly puts it.[31] Among many other things, this means that the world created by these prehistoric artworks relates us to a past in which we were and were not what we are today, just as that same art related early man as he first stepped into the world of humanity to the very world he was uneasily leaving behind. Read as an elaborate archive of this double relation, the art at Lascaux also works against the mobilization of the archival traces that it gathers in the service of this or that identity-formation. In other words, the artworks found at Lascaux refuse to be instrumentalized on behalf of any myth of origin or narrative of foundation, heritage, and provenance that would lend itself to exploitation for purposes of projecting or legitimating an identity. Lascaux is perhaps one of the names of what makes identity impossible. Instead, the archive of works located in the cave preserves another kind of beginning, a liberated mode of dwelling in the world. The irreducible freedom that emanates from these works derives from the fundamental permission they offer not to be oneself, or to be oneself only among other things. To be allowed never to be (only) oneself, to be in communication not simply with what makes one who and what one is but also with what forever disrupts such identification, is inextricably bound up with the experience that makes these works authentic markers of our date of birth.[32]

To insist that the artworks of the cave, through their provision of the experience of non-self-identity and their sanctioning of what makes one's identity impossible, give rise to a certain kind of freedom also is to be hospitable to the ways in which the world that these works set up lives in the shadow of finitude. If these artworks herald not only the triumph of the human as it steps into the world of humanity but also the trepidation that such stepping forward elicits, it is because what we find encoded in the archive of these works is also "the furtive, fearful, indelible trace of man who is for the first time born of his work, but who also feels seriously threatened by this work and perhaps already struck with death."[33] As markers of mortality and as commemorations of a death that has always long since occurred—sometimes many millennia ago—but is nevertheless still to come, they belong to a world that has both perished and is in the process of shaping itself anew. For the early human being who steps into humanity for the first time by creating a world in which works of art exist, the fashioning of the work cannot be separated from the intimations of his finitude. The work, created by the living, will outlive its creator and, in fact, has no need of him, even while he is still alive.[34] It functions in his absence. To construct a world by making a work of art is to render oneself superfluous, even if by creating the work one has opened another world. Here, life and death are once more no longer so radically separate. They touch each other—indeed, live inside one another—in all the remarkable and haunting ways that the complex simplicity of the enigmatic artworks at Lascaux will have made vivid for eternity.

88

If Blanchot's reflections on the prehistoric art at the Lascaux cave that was rediscovered in 1940 were animated in decisive ways by those of Bataille before him, they are imbued with renewed significance in light of the more recent discovery, in 1994, of a similar but older cave. The two distinct caves in present-day France are conceptually linked, as if through a subterranean connecting path. The older cave is situated in Chauvet-Pont-d'Arc, near the small town of Vallon-Pont-d'Arc in the south of France, dating back to the Last Glacial Period in Paleolithic Europe, a time during which early modern European humans (Cro-Magnons) and Neanderthals coexisted. The earliest artworks at the Chauvet cave, which was dedicated to the creation of art for many thousands of years by various early human societies, date back to about 36,000 years ago. In 2010, the German filmmaker Werner Herzog created a meditative documentary film about the Chauvet cave and its art, entitled *Cave of Forgotten Dreams*, for which he had been granted exceptional and exclusive permission by the French Ministry of Culture to shoot footage in the cave itself (which, because of its fragility, is not open to the public), for a very short time (a matter of a few hours across the span of only a few days) and under severely restricted conditions.[35] As Herzog explains in his "Director's Statement," the opportunity to create a film about some of the oldest known pictorial representations created by human beings held special meaning to him. It is noteworthy that the origin of his aesthetic and conceptual interest in the cave art at Chauvet can be traced back to his early childhood fascination with the Lascaux cave:

> My intellectual, my spiritual awakening was in a way
> connected to Paleolithic cave paintings. I alone discovered
> it for myself, it was my first independent quest. At the
> age of twelve, I spotted a book in the display window of a
> bookstore with a picture of a horse from the Lascaux cave
> on it, and an indescribable excitement took hold of me: I
> wanted this book, I had to have it. I wanted to know about
> these paintings before the time of the domestication of
> animals and before the invention of agriculture.

As my pocket money was only one dollar per month, I
started to work as a ball-boy on tennis courts, and borrowed
money from my brothers. At least once a week, I would check,
my heart pounding, if the book was still there. Apparently, I
believed this was the only one. It took more than half a year
until I could buy and open the book, and the shudder of awe
and wonder has never left me since.[36]

If, for Herzog, to delve into the world of the Chauvet cave as an
artist also is to delve into his childhood—that is, into the world
of his own prehistory as a creator of art—it is with an eye toward
excavating some of his earliest aesthetic impulses as they fastened
upon his imaginative obsession with the prehistoric cave art of
Lascaux. Was it perhaps the cover of Bataille's book on the art of
the Lascaux cave that Herzog had seen on display in the book-
store window? We do not know, and Herzog does not say, even
though this is entirely possible, even plausible, as Bataille's book
was published in a German translation by Karl-Georg Hemmerich
in 1955 as *Die vorgeschichtliche Malerei. Lascaux oder die Geburt der Kunst*
with the Swiss publisher Skira, the same year in which Skira also
brought out the original French text. The book appeared at a time
when Herzog would have been an early teenager and looking with
awe at the brightly lit marvels in the shop windows of his local
bookstores in postwar Germany.[37] Furthermore, Bataille's book
did in fact have the picture of a horse from the Lascaux cave on
its cover, just as in Herzog's recollection (to be precise, the cover
showed the second "Chinese Horse," numbered 43, from the
right wall of the so-called Axial Gallery). *Cave of Forgotten Dreams*
is thus itself a cinematic archive in the double sense: it is hospitable not only to the Paleolithic works but also to the filmmaker's
long-standing obsession with its subject matter dating back to
his youth. The complex animal scenes depicted in the cave art,
along with the ancient crystal formations, the stalactites and sta-
lagmites, fossilized footprints, remains of prehistoric bones and
skulls, bone flutes, and human handprints that populate the cave
are interwoven in Herzog's film not only with the views of archae-
ologists and other scholars and scientists working on the subject
of the cave but also with his own reactions to, and meditations on,

the works and the worlds from which they arose and the aesthetic worlds they set up.

If Herzog here figures as an artist whose work of image-creation communes with the work of artists who created their images tens of thousands of years ago—that is, if his cinematic act of world-opening touches upon the pictorial act of world-opening that so radically antedates his and, in a certain way, first made it possible through a kind of aesthetic inheritance—there are dimensions of the film in which this world-opening relation across the millennia is staged in explicit and self-conscious ways. There is, for instance, the image of the bison, which is depicted on the cave wall not with four legs, as one might have expected, but rather with eight if one looks closely. One can envision this image being viewed by a group of early humans in the dark, with only a small, unsteadily held torch or two providing flickering illumination. As Herzog therefore observes in his narration, for "these Paleolithic painters, the play of light and shadows from torches could possibly have looked something like this. For them, the animals perhaps appeared moving, living. We should note that the artist painted this bison with eight legs, suggesting movement, almost a form of proto-cinema." By the same token, the "walls themselves are not flat but have their own three-dimensional dynamic, their own movement, which was utilized by the artists. In the upper-right corner, another multi-legged animal and the rhino to the right seem also to have the illusion of movement, like frames in an animated film."[38] If it is possible to imagine that the multiple legs of some of the depicted animals were meant to indicate not its standstill but its rapid movement, the earlier artists can be imagined as wishing to inscribe into their paintings the very blur of a velocity that is created by the animal's running. To be sure, it is rather provocative and bold to imagine, with Herzog, that such an image stages a form of prehistorical cinema. And yet Herzog's proposition has legs. After all, it is undeniable that the view of the world evoked by the image of the many-legged bison is sensitive and hospitable to the dynamic dimension of movement, as if the image bore an unconscious historic-technical relation to the rapid sequencing of individual still frames that, in their precipitous celluloid projection, create the impression of cinematic motion. It is as if the Paleolithic world that perished forever along with the prehistoric artists had set up a perspective that would resonate in a much later world—our world—in which the cinematic artwork itself sets up a world of images that seek to capture the dynamism of its subjects. (It is worth noting that in the final part of the film, Herzog self-reflexively pays homage to the proto-cinematic movement of the animal paintings by showing them through a variety of changing and dynamic effects of moving light.) Through his own cinematic artwork, Herzog thus figures as a self-conscious heir to an ancient artistic legacy, receiving and reworking the proto-cinematic inheritance of his enigmatic predecessors in ways that are singular to his own visual idiom and artistic style.[39]

It bears noting that the aesthetically created world to which the viewer of the Chauvet cave paintings is an heir can hardly be reduced to the notion of primitive art that first needed to be developed out of its crudeness into more sophisticated manifestations across the millennia. In that sense, the early art does not figure as a mere seed to grow and develop in various stages across time, eventually blossoming with the splendor of a mature plant. The depth of expression, the affective intensity, and the mastery of technique found in the cave paintings are too profound and too striking not to be considered highly refined forms of art in their own right. Herzog's film captures this view on the world of the Chauvet paintings not only through his meticulous cinematic mise-en-scène of individual works and their constellations in the cave setting; it also explicitly addresses this impression in narrative terms. For instance, about midway into the film, during a panoramic long shot of the Ardèche valley region where the cave is located, Herzog comments in his voice-over: "What the people who lived in this valley left behind is their great art. It was not a primitive beginning or a slow evolution; it rather burst on the scene like a sudden, explosive event. It is as if the modern human soul had awakened here." What suffuses these works of art in a most essential manner is the way in which they self-consciously capture the momentum of this explosive emergence. Giving birth to a decidedly modern artistic consciousness, the artworks, in addition to depicting their particular animal subjects, self-consciously stage their own structure of emergence, which is to say, emergence as emergence, even the emergence of emergence itself. The aesthetic world that these works set up, through their remarkably well-preserved and vivid renditions of bison and lions, aurochs and horses, mammoths and woolly rhinoceroses, is suffused by a sense of potentiality and possibility, openness and marvel, in short by the emergence of a world and a world of emergence.[40]

This essential experience of world-emergence as it comes to pass in the cave paintings at Chauvet is supplemented, even enriched, by a series of phenomena in the cave that were presumably not originally intended as works of art or as meaningful structures imbued with aesthetic significance but that have come to interact with the surrounding artworks in enigmatic and highly suggestive ways. They, too, contribute to the scene of the cave as though it were a kind of *Gesamtkunstwerk* in which the emergence of a world and the world of emergence came to be captured on their own terms, even if, as Blanchot puts it with regard to the Lascaux cave paintings, they are also "already struck with death." For instance, on the floor of the cave, which consists of a soft, almost claylike substance that is rather impressionable and sensitive, one finds preserved, side by side, the traces of a walking child and those of a wolf or early wolf-dog. The child's footprints, which scientists date to about 27,000 to 25,000 years ago, moving visually alongside the animal's prints, constitute a fascinating challenge to any hermeneutic endeavor to arrest their meaning, even as they continually and irresistibly beckon the viewer to interpret them. About one hour into the film, we are shown mysterious, dark outlines from within the cave as we hear Herzog's voice narrate: "The cave transforms into an enchanted world of the imaginary, where time and space lose their meaning." And he continues: "In a forbidden recess of the cave, there are footprints of an 8-year-old boy next to the footprints of a wolf. Did the hungry wolf stalk the boy? Or did they walk together as friends? Or were their tracks made thousands of years apart? We will never know." While the footprints of the child and those of the wolf or wolf-dog will remain forever intertwined in the history of our culture, their relation will continue to pose an enigma.[41] The world that is suggested by the footprints emerges as one in which close historical proximity, even intimacy, cannot be separated from vast historical distance, so that what appears so closely related is at the same time situated at an unimaginably immense remove, an abyss of experience and temporality. One may even speak, paradoxically, of an intimately close abyss of radical separation. It is through this undecidable interplay of relation, indexed in the preserved footprints of the child and the wolf or wolf-dog, that the enigma of an emergent yet unreadable world is given over into presence. As viewers, we are the heirs of this enigma; through an infinite network of mediations, this enigma has passed our own world on to us.

Another striking instance of such enigmatic signs supplementing the pictorial artwork proper is the red print of an apparently deformed hand that can be seen at the entrance of the cave (multiplied in a constellation of handprints) and then again repeated several times throughout it. Some of the images of this hand are positive handprints (in which the color-covered palm is pressed against the cave walls), while others are negative handprints (in which the color appears to have been blown around the hand, so that the hand appears in outline. It is presumed that both the positive and the negative handprints were made from the hand of one and the same man: not only do the prints appear to have the same size and shape, but one can also detect a slightly crooked pinkie and, in certain images, two slightly webbed middle fingers, in addition to a somewhat misshapen or deformed thumb. (It is worth noting that the handprints of the Chauvet cave implicitly convene with handprints found on the walls of other prehistoric caves as well, such as those in the caves of Gargas, in the Pyrenees region of France, where they proliferate, with many of the prints also exhibiting deformations.)[42] As for the man who made the handprints at the Chauvet cave, he was about six feet tall and—according to Dominique Baffier, archaeologist and curator of the Chauvet cave, speaking in Herzog's film—the cave scientists have ascertained that he created the large image of multiple handprints at the cave's entrance by first crouching to press his palm against the wall and then gradually moving up to the highest level he could reach while fully standing and stretching. It is as if we "followed" this man into the cave—as if he were leading us along a path through his world with his handprints, becoming our ghostly guide across the ages.

Yet, beyond this sensation of being "guided" into the cave, what are we to make of these unusual traces? What was the man attempting to accomplish by marking the cave with his red-colored handprint? Is this a case of early graffiti, perhaps marking a territory? What made him select the color red for all his handprints—its striking hues, which make it stand out from a darker backdrop, or rather something else? Was the man one of the ancient artists who, perhaps, sought to provide something akin to a signature or mark of origin for the works? Did he wish to draw attention to the deformity of his hand, recording a silent complaint or a mute pictorial testimony to his suffering? If he was in fact one of the Chauvet artists, was it his wish to emphasize the fact that he was in fact able to create such remarkable works in spite of the handicap placed upon him by the deformation? Or do the prints of his misshapen hand rather serve as signs that explain why, unlike others, he was unable to contribute, or to contribute as fully, to the cave art? Are his handprints a form of early vandalism and disfiguration of the existing artworks? Or do his self-conscious handprints rather constitute something like an artistic response, an aesthetic countersignature, as it were, that blesses and celebrates the works created by others? In the absence of human faces in the art of the cave, is the representation of the human hand a depiction of what was most salient to the early artists—that is to say, not individual faces but rather the hand as the instrument that allowed the works to be created through its artisanal handicraft? What was it that prompted him to set his red handprint on the cave walls multiple times? What was it about the repetition and reiteration of his methodic, strategic, and strangely obsessive and dreamlike self-presentation through the hand that he sought to convey?

Or might one be on the right path in considering the possibility that the early person responsible for the red handprints meant to interject and affirm, in the midst of all the animal scenes and in the near-complete absence of human depictions in the cave, the idea of the human by isolating and emphasizing that most human of human body parts, the hand? It is no accident, after all, that Heidegger explicitly relates the hand and its handicraft, something that animals presumably do not possess, to the human as such. In a number of texts, among them "The Origin of the Work of Art" and "What Calls for Thinking?," Heidegger places special significance on the hand. He pursues the idea that thinking in its essence is a craft, a "handicraft," what in German is called *Handwerk*. For him, the "hand is something altogether peculiar. In the common view, the hand is part of our bodily organism. But the hand's essence can never be determined, or explained, by its being an organ that can grasp. Apes, too, have organs that can grasp, but they do not have hands. The hand is infinitely different from all the grasping organs—paws, claws, or fangs—different by an abyss of essence. Only a being who can speak, that is, think, can have hands and can handily achieve works of handicraft."[43] And he expands upon this thought by noting that

> the craft of the hand is richer than we commonly imagine. The hand does not only grasp and catch, or push and pull. The hand reaches and extends, receives and welcomes—and not just things: the hand extends itself, and receives its own welcome in the hands of others. The hand holds. The hand carries. The hand designs and signs presumably because man is a sign. Two hands fold into one, a gesture meant to carry man into the great oneness. The hand is all this, and this is the true handicraft. Everything is rooted here that is commonly known as handicraft, and commonly we go no further. But the hand's gestures run everywhere through language, in their most perfect purity precisely when man speaks by being silent. And only when man speaks, does he think—not the other way around, as metaphysics still believes. Every motion of the hand in every one of its works carries itself through the element of thinking, every bearing of the hand bears itself in that element. All the work of the hand is rooted in thinking. Therefore, thinking itself is man's simplest, and for that reason hardest, handiwork, if from time to time it would be accomplished properly.[44]

For all the difficulties and question marks that arise out of Heidegger's elucidations of the hand exclusively as a human hand, they do provide a powerful image of the singular hand as that which hold us into Being in a primordial manner.[45] If thinking is a form of handicraft—or *Handwerk*, the work of the hand—there can be no genuine reflection, no commitment to a reflective engagement with how a human being constructs and experiences the world, without engaging with the hand. And when viewed from a certain ontological perspective, all handwork has its root in the reflective act of thinking, since it is to the question of the handiwork of the hand that the questioning human being turns. Holding, carrying, reaching, extending, receiving, grasping, pushing, pulling, catching, and clutching—and even thinking and speaking: the hand reaches into the being of the human in fundamental ways.

Is it possible, from this Heideggerian vantage point of the hand, to read the red handprinter's marks also as a kind of primordial handiwork of Being? If this unknown yet forever immortalized man who created these handprints in such deliberate fashion was in fact experiencing what Blanchot, with respect to the Lascaux cave, refers to as a first step into humanity, do his red handprints mark the experience of that essential step in a primal way? Did he experience himself, through the world created by his work, as the essential creature of the hand? Were his self-consciously, almost obsessively repeated handprints the commemorative markers of an unsettling new experience—the step into humanity—through which the handicraft of the handprints proliferated as though they were ever-multiplying question marks? It is not baseless to surmise that in this stepping into humanity which occurred in and through the art at Chauvet, the human began to experience his own existence as something utterly enigmatic, something worthy of perpetual questioning. Finding oneself on the other side of the stride into humanity means finding oneself surrounded—and suffused—by questions about what it means to be human and what it is to live and to die like a human. This is what our being-in-the-world hands us as a primordially human question—and therefore as a question to be grasped and worked on with the handicraft of our thinking hands.

Are we as viewers of the human handprints at Chauvet not situated as the dramatically belated witnesses of a mute communion with thinking as an accomplished work of human handicraft? To what extent does the red hand of this prehistoric man   cave visitor or resident artist—reach out to us across tens of thousands

of years, seeking to share the hand—the handiness of the hand—
that he and we have in common, to shake our hand across the
ages, to embrace our common finitude through our mutual human
handicraft? Do his two hands and ours thereby "fold into one," to
borrow Heidegger's language, extending to us "a gesture meant to
carry into the great oneness," even as we inhabit a world so foreign, so strange, so radically other to his own world that he might
only—but this already is a lot—recognize our shared hand in it?
We cannot say for certain. Yet each time we attend with care and
patience to the world opened by the art of the Chauvet cave, we
silently agree to shake the red hand that inhabits it so deliberately,
so searchingly, and in a manner that appears so cautiously human.
We accept and—if we are willing and able—return the hospitality
that the hand mutely extends to us across the historical and essential abyss of our shared, infinitely fragile humanity.

To commune, from the world of our own historical vantage
point, with the specters arising from the Paleolithic world of the
early artists, under the sign of a shared and infinitely fragile essential humanity also means to experience an uncanny feeling. Coin-
habiting the world of the cave with the specters of the early artists
who have long passed can create a haunting sensation, as Herzog
notes in his film: "Dwarfed by the large chambers, illuminated by
our wandering lights, sometimes we were overcome by a strange,
irrational sensation, as if we were disturbing the Paleolithic people in their work. It felt like eyes upon us. This sensation occurred
to some of the scientists and also the discoverers of the cave. It
was a relief to surface again above ground." To extend the hand of
human communion, across the abyss of history, to the Paleolithic
painters can be a ghostly experience, even for a modern-day artist, who may come to think of his work in the world of the cave as
a disruption, a spectral disturbance of an ongoing and steadfast
artistic work that started tens of thousands of years ago and that
continues mutely yet unwaveringly to the present day and beyond.
After all, as Herzog observes at another point in the film, "we are
locked into history, and they were not."

Aside from the red handprints, the only other partial representation of a human at Chauvet is found in the deepest part of the
cave, the so-called Chamber of the Lions: an enigmatic image of a

woman's exposed pelvic area that, painted on a protruding rock pendant, doubles as the heads of lions. While in the *Cave of Forgotten Dreams* we are first told by the cave curator that it is impossible to obtain a full image of this pictorial figure because this would require stepping onto the sensitive cave floor, Herzog later does manage to devise a way of capturing the full image for his film. It turns out that, on the other side of the painted rock pendant, one sees the representation of a bull, an imagistic association of a female and a bull that, as the curator points out, stretches from the world of the Paleolithic artists all the way into our own time, as evidenced, for instance, in Picasso's image of a woman and a minotaur. The world that opens from this female pubic area which also represents an animal's head convenes with, even as it differs from, more familiar representations of world-creation through female genitalia as we encounter it in much later artworks, such as Gustave Courbet's canonical oil painting *L'origine du monde* (*The Origin of the World*) (1866), on display in Paris at the Musée d'Orsay. As in the Chauvet painting, and as in the earliest known representations of the human form such as the early Aurignacian figurine named Venus of Hohle Fels—a six-centimeter statuette of a woman's body carved out of mammoth ivory found in present-day Germany's Swabian Alps—the woman depicted in *The Origin of the World* has no head and no face. It is as though, through an irreducible emphasis on reproduction, sexuality, seduction, fertility, coming-into-being, and bodily generativity broadly conceived, the origins of the world as they are depicted in the cave art as well as in our modern art shared a common perspective onto world-opening as such. Here, the individuality of the female—or, indeed, of any—human form is secondary, in the aesthetic imaginary, to its setting forth of a world. What appears to be at stake in the affirmation of life as life is a radical form of natality or birthingness—to borrow the language that Arendt employs in a different context in her refunctionalization of Heidegger's notion of *Gebürtigkeit*.

If the only pictorial portrayal of a human at Chauvet consists in a depiction of a vulva that also serves as an animal's head, this portrait comes into focus even more sharply through the conspicuous absence of a human head or face. (Even the schematically drawn man at the well scene at the Lascaux cave possessed a

rudimentary face.) The world of portraiture without human face
or look not only points to the absence of the human face in the
field of visuality, it also draws attention, by implicit contrast, to the
subtle and multilayered faces and facial expressions with which so
many of the animal figures are endowed. It is as if the expressive
face and complex gaze of the animal assumed the full complexity
that inheres in the idea of a portrait—a genre of painting that, in
our own world of aesthetic conventions, we tend to associate with
the realm of the human and the human face. In his discussion
of the idea of the portrait—more specifically, a certain "visageity"
that emerges through the "visibility of visuality" itself—Jean-Luc
Nancy points out that the "portrait is strongly associated with the
visage" and that "the latter word used to have the same meaning
as the former: A *visage* was a portrait before being a *face*."[46] Here,
the "face [*le visage*] makes visible the vision that, strictly speaking,
itself remains invisible, for the eye 'itself' is not yet vision."[47] In
order to elucidate this perspective on the portrait, Nancy refers
to cave painting, including in his text an image from Chauvet that
depicts the heads of a pride of lions all looking in the same direction, toward the viewer's left. This painting also features prominently in Herzog's film, as the filmmaker is especially fascinated
by its visual impact. "Although cave painting," Nancy suggests,
"offers only a very limited number of faces, it should nonetheless
be emphasized that there are many looks to be seen on the animal heads, those of stags, bison, horses, lions, and others."[48] The
absence of a human face endows the look of the animal with even
greater significance:

> The fact that there are no people represented makes these
> looks all the more important. We might speculate on the
> extent to which they are "fixed" by those who paint them:
> The painter "fixes" them in two senses of the word, visual
> (by observing them) and pictorial (by painting them)—and
> in so doing, he or she makes the power of vision itself arrive
> before his or her very eyes, in what is visible, along with
> what that vision itself retains of tension, traction, attraction,
> and contradiction toward an outside. That way, a "within"
> is revealed, that is, not an "interior" entity or region but

the totality of a projected body toward an elsewhere (prey, obstacle, menace ...). This body is thus revealed as something other than a simple presence positioned here or there: It is shown to be the opening of a place, orientation, and aim, a relation to something and to other bodies in the world.[49]

The network of traces upon which the look fastens and which it gathers for visibility operates on a double plane of aesthetic inscription. The work of the prehistoric artist testifies both to the perception—the look as look—and to a representation of that perception—the look as image. Yet lodged deep within the archive of traces and other looks that constitute any particular look is what one might call an other-directedness, an orientation toward an out-side with which the look and its particular object stand in an open-ended tension. (Although Nancy depicts only the lion image in his text, it is worth noting that this other-directedness through the gaze is at work in additional depictions at Chauvet as well, including an especially beautiful and expressive painting of an ensemble of horses, which also shows the horses all looking to the viewer's left, with each of the horses wearing a slightly different facial expres-sion.) Just as the pictorial representation of the lions' and horses' gaze in the work of art conjures a form of interiority—an interiority that makes the viewer wonder what it is that the animals are see-ing and what makes them ponder so intently—this interiority itself emerges as an effect of an absent (because unrepresented) exterior-ity. This intimated but unrepresented exteriority is the presumed object of the lions' and horses' gaze, their look into the openness that exceeds their interiority—and the artwork itself—even as it also constitutes it. The presence of the gaze as it is depicted in the work thus emerges as a supplement of an absence—the absence, within the sphere of the aesthetic form, of the object of the gaze, which is to say, the absence that is merely a presumed distant presence.

The most important word in Nancy's passage is the final one, "world." After all, it is through the interiority that hinges on an exteriority, and through the presence of the gaze that depends on the absence of its object, that the very idea of a world is called into being. The lions' and horses' shared gaze, fastening attentively on an exteriority— perhaps another animal, prey, an obstacle, a threat, an opportunity, or a looming transformation to be evaluated—creates the very idea of world. The shared gaze upon an exteriority opens up a world in a purely allusive way, a world whose existence is hinted at yet remains shrouded in mystery. If this work of art presents, through its remarkable depiction of the lions' attentive gaze toward an unnamed elsewhere, the idea of a body that is not merely a form of self-identical presence, it is because the body's presence is always already suffused by its orientation to an absence, an other, an emergent elsewhere that cannot be contained by any form of presence-to-self. Through the gaze of the lions, we come to regard the body of a self as something that always already stands *in relation* to another and to other inhabitants of a world, whether that world is explicitly depicted or merely intimated as an absence or an ever-distant presence. In other words, the gaze toward an exteriority here becomes visible as a form of world-relation, even as a way of "worlding," in which the world worlds, to use the notorious Heideggerian formulation. In the depicted gaze upon an other that remains undepicted, the work of art stages an irreducible *relatedness* to a world—to the very idea of a world and to the world as idea.

One might say that the paintings of the Chauvet cave, just like those at Lascaux that so fascinated Blanchot and his friend Bataille, embody a vast archive of such networks of relation in which the idea of a world comes into presence through the work of art. Such relatedness to a world, as the relatedness that emerges in the cave images through a multitude of aesthetic mediations, calls these images into presence, naming the essential experience of dwelling in a world which is constantly being made and unmade, woven and unwoven—like our very being-in-the-world. Learning to inherit the world set up by the cave paintings means learning to be an heir to the legacy of an obscure yet infinitely generative non-self-identity that—within the worlds we inhabit, create, and inherit—makes us who we are. When considered from the vantage point of the caves, are *we ourselves* not the ones who—touched by anticipation and unease, hovering somewhere along the fluid spectrum of life and death—are always only on the brink of stepping more fully into humanity?

3

The Work for a Time without Me and the World Stepping toward Us (Levinas, Celan)

Any consideration of the work of art in relation to the world from which it stems and the other world to which it gives rise requires that one also inquire into the specific status of the work as work, the workness of the work that first is capable of setting forth this or that world. Without returning to the long and variegated history of the concept of a "work" in European thought[1]—which also includes disruptions of the notion of work, as, for instance, when its textually mediated nature causes a fundamental shift "from work to text," as Roland Barthes once put it[2]—it is nevertheless possible to bring into focus a series of abiding questions. How is a world-creating work to be conceptualized *as* work? What are its characteristics? Is it to be thought as being identical to itself, an aestheticized form of ipscity? Or is it rather always on its way elsewhere, leaving behind the sphere that it itself has called into aesthetic presence?

To help us reflect upon these questions, it may help to look to a rather unlikely source or resource, one that is not normally adduced when the question of the work of art is at stake. In his multilayered reflections entitled "Le trace de l'Autre," first translated in 1962 by the American philosopher Alphonso Lingis as "The Trace of the Other," Emmanuel Levinas sets out to provide an account of some of the central preoccupations of his thinking: a subject's responsibility that precedes the subject itself, that is, antecedes the very formation of any self and its consciousness; the question of what an "encounter" in the emphatic sense might signify; the idea of the "face" of the other and its particular dignity and unreadability; and the primordial asymmetry between self and other, in which the other is the absolutely or "wholly" other, not just an other to a particular self. Yet what is often overlooked in Levinas's text is a remarkable passage on the question of the work and the operations of a work in relation to a world. To be sure, the text mobilizes the broad category of the *oeuvre*, the work, in a very general way. Indeed, one may say that *oeuvre*, in its baffling abstraction, here remains at once an under- and overdetermined notion, one that gestures toward a kind of transcendence-toward, without being reducible to any single meaning and instantiation. And yet one might profitably inquire what would happen if one were to engage in an unusual experiment by temporarily emphasizing, or momentarily foregrounding, the particular dimension of *oeuvre* that names the work as a work of art—all the while keeping in mind the spectral existence of the much broader, transcendence-oriented resonances that Levinas attaches to *oeuvre*. In other words, while Levinas does not specify precisely what kind of "work" he is addressing—since he is concerned primarily with the thought of work *as* work, that is, with work as a dynamic transcendence-toward—and while the ideas that he develops about the work can therefore not be restricted to any particular form of work such as the work of art alone, his reflections nevertheless can be understood as *also* encompassing the specific instantiation of the kind of work that we call the work of art. The work of art cannot be excluded from the work; the *oeuvre* inhabits the *oeuvre*, at least among other things. In fact, one might say that it is in the conceptual context of our particular discussion here that a significant dimension of

106

Levinas's reflections on the work and its world become visible in their relevance to aesthetics and the work of art.

When Levinas cautions us that "we must not conceive of a work as an apparent agitation of a ground which afterwards remains identical with itself, like an energy which, in all its transformations, remains equal to itself," he sets the stage for his entire reflection on the work as work.[3] There is a non-self-identity at work within the work, something that does not remain unaltered by the act through which the work comes about as work, that is, through which it installs itself in the world. The world-inducing force of the work is a form of nonidentity. "Nor," he continues, "must we conceive it as a technical operation, which through its much-proclaimed negativity reduces an alien world to a world whose alterity is converted into my idea."[4] The true work, while it may set up or enable a world, refuses to appropriate an existing world in such a way as to conform to a subject's preexisting conception about it. On the contrary, the work's world-creation is predicated upon allowing the radical otherness and unavailability of a world to stand as such. No dialectical force of negativity is capable of sublating the world, and no strategic movement of assimilation will incorporate an alien world into one of sameness and identity. "Both conceptions" (that is, the self-identical agitation of an existing ground and the merely technical operation reducing an alterity) will "continue to affirm being as identical with itself and reduce its fundamental event to thought which is ... thought of itself, thought of thought. *A work conceived radically is a movement of the same unto the other which never returns to the same.*"[5] One might say that if Levinas emphasizes the idea of work as a movement toward the other and, indeed, toward otherness as such, it is because the work-character or work-being of the work comes to the fore most emphatically only when its opening onto the otherness of the other no longer leads it back to a particular world that would grant it something like transparent self-identity. The radical work rather remains at odds not just with any world of otherness onto which it may open, but also with respect to itself— which is to say that the radical work never simply returns home. There is no homecoming celebration for the radical work once it has reached out to a radical otherness, that is, after entering its orbit of absolute alterity. In this sense Levinas emphasizes how, to "the myth of Ulysses returning to Ithaca, we wish to oppose the story of Abraham who leaves his fatherland forever for a yet unknown land, and he forbids his servant even to bring back his son to the point of departure."[6] Abraham in Ulysses' stead, eternal dispersion in place of homecoming: the work enters a world in which it can never return to itself. Its errant movements cannot be reinscribed as a path home, a map that would lead it back to its origins, whether they be real or imagined.

Having thus articulated a radical departure of the work accompanied by no return, that is, the idea of nonreciprocal relation, within the work and its world, even between departure and return, Levinas employs the language of gratitude and ingratitude to provide this thought with further contours. "A work," he suggests, "conceived in its ultimate nature requires a radical generosity of the same who in the work goes unto the other. It then requires an *ingratitude* of the other."[7] This is so, according to this model of thinking, because "gratitude would in fact be the *return* of the movement to its origin."[8] At this point, one might understand Levinas as arguing that the true work must be conceived in radical generosity because there is no return on multiple levels: no homecoming, no exchange of gratitude in return for a gift, no return on investment, so to speak. And yet, as he is quick to add, the work cannot be reduced to a form of "pure expenditure," as such a conceptualization of the work would confine it to the model of "pure loss," and, at any rate, "it is not enough for it to affirm the same in its identity circumvented with nothingness."[9] The nothingness that may obtain in and around the work can itself not be the basis upon which reciprocity is tacitly reestablished by insisting on a pure loss that could be set in opposition to the work's originary expenditure—just as little as an absolutely or wholly other is to be thought as a mere binary opposition to a self, which it would then once again serve to stabilize, even if only negatively. On the contrary, a true "work is thus a relationship with the other who is reached without showing himself touched. It forms outside the morose delectation of failure, and outside of the consolations with which Nietzsche defines religion."[10] Another way to put this idea is to say that even though the work may reach into the world of the other—that is, establish contact with the other as other in a world that is alien to it—that other does not respond by affirming or confirming that it has in fact been reached or addressed conclusively. In this way, failure cannot be redeemed, that is, sublated into a secret triumph of reciprocity and gratitude, or understood as something compensatory, the way in which religion itself has at times—by Nietzsche, whom Levinas mentions explicitly, and by many others—been understood as a discourse of relief and a system of consolation that provides those who have no other source of comfort with a measure of solace.

It is for this same reason that the work, as Levinas helps us to think it, must not seek a triumph of any kind, a victory of this or that conception or world-creation. In other words, it must not wish to be rewarded, even if in a manner that is invisible to most. This is why he emphasizes how the "departure without return, which does not go forth into the void, would also lose its absolute goodness if the work sought for its recompense in the immediacy of its triumph, if it impatiently awaited the triumph of its cause."[11] Here again, the "one-way movement would be inverted into a reciprocity," and the "work, confronting its departure and its end, would be absorbed again in calculations of deficits and compensations, in accountable operations. It would be subordinated to thought."[12] The idea of the work to which these reflections give rise resists any mere calculus of reciprocity as it pertains to the rewarding nature of a triumph or confirmation. Instead, the genuine work that reaches into the world, even setting up a world, must unfold on the far side of quotidian calculation, technical verifiability, and reciprocal remuneration. One might even say that this Levinasian work would be unreasonable, that is, not in conformity with what the history of reason and the metaphysical calculabilities that have emerged from it would affirm—or even tolerate. If the work thus conceived resists even thought itself by refusing to subordinate itself to the dictates of what thought condones and what, in the history of thinking, it has allowed to come to pass—the work sets out on a path without return, penetrating and setting forth a world that remains irreducibly other and in retreat.

It is thus only by virtue of having an eye for the abiding affirmation of an alterity in retreat and a resistance to the conventional dictates of thought that the work is capable of maintaining and affirming its one-way movement as such. What are the conditions of possibility that facilitate the work's capability in this regard? The "one-way action," Levinas avers, "is possible only in patience, which, pushed to the limit, means for the agent to renounce being the contemporary of its outcome, to act without entering the promised land."[13] If the work's reliance on nonreciprocity can only be born of radical patience, such patience should not be equated with passivity or disengagement, since it rather affirms the work as something inhabiting the space in which patience is to be experienced—and exercised—precisely *as* patience. There must be no rush, therefore, to enter any promised land, no business transaction to conduct with regard to the work. The work *is*. To the extent that an agent, a term by which Levinas presumably means a subject or a self understood in light of the work it has created, is a contemporary of anyone or anything at all—for can there ever be true contemporaries?—such contemporaneity does not pertain to anything that the work has achieved in the world, no result or effect. On the contrary, the work, along with the agent who created it and the world it sets up, is contemporary only to itself (without, however, being self-identical), that is, it shares its time with a one-way movement that reaches into a world—a world of alterity—without knowing how it will have affected this world (both now and after its demise) and without hoping to reap any rewards for its act of reaching.

Because the true work is never simply or even primarily contemporaneous with the agent who creates it, its creation points to a futurity that far exceeds the world in which it originates. But this is not to say that the subject or agent who created the work in a particular world may expect to achieve a form of immortality through the work, perhaps through fame and recognition, or through the canonical status that his work may achieve one day. The work is thus not a kind of message in a bottle to a future that is especially hospitable to that work or its creator-agent. On the contrary, Levinas insists that the futurity of a work, if there is any, is unconcerned with the life or death of the agent, subject, or artist:

> The future for which the work is undertaken must be
> posited from the start as indifferent to my death. A work,

distinguished from games and from calculation, is being-for-beyond-my-death. Patience does not consist in the agent belying his generosity of giving himself the time of a *personal immortality*. To renounce being the contemporary of the triumph of one's work is to have this triumph in a time *without me*, to aim at this world without me, to aim at a time beyond the horizon of my time. It works in an eschatology without hope for oneself, an eschatology of liberation from my own time.[14]

If a form of futurity is that for the sake of which the work is created and sent into the world, and if that futurity is indifferent to my death, this is because the work does not generate an immortality on the part of the subject. While the work may well come to be appreciated, recognized, and studied in a world to come, this world will be of a time that is closed to me, an experience and a situatedness that, if it happens at all, will happen without me. This world of the work is a world that, if it is to be at all, is always yet to come: it signifies a world and a time in which I will be absent and to which I cannot have a relation among the living. If there is hope in this world, it is only hope for the other and for others, but not for myself, hope for a world in which I no longer can be among those who have hope, that is, a world without me. One may recall here the sentiment that Kafka expressed when he was asked by his friend and longtime interlocutor Max Brod whether he thought there was any hope at all, a sentiment that resonated with Walter Benjamin who cites it in his seminal essay on Kafka: "Oh, there is enough hope, even an infinite amount of hope—but not for us [*nur nicht für uns*]."[15] Not for us: the work's hope is hope for the other and its world of otherness. And though the work addresses itself *as work* to a world that will no longer include me, it does not mourn my death; it does not even fully acknowledge it in advance because, as a form of sheer future-directedness, it is irreducibly indifferent to my death.

When it comes into view, the work no longer serves as a means of temporal and worldly self-perpetuation performed by a finite being, but rather opens onto the idea of an eclipse of the self, as that self, in turn, opens onto the world of the other as absolutely other. Here, the time of the work—even and especially as that work is effected by a self—is the time of the wholly other. The world of the absolutely other is always the time that does not include me, the time after my death, no matter how long or short a life may be granted to me. This world, characterized as a time without me in the Levinasian line of thinking, also marks a passage to the thought of the other:

> To be for a time that would be without me, to be for a time after my time, for a future beyond the celebrated "being-for-death," to-be-for-after-my-death—"Let the future and the most far-off things be the rule for all the present days"—is not a banal thought that extrapolates one's own duration; it is a passage to the time of the other. Do we have to call what makes such a passage possible eternity? But perhaps the possibility of sacrifice goes unto the end of this passage, and discovers the non-inoffensive character of this extrapolation: to-be-for-death in order to be for-what-is-after-me.[16]

By implicitly distinguishing his mode of inquiry from a Heideggerian "being-for-death" or "being-toward-death," Levinas is able to cast into sharp relief the thought of a being-for-after-my-death. In this scenario, the self that is the agent of certain works is no longer seen primarily as being oriented toward its own death, that is, as projecting its being-there into a future that it still inhabits, but rather as a self that projects its work onto a world that will have superseded it, a world to which it no longer belongs and that comes to pass at and as a time from which the self is forever excluded. To insist on this emphasis on being-for-after-my-death also means to view a self's work as marking a transition or, in Levinas's terminology, a "passage" to the time that is no longer the time of a self: the time of the absolutely other.

Yet, one might ask, what precisely is the structure of the sacrifice that Levinas appears to evoke somewhat apodictically at the conclusion of this thought? On the one hand, it seems as if a religious category were being imported without further justification to serve as an element in an onto-structural framework. But, on the other hand, it is possible to espy in this rhetoric of the sacrifice a logic that is generated from within, even demanded by, the very matter at hand. The sacrifice—or, more precisely, the "possibility of sacrifice"—consists in relinquishing a significant dimension of being-for-death or being-toward-death for the sake of something else. If, in the classical Heideggerian conception of being-toward-death, my orientation toward, and fundamental awareness of, my finitude enables me to design a potentially meaningful life and to project my life—as a being-in-the-world—into the future, this being-toward-death not only imposes a grim limit but also enables a resoluteness or undisclosedness with respect to my dwelling in the world. But if I were to surrender this possibility of charting a being-in-the-world by reassigning the thought of finitude from life-design to an affirmation of something that will no longer contain me—a time that is never my time—then I will have engaged in the work of ontological sacrifice. In other words, to affirm, within the work, what-is-after-me—that is, to devise the work as work precisely "for-what-is-after-me"—is to give up those aspects of my shaping of the world through the work that could have guided my existence as it moved forward and confronted its thrownness into this world, as Heidegger would say, by means of engaging with my finitude as a being-toward-death. One might specify Levinas's position in the formulation that I sacrifice the redemptive potentialities of my ontological engagement with the world in finitude through and as the work for the sake of a world that comes after me and a time that will never include me, never have a place for me.

In contemplating relays between Levinas's elaboration of the work and the specific realm of an aesthetic object, one would do well to bear in mind Levinas's own guardedness vis-à-vis the image and, by extension, the visually mediated artwork. For him, the ethical dimension of thought requires an emphasis on the infinity and inscrutability of the face—the lace of the other—rather than the image, which, in Levinas's eyes, always threatens to perform a certain work of objectification, reification, and ontological closure. It is hardly an accident that, in *Totality and Infinity*, Levinas differentiates the ethical vision of his thought from that of the image as image. There, even though the "first 'vision' of eschatology ... reveals the very possibility of eschatology, that is, the breach of the totality," and even though "ethics is an optics," he emphasizes that "it is a 'vision' without image, bereft of the synoptic and totalizing objectifying virtues of vision, a relation or an intentionality of a wholly different type—which this work seeks to describe."[17] If the image and its potentially totalizing tendencies are bracketed by a Levinasian perspective in favor of an open-ended face of alterity, then visuality and the visual work of art would need to be viewed with an insistent kind of ambivalence, a critical and ethical vigilance that works to keep the openness of the artwork open.

The question then arises as to what kind of world may still be considered in terms of a work that is thought along such Levinasian lines. Here, instead of the visual work of art, it is the literary work of art, specifically a work of lyric poetry, that may be of help. If the work is conceived in virtue of a world that may not include me, yet I am capable of speaking of this world even as I perform or create a work that, like its creator, may itself not feature in this world, how might one conceptualize a possible relation to a world as it unfolds in a poetic work of art? For the third poem in section V of his 1959 collection *Sprachgitter*, Paul Celan includes a brief poem that begins with, and is entitled, "Die Welt," or "The World." Let us focus here only on two lines, the opening couplet, of this often-neglected poem, isolating these lines as a heading or motto that has been removed from its own world and asked to step toward us all by itself, as it were, but that nevertheless contains a reflection on the world as such. Celan's lines read:

Die Welt, zu uns
in die leere Stunde getreten:[18]

The world, stepped toward us
into the empty hour:

These lines stage something of an unexpected counterpart to Celan's much better-known line "Die Welt ist fort, ich muß dich tragen" ("The world is gone, I must carry you") from his later poem "Große, glühende Wölbung" ("Vast, Glowing Curvature"), which was made famous by Derrida's repeated commentary over a number of years, as we saw in the introduction. But while the world of "Die Welt ist fort, ich muß dich tragen" has vanished for good and is now to be lamented as radically absent, the world of the earlier work "Die Welt" performs something like the opposite movement. There, rather than remaining gone, the world now steps forward. The world evoked by the speaking voice of the poem, its lyrical I, was once distant or absent. Indeed, it could only have stepped toward us from that distance, approaching us as if to reconnect temporarily before abandoning us again. "Die Welt, zu uns / in die leere Stunde getreten" thus suggests an encounter that may have been unexpected, an encounter that could not simply have been prepared by the work itself. The world, we are told by the lyrical I of the work, has stepped "zu uns," toward "us." What has caused the world to step toward us? What does it want from us, if anything? And why now? Is this a joyous occasion, or do we have reason to be anxious in relation to this forward-stepping world? Why in the world would this stepping take place at all—and why in the world at precisely this moment?

By the same token, it is not clear to whom, or for the benefit of whom, the world has stepped forward. Who, precisely, is named by the "uns"? Does it refer to the lyrical I's invisible companion or companions, that is, to some form of community or proto-community that is approached by a world that was formerly absent? Or does the evocation of the "uns" rather refer to a kind of spectral bond between the lyrical I and the reader of the poem? In that case, the experience of the stepping-toward that the world performs would be shared by the speaking voice and its listener. Depending on how one interprets the implicit mode of address encoded in the first line—"Die Welt, zu uns"—one either becomes a witness to or a participant in the experience of a world stepping-toward, coming forward to make itself felt.

If Celan populates his opening couplet with precisely nine words, this number self-consciously evokes, among other things, not only the nine muses of Greek mythology but also the nine circles of hell in Dante's *Divine Comedy*. By staging the opening meditation on the world through exactly nine words, the poem points to the nine muses as the inspirational sources of poetry, literature, song, and artistic creation, calling into presence the fundamental relation between work and world as such. But from the beginning, this emphasis on the relation between the created work and the world is modulated by the threat of a certain darkness, namely the nine circles of hell that structure Dante's *Inferno*, the first part of the *Divine Comedy*. If we pay attention to the numerical dimension of the two lines that open "Die Welt," the world created by the work here is implicitly exposed already to its decline.

Yet what these nine words leave undetermined is the reason why the world was previously absent and the circumstances under which it has now decided to approach the "uns," however this plural entity may be defined. Did the world have a reason to absent itself previously? Did "we" perhaps cause it to vanish in the first place? And what kind of world is being signified here? If there is more than one world—for instance, the world, as one says, of literature, or the world of academia, of geology, of journalism, of sports, etc.—then according to what logic does the lyrical I here speak only of "*the* world"? Why does Celan not write "Eine Welt," a world, as he easily could have, employing the indefinite article rather than the definite article? "Eine Welt, zu uns / in die leere Stunde getreten" could have signified the stepping-forward of a particular world into the situation of our unique circumstances. But what appears to be at stake in Celan's lines is not this or that particular world, "eine Welt" in the sense of "irgendeine Welt," any world, but rather the world as such, the world *as* world, the worldliness of the world. Stepping toward us, then, is the world as the very idea and embodiment of the world, a world that adds itself, as it were, to "our" shared being, rather than always already having been there, fully formed, more or less stable, and simply waiting to be populated by beings that enter it. It is in and through the address of the poetic work that the world steps forward and toward us, insisting that we learn to relate to it in a way that will not annihilate its specificity *as* world.

Yet for all its stepping-forward toward us, "die Welt" also remains forever separated from us. The world steps toward us, approaches us, addresses us—even if silently—and places demands on us merely by being the world that will have joined us. But the world will never be one of us, will not simply remain with us, or become legible in a fully transparent manner and according to principles imported into it from the outside. This is perhaps one of the reasons Celan carefully inserts a comma between "Die Welt" and "zu uns" in the first line. There, the comma both conjoins and separates "the world" and "us," the ones who forever must reside on the opposite side of this punctuation mark.[19] Understood in this way, the comma not only specifies a world that has stepped forward (that, by means of a comma, becomes identifiable as precisely the world that has stepped toward us); the comma also demarcates an abiding border line, hardly permeable, between, on the one side, the lyrical I—along with the other that it addresses—and, on the other side, the very world that is identified as stepping forward. "Die Welt, zu uns" thus inaugurates an inquiry into the shifting set of relations that the forward-stepping world has spawned yet leaves radically open and underdetermined.

The world, then, dwells on one side of the comma, and we dwell on the other. Both united and separated by a punctuation mark—and thus by language—the world faces us and we face the world in an uneasy relation that remains to be determined. But, one might ask, where, precisely, did "we" reside before the world stepped toward us? In something other than a world? What was, or is, "our" location? Celan's lines provide a surprising and enigmatic answer: we reside in the "leere Stunde," the empty hour, since the world is "zu uns / in die leere Stunde getreten." The paradox of mobilizing a temporal marker, "leere Stunde," to designate a location to be accessed is underscored by Celan's use of the accusative case in the phrase "in die leere Stunde." In German, "in" is a two-way preposition that, depending on context, sometimes requires the accusative case and sometimes the dative. If Celan had chosen to mobilize the preposition "in" with the dative case, as he easily could have, this would have yielded "in der leeren Stunde," rather than "in die leere Stunde." Employing the (equally acceptable) dative case here would have emphasized a more expected or common signification, since a subject ("die Welt") would have stepped toward us at a specific temporal point, namely, in the "leere Stunde," the empty hour as if making use of a momentary emptiness in time to step in and make itself felt. But Celan self-consciously departs from this temporally mediated image in which the world steps toward us by pairing his preposition with the accusative case. In so doing, he provides us with an image of the world stepping toward us—"in die leere Stunde getreten"—as if the empty hour were the precise location where we found ourselves. The uneasy site of our dwelling, the "leere Stunde" of the accusative case suggests something even more unsettling and less familiar: an empty time-space, what in German is called a *Zeitraum*, in which our being takes place. If, in fact, our being takes place in the strange space provided only by the emptiness of time itself, then it is here that the world must meet us, stepping toward us to make itself felt. The world becomes palpable *as* world when it reveals itself as having ambulated toward us in the empty time-space that is our transitory dwelling in life.

The figure of the "leere Stunde" into which the world has stepped in order to meet us also convenes with another figure of the hour, one that Celan includes in his 1949 constellation of fragments and aphorisms entitled "Gegenlicht." There, one entry reads: "Die Stunde sprang aus der Uhr, stellte sich vor diese und befahl ihr, richtig zu gehen [The hour leaped out of the clock, positioned itself before it, and commanded it to keep time correctly]."[20] This striking image of personification, in which an hour emancipates itself from the instrument that keeps time, suggests a form of temporality that is aware of itself and of how it is measured (or fails to be measured). Time here is not identical with its mechanically achieved measurement. Celan's personified hour self-consciously places itself in (critical) relation to its measuring in the world by springing forward into that world itself, intervening in it for the sake of an intervention in how the world conceives of, and keeps, time. The world keeps time, through its clocks, even though time refuses to be kept, that is, kept in place and subordinated to its measuring. What, then, would be the way in which the time of an hour could be kept correctly? What form of timekeeping would be appropriate to a time that is always on the verge of escaping, a time that will not remain self-identical? Celan's peculiar image of an hour's gesture of self-emancipation conjures a world in which the experience of time and its measurement have become asynchronous. As the hour springs forth from its containment by the clock, it presents an ever-deepening enigma. The *Stunde*, one might say, becomes visible as a *leere Stunde*, defying our understanding as it withdraws from transparent accessibility and a unified, stable meaning.

Unlike Celan's aphorism, where we are presented with the image of an hour approaching its clock in order to engage with it and to rectify its presumably faulty timekeeping, in the poem the world does not approach us in order to correct anything, to fill the empty hour of our existence by giving it meaning, purpose, or fulfillment. Rather, "Die Welt, zu uns / in die leere Stunde getreten" suggests the image of a world that has befallen us, accosting us in a peculiar way and making demands that we can hardly fulfill. Celan here is closer to Wordsworth's insight that "the world is too much with us," as his 1807 sonnet of that name has it, which is to say that the world occupies us with its material and intellectual demands, beckons us to yield to its pressures and seductions, while ultimately remaining inscrutable to us.[21] We could not have prepared for the world to step toward us and impose itself, not even in the barren time-space of the "leere Stunde," the "empty hour" in which we dwell. No work, no oeuvre, not even a poem could have set the stage for our engagement with a world that descends upon us. The world makes itself felt as world by stepping forward, and all that an artwork, even a poem, can do—but perhaps this already is a lot—is to bear witness to the event of making-itself-felt. If the work bears witness to an enigmatic world stepping toward us, it does so by recording and archiving the traces of this encounter.

In Levinasian terms, the work cannot and must not anticipate any specific place in a future world on the basis of what has been accomplished in and as the work itself, yet it is in artworks such as Celan's poem that the ways in which the world nevertheless makes itself felt are inscribed. "Die Welt, zu uns / in die leere Stunde getreten" not only bears witness to a world that approaches us even in the emptiness of our withdrawal from it—or in our inability to locate a place in it through our work—but it also makes visible the irreducible and ongoing pull that the world never ceases to exert on us. Without wishing to fill, even saturate, our "leere Stunde" with the lush worldliness of world, the work becomes a silent witness to our infinite conversation with, and interminable interrogation of, the world, even as the work knows that we will forever remain, as Celan's fateful comma serves to remind us, on the other side of that world.

4

Inheriting the World of the Subcutaneous Musical Artwork (Adorno, Schönberg)

When we consider the perished nature of the world
in which an artwork once came into presence, along with the other
world—the aesthetically mediated world—that the artwork sets up
according to its own singular terms, it becomes imperative to take
account of questions of legacy, tradition, heritage, and inheritance.
What is the relation of a work of art—precisely by virtue of belonging to a lost world and by setting up another world in turn—to
the tradition out of which it arose and with which it may simultaneously break? What kind of world does the artwork inherit as a
legacy and what kind of inheritance does it in turn make available
to future heirs? How does an artwork inherit—even, at times, by
refusing an inheritance—the tradition associated with the world
of its provenance? How does the work relate to the futurity of
the world that it sets up and that demands permanently to be
reworked, reengaged, and reinherited by those who would con
front it in a serious manner? If the act of inheriting worlds by

means of an artwork—both the world that has fallen away and the world that the artwork sets up—cannot be reduced to a straightforward transfer of certain stable contents or delimited properties, then the worlds that emerge as legacies to be handed down in and through a work begin to become visible as abiding question marks. Such worlds incite a thinking that will not be appeased by any appeal to a conservatively minded, reassuring, or reified notion of a self-identical and transparently readable tradition. Rather, this inheritance of world—and of the idea of world as such—takes place in relation to a work of art that inscribes itself in a tradition precisely by calling into question the precepts and premises of that very tradition, thereby rendering the legacy that suffuses that tradition a contested matter of perpetual reinterpretation and renewed examination. The Latin *tradere* from which our word and modern concept of tradition derive names a handing-down that also consists in a surrender or handing-over of worlds. These worlds remain lodged at the very core of the artwork, whose persistent engagement with the refractory inheritance they embody will not cease to impose itself upon their reader-heirs.

On matters of intellectual and artistic inheritance and the concept of tradition, especially as these relate to the conjunction of the artwork and speculative thought as such, Adorno's variegated oeuvre offers an unusually rich archive of reflection. Adorno's texts often include direct or indirect meditations on the complex question of inheriting an intellectual and artistic tradition—for instance, the question of how to inherit Hegel in his *Hegel: Three Studies*.[1] There are even entire essays and seminal sections of books that are concerned with nothing else, such as the 1966 study "On Tradition" and the section "Tradition and Cognition" in *Negative Dialectics*, in which tradition is shown paradoxically to remain alive only by denying itself to that in which it occurs.[2] There, Adorno demonstrates that what tradition is and can be remains fundamentally predicated upon what escapes tradition, and tradition for its part only comes into its own as a concept to the extent that it engages with what cannot be inscribed into the very logic of tradition. The far-reaching works he devoted to problems of music—the kind of artwork that constitutes the very heart of his aesthetic and conceptual concerns—include his early meditations on "Beethoven's Late Style" (written in 1934) and the unfinished book on Beethoven (posthumously published by Adorno's editors in 1993), his reflections on Schubert, Brahms, Wagner, Stravinsky, Ravel, and Bartók, his countless other essays on musical figures and musicological issues, his critiques of pop cultural phenomena such as the programming of radio music, the phenomenon of jazz, and the music of Hollywood film soundtracks, his far-reaching musical aphorisms, and his programmatic *Philosophie der neuen Musik*, conceived as a musicological elaboration on aspects of *Dialectic of Enlightenment* and published, in 1949, as his first book following his return to Germany from American exile during Hitler's regime. In addition, his extensive monographic studies of composers such as Gustav Mahler, Arnold Schönberg, and Alban Berg figure centrally in this area of his thought. Taken together, these studies exemplify the practice of what Adorno liked to call "mit den Ohren denken," "thinking with one's ears." What comes to pass in these works in various modulations and ever-changing contexts is an abiding engagement with the musical tradition and its genealogies that places music at the very core of philosophical aesthetics in a way that later allows Adorno, in his *Aesthetic Theory*, to speak of a *Musikähnlichkeit*, a certain "music-likeness," with respect to all genuine works of art, not just the musical ones.[3] This irreducible *Musikähnlichkeit* of all true art and its legacies also propelled him forward in his own musical compositions, guided by the example of his composition teacher and musical master Berg, with whom he studied in Vienna after he had finished his doctoral dissertation on Husserl. And if, for Adorno, Beethoven is indeed Hegel set to music, this particular setting to music of the conceptual realm also deserves to be contextualized within the realm of the musical and philosophical traditions along with the complex modes of inheritance they call into presence.

What is of particular concern to us here, however, is a little-known and typically neglected text from 1954 that was not published during Adorno's lifetime but that his German editors included toward the end of the massive fifth volume of his collected writings on music, the *Musikalische Schriften* (that is, volume 18 of his *Gesammelte Schriften*). This text, a lecture that Adorno apparently did not intend for publication and that has been largely overlooked by readers and scholars, bears the title "Das Erbe und die neue Musik" and is thus far unavailable in English translation.[4] It is, however, a crucial and highly illuminating document that sheds unexpected light on our present concerns. The title could be translated as "Inheritance and the New Music" or "Heritage and the New Music" or even "Legacy and the New Music," depending on which valence of "Erbe" one wishes to emphasize most fully. In this defense of the New Music—a shorthand term by which Adorno does not mean any new, recent, or contemporary form of music in general but specifically the Second Viennese School comprising Schönberg, Berg, Anton Webern, and their associates—one finds a trenchant engagement not only with the world of tradition that a challenging musical work of art opens up but also an abiding reflection on the concept of inheriting a legacy, tradition, or heritage in art as such. The perspective thus opened up works to enrich our thinking of an artwork's worlds—the decayed world from which it stems and the new world it sets up in and through itself—in decisive ways.

One might say that on a formal and methodological level, "Das Erbe und die neue Musik" exemplifies Adorno's understanding of what it means to think a phenomenon conceptually in a rigorous yet open-ended manner. As early as his academic inaugural lecture "Die Aktualität der Philosophie" from 1931, which is methodologically indebted to his older friend and mentor Benjamin, to whom Adorno wished to dedicate the lecture and whose *Trauerspiel* book is explicitly cited in it,[5] Adorno demands a special kind of gesture or attitude of philosophical reflection that allows its object to be illuminated in an unexpected way. (In fact, he considered this demand so central to his intellectual concerns that he sent a copy of the lecture manuscript to three of his most significant interlocutors at the time, Benjamin, Siegfried Kracauer, and Ernst Bloch, all of whom studied the manuscript carefully and discussed it intensively with each other and with its author.) "Genuine philosophical interpretation [*Deutung*]," Adorno argues, "does not aim at a meaning that already exists and perseveres behind the question but rather illuminates the question in an abrupt and instantaneous way while distorting [*verzerren*] it at the same time."[6] Such interpretation proceeds by allowing "the singular and disparate elements

126

of a question" to enter freely "into different configurations [*Anord-nungen*]" until "they coalesce or shoot together [*zusammenschießen*] into a figure from which the resolution springs forth while the question disappears."[7] For thinking to proceed in this manner it must be able to enter into relation with the world of ideas and the world of phenomena in a way that is rigorous yet free and open, deliberate yet unsaturated by the conventional constraints of instrumental reasoning. If such thinking arrives at any kind of resolution, such resolution is not merely a result, understood as a fabricated entity of knowledge. On the contrary, when the different configurations of thinking an object, idea, or phenomenon philosophically convene to yield an insight, this insight is on the level of a figure (*Figur*) that in turn requires further interpretation and continued commentary, as if it were an especially challenging text to be deciphered. Such figures would presumably also include, in the musical realm, *Klangfiguren* (sound figures), to evoke one of Adorno's privileged terms. If the act of philosophical reflection upon such figures can be made vivid in relation to the thinking of a world as it is fashioned by a musical work of art, this world, too, would appear only as a figure, a suggestive enigma that invites continued interpretive engagement and careful critical judgment.

To be sure, in his lecture on inheriting a musical work of art, Adorno does not explicitly mobilize the terminology associated with the movements of world-decay and world-opening that concern us here. Yet his meditations do provide an indirect illumination of the issues pertaining to the relation between a work of art and the idea of a world, an illumination that is no less suggestive for operating on an indirect level. After all, Adorno is careful in his defense of New Music—precisely against those who would see in its emphasis on atonality and dissonance merely a violent departure from the venerable tradition of classical musical composition and a misguided experimental self-indulgence—to emphasize the human madeness of this music, its irreducible status as a humanly created product. "Artworks," he argues, "musical ones no less than the others, are human products [*von Menschen Gemachtes*]; consciousness and spontaneity of humans enter into them, and, through their intervention, continuity is always again disrupted [*stets wieder wird durch deren Eingriff die Kontinuität durchbrochen*]."[8]

One might say that in order to approach the dimension of legacy and inheritance both in musical works of art and in other art forms, it is imperative to remain cognizant of the ways in which the so-called tradition of a particular art form does not unfold according to the model of natural progress but rather is subject to the modes of world-creation with which human agents suffuse their works of art, whether intentionally or not. It is for this reason, too, that Adorno emphatically rejects the notion of "organic growth" when it comes to thinking the unfolding of an artform across time, as the laws of nature must not be confused with the movement of spirit, mind, or intellect, in short with what Hegel and others have taught us to think under the term *Geist*. Adorno's examples, including the "invention of the operatic form by a circle of Florentine literati at the end of the sixteenth century, the ascetic reform of opera through Gluck, the romantic short forms of the children's scenes in Schumann or the preludes of Chopin" and "Wagner's musical drama which he intensively developed in his programmatic writings," suggest a history of radical experimentation that long precedes both Second Viennese School works such as Schönberg's *Pierrot lunaire* or, beyond that school, compositions such as Igor Stravinsky's *Sacre du printemps*.[9] It is hardly admissible to think of the history of music as being divisible into a phase in which it adhered to classical precepts and was created in conformity with the movements of its own progressive unfolding, and another phase in which it was allegedly threatened, even compromised, by excessive experimentation and deviation from tradition. The ideological premise that is based on an analogy between the history of music and the botanical model of developmental growth therefore deserves to be rejected in favor of a differently inflected thinking of how the world of a musical work of art—or, indeed, a work of art from any aesthetic provenance—calls us into a singular form of presence and a unique world of reflection. What comes to pass in this unique world of reflection opened up by the artwork cannot simply be superimposed on it from the outside; it cannot be the object of an assigned meaning but is intimately tied to the experience of a total immersion in the world of a singular work, that is, it requires an "uncompromising sinking-into the phenomenon [*rücksichtslose Versenkung ins Phänomen*]."[10]

When it comes to the musical work of art, this uncompromising sinking-into is achieved in a manner that differs from that demanded by other forms of art, such as the poetry of a writer like Hölderlin, whom we encountered in chapter 1, or the prehistoric paintings at Lascaux and Chauvet, with which we engaged in chapter 2. What the musical work of art demands of us when we sink ourselves into it—that is, when we enter the particular world that it sets up—is that we engage with what Adorno, following Schönberg, names its "subcutaneous" dimension. Adorno derives the notion of the "subcutaneous [*Subkutanen*]" from "Schönberg's final book," where he uses the term, "in the context of metrical problems," as something that refers to "an irregularity that takes place under the skin of the regular [*einer unter der Haut des Regulären sich abspielenden Irregularität*]."[11] The concept of the subcutaneous to which Adorno refers in fact appears in a number of Schönberg's writings, including his "Brahms the Progressive," an essay collected in Schönberg's *Style and Idea*; it also makes an appearance, in various modulations, in other Adornian texts, including a 1952 fragment intended for his book on Beethoven, as well as the essays "Arnold Schönberg 1874–1951" and "Toward an Understanding of Schönberg."[12] In the present context, Adorno generalizes Schönberg's notion to all musical works of art, averring:

I believe that this concept of subcutaneous structuring is valid for all music of genuine quality in all its aspects. By this I mean nothing other than the capability to develop all aspects of that which sensuously appears now and here as aspects of a unified sense that obeys its own logic. This sense is neither to be understood as something that is presented by music, nor as its expression; it does not exist detached from the music itself, but rather is, again according to a phrase by Schönberg, something that is sayable only through music.

Ich glaube, dieser Begriff der subkutanen Gestaltung gilt für jegliche Musik von wahrhaftem Rang in all ihren Aspekten. Ich meine damit nichts anderes als die Fähigkeit, alle Momente des jetzt und hier sinnlich Erscheinenden zu entwickeln als Momente eines in sich einstimmigen und seiner eigenen Logik gehorchenden Sinnes. Unter diesem Sinn ist nicht ein von der Musik Dargestelltes, auch nicht ihr Ausdruck zu verstehen; er existiert überhaupt nicht abgelöst von der Musik, sondern ist, abermals nach einem Wort Schönbergs, etwas nur durch Musik Sagbares.[13]

To enter the world set up by the musical work of art means to penetrate to a layer beneath the surface: to recognize "under the skin," that is, subcutaneously, "unter der Haut," a pattern of irregularity that is operative behind—and thus concealed by—the apparent regularity that structures the surface. It is as if there were a second world beneath or behind the surface world that the musical work of art sets up, a structure of elements that precisely undermines the apparent regularity that is visible or audible in the realm of the work's immediately palpable world. To find a relation to the subcutaneous, then, means to listen to a world behind or beyond the world, to entertain an open and hospitable relation to the pulse of irregularity behind or beyond regularity. Yet Adorno is careful to note that this subcutaneous element of the musical work of art is not something that is presented or expressed in music, nor does it unfold on the level of this or that content. There is no primacy of subcutaneity that merely waits, in an act of secondary transposition, to be cast into artistic form. In other words, the artwork does not present a world that has been decorated by irregularity within regularity, as if its subcutaneous layers were a secret puzzle to be solved by its listener. Rather, if there is any "sense [*Sinn*]" to be found in the subcutaneous world of irregularity, it must be engaged in that which can only be said by music in the first place, "etwas nur durch Musik Sagbares," as Adorno puts it in his borrowing of Schönberg's dictum. Consequently, whatever sense emerges from the subcutaneous world of the musical work of art does not submit to the requirements of sense as posited by a world assumed to be outside the aesthetically mediated world that was set up by the artwork. The subcutaneous world set up by the work does not plagiarize from the world in which the work is created but rather ceaselessly posits its own sense of what sense is in the first place, its irreducibly singular and idiomatic sense of sense.

Interpreted from this perspective, Adorno's emphasis on the subcutaneous dimension of the world created by the musical artwork gives rise to an understanding of the generative dimension of the artwork. Such an understanding breaks with conventional expectations pertaining to the relation between surface and hidden layers, inside and outside. What may seem inexcusably "abrupt" and "torn [*zerrissen*]" in the compositions of the Second Viennese School in reality marks a radical faithfulness to the unrelenting demands of the subcutaneous. Here, "the subcutaneous," in the form of "the fabric of individual musical events [*Gefüge musikalischer Einzelereignisse*] as the bearer of a unified sense," becomes visible as it "breaks the surface [*die Oberfläche durchbricht*]" in order to "affirm itself, free of any schema." In this movement, "the inside steps into the outside [*das Innere tritt nach außen*]."[14] When the musical work of art prompts its internal subcutaneous layers to step forward into the outside, it sets up a world in which the question of sense demands to be posed in a different manner altogether. The unexpected dissonances and peculiar placement of intervals, for instance, that one might encounter in Schönberg and his circle do not work to set up the mere disruption of a world, a world that is otherwise assumed to be already fully formed, transparent, and the product of a self-evident givenness. On the contrary, these compositions, through their subcutaneous inversions, project a mode of listening in which the world as world first demands to be formed, that is, in which it is incumbent upon the listener actively to forge a relation to the very notion of a world, a relation that would not already have foreclosed the free, open, and shifting ways in which the artwork interacts with the world and its idea by superimposing ossified premises about the worldliness of the world onto that world. One might say that the world that emerges from the subcutaneous layers of the musical work of art is always only in the process of forming and on the brink of appearing. It is always only stepping into appearance, never a stable presence that has settled its own status as world—and as world-sense—once and for all.

Once it becomes possible to think the subcutaneous in relation to a world stepping into appearance, the presumed break between the tradition of musical history and the supposedly disruptive works of the Second Viennese School becomes increasingly problematic. It is no accident, therefore, that the musical examples with which Adorno interweaves his lecture work steadily to undermine the tacit binarism of tradition and a departure from it vis-à-vis the worlds set up by the musical artworks. For instance, he points to an air by Bach, playing the first eight measures on violin and piano twice in a row, as a subcutaneous movement. The first time around, Adorno plays the composition "without sense [*sinnlos*]": here, a richly textured melody is performed without articulation and phrasing, so that its sense and purpose remain opaque. The second time he plays these eight measures, Adorno includes phrasing and articulation in such a way as to articulate a network of relations among the individual notes, so that what steps forth from the subcutaneous level of the composition is a rich sense of interconnectedness, in which all sounds attain their purpose in relation to the totality of all other sounds with which they constantly interact. While this performative engagement with the subcutaneity of the musical work of art allows a certain interconnected simultaneity to be heard, the unphrased and unarticulated way of performing these same eight measures yields only "an agglomeration of sounds [*ein Agglomerat von Tönen*]."[15] The movement of Adorno's argument is to suggest that this very same principle, so evident both in Bach and in the works of Viennese classicism, is shared by the experimental compositions of the Second Viennese School, albeit in a singular and idiomatic way. The specific example that Adorno plays comes from Schönberg's *Lockung*, opus 6, specifically the opening measures by the piano up to the point at which a singing voice enters. What he wishes to demonstrate is the way in which Schönberg's composition, too, is concerned with articulating a subcutaneous and polyreferential network in which the individual sonic elements enter an abiding and purposeful relation. One might say that it is in this purposeful relation that these sonic elements first become true *Klangfiguren*. What is "revolutionary" about this experimental Schönbergian way of setting up a world through the musical work of art is not its penchant for dissonances but rather its strategic ways of "reducing music to the elements of its sense" while eschewing conventional mechanisms that "apparently make listening-along easier, but in truth often occlude sense [*in Wahrheit aber oft sich vor den Sinn schieben*]."[16] What connects Schönberg to a subcutaneous tradition—even as he breaks out of that tradition—is the way in which the world that his compositions set up are populated by highly differentiated sonic events that nevertheless are infinitely related to each other, emerge from each other, refer back to each other and the broader, all-encompassing texture in a most compelling manner. In order to "remain faithful to its inheritance," this music "had to forget its apparent inheritance,"[17] which is to say that remaining true to the subcutaneous inscriptions of its own world-creating movements required the artwork to abandon its external scaffolding, the enabling (but ultimately misleading) façade—what Adorno terms music's "Außenarchitektur"—for the internal structure of its normally hidden inner logic to emerge and to be self-reflexively exposed as such.

One of the lessons to be drawn from these musical examples with regard to the question of what constitutes the genuine inheritance of an artwork is the idea that an authentic relation to a tradition also unfolds, as it were, subcutaneously. "To inquire into the legacy or inheritance of New Music [*Nach dem Erbe in der neuen Music zu fragen*]," Adorno suggests, "would therefore mean to inquire into the secret that serves to connect music's authentic works with those of the past without a resemblance being visible on the surface [*ohne daß eine Ähnlichkeit obenauf läge*]."[18] For a musical work of art—as perhaps for any artwork—being connected to the tradition of a past does not mean exhibiting obvious ties to that past. An authentic relation to the tradition does not consist in sharing particular features, readily identifiable markers, or citable elements with works that came before. For a musical work of art—along with the unique world that it sets up—to entertain a genuine relation to the tradition of the past, it must not repeat, recycle, or appropriate the visible signatures of what came before. Rather, to enter into a genuine, refractory relation with the past and the musical traditions inscribed in it, the work of art "makes the elements borrowed from the musical idiom speak" in such a way that it is no longer "the familiar husk [*die vertraute Hülle*]" that sponsors the connection to the tradition. It is, rather, the "presentation" of its specific way of being composed, a "composedness

[*Komponierten*]," that assumes an idiomatic function within the new work.[19] Another way to put this is to say that it is the very composedness of the musical idiom as such that makes itself felt on the subcutaneous level at which the surface structure of the work begins to be disrupted. One might thus say that an indifferent, imitative, or unfree relation to the tradition takes place on the surface of the aesthetic phenomenon, its recognizability as form; but a genuine, transformative relation to the tradition is hidden within the invisible (or inaudible) layer of the subcutaneous, in which authentic and surprising relations to the tradition can be forged in ways that necessarily betray the tradition precisely in order to remain faithful to it. Its inheritance becomes most forcefully palpable at the conceptual and performative point at which it is no longer possible to differentiate between faithfulness and betrayal in any reliable way. Inheriting the world of the musical work of art is an act of the most faithful betrayal imaginable.

*

In order better to understand this perspective on inheriting a tradition, it is helpful to consider Adorno's reflections on what might constitute *das Neue*, "the new." For it is in relation to the thinking of the new that the genealogical dimension of the subcutaneous is modulated. Even though the subcutaneous is best thought on the structural level as vectorizing seemingly disparate elements into a constellation of previously hidden yet highly significant structural or spatial relations, it also has an irreducibly temporal dimension, entertaining an abiding relation with the notion and experience of time. Without such an engagement with its own temporality, the subcutaneous could not be mobilized as an aid to thinking the problem of tradition, which must always be considered in historical terms, that is, with an eye (or, in the case of the musical artwork, an ear) to its temporal grownness and its relation to the past. Indeed, it is only through an engagement with this temporal and historical dimension that a category such as "the new" could first come into focus, since the new always marks a rupturing of that which is in terms of its departure from what came before, from what has already been the case at some point in the past.

134

There is no thinking of newness without its other, the old or something already in existence.

When it comes to the world set up by a musical work of art, however, the newness of the new as such demands to be called into question. "After all," Adorno argues, "it would be naïve to assume that, within art, something absolutely new could ever appear in an unmediated way [*es könne in der Kunst ein schlechterdings Neues unvermittelt erscheinen*]."[20] One way of understanding this insistence on questioning the newness of the new is to acknowledge that whenever the ostensibly new announces itself as new, bursting onto the scene of that which is, it does so with a gesture of departure and with a promise of something unprecedented.[21] But these claims tend to be based on a denial or attempted erasure of the very roots from which the new has emerged and which first have made the supposedly new possible.[22] The new, when it announces itself as such, therefore always erases its own genealogical having-becomeness, that is, its radical indebtedness to what is now to be considered old, even if that indebtedness takes the form of having received the impetus from the old to criticize, modify, or even overthrow it. Adorno, for his part, offers an image borrowed from Hegel to illustrate his thinking of the new, both in relation to the art termed New Music and with respect to the newness of the new in art as such:

> Especially where the new becomes visible in a striking and overwhelming manner, one can be certain that it—to speak with a parable by Hegel—has formed itself for a long time as if under a cotyledon, until it was capable of shucking its shell; and only that which has nourished itself on the juices of tradition possesses the strength to confront tradition as an other, while an unauthenticated beginning will always defenselessly fall victim to the powers of what is, powers that it has insufficiently negotiated and overcome within itself.

> Gerade dort, wo das Neue schlagend, überwältigend sichtbar wird, kann man sicher sein, daß es, mit einem Gleichnis Hegels zu reden, wie unter einem Keimblatt sich lange gebildet hat, bis es fähig ward, die Hülle abzuwerfen, und

nur was mit den Säften der Überlieferung sich nährte, hat wohl überhaupt die Kraft, der Überlieferung als ein anderes gegenüber zu treten, während der unverbürgte Beginn stets wieder wehrlos den Mächten dessen was ist zum Opfer fällt, von denen es allzu wenig in sich selber bewältigte.[23]

It is hardly an accident that Adorno here employs, via Hegel, the botanical rhetoric of a *Keimblatt* (literally "seed leaf"), or cotyledon. If he mobilizes the figure of the cotyledon in his reflection on the new it is because, in our commonplace relation to the newness of the new, the quality of the new as something that has gradually grown and nourished itself on that which exists has been obscured. As a crucial element in the embryo of a plant seed, the cotyledon functions as an embryonic leaf that becomes visible when a seed germinates. As such, the cotyledon is the visible manifestation of early growth having taken place within the seed of a plant; the flowering both demonstrates and symbolizes its own history of nourishment and transformation. One might say that in order for the new to be of a genuinely transformative nature—as in the case of a political revolution, the invention of a medication or vaccine that will alleviate unnecessary human suffering, or an apparently unheard-of musical sound bursting onto the scene—it must have grown out of the tradition of what came before, wrestled with the authority of the status quo found in the existing world, and nourished itself on its persistent engagement with the ostensibly old. It is only by traveling in a most intimate manner through the forces and logic of what already exists—engaging with that which belongs to the authority of a tradition—that the new becomes capable of positing itself as an other to that tradition. It must already have absorbed within itself something prior, a predecessor in relation to which it wishes to posit itself as a genuine alterity. The new must have deliberately suckled on the juices of tradition ("Säften der Überlieferung") for a long time before it could wean and become the kind of otherness that may call itself "new" in any genuine sense. If it fails to nourish itself on what the legacy of its heritage has to offer it—and, by extension, if it fails to confront the internal tensions and contradictions of that legacy—it will hardly be able to hold its own when it faces the authoritative force of the

136

powers that be, the powers in relation to which it wishes to be an other. In other words, in order to become a true other—a radical form of alterity to the status quo—the new must already be the old, at least *among other things*. It is incumbent upon that which announces itself as the new to have internalized the otherness of its very own other—the always already prior tradition—without simply being identical to that otherness or even to itself.

If it is the case that the new only emerges out of a nourishing and lasting engagement with the legacy of its inheritance, to which it remains tied even as it separates from it, the question arises to what extent this abiding imbrication between the new and the traditional informs the kind of world that a work of art sets up, especially if that work of art, as is the case for the "new music" of the Second Viennese School, sails under the banner of newness. Does the world that is set up by the artwork conform to the precepts of newness? Is the world that emerges from it in fact a "new" world at all? If it is a "new" world, in what relation to other, perhaps older, worlds does the ostensible newness of the new world stand? Does that which is said to be new about the new world as it emerges from a work of art break with other, older worlds, or does it also perpetuate the latter in some way? How would our thinking of the singular world that is set up by a particular work of art have to be inflected if we wished to account for the ways in which other, older worlds continue to be operative in that new world, even on a subterranean or subcutaneous level?

To affirm that a genuine work of art, especially one that posits itself as new, stands in an abiding relationship to the legacy of the tradition in which its predecessors are inscribed is also to open up the possibility that the world created by a new work of art is tacitly suffused by elements of other, older worlds, which continue to make themselves felt. The world that a new work of art sets up in its own idiomatic terms can then be apprehended as a ghostly archive in which traces of previous worlds continue to haunt and silently to live on. One consequence of thinking the relation between these new and old worlds in the realm of that which is set up by the work of art is that every world emerging from a work of art is related to vast networks of other, older worlds that make themselves felt in the space of a particular world, even as these other worlds were set up by other artworks in very different times and under incommensurate circumstances. Learning to read in an emphatic and responsible manner a single world as it is set up by a particular work of art therefore always also means learning to read a vast, even infinite, network of other worlds. To read a world is to read *other worlds*.

How, then, is it possible to conceptualize the particular way in which tradition is present in the works that set up such worlds? What are the modes of dwelling assumed by particular traditions within the singular world that an artwork calls into presence? Or, as Adorno puts it, "where in New Music today is the legacy contained [*das Erbe geborgen*]?"[24] The relevance of the question concerning the *Erbe*—the tradition, legacy, or inheritance—of musical works of art cannot be reduced to its supposed historical interest. After all, the "question concerning tradition, the genuinely present inheritance within New Music, is so urgent because today, no less than during Hitler's time, much mischief is committed by means of the concepts *Erbe* and *Tradition*, and they are used to throttle the mind or spirit [*Geist*] that is in the process of forming."[25] If to think genealogical concepts such as inheritance, legacy, heritage, and tradition in a manner that wrests them from reactionary or conservative mobilizations is paramount to Adorno's understanding of the musical work of art, it is because he espies in the historically saturated dimension of the work a transformative yet persistent relation between past and present, a relation that cannot be reduced to mere preservation, continuation, or an inflexible insistence on traditional norms that have been handed down by an authority. "Tradition," seen from this vantage point, "hardly is a resemblance to that which, within history, follows upon something else." Rather, what "bestows such force on tradition" is "something subterranean [*etwas Unterirdisches*]," so that tradition "does not form itself within that in which someone obeys his predecessor."[26] The world that the genuinely traditional work creates also breaks with tradition; it conforms to tradition only by disobeying or, literally, by refusing to listen to it in the way that it conventionally commands (*gehorcht* is the word that Adorno uses, meaning both obeys and, as a form of *hören*, listens or harkens). Honoring the tradition by disobeying it, the world of the genuine artwork opens up a different kind of listening or harkening. One might say that the acoustic world created by the musical work of art is informed by the inheritance of tradition even—and especially—as it departs from it; the world that the work sets up feeds on tradition, yet is hardly recognizable in relation to that very same tradition.

Adorno here thinks the inheritance of a tradition in terms of a strategic refusal to allow the ready-made historical and conceptual categories supplied by a naïve relation with tradition to determine how a musical work of art is understood—and, by extension, what kind of world it is presumed to set up. In fact, by rejecting the assumption that the tradition is best understood as a self-identical provider of meaning to newer forms of artistic production, he keeps alive the very idea of a world—set up by the work of art—in which the musical realm and the philosophical realm can relate to each other in transformative and surprising ways. Adorno expresses this thought, again with regard to the example of Schönberg, in his *Negative Dialectics*, where he argues:

> An experience that Schönberg noted with regard to traditional music theory is confirmed in the case of philosophy: one actually only learns from it how a movement begins and ends, but nothing about the movement itself, its course. Analogously, philosophy would need first not to turn itself into a series of categories, but rather, in a certain sense, to compose itself. It must, in the course of its progression, relentlessly renew itself, as much from its own strength as from the friction with that against which it measures itself; it is what happens in philosophy that is decisive, not a thesis or propositional fabric, not the deductive or inductive single-tracked train of thought. Therefore philosophy is in essence not summarizable [*referierbar*]. Otherwise it would be superfluous; that most of it allows itself to be summarized speaks against it.[27]

Read in the context of the problem of tradition and its relation to the new in the realm of music, this rich passage suggests, among many other things, that a philosophical reflection on music and the kinds of world that it sets up ought not to be deaf to genuine music's own demands. In this world opened by the musical artwork, music and philosophy share a common principle of composition. Far from being identical to each other, they enter a special and irreducible relation in which they each expose their compositional principles in a self-conscious manner.[28] Eschewing summary and paraphrase, both music and philosophy self-reflexively exhibit the traces of their having-becomeness as form. In the case of musical works of art, it is the movement of music itself that steps into the foreground; and in the case of philosophy, what is central is the active journey and the experience of how its propositional content and claims to validity came into being, not the mere end products of knowledge, its so-called results. A rigorous and innovative engagement with tradition, conceived in a nondogmatic way, enables such foregrounding of the process and movement of both musical composition and philosophical thought. And the genuine work of art creates a world that is hospitable to a thinking of tradition in those terms, that is, a consideration of the relation between music and philosophy that respects both their singularity and their elective affinity. This world set up by the artwork and the aesthetic experience it sponsors enables a perpetual interplay between the wish to remain radically faithful to a tradition and the need to break with it at the same time.

One way of expanding the reach of this insight is to place it into syntactical relation with Alan Badiou's remarks on the relationship between Adorno's *Negative Dialectics* and the latter's views on the music of Wagner, especially as they are formulated throughout the early work *In Search of Wagner*. In the course of his reflections on this relation, the French philosopher arrives at a generalized characterization of Adorno's negatively dialectical perspective on music. As Badiou suggests, "Adorno's view is that music should *not* sublate its negativity but instead let it be and preserve the negative imperative of its being."[29] From this perspective, one "might say, then, that Adorno's position on music" finally "amounts to a thinking of formless form or informal form in the post-Auschwitz situation and consequently in the world today."[30] Badiou continues by arguing that three "aspects are involved" in such a determination:

140

First, it is music that terminates the unifying processes of form and consequently tolerates real difference or multiplicity, that is, the genuinely heterogeneous, or, in other words, things that have nothing to do with one another. Second, it is music with no resolution, music that is endless, in a manner of speaking, almost in both senses of the term: it has no ending that is truly essential to it nor does it have an end in the sense of a *telos*; it does not resolve the system of tensions it creates. Third, it must be music that does not sublate its own negative elements and therefore allows within itself the possibility for something different from itself.[31]

If Badiou is right that music for Adorno pivots on the capacity for difference and multiplicity, on being without ending and without end or telos, and on respecting a nonsublatable remainder within its own non-self-identity, one might say that these qualities also reinforce the capacity of a musical work to open onto the radical heterogeneity of its own tradition. After all, is it not the very ability of the musical artwork to set up a world in which the legacy of its own tradition becomes visible as problematic and refractory that predicates the work's capacity to confront its own negativity? In other words, the extent to which the world as set up by the musical work of art operates—as if through a negative capability—in a manner that pivots on its own self-differentiation and internal multitude determines how rigorously and sensitively the work is able to engage with both its being anchored in tradition and its perpetual breaking with that same tradition. If such music has no "resolution," as Badiou rightly observes, then the world that it projects out of itself also is not structured according to any logic of resolution—a resolution that could adjudicate once and for all how the world that is set up by a specific musical artwork is to relate to the competing demands of remaining faithful to a tradition while not following it at the same time. Taking up the language that Badiou mobilizes in his interpretation of Adorno's concept of music, one might say that such a world set up by the musical work of art "allows within itself the possibility for something different from itself," including, one might now argue, first and foremost the concept and force of tradition itself. Only in this hospitality, this willingness to invite and to provide shelter, within the same bounds, precisely to what does not fit, to what radically differs from a self-identity, can the ability to relate to a tradition—even to the tradition of tradition—be cultivated.

To argue that the acoustic world set up by the musical work of art finds itself inscribed in a tradition precisely when its breaks with it also is to suggest that one's relation to the precepts of an inheritance does not take place exclusively on a conscious level. On the contrary, there is a strong unconscious component that modulates the genealogical imbrication of an artwork and the legacy of artistic production to which it stands in relation. In order to illuminate this idea, Adorno cites a pivotal passage from the section on "Latency and Tradition" in Freud's *Moses and Monotheism*, in which the latter, as so often in his mature writings, engages with explicitly historical questions to supplement the more overtly structural questions that his earlier explorations of psychoanalysis had engaged. In this late work, Freud devotes his attention to the problem of tradition by engaging with a verse by Schiller. The final two lines of the second version of Schiller's poem "Die Götter Griechenlandes"—a revised version of his original 1788 poem that was published in 1804 and involved the cooperation of his friend Goethe—read:

> Was unsterblich im Gesang soll leben
> Muß im Leben untergehen.[32]

> What is to live immortally in song
> Must perish in life.

That which becomes immortal within the work of art can only become so if its empirical existence ceases. In other words, only in light of its death in the world out of which it arises can something live on, through a kind of immortality, in the songs, artworks, and legends devoted to it. To survive forever, it must first die; its death is the precondition for its inability to die. To be sure, one may recall here the Christian narrative of the life and death of Jesus, who died and became immortal as God, a process upon which Ernst Bloch once commented that "even the death of Christ was only his beginning." Yet the reach of Schiller's lines extends beyond any one religion, even beyond the confines of religion as such. What is at stake, more broadly, is the idea that the phenomenon or even the world that lives on in the artistic creations and cultural narratives of a civilization presupposes the real-life perishing of what is to survive in immortality and historical perpetuity. The continued existence in life of that which is to become immortal in song or art would only compete with, even impede, its transfiguration into an aestheticized work that may come to inform the world of a tradition. In perishing, that which is to survive leaves behind a trace. Here, the trace of an absence marks a former presence, and this mark indicates the site where what is now absent but lives on in an elsewhere can assume the form of song, art, and the narrative of cultural legend. The trace of an absence here figures as the ghostly founder of an aesthetic and cultural tradition, a tradition which then itself becomes, among other things, the archive of such spectral traces.

What could be said about such a tradition when it makes itself felt? How do its ghostly traces shape what we perceive to be the case in our world of experience, and how are we compelled to relate to a tradition thus articulated? Adorno cites the passage in which Freud comments on the two lines from Schiller that the latter has just quoted. Freud argues that a

> tradition that is only based on communication [*Mitteilung*] could not create the compulsive character [*Zwangscharacter*] that is characteristic of religious phenomena. The tradition would be listened to, judged, and possibly rejected like any other message coming from outside and would never attain the privilege of being free from the compulsion of logical thinking. It must first have experienced the fate of having been repressed, the condition of tarrying in the unconscious, before it can have, upon its return, such powerful effects and can compel the masses to be mesmerized by it, the way we have observed in the case of religious tradition with such astonishment and, thus far, without understanding."

In Freud's perspective, there is something more powerful at work in tradition—and especially religious tradition—than could be transmitted through direct and explicit communication between generations. Considered within a psychoanalytic framework, tradition also—and especially—works its powerful effects when its individual elements are not handed down explicitly but rather come to influence a subject on an unconscious level. (Elsewhere in the text, Freud also evokes the notion of an enigmatic "archaic inheritance," in which certain primal experiences are received by a new generation as a fundamental part of their tradition, even though they themselves never had these particular experiences themselves, nor were they explicitly instructed about their meaning or even existence.) Freud's interpretation of tradition as it unfolds in relation to the lines from Schiller are especially instructive for Adorno because they point to something that is also fundamental to the world of the artwork. While Freud's "sentences refer directly to religious tradition," as Adorno point out, it is "as if they were also valid with respect to artistic tradition."[34] This is so because the tradition involving art and artworks also constitutes "a memory of something unconscious [*Erinnerung an ein Unbewußtes*], even something repressed."[35] Vectorizing Freud's intuition about religious tradition in the direction of aesthetic production, Adorno locates the most powerful effects of the tradition away from a model of explanation that would rely on straight lines of continuity and the superficial consciousness of being the heir of a transparent legacy. Instead, he places the emphasis on a view of the force of tradition that "prevails especially where what is unconsciously remembered explodes such continuity [*wo das unbewußt Erinnerte jene Kontinuität aufsprengt*]."[36] This blasting open of continuity reveals an even deeper connection to the tradition, one that is based not on straightforward succession or compliant reception but rather on an unacknowledged, unconscious—and therefore all the more powerful—relation to what has come before.

It is therefore hardly an accident that Adorno advances the idea that, in the world of art, artists themselves have had at least an intuition, however inchoate, of this state of affairs. While one cannot speak of knowledge in this regard—after all, the unconscious can never be reduced to, or translated into, simple knowledge without ceasing to be unconscious—it is possible to speak of an "Ahnung," as when Adorno suggests of certain artists that "eine Ahnung davon" was not entirely alien or strange to them ("nicht fremd gewesen").[37] He specifically cites the cubist painter Juan Gris, who is said to have argued that "the tradition of French painting is alive in those modern artists who have freed themselves most energetically from this tradition, rather than in those who claim to be based on that tradition in an immediate way."[38] Tradition thus is present precisely in those artistic works that self-consciously break with it. And to claim to perpetuate tradition in a linear and straightforward line can be a way of betraying it, a manner of not engaging with what is most essential in it—and thus rendering it static and lifeless. It is from this perspective that Adorno makes a case for the experimental music he holds in such high esteem: precisely by continuing to engage with the tradition in a way that also breaks with it, this new music keeps that tradition alive much more effectively than do those works that portray themselves as the true heirs of the musical tradition, the self-appointed guardians of, and successors to, a supposedly fixed and self-identical auditory heritage of composition, performance, and reception. Reading Freud reading Schiller, Adorno thus advances an argument about tradition that privileges the experimental critique of tradition rather than any submissive adherence to it. Yet it is precisely in this apparent turn away from tradition that tradition is able to make itself felt most powerfully as a ghostly and haunting presence, as something undead that continues to hold us in its sway. We share with it its world of specters that return each time we allow ourselves to enter into the very world the genuine work of art has opened up for us—that is, when we become *attuned* to it.

The question may arise, at this point, in what precise form the tradition lingers within the world set up by experimental works of musical art that, at first sight, seem to reject tradition. Even the subcutaneous level of the musical artwork demands a certain phenomenological resonance in order to make itself felt. What relates experimental works such as those of the Second Viennese School to significant works of the tradition is not, from Adorno's perspective, to be found in "analogies" such as "the use of similar form-types," not even in what "one generally calls motivic-thematic work."[39] To

145

the contrary, "it is especially in the eccentric and alienating traits [*exzentrischen und befremdenden Zügen*] of New Music that the inheritance [*Erbe*] lives on."[40] In order to render vivid the world of "a subterranean tradition [*unterirdische Tradition*],"[41] Adorno plays a number of passages, both from the tradition of so-called classical music and from the experimental music that reengages with that tradition in unheard-of ways. (Adorno was animated by a particular fascination in the musical realm with what he called *schöne Stellen*, "beautiful passages," a topic to which he devoted an entire essay in 1965.)[42] In the text on musical inheritance, he places, for instance, Beethoven's String Quartet no. 7 in F Major, op. 59, no. 1, in comparative relation to the beginning of another *Quartettsatz*, taken from the "Andante amoroso" of Berg's six-movement work for string quartet entitled *Lyric Suite* (1925–1926). What Adorno finds, throughout his careful, painstaking, and patient microanalyses of these musical moments, is a highly differentiated engagement with the tradition that connects Beethoven and Berg in unexpected but decisive ways. The ways in which Adorno's composition teacher Berg relates to the musical tradition and its inheritance may be subcutaneous and infinitely demanding of its listeners; but, as such, it is all the more compelling.

One is thus able to appreciate the idea that the legacy of a tradition places an enigmatic yet powerful inheritance at the feet of the heir. The heir stands before a riddle that demands to be interpreted carefully and caringly, even daringly. The inheritance and the tradition out of which it arises are never a transparent given but only come to exert their force most fully when they are reengaged and reinterpreted in a ceaseless and infinitely close act of reading. It is from this perspective, and having demonstrated an uncanny connection between such unlikely relatives as Beethoven and Berg, that Adorno can insist on a certain responsibility toward the tradition that also breaks with it. For him, only where "the capacity obtains" to invite "an intensification of the capacity to realize musical sense in each trait" can one genuinely "be loyal to the tradition [*wird der Tradition die Treue gehalten*]."[43] This is so because "tradition is nothing thing like [*nichts Dinghaftes*] but rather a force field that tears all moments of the work of art into itself [*alle Momente des Kunstwerks in sich hineinreißt*]." And the "stronger a formed entity [*ein Gebilde*] follows this compulsion—that is, the more responsible it shows itself to the inner claim, requirement, and address [*Anspruch*] of tradition—the more fully and necessarily it must today distance itself from the façade of tradition."[44] One might say this distancing that Adorno evokes is simultaneously an approaching. By distancing itself from the façade or apparent surface structure of a tradition, the musical work of art is in a position in which it can first be receptive to the lingering, unresolved, and continuously relevant aspects of an artistic inheritance. The world that the genuine musical work of art sets up allows for this movement of distancing-as-approaching, this unyielding responsibility to brush the legacy of a tradition against the grain in order to preserve it as a question mark that has a future and, in turn, may spawn a future world.

If the world that the musical work of art sets up for those who are attuned to its requirements is one that cannot do without the tradition with which it simultaneously breaks, this world also names the gesture of a discarding that simultaneously is a form of gaining. Adorno expresses this idea as follows: "If, in response to the question concerning the inheritance [*die Frage des Erbes*] within New Music, one wished to apply Goethe's demand to acquire it in order to own it, then this would amount to the same thing as the biblical one: Cast away so that you may gain [*Wirf weg, damit du gewinnst*]."[45] The apodictic allusion to "Goethe's demand" is in fact a reference to a specific moment in Goethe's *Faust* that is explicitly concerned with the difficult problem of inheriting. At night, in his Gothic study, Faust not only considers the relative advantages and disadvantages of science and scholarship for one's understanding of human life, but he also explicitly includes among the most urgent questions of one's being-in-the-world the problem of inheritance.[46] In a multilayered soliloquy, Faust says: "What you have inherited from your fathers, / Acquire it to gain possession of it [*Was Du ererbt von deinen Vätern hast, / Erwirb es, um es zu besitzen*]."[47] Goethe is not merely concerned, in an allegorical mode, with problems of aesthetics, such as the question concerning modern appropriations of the classical Greek heritage or the dramatic legacy of Shakespeare, which often claim his attention. After all, according to Faust's statement, what has been inherited—and thus presumably already transferred to the property of another—does not simply *belong* to that other without further reflection. What has been inherited first demands to be acquired not only in the juridical, economic, or material senses. The inheritance demands to be inherited *as inheritance*. In other words, a proper inheritance requires that one learn how to inherit *as such*.

Like Freud, who much appreciated this line by Goethe and was fond of citing it himself (for instance, in *Totem and Taboo*), Adorno mobilizes Goethe's reflection in order to emphasize the abiding need to learn what an inheritance is and what can really be meant by the idea of a tradition and the concept of a legacy that is to be taken up by an heir. Yet unlike Freud, Adorno predicates this meditation upon the need first to acquire an inheritance so that it may become one's own in any genuine way in terms of another impetus: to throw away in order to acquire. Adorno felt a special elective affinity to this phrase—"Wirf weg, damit Du gewinnst"— employing it multiple times in a number of passages throughout his work, including in *Minima Moralia*.[48] Yet if he mobilizes it in the current context, it is with a specific and circumscribed purpose: it points to the necessity of throwing the tradition away in a proper and deliberate manner so that it may tacitly be regained *as* tradition. Here, to shun also means to invite, and to depart from also means to be hospitable to. When set into dialectical relation with Goethe's emphasis on gaining possession of an inheritance—truly possessing by first learning how to acquire it in a genuine way—the injunction to discard or cast aside an inheritance in order possibly to gain it sheds new light on the concept of tradition and the artistic world in which it can come to pass. Considered from this perspective, the supposedly opposite movements of acquiring and throwing away no longer stand opposed. On the contrary, with regard to the inheritance of tradition that is only available to the world of an artwork as a function of the work's departure from it, to acquire and to throw away turn out to be the same thing. When it comes to the relation that the world set up by a genuine work of art entertains with the tradition, to gain is to cast aside, and to cast aside is to gain.

The subcutaneous movement of acquiring and discarding that structures a truly nonforeclosed and radically open relation to the inheritance of a tradition informs the world set up by the genuine musical work of art in decisive ways. When we risk entering the unfamiliar aesthetic world that a specific work has prepared for us—even and especially when the world in which the work itself came to be has perished once and for all, Berg's no less than Beethoven's, Schönberg's no less than Bach's, we should not only be prepared to engage patiently and caringly with its sonorous offerings. We also should be willing to endure the experience of no longer being able to tell the difference between acquiring and casting away. After all, the capacious world set up by the artwork itself hauntingly holds this very difference in abeyance.

How do we relate to this world fashioned by the musical work of art? How do we find our bearings in it? Can we ever supply an appropriate response to the questions we feel it addresses to us? Among the earliest notations that Adorno recorded for his planned book on Beethoven—a plan that he carried within himself, indeed that weighed heavily on him, for his entire lifetime but that he did not manage to carry out before his untimely death in 1969—we find the following enigmatic reflection:

> We do not understand music—it understands us. This is
> true for the musician as much as for the layperson. When we
> consider ourselves closest to it, it addresses us and waits with
> sad eyes for us to respond.

> Wir verstehen nicht die Musik—sie versteht uns. Das gilt für
> den Musiker so gut wie für den Laien. Wenn wir sie uns am
> nächsten meinen, dann spricht sie uns an und wartet mit
> traurigen Augen, daß wir ihr antworten.[49]

The world that the musical work of art sets up may defy our comprehension, while nevertheless comprehending us. How, one might ask, can this be? What is the rhetorical function of this personification of music? It is as if there were something within the world set up by music that manages to grasp something about us that we ourselves do not understand—about music, about ourselves, and about our shifting and enigmatic ways of sharing the world with music. One might say that the world fashioned by the musical artwork understands that we do not understand. That is to say, it possesses a kind of knowledge of nonknowledge, grasping our very inability to grasp and reflecting this inability back to us. The proximity we may feel to music within the world that it has set up is occasioned by the act of an address: when it resounds, it speaks to us, soliciting our response. Yet if it waits with sad eyes ("mit traurigen Augen") for us to respond, this is because it knows that we do not know how to respond. Music calls on us to act on our responsibility, or answerability, in the face of the *Klangfiguren* that populate the world set up by the work; yet it knows, in its own musical way, that we must fail to answer and that we will remain silent, no matter how much we may say and write about it. Such melancholic knowledge of nonknowledge not only resounds in the sound figures that we call the musical work of art; it also names its abiding subcutaneous inheritance.

A World of Gray: Color, Grayness, and Utopia in the Work of Art (Adorno)

W hen we think of the world, does it have a color? Or does it not sometimes also appear in gray, almost as if it belonged to the sphere of an old photograph or a black-and-white film? What are the stakes of considering the world in either gray or colorful hues? If, in the course of our reflections, we encounter a world of gray, is this encounter to be lamented or invited? If the world that is set up by the work of art is suffused by gray—or even is fully immersed in grayness—how may we begin to relate to that gray world? And when the world is our concern, what is it that appears to imbricate grayness with thinking and the work of art?

At first glance, there is nothing self-evident about the connection between the color gray and any particular kind of intellectual activity. And yet, upon closer inspection, our engagement with gray, which is often considered a noncolor that figures as a gradation between black and white, a shade on the achromatic scale, is intimately intertwined with philosophical thought itself—and therefore with a consideration of the world. Unlike colors whose distinctness and intensity may distinguish them rather clearly from other pigmentations, gray lives predominantly in a world of shades. Located somewhere on the spectrum between the poles of black and white, what is called gray draws attention, each time it is perceived, to its own differential gradation, a gradation that sets each gray apart from other instances of grayness by merely a hue, more accessible perhaps to the eye than to the word. Like the experience of philosophical thinking itself, our encounter with gray thus pulls us into a world of nuances, subtlety, and the exacting experience of fine differentiations. When we encounter grayness in the world, we may speak, for instance, of a warm gray or a cool gray, a light gray or a dark gray, an ashen gray or an anthracite gray. As the German art historians Magdalena Bushart and Gregor Wedekind point out, it behooves us to regard gray "not as a negation and a noncolor" but rather "dialectically, as a quality that consists in being nothing and yet something, an absence and a fullness, dead petrification and living bravura, a mode and a form of being."[1] This intricate form of being manifests itself in a plurality of perspectives. In the world of older art, we may be drawn to modes of philosophical reflection that are opened up by the complex grisaille technique in medieval panel painting and in baroque oil painting, or by the subtly gray-suffused portraiture that we associate with masters such as Rembrandt. From among the most well-known paintings of the modern Western canon, we may be especially hospitable to the modes of conceptual inquiry instigated by the gray tonalities of Picasso's *Guernica*. Even though Picasso experienced a so-called blue period and a rose period but no gray period, it can be said with confidence that, without his seminal engagements with gray, our concept of modern painting would be radically different— and impoverished. In the world of more recent artistic production, we may find the impetus for theoretical meditation in the modernist experimentations with gray by American painters such as Jasper Johns and Cy Twombly or the sustained explorations of grayness and its overdetermined historico-philosophical valences in contemporary German artists such as Anselm Kiefer and Gerhard Richter. In the world of early photography, we may be particularly attentive, as were pioneering philosophical interpreters of photography such as Benjamin, to the shades of gray that intermingle with conceptual reflection in Eugène Atget's masterful images of ghostly Parisian street scenes. In the sonic realm, some of us who lived in Europe in the early 1980s may have listened to the dreamy rhythms of "Fade to Grey" by the British new wave band Visage—with its hauntingly interjected French refrain "devenir gris"—as the soundtrack to our conceptual buckling up for a protracted journey through a world that was beginning to be dominated by the Thatcher-Reagan-Kohl paradigm.

One might also say that the experience of the world of gray is linked to theoretical reflection through its tendency always to open onto something other than itself, an alterity that will not remain within the realm of any form of self-identity. Indeed, as the literary scholar David Scott Kastan and the painter Stephen Farthing suggest in their recent collaborative work *On Color*, "it is rare that gray is not something other than itself," as when it becomes, for instance in older photography, precisely the "color of colorlessness."[2] As happens under the philosophical gaze with its operations of increasing differentiation, the objects of one's reflection, when they are regarded as shades or gradations within a gray-toned framework, may begin to change subtly but dramatically, and we may end up viewing and understanding these shades in rather differently modulated terms. Gray, when seen from this perspective, is one of the names for what refuses to remain simply itself yet continually demands to be thought and interpreted.

Its very status as a noncolor, or as an other to color itself, casts gray as the embodiment of larger, unresolved conceptual issues and theoretical speculation pertaining to color and its interpretation. To be sure, the canonical view of gray holds that it, like black and white, is not a color at all because it does not have its own place on the color wheel, and should strictly speaking be referred to as a so-called neutral. But art historians such as Frances Guerin are beginning to complicate this traditional conceptualization of gray. As she suggests in *The Truth Is Always Grey: A History of Modernist Painting*—a study that works to establish gray as a legitimate color and even as a privileged key to seminal issues in the relationship between painting and modernity—one may well wonder if "the 'noncolor' of grey" signifies "merely a convenient way to deal with the uncomfortable space between the visual and the linguistic designation of colors." In other words, "to call grey a 'noncolor' is perhaps an unimaginative way of describing the constant ineffability of grey," and, in fact, the "designation of grey as a noncolor might be a convenient repository for a much larger unknown," so that "the indeterminacy of all colors" may appear "projected onto the nebulousness of grey."[3] Considered from this angle, the indeterminacy of gray, its very resistance to being assigned any particular stable significance, figures as a prime instantiation of some of the most fundamental problems concerning our perception and interpretation of color as such. The world of gray, in its withdrawal, opens onto the question of meaning itself.

Yet philosophical reflection on the very grayness of gray is always also called upon to consider the manifold associations that are tied to the world of gray as well as its traditional experiential valences and culturally mediated connotations, such as tristesse, neutrality, nonspecificity, boredom, indistinguishability, barrenness, sobriety, a lack of stimulation or excitement, nebulosity, belatedness, old age and death, even spectrality. It is no accident that, in what could be considered one of modernity's primal scenes of the world of gray and grayness, Goethe's Mephistopheles warns his pupil: "Gray, dear friend, is all theory, and green alone life's golden tree [*Grau, teurer Freund, ist alle Theorie und grün des Lebens goldner Baum*]."[4] Whenever Goethe throughout his oeuvre takes recourse to the rhetoric of color, it behooves his readers to pay especially close attention, in light of his extensive engagement with fashioning a comprehensive non-Newtonian *Farbenlehre*, or theory of color. (In the *Farbenlehre*, Goethe largely denigrates the supposedly neutral gray in favor of the other, more vibrant colors, to whose full apperception, however, gray may contribute by way of contrast.) In its dominant interpretations, Goethe's line from *Faust* has been taken to favor a certain empirical pragmatism, an intense and experience-based engagement with the supposed fullness and richness of life itself, over mere detached speculation, abstraction, and exclusively conceptual modes of relating to one's lifeworld. Whereas, according to this model, "theoretical" modes of being in the world appear to be connected to a drab, dry, and anemic grayness—that is, to the lifelessness one might associate with a noncolor or an achromatism—life itself is to be experienced as something vital, vivid, and organic, as expressed in the color green. This vital greenness is regarded as harboring the true value—as it were, the gold standard (expressed in Goethe's locution *goldner Baum*)—of life. When Hegel, in the programmatic preface to his *Philosophy of Right*, implicitly takes up Goethe's rhetoric without mentioning him by name, he retains Goethe's sense that the world of gray and grayness are to be considered modes of decline, decay, and immobility, even as Hegel vectorizes this thinking toward a slightly shifted purpose. He writes: "When philosophy paints its gray in gray [*Wenn die Philosophie ihr Grau in Grau malt*], one form of life has grown old, and by means of gray in gray it cannot be rejuvenated [*nicht verjüngen*], but only cognized [*nur erkennen*]; the owl of Minerva begins to take its flight only with the falling of dusk [*erst mit der einbrechenden Dämmerung*]."[5] Even though Hegel's well-known formulation elaborates upon the ambivalent conjunction between grayness and the philosophical reflections to which it may be linked in ways that are perhaps more subtle and complex than has typically been appreciated, dominant interpretations of Hegel's passage emphasize the ways in which philosophy is struck by a certain belatedness, a sense in which, when it finally does appear, it is unable to capture the full richness of lived experience in a world that is about to move on, shucking the forms of previous experience to which it had given rise. Viewed in this light, the speculative activity of painting gray in gray would suggest an inability in the face of a particular form of being alive in the world, an impotence with regard to providing a new impetus and vision to sustain an ever more exhausted world. When seen from this perspective, the gray in gray that philosophical thought paints becomes the very figure of lateness itself. Its theoretical apparatus is reduced to mere knowing (even while the status of that "knowing" is itself rather shaky), as it cannot "rejuvenate" a world and a form of living that are about to vanish for good. The theoretical interpretation offered by philosophical speculation, like the owl of Minerva itself, only first takes off amidst the darkness that descends upon it and the forms of life in relation to which it wishes to think, that is, amidst the achromatic shades of gray that dusk visits upon thought just as it begins to come into its own.[6]

There are few thinkers for whom this constellation of problems has played a more significant role than Adorno. As the present chapter shows, crucial elements in his conceptualization of a negative dialectics in general and of his theory of the aesthetic in particular cannot be fully appreciated outside the framework of a thinking that incorporates both the threat and the hidden potentiality of its grayness. In fact, the world of gray emerges as one of the keys to accessing core aspects of Adorno's philosophical preoccupations. In his often overlooked "Marginalia on Theory and Praxis," which first appeared in his late collection of philosophical essays, *Stichworte* (*Catchwords*)—in turn figuring as the second volume of his *Kritische Modelle*, or *Critical Models*, in 1969, the year of Adorno's death—we encounter the following observations:

> "All theory is gray," Goethe has Mephistopheles preach to the student he is leading around by the nose; the sentence was already ideology from the very beginning, a fraud about the fact that the tree of life the practitioners planted and that the devil in the same breath compares to gold is hardly green at all; the grayness of the theory is for its part a function of the life that has been de-qualified. Nothing should exist that cannot be fastened upon by both hands; not thought. The subject, thrown back upon itself, divided from its Other by an abyss, is supposedly incapable of action.

> Daß alle Theorie grau sei, läßt Goethe Mephistopheles dem Schüler predigen, den er an der Nase herumführt; der Satz war Ideologie schon am ersten Tag, Betrug darüber, wie wenig grün des Lebens Baum ist, den die Praktiker gepflanzt haben, und den der Teufel im gleichen Atemzug mit dem Metall Gold vergleicht; das Grau der Theorie seinerseits ist Funktion des entqualifizierten Lebens. Nichts soll sein, was nicht sich anpacken läßt; nicht der Gedanke. Das auf sich selbst zurückgeworfene, durch einen Abgrund von seinem Anderen getrennte Subjekt sei unfähig zur Tat.[7]

If Adorno espies in Goethe's Mephistophelean pronouncement a decidedly ideological component, it is because the grayness that is said to saturate all theory and, therefore, is to be abhorred is, in actuality, something else entirely. It is the very instrument by means of which the grayness that permeates the world of quotidian life and its various contexts of domination and oppression can be submitted to critique in the first place. Adorno reminds us that Mephistopheles, rather than enlightening his hapless pupil, actually leads him only "by the nose," which is to say, he indoctrinates him with an ideology that prevents his pupil from availing himself of genuine theoretical reflection—which is simply dismissed as "gray." Just as fatally, Mephistopheles creates the false impression that the tree of life is in fact colorful—green and vital—as the pragmatists who apparently placed it there for undisclosed reasons wish us to believe. The supposed grayness of theoretical reflection, in Adorno's reading, is in reality the expression of an "entqualifiziertes Leben," literally a kind of "de-qualified" life that has lost its essential characteristics in deference to a mere functioning or seamless submission to the logic of domination and exploitation in which it is immersed. The aversion to the world of gray, along with the grayness of theoretical reflection, therefore emerges as an ideologically motivated attempt to negate all true thinking by means of a pragmatist precensorship that only considers as real that which can be grasped in the most concrete terms while excluding any consideration of the idea that things could be *entirely different*. The pragmatist disqualification (or de-qualification) of theoretical reflection as merely "gray" thus not only paints a deceptive picture of a supposedly "green" world and vivid tree of life, it also evinces a fear of genuine thinking, whatever the content of that thinking may be in a particular context. Adorno's critique of the de-qualification of theoretical thought as gray is evocative of Arendt's incisive dictum from *The Life of the Mind*: "There are no dangerous thoughts; thinking itself is dangerous."[8] One might say that those who would wish to denigrate theoretical thought by associating it with the supposedly undesirable quality of grayness in reality wish to erase thinking itself by making it disappear under thick and impenetrable layers of gray.

Yet, when seen from another vantage point, layers of gray can at times also aid the mobilization of sustained philosophical and aesthetic practice. For instance, in a 2012 filmic installation entitled *Adorno's Grey*, the German artist Hito Steyerl takes as her point of departure the persistent (but likely apocryphal) legend that Adorno had his seminar and lecture halls at the University of Frankfurt painted gray in order to minimize distraction and thus to enhance his students' ability to concentrate on the task of thinking. In the course of the video projection, which lasts 14 minutes and 20 seconds, the black-and-white images of the film show two lab-coat-clad conservators at work in Adorno's former classrooms at the University of Frankfurt as they meticulously attempt to remove the top layers of wall paint in order to ascertain whether there is in fact a layer of gray paint to be found underneath.[9] This quasi-palimpsestic approach to the world of Adorno's gray and its institutional history functions as a prismatic lens through which various aspects of his lifeworld, politics, and thought come into view. Although the conservators' investigative efforts yield only inconclusive results, their scraping and chiseling frames the film's own investigation of gray, even the very grayness that insinuates itself into the world of what we rather imprecisely call a black-and-white film. Here, it is the abiding mysteriousness of gray itself that propels both conceptual thought and artistic practice forward into the world.

One might say that especially for the late Adorno, who devotes himself ever more relentlessly to a philosophical exploration of the work of art and, through it, to his unfinished *Aesthetic Theory* (the completion of which was interrupted by Adorno's death), such considerations of theory and its alleged imbrication with grayness deserve to be thought first and foremost in relation to the world of artistic production. For instance, in a remarkable and, at first glance, rather enigmatic passage from *Aesthetic Theory*, Adorno takes up the question of grayness once again, this time in relation to a certain unconventional utopian potentiality that he hopes to develop conceptually through recourse to the work of art:

> Each artwork is utopia insofar as through its form it
> anticipates what would finally be itself, and this converges
> with the demand for the abrogation of the spell of self-
> identity cast by the subject. No artwork is to be ceded to
> another. This justifies the indispensable sensual element

of artworks: It bears their *hic et nunc* in which, in spite of
all mediation, a certain independence is maintained; naïve
consciousness, which always clings to this element, is not
altogether false consciousness. The nonfungibility, of course,
takes over the function of strengthening the belief that
mediation is not universal. But the artwork must absorb
even its most fundamental enemy—fungibility; rather than
fleeing into concretion, the artwork must present through
its own concretion the total nexus of abstraction and
thereby resist it. Repetition in authentic new artworks is
not always an accommodation to the archaic compulsion
toward repetition. Many artworks indict this compulsion
and thereby take the part of what Haag has called the
unrepeatable; Beckett's *Play*, with the spurious infinity of its
reprise, presents the most accomplished model. The black
and gray of recent art, its asceticism against color, is the
negative apotheosis of color.

Utopie ist jedes Kunstwerk, soweit es durch seine Form
antezipiert, was endlich es selber wäre, und das begegnet
sich mit der Forderung, den vom Subjekt verbreiteten
Bann des Selbstseins zu tilgen. Kein Kunstwerk ist an ein
anderes zu zedieren. Das rechtfertigt das unabdingbare
sinnliche Moment an den Kunstwerken: es trägt ihr Jetzt
und Hier, darin bewahrt trotz aller Vermittlung sich auch
einige Selbständigkeit; das naive Bewußtsein, das stets
wieder an jenes Moment sich klammert, ist nicht durchaus
das falsche. Allerdings übernimmt die Unvertauschbarkeit
die Funktion, den Glauben zu bestärken, jene wäre nicht
universal. Noch seinen tödlichsten Feind, Vertauschbarkeit,
muß das Kunstwerk absorbieren, anstatt in Konkretion
auszuweichen, durch die eigene Konkretion den totalen
Abstraktionszusammenhang darstellen und dadurch ihm
widerstehen. Wiederholungen in authentischen neuen
Kunstwerken bequemen nicht stets dem archaischen
Wiederholungszwang sich an. In manchen verklagen
sie ihn und ergreifen damit Partei für das von Haag so
genannte Unwiederholbare; Becketts Play mit der schlechten

Unendlichkeit seiner Reprise bietet dafür das vollkommenste Modell. Das Schwarz und Grau neuer Kunst, ihre Askese gegen die Farbe ist negativ deren Apotheose.[10]

What is utopian in the work of art, or what points to the world of a utopian elsewhere that is not coextensive with what is merely the case in the worldly and intellectual setting in which a work is situated, cannot be found on the level of its content, that is, on the level of what it appears to be about, its "theme" or apparent subject matter. If no artwork is to be "ceded," as Adorno puts it, to another, that is, if the artwork persists in the irreducible and unsublatable singularity that makes it absolutely other from all other works—even as it also necessarily remains connected to these other works *qua* its work-character—this is because the utopian element anticipated by the work comes to pass precisely in its form, that is, in the formal features which alone relate it to its situatedness in the world of the here and now. To actualize its utopian pull, the artwork absorbs within itself even that which it resists, its own *Vertauschbarkeit*, the fungibility or exchangeability in a system of exchange and exchange relations. To fulfill its own movement of concretization, the work of art incorporates, and then serves as a hospitable world for, the negatively charged system of mere abstraction and bad infinity in which, under the conditions of modernity, it comes to pass. As so often is the case in Adorno's aesthetic theory, Beckett's work represents a prime instantiation of that refractory knowledge and its artistic consequences. For instance, repetition here must not be *mere* repetition because the genuine work of art—such as Beckett's—may well mobilize the movement of repetition precisely to call into question art's repetition compulsion, whether in its relation to mimesis or with an eye toward its position vis-à-vis the world of mass-cultural production.

It is striking that Adorno's thought concludes by referring to the "black and gray [*Schwarz und Grau*]" of contemporary art. After all, as we have seen, the discourse of color and noncolor—and especially of gray or grayness—plays a pivotal role in his reading of Goethe and Hegel, as well as in his own thinking. At this point in Adorno's meditations, the emphasis on gray and grayness in what was then "new" art, its guardedness and quasi-ascetic stance in relation to the world of color, does not merely represent a turn away from specific colors or the very idea of color and its potentialities. On the contrary, the utopian-liberatory streak that may mutely traverse the gray work of art is precisely to be located in its indirect or silent preservation of color as a negativity, an other that is kept alive, even made the object of an apotheosis, when it is seemingly eschewed or repressed. The trace of otherness that is inscribed through the absence of color in the gray work of art perpetuates the potential thinkability and return of color itself.

The precise logic of this movement is further concretized when we recall a particular passage from *Negative Dialectics* where, at a point in the argument that might be read as an indirect response to Hegel's (and, by extension, Goethe's) statements on the grayness of theoretical thought, Adorno emphasizes:

> Total determinism is no less mythical than is the totality of Hegel's logic. Schopenhauer was an idealist *malgré lui-même*, a spokesman of the spell. The *totum* is the totem. Consciousness could not even despair over grayness if it did not harbor the concept of a different color, a scattered trace of which is not absent from the negative whole. The trace always comes from the past, and hope comes from its counterpart, from that which was forced to go under or is doomed. Such an interpretation [*Deutung*] may very well be in accord with Benjamin's text on *Elective Affinities*: "Only for the sake of the hopeless ones have we been given hope."

> Totaler Determinismus ist nicht weniger mythisch als die Totale der Hegelschen Logik. Schopenhauer war Idealist malgré lui-même, Sprecher des Bannes. Das totum ist das Totem. Bewußtsein könnte gar nicht über das Grau verzweifeln, hegte es nicht den Begriff von einer verschiedenen Farbe, deren versprengte Spur im negativen Ganzen nicht fehlt. Stets stammt sie aus dem Vergangenen, Hoffnung aus ihrem Widerspiel, dem, was hinab mußte oder verurteilt ist; solche Deutung wäre dem letzten Satz von Benjamins Text über die Wahlverwandtschaften, "Nur um der Hoffnungslosen willen ist uns die Hoffnung gegeben", wohl angemessen.[14]

Just as in *Aesthetic Theory* the grayness in modern works of genuine art preserves what it simultaneously occludes or neglects (that is, color itself) by keeping alive within itself an awareness of this repressed otherness and the worlds to which this otherness may give rise, so *Negative Dialectics* argues that there can be no consciousness that is capable of feeling despair in the face of a particular experience of grayness without also having a strong intimation of color, a different color, even of the concept of color itself. And the place where this implicit or hidden knowledge is preserved is in the negative whole, in other words, in the very fibers where the despair associated with the supposed bleakness of gray is said to originate. If Adorno here prefers to speak not of archives, supplies, or storage facilities but merely of elusive traces ("Spuren"), this is because the dispersed traces, aleatory remnants, and spectral remainders of our knowledge of color permeate even and especially the gray works of art that may appear to have turned their backs on the ideas of hope and utopian longing altogether. In this sense, Adorno evokes his friend Benjamin, who in the memorable last sentence of his 1924–1925 essay on Goethe's *Elective Affinities* gives voice to the idea of receiving hope only in the name of, and for the sake of, the hopeless, that is, those who in principle are not able to receive any hope at all. No despair over this Goethean-Hegelian gray would even be possible if the knowledge—mediated by history, unsaturated experience, and a hope for radical alterity—of another colorful way of being in the world did not inscribe itself as an invisible, unruly, spectral otherness in the discourse of nonknowledge and even of despair.

The "versprengte Spur," or dispersed trace, of color that, according to Adorno, necessarily suffuses the experience of any grayness that is capable of evoking despair over its own abject condition deserves to be further explored. One may turn, with this purpose in mind, to a text first published in 1960 and later entitled "Blochs *Spuren*" ("Bloch's *Traces*"), in which Adorno engages not only with Ernst Bloch's 1930 collection of thought-images, the literary-philosophical miniatures entitled *Spuren*, but also with the relation among trace, color, and the principle of hope broadly conceived. While Adorno, especially in the early phases of his thinking, is not unreceptive to many of Bloch's philosophical lessons, thinking highly enough of Bloch's reflections on utopian principles to engage with Bloch in public settings such as a radio discussion on "Contradictions in Utopian Longing," Adorno is careful to demarcate where his thinking deviates from Bloch's utopian project. Adorno draws this line when he once again takes recourse to the language of grayness and color. He writes: "For the trace itself is the involuntary, inconspicuous, intentionless. [*Denn die Spur selbst ist das Unwillkürliche, Unscheinbare, Intentionslose.*] To reduce it to an intention is to violate it, just as examples violate the dialectic [*Beispiele an der Dialektik freveln*], as Hegel recognizes in the *Phenomenology*. The color that Bloch is after becomes gray when it becomes total [or: totality, *als Totale*]." And he continues: "Hope is not a principle. But philosophy cannot fall silent in the face of color [*Philosophie kann aber nicht vor der Farbe verstummen*]. Philosophy cannot move within the medium of thought, of abstraction, and then practice asceticism when it comes to the interpretation [*Askese gegen die Deutung*] in which such movement terminates. If it does, its ideas become enigmas."[12] In specifying how his own thinking of the trace differs from that of Bloch, Adorno stresses that the trace traverses an aleatory world of fleetingness, nondetermination, and nonintentionality.

In contrast to Bloch's idea of the trace, Adorno's conception of the trace cannot simply be mobilized by a sovereign, knowing consciousness in the service of any particular program or agenda. Closer to Derrida's later conception of the radical trace than to Bloch's intention-bound utopianism of the trace, Adorno fastens upon the noncontainability of the trace, its internal fissures and deviances, its unruly aberrations and disruptions. It is no coincidence that Adorno once again refers back to Hegel, who argues that examples of the dialectic can never catch up with it—that is, examples never merely illustrate a dialectical process which is always already operative beyond the very logic of exemplarity. Like the example that cannot match the requirements of the dialectic whose workings it is meant to illustrate, intentionality and its consciousness-bound modes of conceptualization cannot account for the aberrant potentiality of the trace, whose inherent utopian potential and liberatory force are inextricably intertwined with its resistance to any intention-bound, knowing subject's instrumentalization.

In his qualification of Bloch's conception of the trace of utopian hope, Adorno notably employs the language of grayness to describe how Bloch's hopefulness or "color" ("Farbe") tacitly turns gray ("wird grau") when it enters the world of totality. This movement of unwitting exchange, in which color transforms into grayness, is the price—according to Adorno's reading—that Bloch's model must pay for seeking to harness the utopian potentiality of the trace in the service of a prescribed political program with a predetermined image of the world, including the particular color combinations it is meant to possess in the future. For Bloch, the utopian force of an artwork is realized by means of a "principle," more specifically a "principle of hope," as his magnum opus, the three-volume *Das Prinzip Hoffnung* (1954–1959), names it. For Adorno, however, hope "is not a principle," but a concept that demands to be thought in different terms and according to different models. While Adorno does not say just what hope precisely is if it is no principle, he does intimate that hope must still assume the responsibility of engaging with the world of color and colorfulness that the gray of nonfreedom—along with the gray of totalization that paradoxically works against its own intention precisely by remaining attached to the category of intentionality—threatens to paint over. One might suggest that Adorno also hears in the threat of gray (*Grau*) a certain *Grauen* (horror), a *Grausen* (a shudder in the face of something uncanny), something *grauenvoll* (gruesome) or *gräulich* (horrible), perhaps even a *Grausamkeit* (cruelty).

In Adorno's world of thought, to face this threat rigorously also means to affirm that "philosophy cannot fall silent in the face of color." In other words, philosophy cannot abandon its responsibility, perhaps even its infinite responsibility, to a lifeworld demanding to be liberated, a world wishing for emergent color to undo its saturation in grayness.[13] It is perhaps no coincidence that Adorno's formulation takes recourse to the rhetorical figure of synesthesia, in which the experience of one sensory impression is expressed in terms of another. Philosophy must not "fall silent," he argues, before color, even though color is perceived visually, as an object of one's sight, not one's voice. Why, then, is the sound of philosophy's voice and not the faculty of sight addressed in Adorno's formulation? It is as though philosophical thought must not content itself

166

with merely taking in the color images of the world as it presents itself—or as it might be imagined once its grayness is replaced by color. On the contrary, any perceived or imagined color, or even a perceived or imagined distinction between color and grayness, would require philosophical thought not only to look at it but always also to address it, *to speak to it*. The demand for philosophical thought to "Speak the speech, I pray you," as Shakespeare's *Hamlet* has it, is inextricably intertwined with the demand that philosophy not fall silent ("verstummen" is Adorno's word) vis-à-vis the color, real or as yet only imagined, without which the world in which philosophical thought is immersed could hardly be conceived.

The demand that philosophy not fall silent in the face of color ("nicht vor der Farbe verstummen") also entails exposing itself to the exacting and exhausting requirements of explication and interpretation ("Deutung"). The object of this explication and interpretation may be the appearance of a specific color, the general idea of color, or even color as it comes to suffuse, for instance in the form of a trace, a specific area or even a world of grayness. Yet the object of this "Deutung" is also the very thought that philosophy produces. In other words, the thinking to which philosophy gives rise in the face of color first must be understood as such; it cannot simply be assumed to be a transparent, self-identical form of communication, offered in the form of straightforward propositional argumentation. Thinking and (its) understanding are themselves in need of thinking and understanding. Philosophical thought therefore cannot eschew the task of interpretation while embracing a certain "ascesis" of meaning. It is not necessary to revisit Nietzsche's trenchant critique of ascetic ideals in the third section of his *Genealogy of Morals* ("What Is the Meaning of Ascetic Ideals?") in order to appreciate Adorno's guardedness with regard to the ideal of ascetic abstention here. Not engaging with the difficult demands of an ongoing and treacherous "Deutung" would be akin to a kind of "Verstummen," a falling into silence before the world of color. By advancing his argumentation in this way, Adorno does not mean to suggest that the task of philosophical thought is to impose a closed and unalterable meaning upon a phenomenon or to interrupt the movement of a signifier in virtue of this or that achieved stable meaning. Rather, what comes to pass in the medium of thought cannot simply be held in abeyance as if it had no meaning at all, that is, as if it did not explain anything, as if it did not make a significant argument or expound an intelligible position. Whatever comes to pass, therefore, in and as philosophical thought in the world of color—and, by extension, what refuses to fall silent in the face of color—is intimately bound up with the Sisyphean task of reading and interpretation, of obsessive analysis, even when this analysis cannot come to rest in the safe harbor of achieved hermeneutical stability once and for all, because its encounter with the object to be understood keeps running awry. The relentless and obsessional nature of this analysis might itself be best conceptualized as gray: as a form of immanent repetition compulsion that enables fine-grained difference and nuance to emerge.

Genuine artworks, in Adorno's sense, are capacious, heterogeneous, and non-self-identical enough to open up the possibility of both soliciting interpretation and complicating any achieved understanding at the same time, and gray figures as a provisional name or tonality for this resistance, reticence, and perpetual unthoughtness. In this demanding gesture of invitation and withdrawal, they set up a world in which the intentionless trace of color almost imperceptibly—yet therefore all the more powerfully— traverses any saturated space of grayness. If the artwork does indeed harbor any liberatory, even utopian trace, such a trace also signals a certain complication, even rejection, of the commodified forms of consciousness into which the world of modernity has so dramatically fallen. In this world of exchange and exchangeability, everything and everyone is assigned a certain value in a system of equivalences, leaving no singularity, no idiomaticity, no disruption exempt from the powerful imposition of forms of equivalence onto every object, person, and aspect of experience. But this "equivalent form [*Äquivalentform*]," Adorno emphasizes in his thought-image "Kaufmannsladen" from *Minima Moralia*, "disfigures all perception. What is no longer irradiated by the light of its own self-determination as 'joy-in-doing,' pales to the eye." With respect to gray, one might say that this Adornian "irradiation" effected by "the light of its own self-determination"—which can always also be a form of indetermination—suggests a gray that is not concerned with general equivalences or fungibility but rather with acts of immanent, nuanced coloring. He proceeds, implicitly taking up the Hegelian distinction between a "for-oneself" and a "for-another," to observe how "organs grasp nothing sensuous in isolation, but notice whether a color, a sound, a movement is there for its own sake or for something else; wearied by a false variety, they steep all in gray [*tauchen alles in Grau*], disappointed by the deceptive claim of qualities still to be there at all, while they conform to the purposes of appropriation, indeed largely owe their existence to it alone."[14] One might say that the slender trace of color within a vast sea of gray commodity equivalences consists in the insight that "only when purified of appropriation would things be colorful and useful at the same time [*bunt und nützlich zugleich*]: under universal compulsion the two cannot be reconciled."[15] The grayness of one's experience of the commodity-world is sustained by a compulsory emphasis on exchange relations and the thinking of equivalences that are in principle deaf and blind to the singularity of any particular object, person, or experience (except in those particular instances when singularity itself is seen as commodifiable, as in the case of a rare painting by a canonical artist, for example, or the unique misprint on a collectible record label). It is the utopian trace in a genuine work of art that interrupts the system of equivalence in such a way as to render the objects within it no longer gray ("grau") but "colorful" ("bunt") and useful ("nützlich") at the same time (even though, as the present discussion has shown, it would ultimately be necessary to have at least some minimal traces of grayness that persist in any authentic work of art). To employ a more familiar Marxian terminology, within such a world the use value of an object is no longer eclipsed by its exchange value within the larger system of forced equivalences.

In his 1969 reflections on "Free Time," Adorno emphasizes that, for the human subject situated within an economy of mere exchange relations, "boredom is the reflex reaction to objective grayness [*das objektive Grau*]," while art behaves rather differently in relation to this objective grayness, presenting a provocation and potential subversion of the dominant gray, regardless of whether or not a particular work of art is commonly characterized as utopian or reactionary, progressive or conservative.[16]

"Art," he had underlined three years earlier in his musicological meditations concerning the "abused baroque," "separates itself through its mere existence from the gray of normal bourgeois self-preservation; the non-normal is its apriori, its own norm."[17] The artwork thus breaks with the grayness of quotidian experience in an administered world merely by existing, that is, prior to this or that content or intention. Its utopian otherness does not lie in the propositional statements or political agenda it may seem to offer but rather in its multiple aberrations from the self-sustaining norms of a conventionally bourgeois mode of being in the world, that is, the familiar models of mere self-preservation. If its norm is precisely to deviate from any norm, and if it affirms only the undoing of any affirmation, the genuine work of art opens itself to the rays of color that penetrate even the most saturated grayness. Perhaps the utterly unconventional utopian streak traversing the work of art even allows—for all its celebration of color and its associated possibilities and liberatory promise—a renewed appreciation of the utopian potentiality of gray itself, its often-hidden beauty and dignity. After all, it is hardly an accident that, in a 1928 review of Manuel de Falla's ballet *Le Tricorne* as performed in Frankfurt at the time, Adorno remarks that what was "most beautiful [*das Schönste*]" about it was the "Spanish stage set by Picasso; with dreamy arches of the bridge, little windows that hang like flags in the wind, and a gray in which there is more sun and more Southern essence that in any radiant yellow [*einem Grau, in dem mehr Sonne und südliche Essenz steckt als in allem strahlenden Gelb*]."[18] Dreamy painterly strokes of gray such as Picasso's here work to raise into consciousness the aesthetically mediated grayness that opens rather than forecloses, even in a world in which it is so difficult to tell apart the movements of opening and foreclosing at any given moment.

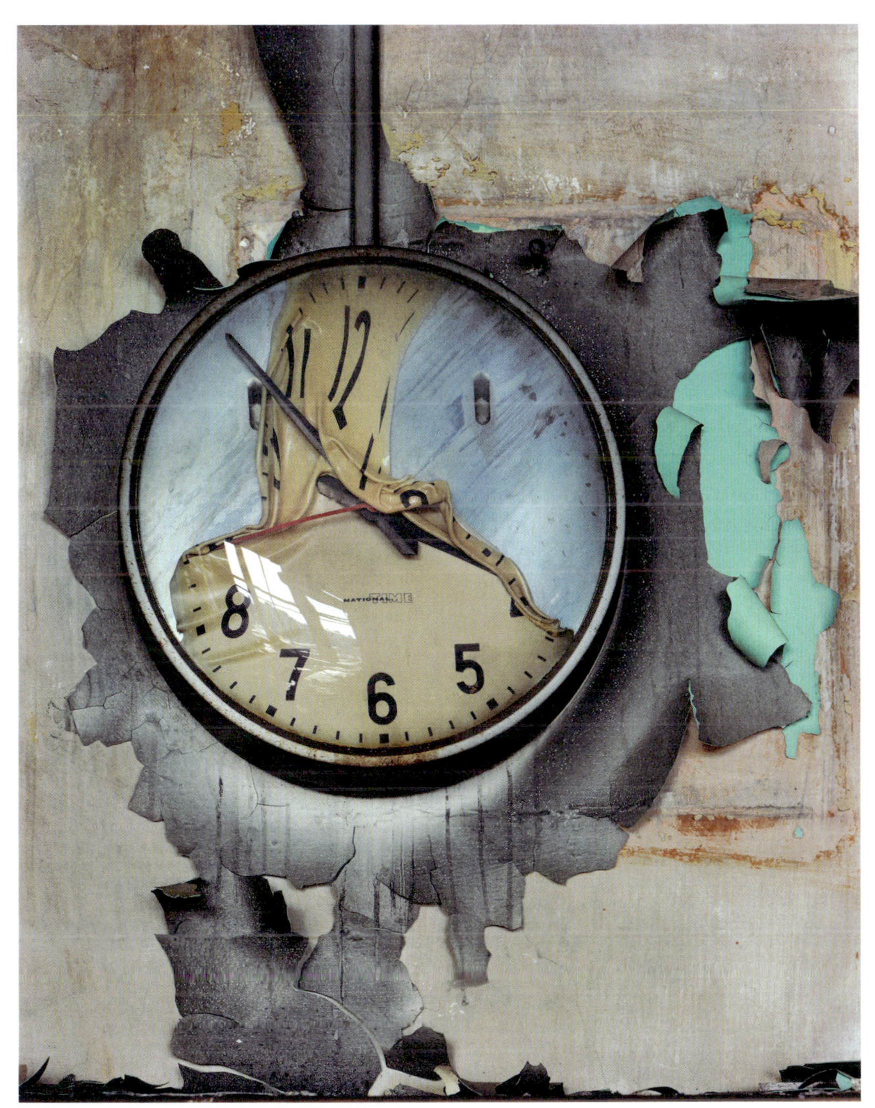

12
8
7 6 5
NATIONAL TIME

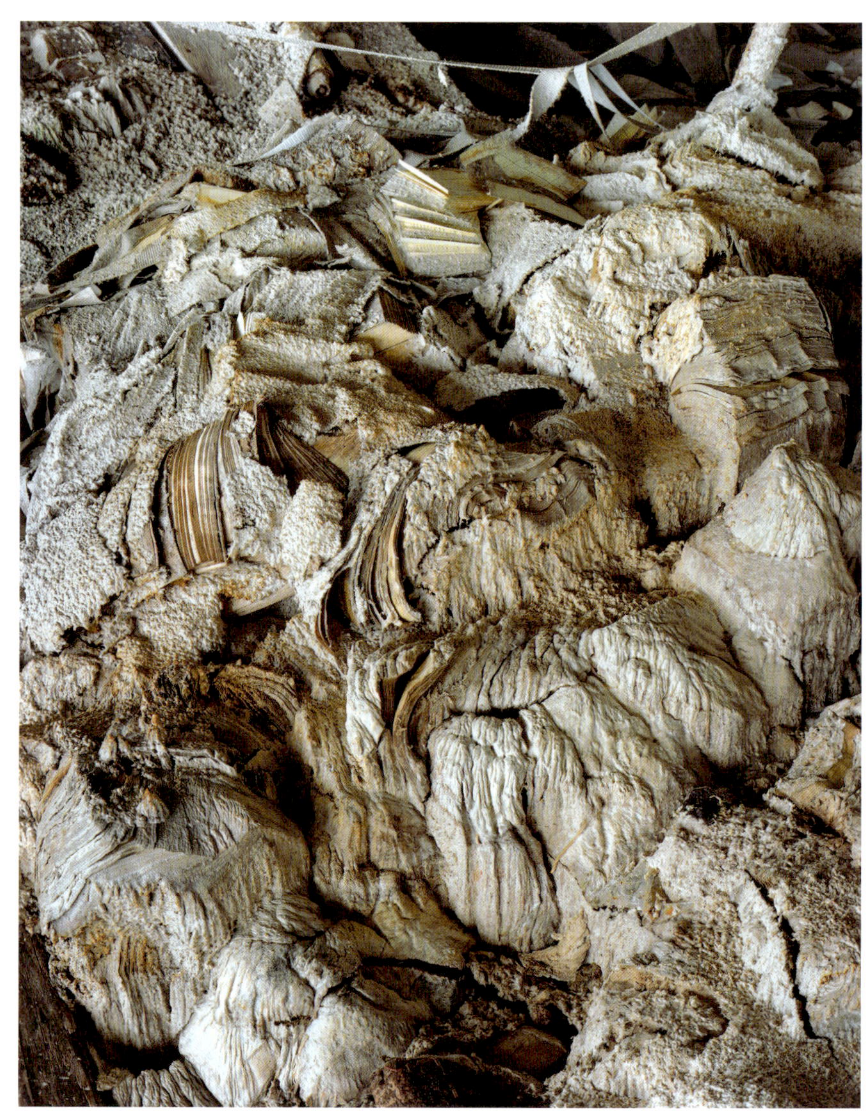

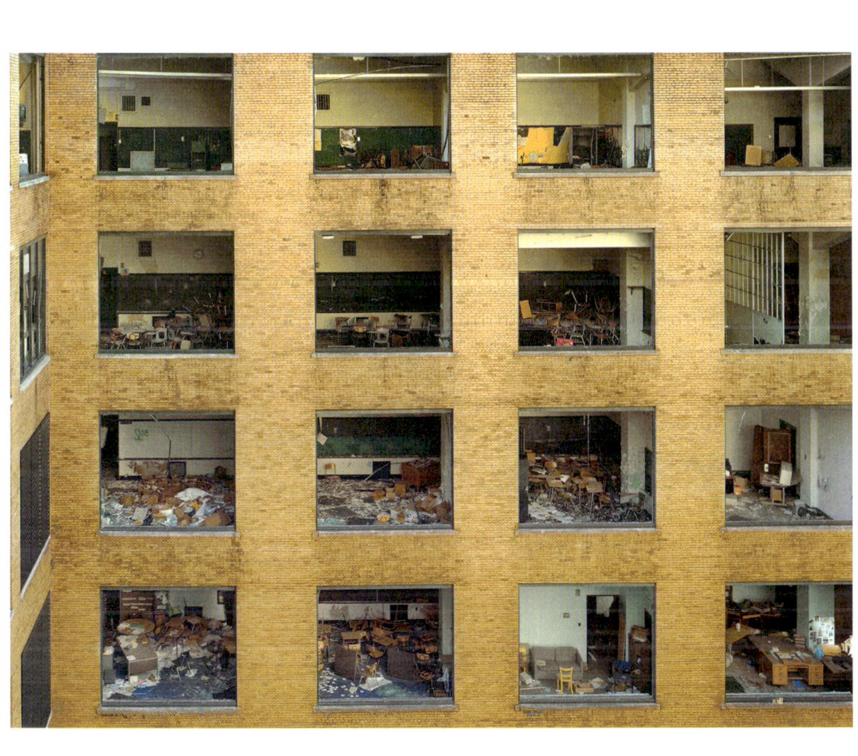

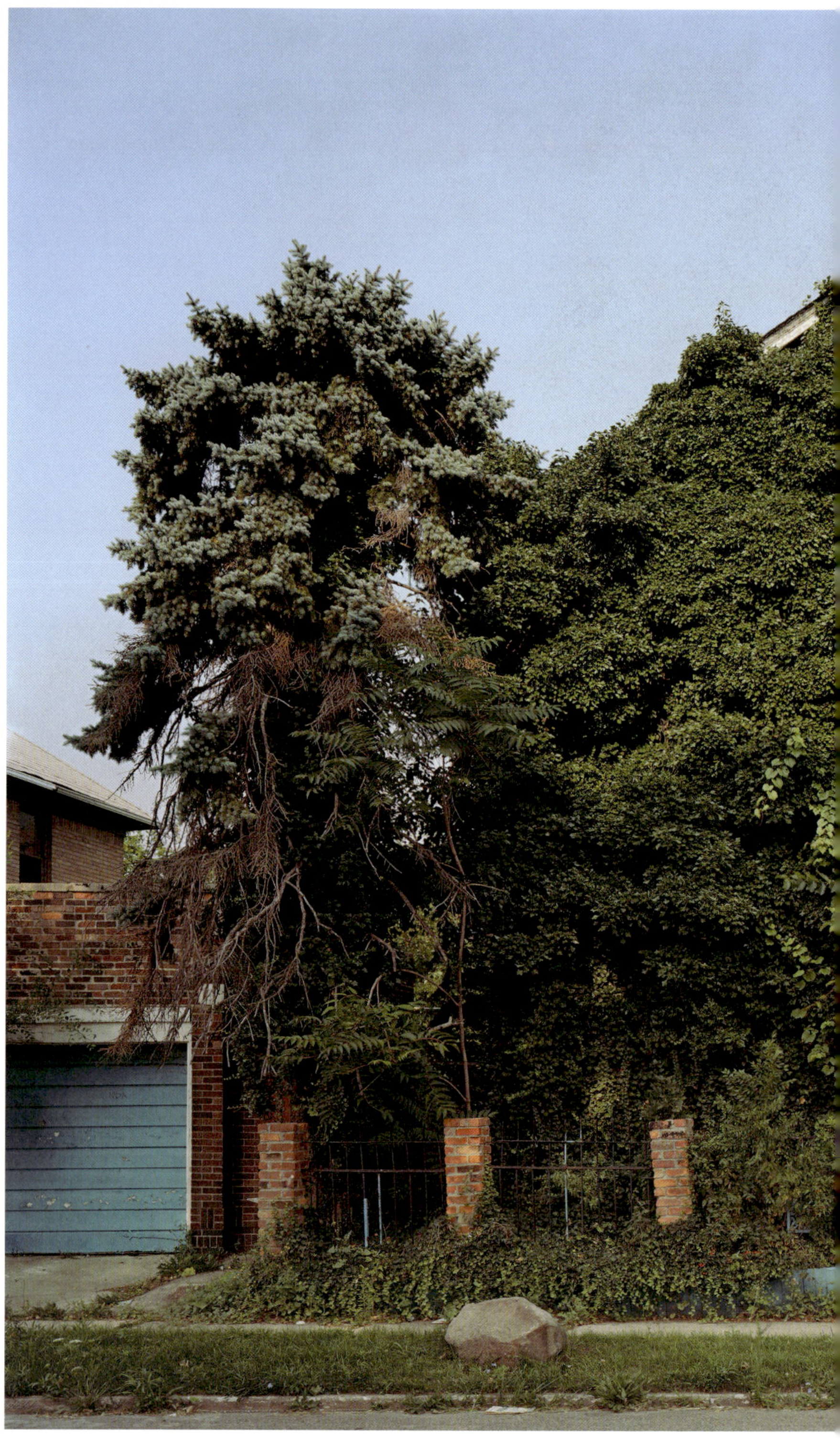

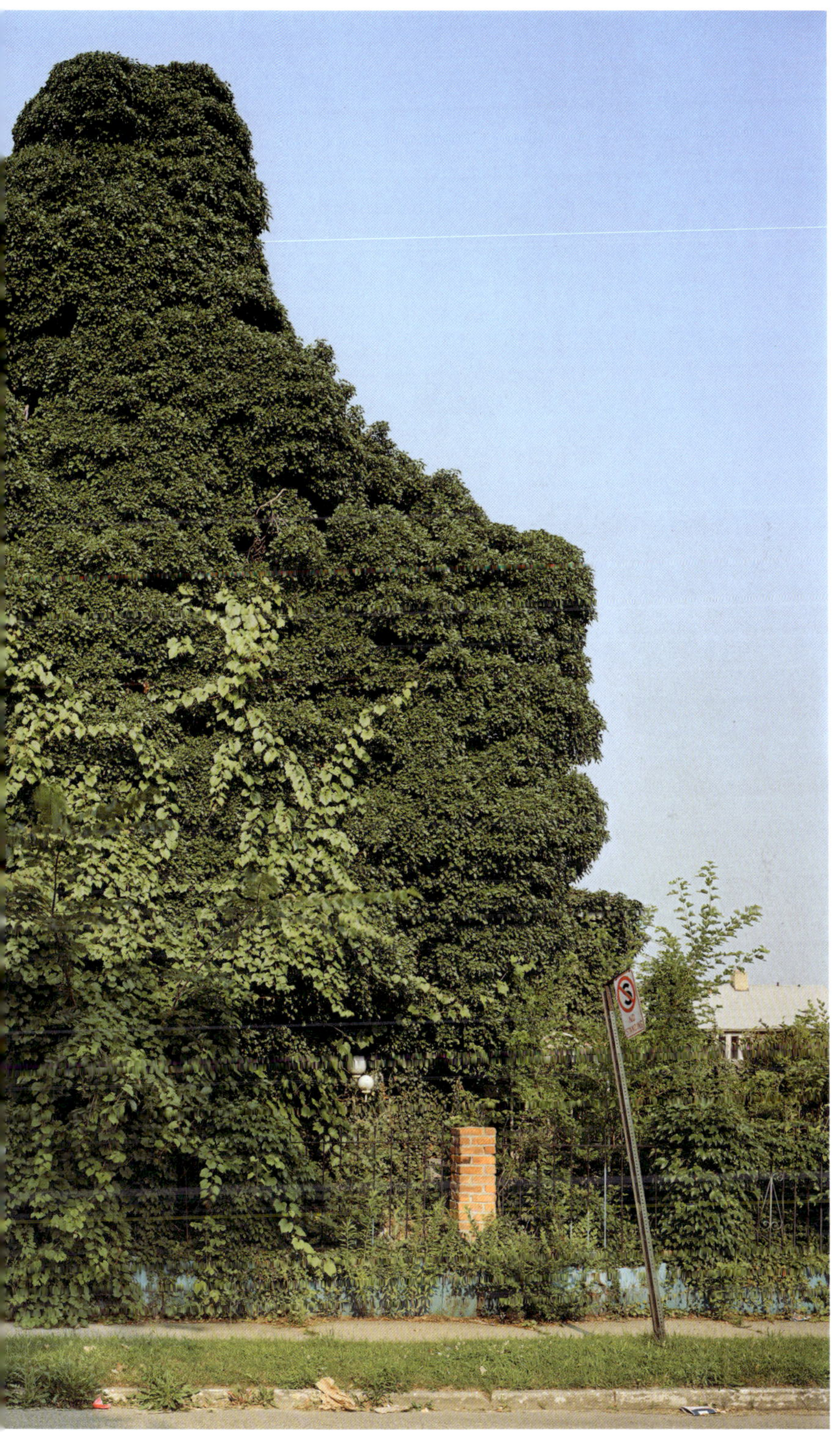

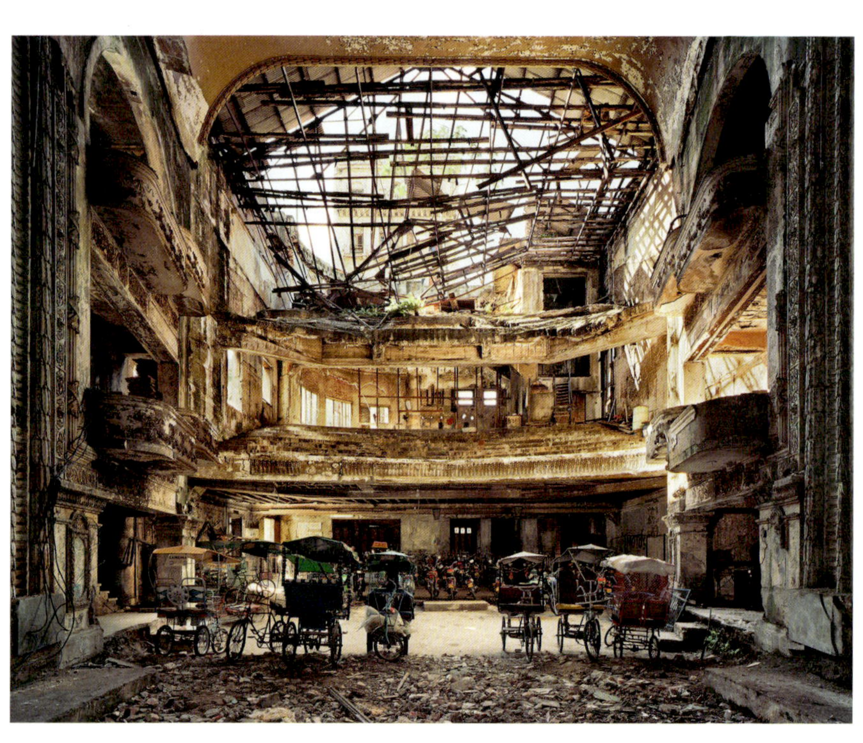

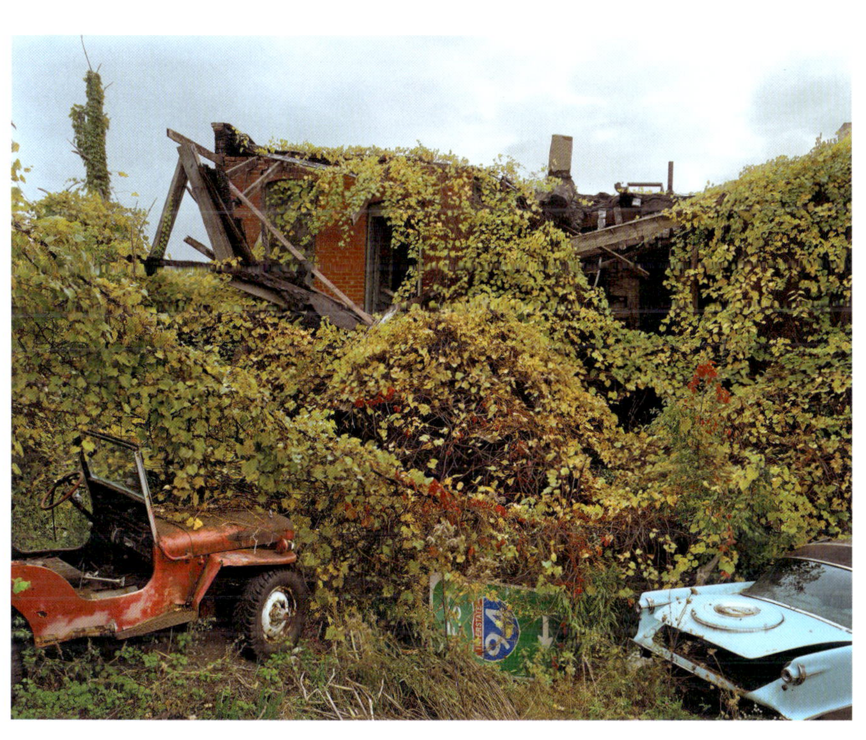

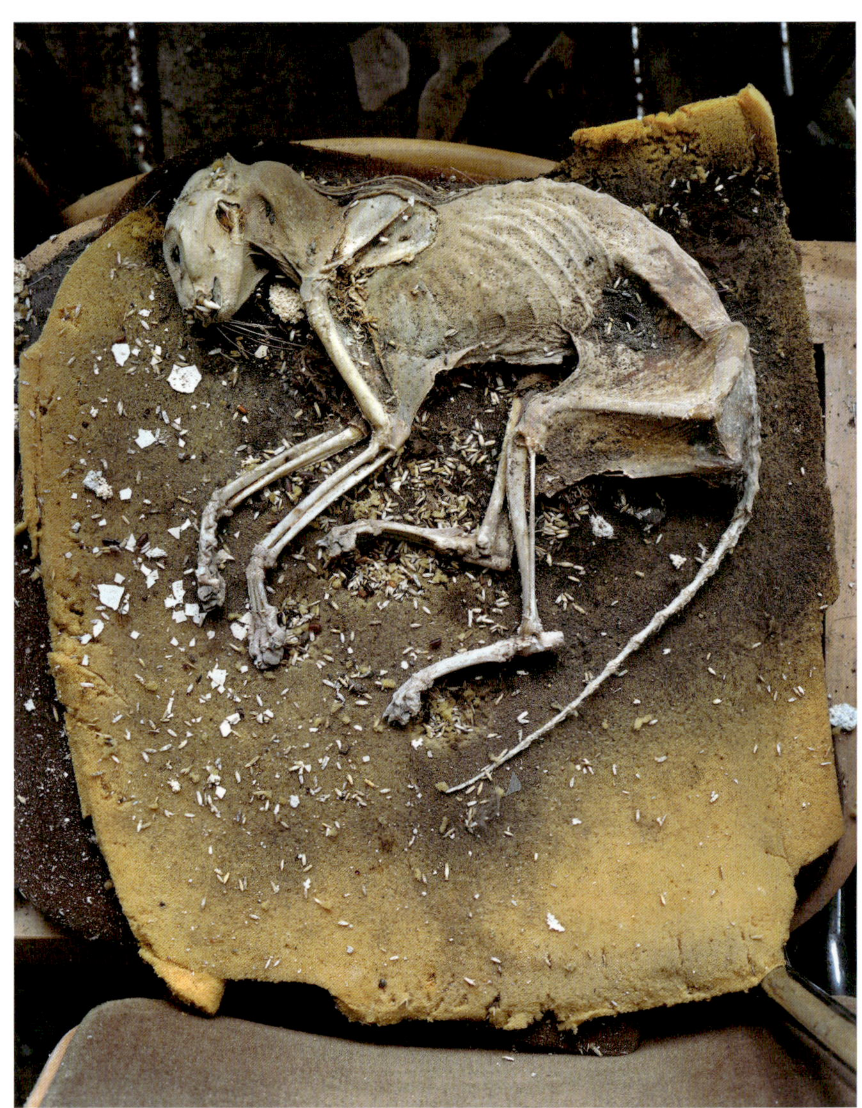

Conjoining the Intimate with the Infinite: On World-Decay in the Photographic Work of Art (Benjamin, Andrew Moore)

So far we have explored the link between an artwork's world-decay and the manifold ways in which it sets up a new world in the realms of poetry, (cave) painting, film, music, and even the color gray. It is now time to investigate this relation with respect to an artistic medium not yet explicitly addressed, photography. The question to be pursued in this chapter concerns the particular demands made by a photographic work of art as it sets up a world that is itself already in decay. In other words, we will examine how our thinking of the relation between the artwork's two worlds—the one in which it was created that is now decayed, and the one that it projects on an aesthetic level—is inflected when the world set up by the artwork itself becomes touched by decay and a ruinous way of being. What if the artwork places into the world a kind of disappearance of world, a decaying realm of existence, a world of ruins? To what extent does the work itself then become touched by the world-decay that modulates its act of world-creation in the aesthetic form? And how is our understanding of the artistic medium itself—in this case, photography—affected by the world-decay that it both sets up and captures in the form of the image?

In order to approach these concerns, we will be guided by our ongoing reflections on a seemingly apodictic remark—often neglected yet far-reaching in its consequences—made by Benjamin in section 3 of his 1938 text "Das Paris des Second Empire bei Baudelaire," entitled "Die Moderne."[1] There, Benjamin writes the following remarkable sentence:

> That of which one knows that one soon no longer will have it in front of one, that becomes image.

> Das, wovon man weiß, daß man es bald nicht mehr vor sich haben wird, das wird Bild.[2]

Under Benjamin's melancholic gaze, the image becomes what it is only from the perspective of what it will have been and what it will have ceased to be even before it has become it. The image is oriented toward its imminent absence, future decay, and departure. Its presence-toward-absence is precisely what allows it to become a Benjaminian image in the first place—a mnemonic image *avant la lettre*, perhaps, the image of something in anticipation of its disappearance for good. While it would be necessary to place this image of the image into syntactical relation with other images of the image that traverse Benjamin writings, such as the dialectical image, the filmic image of reproducibility, the image of the gesture, the more narrowly photographic image, even the image of Proust and Kafka, the *Denkbild*, or "thought-image," and so on, the image for Benjamin encrypts the futurity of a decline or decay, a ruinous absence, the trace of a withdrawal that is already silently at work within it.

"That of which one knows that one soon no longer will have it in front of one, that becomes image [*das wird Bild*]." Benjamin imagines an image in withdrawal, an image that can become what it is only to the extent that what it shows is depicted in terms of what it is not yet. The Benjamin of the Baudelaire material here

174

convenes with the one on view in the initial outlines and notes for his *Arcades Project* entitled "Pariser Passagen 1," composed in 1927. There, Benjamin exhibits his fundamental theoretical obsession with the appearance of things in the moment when they are about to disappear, that is, "things in the moment of the 'being-no-longer' [*Dinge im Augenblick des Nicht-mehr-seins*]. Arcades are such monuments of being-no-longer. ... And nothing of them lasts except the name: *passages*."[3] One can place an image that is about to disappear for good—"das wird Bild"—into syntactical relation with the *Augenblick*, the "moment" or, literally, the "blink of the eye," in which nothing remains what it is—"im Augenblick des Nicht-mehr-seins." This obsession with disappearance and melancholic decay also can be seen in the emphasis that Benjamin places on the figure of the ruin across the wide spectrum of his meditations, such as, for instance, in the *Trauerspiel* book, his study of the German baroque mourning play, in which he suggests that "allegories are in the realm of thoughts what ruins are in the realm of things [*Allegorien sind im Reiche der Gedanken was Ruinen im Reiche der Dinge*]."[4] To imagine the image of something in terms of its future decay, its status as a ruin—just as allegory, in its deferring temporality works to render what is figured as always already slightly disfigured—is to capture an image in its withdrawal, the fragmented image of ruinous retreat. If, as Adorno once observed, Benjamin's constellation of images "throughout laments the irretrievability of what, once lost, congeals into an allegory of its own demise,"[5] this allegorical demise structures the ways in which Benjamin's restless thought encounters the world of objects and images in the first place, as though this world always already were conditioned by the movement of a constitutive withdrawal.

Yet even this image of the ruin and fragmentation hardly would remain immune to political co-optation or "entirely useless for the purposes of fascism," as Benjamin famously puts it in his preface to the "Artwork" essay.[6] After all, even Hitler's architect Albert Speer developed what he called a "theory of the value of the ruin" (*Theorie vom Ruinenwert*) prior to World War II, in which he emphasized the importance of designing buildings that could be imagined in advance as beautiful ruins, architectural structures that, as future ruins, in hundreds of years still would impress us with their beauty and fragmented grandeur.[7] Rather, Benjamin's image in withdrawal, the fragmented and ruinous trace, must show itself responsible, always one more time, to the ways in which nothing in its internal structure is guaranteed once and for all, nothing is permanently inscribed in the framework of this or that stable signification. This image in withdrawal takes risks and exposes itself radically and strategically to its own contingency. As Benjamin writes in theses V and VI of his 1940 theses on the concept of history, while the "true image of the past *flits* by" and "the past can be seized only as an image that flashes up in the moment of its recognizability, never to be seen again," it is also the case that "only that historian will have the gift of fanning the spark of hope in the past who is firmly convinced that even the dead will not be safe from the enemy if he wins. And this enemy has not ceased to be victorious [*Und dieser Feind hat zu siegen nicht aufgehört*]."[8]

The image in withdrawal or decay cannot simply be an image *of* something. It would still be an image, but without the "of," if the genitive preposition is meant to signify possession in the sense of mimetic belonging or a parallel creation. Rather, the image in withdrawal partakes of a perpetual leave-taking, indeed stages the very scene of leave-taking precisely there where it is no longer an image of something. This does not mean that it is simply an abstract image, as in an abstract painting, which, after all, is always to some extent still an image *of* abstraction. It is more radical than that. "How much more easily the leave-taker is loved [*wie der Abschiednehmende leichter geliebt wird*]," Benjamin says, how "the flame for the one who is distancing himself burns more purely [*die Flamme des Sichentfernenden reiner brennt*]."[9] The image in withdrawal, even the image itself as leave-taker (*das Abschiednehmende*), would become what it is only to the extent that it steps into something other than that which is merely the case, waiting to be reproduced, in however mediated a fashion. As an originary image, the image in withdrawal claims our attention there where it refuses to leave its own world of appearance, and our experience of this appearance, untouched.

The variegated image-worlds created by the contemporary American photographer and filmmaker Andrew Moore appear particularly sensitive to these Benjaminian concerns. His large-format photographs often exhibit worlds of decay, ruin, decline, and immanent absence, especially as these come into focus in the images of apparently abandoned or declining metropolitan spaces in such locations as Detroit, New Orleans, Havana, Russia, or Governors Island in New York City. Both in his exhibitions and collections of photographs such as *Inside Havana* (2002), *Russia: Beyond Utopia* (2005), *Detroit Disassembled* (2010), and *Cuba* (2012), but also in more recent work such as *Dirt Meridian* (2015) and *Blue Alabama* (2019), what makes itself felt is a quasi-Benjaminian impetus to grapple with the ruinous nature of the image, the way it comes into presence both as a form of archiving or commemoration and as a way of mourning an absence, the felt absence of something that has already come to pass and that of something that will have come to pass in a futurity to which the image addresses itself already in the moment of being created. If Moore's images work collectively to set up a world that is often suffused by decay and imminent death, they tacitly place themselves in syntactical rela tion with Benjamin's insistence on how "that of which one knows that one soon no longer will have it in front of one, that becomes image." It is as if the world that emerged from these photographs knew about its own inscription in finitude, the scene of mourning in which every photographic image, no matter how affirmative of a life and its world it appears to be, is also embedded.

This relation to world—a world that is set up by the photograph as specifically aesthetic, but withdraws as it perishes into oblivion—becomes a self-reflexive central concern of these images. As Moore himself observes about his art in a conversation with Lyle Rexer:

> I am profoundly interested in the fact that human beings'
> attempts to mark their passing, to establish a permanence,
> take place on a longer timeline, within a wider context.
> I've read Giambattista Vico and Jorge Luis Borges, so I am
> thinking about historical cycles but also natural processes.
> In the Detroit photographs, nature absorbs all our efforts.
> As opposed to the formlessness of nature, its fecundity, the
> geometry of buildings—of man-made structures represents
> the trace of human ambition, and in their decay we can read

the failure of dreams, for all the complex reasons history presents. But I want to add one thing: as bleak as the Detroit pictures may seem, they are not empty. In terms of nature and culture, what I show is a repurposing of that landscape, and a resilience.[10]

If Moore's photographs grapple with human beings' attempts to inscribe their ways of being in the world and thus of "marking their passing," the images must also find a way of relating, through their aesthetic form, to the increased sense of temporality and the broader context in which such attempts are always also embedded. One way of shedding light on this temporality and this human contextualization is to consider the interaction between the forces of nature and those of culture, an interaction that shifts its balance and its center of gravity depending on how far a process of decay has progressed. To the extent that nature can be conceptualized as reimposing formlessness on the forms that the ambitions of human culture have created—what Moore refers to, among other things, as the geometrical shape of human dwellings—this gradual slide of highly constructed form into a state of formlessness stages within the photographic image an erasure of plans, dreams, and hopes, in short: an erasure of affirmations of futurity. In Moore's images, this transformation of human-made geometrical struc-tures into the states of apparent formlessness associated with a takeover by nature has not yet fully occurred. Rather, it is con-tinually in the process of taking place, and the image chronicles one particular stage of decay, entering the scene, as it were, always at a certain moment along a broader trajectory of physical and historical decline. Moore's images are invested in the Benjamin-ian moment of "that which one knows that one soon no longer will have it in front of one," and they affirm the multiple ways in which this moment makes an image what it is. As if, in the moment of capturing a point along the trajectory of decay and disappear-ance, these photographs say to the observer: "das wird Bild," "that becomes image."

One might note that, in more ways than one, Moore's photog-raphy of decay and imminent withdrawal convenes with that of an aesthetically and conceptually congenial nineteenth-century

French predecessor, Charles Marville, whose work focuses on the streets and public spaces of Paris on the eve of its urban transformation.[11] While Benjamin in his reflections on photography (such as his 1931 "Little History of Photography") does not refer to Marville—focusing instead on the work of such other nineteenth-century photographers as Nadar, Eugène Atget, and David Octavius Hill—the remarkable images of impending absence and withdrawal created by Marville speak directly to Benjamin's concerns with both the photograph in retreat and the historical urban changes that propelled Benjamin, in his *Arcades Project*, the Baudelaire project, and elsewhere, to regard Paris as the capital of the nineteenth century. Like Moore in our time, Marville trained his photographic gaze relentlessly upon a historically grown city on the brink of its de facto disappearance. As a photographer with an eye for the poetic intricacy and historical significance of a mature cityscape, Marville was entrusted by the French authorities to serve as the official photographer of Paris, documenting many of the ancient Parisian streets, squares, bridges, and architectural sites that were slated for annihilation in the wake of a radical modernization program inaugurated by Emperor Napoleon III's urban planner, Baron Haussmann. (It is no accident that Benjamin regularly refers to the "Hausmannization" of nineteenth-century Paris in the *Arcades Project*.) Among Marville's images, we find, for instance, the destruction of the ancient working-class neighborhood of Butte des Moulins, the about-to-be-razed-and-replaced rue de Constantine, and the destroyed space that was to become the grand Boulevard Henri IV in the fourth arrondissement. Even though Marville created significant images of the new, post-Hausmannization Paris with its impressive boulevards and grand urban architectural topography, it is his haunting and beautiful photographs of quaint Parisian streets, quarters, and squares, many of them centuries old, just as they are about to disappear forever, that lastingly inscribe his legacy in the history of photography. If Moore's photographs attend to the traces of an imminent (or already effected) absence in modern-day cities such as Detroit, they always also stand in ghostly dialogue with those of Marville and the impending withdrawal, even destruction, of old Paris.

It is perhaps no accident that Moore evokes the figure of the "trace" when he addresses what concerns him in his photographs. If the human-made structures are shown to be in a state of ever-progressing decay, a state of decline that allows them to be reclaimed by natural forces, there is always also a certain remainder at work in these images, a residual trace of human ambition and desire. No matter how much the world that is depicted in the images is in decay, it has not disappeared for good with the humans who have abandoned these buildings and sites. The human ambition and affirmation of what was once a futurity continues in various intensities to pulsate through these images, as if the commemoration of the lost world that the photographs enact also bore the traces of an archive. Viewed in this way, one might say that so many of Moore's photographs act as grave markers, even headstones, memorializing a perished world of human dreams and ambitions, while also serving as archival traces that preserve—however mutely, however faintly—a former world of human striving. If these photographs are poetic markers of history, the view of history they archive is hospitable both to the irreducible finitude that they chronicle and to the world-affirming, world-making traces created by thinking, feeling, and dreaming human beings.

In the context of this double perspective or this double hospitality, the photographs come to serve as primers for learning how to read images—the specific images of Detroit, for instance, but also images more generally. Every photographic image teaches us how it wishes to be read, setting up a singular world according to its own terms, challenging us to become sensitive and informed image-readers. To read Moore's Detroit photographs, taken in 2008 and 2009, one must learn how to read the variegated traces of decay. If, as the photographer suggests with respect to the human-made structures on display in his images, "in their decay we can read the failure of dreams," we are called upon not only to learn to read world-decay as world-decay, but also, in the traces of this very world-decay, to read another decay: the decay and ultimate failure of dreams. In this sense, becoming a good reader of Moore's photographs also always means becoming a good reader of dreams and their failure. The rigorous activity of *Traumdeutung*, or the interpretation of dreams, that Freud pioneered within the realm of psychoanalysis thus demands to be supplemented, even enhanced, by a kind of *Bilddeutung*, an interpretation of images. Through such *Bilddeutung*, the world-decay that traverses Moore's photographs of sites such as Detroit opens onto a dream-decay that nevertheless continues to structure, even haunt, the world that is set up by these carefully composed images.

The double hospitality to the historical trace that is evident in the world-making space of Moore's images cannot be reduced to the idea of a mere rescuing or redemption. So what is it that these traces of decay and historical transformation leave for us to reflect upon? As Moore himself puts it, his images wish "to—not redeem, that's too grand a word—discover something of value in these traces."[12] Referring to the images gathered in *Dirt Meridian*, he adds that on "the Great Plains, the footprint of a sod house is still visible after 100 years. The houses I photograph were all built by their owners, usually from plans and materials ordered from a Sears Roebuck catalogue." And Moore continues by pointing out that one of his "subjects, the Murray house, was constructed of concrete blocks shaped to recall Renaissance stone work, and the concrete was made from the very sand the house stood on. The passing of all this is sad, even tragic, but it speaks to a landscape that inspired the inhabitants to dream, to imagine."[13] Revealing something of value in the traces of an absence, the images work to affirm a world even as it finds itself in irreversible decay. They are vectorized toward a process not of rescuing or redemption but of perpetual discovery, a disclosive encounter pivoting upon a world-decay that simultaneously opens up another world still inhabited by the spectral traces—themselves subject to varying degrees of potential legibility—of former worlds.

If photographic works of art connect us with multiple worlds at once, including the spectral traces of perished worlds, they guide us in our mourning as it fastens upon "an American city," as Moore reminds us, "whose decomposition is barely comprehensible." They open, for instance, onto a Detroit whose "transfiguration has led it beyond decay into a surreal landscape, where the past is receding so quickly that time itself seems to be distorted."[14] It is to this relation to time as a distortion that we owe some of Moore's most striking images. The decay and decomposition that touches these photographs, even ones that lie on the far side of what is comprehensible, emerge as belonging to a world in which the forces of life and death, culture and nature, construction and destruction, eros and thanatos, affirmation and annihilation, building and unbuilding have entered an eternal struggle.

Moore's photograph of a house on Detroit's Walden Street, for instance, stages in the most vivid terms the process by which nature reclaims a human-made dwelling in decay. An almost forest-like greenery appears to have swallowed the house whole, and only the remainders of the short red-brick pillars that were part of its fence—now crooked and broken—as well as a tiny part of the roof barely visible in the upper left portion of the structure along with two small lights at the bottom right, provide traces of the more orderly, more geometrical, more ambitious form of life that once found shelter here. It is as if the life surrounding the swallowed house were also gradually succumbing to a world of decline, as embodied by the street sign in the lower right quadrant of the image, bent out of shape and now standing crooked like the brick pillars in the middle of the rotted fence. The city street in front of the house, too, seems to be suffering the same fate, as a substantial boulder on the grass strip encroaches onto the scene. While it is unclear whether the garage with the chipped blue paint in the lower left corner of the image belongs to the swallowed house or rather to the structure on the other side of the garage (a brownish building just barely visible on the far left), the viewer is invited to wonder just who might park a vehicle here or, indeed, when the last time may have been when this garage had a purpose. It is striking that such decay could happen in the midst of an urban setting and that an American city of the prominence of Detroit would be allowed to decline in such a drastic way. As Moore confesses: "I have to admit that I am also attracted to the pathos of decline, the symptoms of a late empire, whether it's Russia, the United States, or Cuba."[15] The pathos of decline in the Walden Street photograph is palpable, as the image of this aptly named street ("Walden" evokes Thoreau's Walden Pond, but *Wald* also is the German word for forest) stages a scene of abandonment that can indeed be viewed as symptomatic of a late, falling empire.

Unlike the human-made dwelling obscured behind a forest-like greenery in the Walden Street house that is still standing, the thematically related image of Detroit's former Carwash Café depicts a structure that already has collapsed. The remains of this building are also in the process of being reclaimed by nature and disappearing for good among the leaves and shrubbery. Here, however, the decaying building is framed by the decrepit remains of two old cars (a red Jeep on the left, a blue Chrysler on the right), separated by a fallen traffic sign for Interstate 94. Did these rusty cars and the Interstate sign once serve as decorations at the erstwhile Carwash Café, or do they have a different story to tell? Who or what moved them into this position? Are they the spectral remains of vehicles that once frequented the Carwash Café? Are they symbols of the widespread decline that has befallen Detroit's once prosperous and powerful car-manufacturing industry? One thing is clear: no car is being washed at this carwash any longer, no coffee being served; no human community gathers here anymore, only insects, birds, and other nonhuman animals. Stripped of its livelihood, this scene is one of absence and ruination, a world abandoned by history and framed by an appropriately dark cloud hanging over it.

The entropic impulse that circulates through Moore's Detroit photographs makes it possible to espy a syntactical relation to the world of his earlier Havana photographs, created over a span of years when he was residing in Cuba. Inviting comparison to the pioneering work of photographers such as Atget, Charles Edward Doty, Berenice Abbott, and Walker Evans, Moore's Cuban images shows themselves hospitable to a constellation of decay, tenderness, historicity, documentary-style sobriety, poetic resilience, and self-conscious inventiveness. Whether in street scenes of a domino game, acts of reading a book in the remarkable interiors of once-grand but now declining buildings, parlors in peeling mansions still suffused by the elegance of their former beauty, or in the portraits of two Cuban youths defiantly bearing make-shift particle board surfboards, the world that is set up by these photographs is conscious of, but not crushed by, the indelible traces of its own decline. As the art critic Andy Grundberg suggests in "The Photograph as Territory," his preface to Moore's Havana project, Moore's "elegant, elegiac color photographs of Havana and environs" are suffused with "decay and contradiction." Their "beauty is the beauty of dissolution, of order giving way to entropic forces." It is no coincidence, then, that "virtually every ceiling Moore photographed has lost patches of plaster, so that the lathe boards have become part of the country's interior decoration" and paint "has peeled from many of the walls, creating a pentimento effect that denotes earlier times."[16] The elegiac beauty of the world that Moore's photographs set up owes itself to its receptiveness to the forces of entropy, that uncontainable drive of formlessness that encroaches upon every formal construct. It is as though the highly ordered and yet dynamic composition of his large-format images itself is called upon to engage with, even wrestle, the impulses of destruction that propel the forces of formlessness and decay. As Goethe's Mephistopheles memorably says to Faust in verses 1338–1340, "Ich bin der Geist, der stets verneint! / Und das mit Recht; denn alles, was entsteht, / Ist wert, daß es zugrunde geht" ["I am the spirit that always negates! / And justifiably so; for everything that comes to be, / deserves to perish"].[17] In Moore's images, Mephistopheles's entropic element of negation threatens what was posited by ambitious and vigilant human beings in the orbit of their worlds, engaging in an eternal struggle with these human-made worlds and their genealogies. The photograph captures moments of intensity when this struggle between world-creation and world-destruction itself is thematized in especially striking ways.

The fine-grained sense of ruination, finitude, decay, and death that permeates so many of Moore's photographs opens onto a thinking of certain characteristics that are shared by all photographs, and thus by all the worlds that photographic images create. Contemplating an 1865 photograph by Alexander Gardner of Lewis Payne, a young man in handcuffs waiting in his cell to be hanged, Roland Barthes remarks: "The photograph is handsome, as is the boy: that is the *studium*. But the *punctum* is: *he is going to die*. I read at the same time: *This will be* and *this has been*; I observe with horror an anterior future of which death is the stake." He further notes that by providing "the absolute past," the "photograph tells me death in the future. What *pricks* me is the discovery of this equivalence. In front of the photograph of my mother as

184

a child, I tell myself: she is going to die: I shudder, like Winni-cott's psychotic patient, *over a catastrophe which has already occurred.* Whether or not the subject is already dead, every photograph is this catastrophe."[18] The photograph, especially if it depicts some-one or something that already has died empirically, always antic-ipates a death to come, even as it tears its subject out of the flow of time, arresting its current state in the form of a frozen image. In observing a photograph, we become witnesses to how it strug-gles to hold death at bay while always also foretelling a death to come. He who, and that which, is pictured is going to die; the pho-tograph stands as a visual testimony to this demise. While Bar-thes's reflections are organized around his mother's recent death as well as a photograph of her in the Wintergarden (an image that itself he never actually shows), they touch upon the death that is encoded in photography as such. The ruptured temporality of a photograph makes us look with concern to something that, liter-ally or figuratively, has already come to pass: the work of finitude. Like the photograph of Barthes's mother as a child—the image that makes him shudder over the catastrophe of her death not only from the perspective of her actual death but also from the moment in time at which the image was created—every photo-graph has the potential to make us shudder *"over a catastrophe which has already occurred,"* over a death that will happen yet has already happened. If a photograph sets up a world in which this world— even world as world—is also already in decay, it is "because each photograph always contains this imperious sign of my future death, however attached it seems to be to the excited world of the living."[19] The photograph, in other words, always speaks two sentences at once: it has been, and it will be. The catastrophe has already come to pass, and it is still coming. Learning to read this technical and aesthetic attachment to the photograph's double affirmation requires learning to relate to finitude itself—the very finitude that gives us death and the ruin to think within the world of the captured image.

One might say that Moore's photographs are especially hos-pitable to the double affirmation that arises out of the thought of finitude itself and upon which Barthes's reflections fasten in such vivid detail. The courtyard photograph of a façade at Detroit's Cass

Technical High School provides a frontal view onto a classroom building. Here, the missing windows confront the viewer with sixteen openings, frames, or stills that display eerily abandoned classrooms in utter disarray, with tables overturned, chairs wildly strewn about, heaps of papers and books on the floor, as if a grenade or tornado had unleashed its rage on the school building. No pupils or teachers are to be seen anywhere, only the unruly traces of their absence. In some of the classrooms, what appear to be writings or markings can still be seen on the blackboards and white boards, as if the classrooms had been abandoned not in a slow historical process of decline, but somehow in a hurry, leaving certain aspects of the scene in suspended animation. What could have happened here to transform the classroom building of a school in the middle of the United States into such an eerie wasteland? Is this the photograph of a catastrophe that has already happened, as in Barthes and Winnicott, or of one that is yet to come? Does this photograph provide a vista onto an unfortunate exception to an otherwise intact world—that is, does it relate to its subject matter as a singularity, an aberration of history—or does it rather embody a melancholic commentary on the world of American education as it already presents itself as a matter of course today? "We don't need no education; We don't need no thought-control," Pink Floyd memorably sang in "Another Brick in the Wall" (1979), criticizing a rigid and oppressive British educational system. But in Moore's photograph, the wall has long begun to fall apart, its bricks coming lose, windows gone, classrooms devastated; and the very idea of education—even an education that deserves to be subjected to critique—appears as little more than a distant dream.

Engaging with the images of a different artist—those of Belgian photographer Marie-Françoise Plissart—Derrida remarks: "You could speak of these photographs as of a thinking, a pensiveness without a voice, whose only voice remains suspended."[20] What Derrida suggests with regard to Plissart's photographs also applies to Moore's. After all, the latter's photographs perform a kind of thinking that remains mute; a pensiveness puts itself on display without becoming fully voiced. His haunting photographs of Detroit and other scenes—often indissociable from ruin, death, and decay—enact a silent thinking that nevertheless demands to be heard. If the observer of Moore's photographs responds affirmatively to this pensive call for thinking, he enters a world of finitude in which that finitude is not simply feared, resented, or kept at bay, but in which finitude *as* finitude works to disclose certain vistas—if we are willing and able—onto a world that otherwise would not be available to us as such.

Among the most striking images of finitude in the archive of Moore's Detroit photographs is that of a cat's remains at the Mark Twain Library. Rolled up on top of the foam remnants of a decrepit chair's upholstery, the feline's skeletal remains have been consumed by time. Did this cat "belong" to the library in some way? Was it a kind of mascot, perhaps the pet of a former librarian? Did it visit with patrons as they read their books? Or was it a stray cat with no obvious or reconstructible connection to the place of its passing? How did the cat die in the library? Was it accidentally left behind one day when the doors were locked, perhaps for the final time? Or did it enter the library building by chance, and find itself unable to escape? And what is a cat's death? Heidegger believes that only human beings are capable of dying (*sterben*) because they fully inhabit a world, while animals, who are poor in world (*weltarm*), merely perish (*verenden*). (Inanimate objects, in the Heideggerian pattern, are entirely worldless—*weltlos*—and they are capable neither of being alive nor of dying or perishing in any ontic sense.) But who is to say that a cat is truly *weltarm*? Did this particular cat at the Mark Twain Library die or perish? If it has neither a grave nor a grave marker, neither a plot nor a headstone, one might say that the entire library serves as its cemetery—a mausoleum lined with books and shelves, a garden of remembrance watched over by the inherited wisdom and ambition of the ages, itself in a state of decay.

Moore's photograph of the cat's mortal remains also evokes the more general question of the relation between the image and the corpse. One might recall Blanchot's far-reaching reflections on this relation. For him, the "image does not, at first glance, resemble the corpse, but the cadaver's strangeness is perhaps also that of the image. What we call mortal remains escapes common categories." Blanchot continues:

Something is there before us which is not really the living
person, nor is it any reality at all. It is neither the same as
the person who was alive, nor is it another person, nor is
it anything else. What is there, with the absolute calm of
something that has found its place, does not, however,
succeed in being convincingly here. Death suspends the
relation to place, even though the deceased rests heavily
in his spot as if upon the only basis that is left him. To be
precise, the basis lacks, the place is missing, the corpse
is not in its place. Where is it? It is not here, and yet it is
not anywhere else. Nowhere? But then nowhere is here.
The cadaverous presence establishes a relation between
here and nowhere. ... The place where someone dies is not
some indifferent spot. It seems inappropriate to transport
the body from one place to another. The deceased cleaves
jealously to his place, joining it profoundly, in such a way
that the indifference of this place, the fact that it is after
all just a place among others, becomes the profundity
of his presence as deceased. ... The deceased, it is said, is
no longer of this world; he has left it behind. But behind
there is, precisely, this cadaver, which is not of this world
either, even though it is here. Rather, it is behind the world.
It is that which the living person (and not the deceased)
left behind him and which now affirms, from here, the
possibility of a world behind the world, of a regression, an
indefinite subsistence.[21]

There is much to be said about Blanchot's passage, but let us
only emphasize, with an eye to our present context, the idea that,
within the image, the relation between death and place is called
into question, even suspended. If the image not only works to document a location at which death has occurred but rather also que-
ries, in the same breath, the very idea of a relation between place
and finitude, this is because the image gestures toward the notion
that the corpse it depicts has left a world while simultaneously
hinting at another form of world, the possibility of more than one
world. This other world does not necessarily suggest any kind of
transcendence in an otherworldly realm; its idea subsists as pure

potentiality, a disruption of our quotidian and quasi-automatized understanding of the relation between body, place, and world. To be sure, Blanchot is speaking of a human corpse—rather than an animal corpse—and its relation to the image and its place. And yet, when pondering Moore's photograph of a cat's corpse at the library, the radical differentiation between a human corpse and an animal corpse—and therefore also between a human death and a nonhuman animal's death—no longer appears so rigid and categorical. Does not the image of the cat's corpse, curled up as it is in the library, also give rise to the question of how the life and death of this being relates to the place in which it came to an end? Does this photograph not also invite the observer to reflect upon the very idea of mortal remains—that is, remains that, while now dead, once were animated by a life, and therefore cannot be considered merely to belong to the world of inanimate objects that never were alive—and upon how these remains demarcate a place within the image? One might say that the photograph of the cat's corpse stages the idea that "it is not here, and yet it is not anywhere else," which is to say its strangely acute nowhereness, in particularly probing terms.

What is the "place" of the cat's corpse—if, following Blanchot, one can still speak of a place in any ordinary sense at all—in Moore's image? What does it suggest about its surroundings, the location of this particular death? One might say that, like the cat's skeletal remains, the library itself is in ruins, its treasures exposed to neglect, decline, and the threat of oblivion. The library, as archive, is threatened by the erasure of the historical traces to which is has shown itself so hospitable. Through Moore's photograph of the cat's remains, Detroit's Mark Twain Library becomes visible as the scene of erasure, a threat to the textually and visually mediated archival function that has been touched by catastrophe in libraries from the Great Library of Alexandria in Egypt all the way to the grand Duchess Anna Amalia Library in Weimar that was ravaged by a devastating fire in 2004. As Eduardo Cadava reminds us in his richly textured reading of another image of a library in ruins—the well-known photograph of the Holland House Library in London following its destruction in 1940 in the course of Nazi air raids—the photograph "bears witness to the enigmatic relation between death and survival, loss and life, destruction and preservation, mourning and memory," so that the photographic image often tells us that "what dies, is lost, and mourned within the image ... is the image itself."[22] To create a photograph of a library in ruins and its archive touched by death—literally and figuratively—is therefore to suggest something of photography's relation to finitude itself. Moore's photograph provides us not only with an image of the remains of a cat in a decaying library; it also speaks eloquently—without having a voice and without saying a single word, that is, mutely—to the imbrication of the photographic image with the ruin and with death as such. The ruins of the decaying library in Detroit thus also become visible as the ruins of photography itself—the secret crypt lodged at its very core.

The idea of a library in ruins is powerfully elaborated by a photograph of moldering books in the Detroit Public Schools Book Depository. Having decomposed almost beyond recognition, the paper that once comprised these books has metamorphosed into an indefinable whitish-gray mass that is shot through with brown and rust-colored hues. Only the occasional remnants of some book pages are faintly visible in this heap of alien material, as are some paper edges and spectral spines. The mass of moldering books gives the appearance of a geological formation that is itself partially covered by the growth of vegetation—perhaps a kind of moss—as becomes visible especially in the lower right and upper left corners of the image. Exuding the atmosphere of a postapocalyptic world of decay, the photograph commemorates the decomposition of books, along with the words, sentences, paragraphs, and chapters they once contained—one is tempted to say: along with language itself. There is a muteness to this sight, of a wordless and voiceless site in which books and the learning contained within them, their arguments, views, and visions—in short: their worlds—are but a distant memory. In a mute world that has outlived itself, who still needs books? What happens to books when their "depository," which is to say, their archive, recedes into oblivion? Unlike in the dystopia of Ray Bradbury's *Fahrenheit 451*, where books are systematically destroyed by fire at the hands of a totalitarian regime while some of their content survives because a few human rebels have memorized them, the books in Moore's image are not consumed by the fury of a flame but rather die slowly through organic decomposition. And the observer is not given to believe that a tacit survival of their contents through rebellious human intervention staving off the other forces of ignorance and forgetting is likely to be part of any future world.

Yet the abiding and relentless decomposition of books and words that is at work in the world of the Detroit public school supply depository is inextricably intertwined with another trajectory traversing the very same site. As Moore explains, this depository, "abandoned for many years," became, "in winter 2009," the "scene of a grotesque discovery: a homeless man had plunged head down into the bottom of a flooded elevator shaft and disappeared into a deep block of ice except for his protruding feet." He continues by recalling that on "the top floor of this same depository, where the concrete roof has partially collapsed, is another scene of human endeavor stood on its head. Amid a dense matting of decayed and burned books, a grove of birch trees grows from richly rotting words." Here, in the midst of "crooked I-beams, jagged slabs, and blackened soil, the trees' white trunks rise straight into the sky."[23] Growing from the remains of decomposed books, these birch trees emanating from the ruins not only bespeak the decay of a once flourishing and functional American city; they also suggest, through a kind of takeover by nature, the possibility of renewal and the idea of rising from the ashes, as Moore's images of these strange, book-based birch trees also document. After all, if trees grotesquely grow here out of decayed books, a strangely poetic cycle is at work, in which these trees are growing out of the very material for which they had been cut down and instrumentalized.

The odd cycle captured by the tree scene evokes a defamiliarizing dimension of photography as such. On the one hand, one could say that there is nothing abnormal about witnessing the physical processes by which books decay and new trees grow out of soil and organic matter. After all, science could explain these processes according to certain established principles of causation. Yet, on the other hand, these images startle the observer, transporting him into a space of reflection that marks the fundamental disruption and disorientation that the subjects of these photographs occasion. If Moore's images here give rise to thought, it is a thought that also is at odds with itself. As Nancy suggests apropos of photography in general, "thought remains here fundamentally a thought of its own strangeness." If, from a certain perspective, within "a photograph there is always something hallucinatory, something that has lost its way or is out of place," the thought to which it gives rise must find a way of relating to this out-of-placeness, its peculiar strangeness. Indeed, the "secret of the photograph, the very mystery of its being lost and straying, is its flight into the strange in the very midst of the familiar," which is to say that the "photo *captures* the familiar, and immediately, instantaneously, it strays into strangeness," so that by "capturing its own straying, it leads what it captures astray."[24] If, in this process of straying, the photograph emerges as "the prodigious image of our strangeness,"[25] it is because the intricate imbrication of the familiar and the strange that it gives us to view also captures the fundamental tension of familiarity and strangeness that makes us who we are—even, and especially, in front of ourselves. Moore's photographic inflections of this straying into strangeness take many forms in his oeuvre, and the birch trees growing on and through moldering books toward a sky that nevertheless remains out of reach in the here and now of the image stage a particularly striking instantiation of this straying. The ruins that populate the photograph belong to a world that is itself meandering off course, both in a decaying archive in Detroit and in a much larger world in which this irreducible straying itself is incessantly operative.

Reflecting upon ruin, decay, and finitude in the world of the photographic image also demands reflecting upon the ways in which the photograph relates to time itself. It is as if the photograph had its own time, an aesthetic temporality proper only to itself, that operates on several levels. The photograph relates to time in that it interrupts it, as it were, when the shutter is released and a moment in time is arrested for good. That moment is removed from time, wrested from its flow, even as it addresses itself to time's very existence. A temporal point is captured by the photographic image as a confirmation, an archive even, of the "there and then," in a manner that always both disrupts and preserves time. The photograph performs something of a Hegelian *Aufhebung* of temporality in the sense that time is both preserved and canceled within the parameters of the photograph and the experiences of taking and viewing to which it gives rise. Photography creates a world that is modulated by its own relation to time. By the same token, that very relation to time is itself the subject—sometimes only implicitly, sometimes explicitly—upon which photography pivots. Photography sets up a world in which the creation of images becomes visible as a radically time-based aesthetic practice, and its self-reflexive knowledge concerning this world of temporality makes a photograph what it is. Viewed through the lens of the photograph, time is at odds with itself: it can be captured and removed from the apparent sequentiality of a flowing stream and transposed into very different temporal points or sequences, as becomes most striking when we observe especially old photographs.

If the world set up by the photographic artwork is suffused with the time of finitude and absence, it always also gives rise to the experience of mourning and commemoration (themes to which we will return at greater length in chapter 8). As Derrida points out in his readings of Jean-François Bonhomme's photographs of Athens, when it comes to relating to such photographs "each one of them remains in its turn what it becomes: a funerary inscription with a proper name. Having to keep what it loses, namely the *departed*, does not every photograph act in effect *through* the bereaved experience of such a proper name, through the irresistible singularity of its referent, its here–now, its date?"[26] Extending Derrida's observation, one might say that the world of the photograph is populated by funerary inscriptions on multiple levels, among them the commemoration—precisely *as* image—of what is about to disappear in the Benjaminian sense; the memorial identification of a specific absence—such as that of a certain person, place, animal, or thing; and a general commemoration, through the photographic image as a kind of memento mori, of the passing of time, which is to say of finitude and death, of loss as loss. As a funerary inscription with a proper name—a name that may resonate in, but need not of necessity be limited to, the referential range suggested by a photograph's title—the photograph stages a relation to finitude in such a way as to make this relation capable of being revisited, the way one might revisit a specific grave according to certain temporal or seasonal rhythms. The photograph, through its status as a funerary inscription with a proper name, works to make our relation to finitude *citable*.

The finitude that is the experience of every being in time is staged in the world set up by Moore's photographs according to particularly self-conscious visual protocols. Here, time announces itself as an explicit and abiding concern, one that runs like a red thread through the world of these images. As the photographer puts it, his "photographic interests have always lain at the busy intersections of history, particularly those locations where multiple tangents of time overlap and tangle," and in "Detroit, the forward motion of time appears to have been thrown spectacularly into reverse."[27] One might say that a photograph from the Detroit series entitled *National Time Clock, Former Cass Technical High School Building* stages this perception in particularly stark terms. Here, a damaged and defaced wall clock inscribes the motif of ruptured or reversed time into the core of the constellation of images in which it is embedded. The face of this clock—set in a rusty rim and hanging on a decaying wall with remnants of peeling wallpaper perched on a stained and weather-beaten foundation—has partially melted away, so that only a few of the lower numbers are still legible in full. The numbers at the top—eleven and twelve—appear strangely elongated and distorted, apparently due to the extreme heat that has caused the hard plastic of the clock's face to decompose. The melted plastic has engulfed the hands of the clock, preventing them from ever moving again. Time appears to have come to a standstill here; or at least it can no longer be measured by mechanical instruments according to the conventional logic of clock time. The time is out of joint, as Hamlet memorably puts it. The photograph seems to be saying that Detroit's time is up; time itself has run out, and there is no point in attempting to measure it anymore. And what are we to make of name of the clock's manufacturer, National Time? Does it figure as a harbinger of things to come for the nation as a whole, if Detroit time were to become the national time as well?

The National Time clock melting from the peeling wall of a Detroit high school belongs to an archive of abandoned yet lingering items that populate the world of Moore's photographs. So many of the things one encounters in the object-world of these images have lost their use-value, their quotidian purpose, literally their place in the world. And yet they continue to dwell in this world as if they were still capable of making a claim on it, insisting on their residual membership. As such, they acquire a certain dignity, even and especially in their decay and forced retreat from the world. As the poet Philip Levin puts it in his essay "Nobody's Detroit," Moore's photographs exhibit a "dignity of the isolated and inconsequential, of all that refuses to not be," that may be likened to certain dimensions of the poetry of William Carlos Williams.[28] If Moore's images are suffused by such a dignity of the isolated and inconsequential, and if what they show refuses not to be, but rather affirms that it belongs to life—a form of life even in decay and death—then the decrepit things that are on display in these photographs bear historical and ontological witness to this dignity and this affirmation. Like the nonfunctional melted National Time clock, the objects that live in Moore's photographs refuse simply to die completely, even when their time is up. By insisting on their dignity even in a state of irreducible isolation and apparent inconsequentiality, these items bear witness to a life that is not simply and not exclusively the opposite of death, but rather is always strangely interwoven with it.

Even as Moore's photograph documents the National Time clock's dignity as an object that refuses merely to vanish from the world, the image also inscribes itself into an art-historical genealogy, self-consciously evoking the melting clocks of Salvador Dalí's surrealist paintings. Detroit's time here not only becomes national time but also enters into syntactical relation with the very time of art history. One thinks, for instance, of the melting clocks and watches in one of Dalí's most iconic paintings, *The Persistence of Memory* (1931). Evoking Dalí's dreamlike images of melting clocks and watches along the shoreline of his native Catalonia, Moore's photograph allows a blue-hued surface of light to appear on the clock's face. While in Dalí's surrealist depiction this layer of blueness already is the very foundation of the melting clocks' and watches' face, in Moore's image the blueness appears just *beneath* the standard white face of the clock. As a result, the incommensurate blueness of the clock becomes visible only where the standard white has melted away, revealing a deeper, hidden layer of color beneath its apparent whiteness. By placing itself into syntactical relation with the blueness of Dalí's melting clocks, does Moore's photograph gesture toward a surreal time beneath the veneer of officially measured time? Is Detroit's time also the time of decayed dreams that never cease to haunt in the collective imaginary? Is time here out of joint, opening onto dream-time, phantasmagoria, and suspended disbelief, in which an optical unconscious supersedes the claims of reason?

One might say that this self-reflexive awareness of temporality and finitude as it relates to the world opened up by a photograph inflects the sense of singular historicity that emerges from Moore's photographs. Without such singular historicity, the photographic image does not fully connect to the world of its place, which can be both the place at which it was created and the place that it takes as its subject. This view is confirmed when Moore, in a conversation about his art with Tsuyoshi Ito, explains that "I find that there is no sense of place in a photograph unless it alludes to time and history, that an image has to be grounded in the currents of history that flow through a particular place as well as some sense of the current moment that the photographer lives in." This also means that, "as contradictory as this may sound, what I want an image of place to display is not so much a particular geographic point on the map, but how that location has been shaped through time both by the events past as well as the present."²⁹ Place here is not conceived as a mere location or a spatial point that can be reduced to its world coordinates. Rather, place names a particular constellation of the traces of temporality, the archive of its genealogy, it very having-becomeness. If place, at least from the perspective of the photographic image, cannot come into its own without also opening up vistas onto its own historical grownness—that is, without also giving an account, as Nietzsche would put it, of how it became what it is—then the photographic image that wishes to capture (a) place must find a way to welcome the more or less invisible specters of its past. Even though a place can only occupy one space at a time, it is built upon, indeed dependent in relation to, all the other places that once stood in its very space. To recall Freud's famous example of the city of Rome—which, as a site, can only ever exist in one space and in one time at once, even though it is built upon more or less invisible ruins of past versions of itself—a place is never just what meets the eye. Like the psyche, as Freud reminds us, for which—unlike the city of Rome—different realities and different worlds can exist at the same time and in the same space, the photograph shows itself responsible to the demands that time and history always make on the present moment. Such an image cannot close its eyes before the ghostly traces of previous worlds that traverse every photographic document. Indeed, the world that a photograph opens up in a rigorous and searching way always also opens onto *other worlds*, worlds populated by past concerns, previous ambitions, and long-forgotten dreams, in short, by the fateful inheritance of the dead. To understand the world of a particular photograph, one must understand another world.

In Moore's photographs of Havana, the question of coming to understand a world by coming to understand another world—a different world altogether or, sometimes, a world *inside* of a world, as in the many interior shots that populate the Havana collection—is modulated by an emphasis on temporality, on bearing witness to the place of time. As the Cuban architect and architectural historian Eduardo Luis Rodríguez puts it in "Poet in Havana," his introduction to Moore's *Inside Havana*, "time is the protagonist of this book as it deciphers the skein of architectural elements to us as the scars of daily life, the aging of the physical, and the ennobling of existence through the passage of time." Here, "doorways and columns, gates and windows, arches and stained glass appear to be the subject of these photographs, but a careful reading shows us that they are only the 'incorruptible witnesses,' the setting against which history and time are played out." What comes into focus is "time passed and now static, letting itself be read," yielding an image of "time as the absolute receptacle of history, architecture, and society."[30] If time itself is the protagonist of Moore's photographs, they exhibit a world in which we as the observers are enjoined to witness the witnessing of the passage of time and history as it is staged in these images. Our reading of these photographs must attend, with a kind of double focus or double intensity, both to the temporally mediated worlds they

197

capture and to the silent witnesses that populate these images, whether the incorruptible witnesses be inanimate objects such as peeling walls, caving roofs, and shattered mirrors and windows, or human beings who traverse them as if they were both anchored in space and time yet somehow also lost in history, not quite contemporaneous with their own time and world, even as they appear fully immersed in them.

Moore's 1999 photograph *Campoamor, Vista Oeste*, taken in La Habana Vieja, condenses some of these conceptual concerns into the formal principles of a single composition. The image, which figures as plate 8 of *Inside Havana*, shows the current state of the Campoamor theater, which, as Moore adds in the brief endnotes following his archive of images, was originally designed for the performance of light opera. He points out that Placido Domingo's parents, both singers, regularly performed at the Campoamor and that authors such as Federico García Lorca and Ernest Hemingway gave readings there. The structure, once a grand, representative palace of cultural performance, now stands in decay, with its roofs largely missing, its walls peeling, its balconies growing moss, and vegetation encroaching ever more noticeably upon the scene. What the observer encounters along the bottom center of the photograph is a row of bicycle rickshaws, one of which is labeled "Taxi"; and across cleared space now serving as a makeshift courtyard, one sees a row of parked mopeds and motorcycles. (Here the image enters into a spectral relation with a later photograph from Moore's Detroit project, in which, grotesquely, a parking deck has been built inside the formerly majestic Michigan Theater, whose once-grand features—with ornate arches and painted ceilings—are still visible.) If the bottom third of the image and its outer "frame" are dark, the top two thirds of the photograph are flooded in sunlight, as if the world of today were attempting to illuminate the increasingly dim and obscure past of this formerly glorious dwelling. It is, however, precisely the darker part of the image and the building that shelters the structure's current usefulness, that is, its function as a parking area for bicycle taxis and motorcycles. What is illuminated is a moss-laden history that is caving in on itself, while the world of shadows and obscurity ties the building to the here and now of the photographic scene.

Is it admissible to consider, for a moment, whether the lower third of the image is steeped in pure immanence, while the upper two thirds stage a kind of transcendence? The interplay between immanence and transcendence gives itself its own frame: not an external picture frame added to the photograph after the fact, but a self-conscious framing that occurs inside the photograph itself, an internal delimitation, as the dark ornate pillars on the left and right conspire with the debris-cluttered ground to enframe the image. But, as if to accentuate the idea of a photographic transcendence, this "frame" only features three sides, because the fourth side of the frame, at the top of the image, is missing, so to speak. No dark border is to be found there, but rather the bright sky as daylight floods in through the decayed roof, a light that is reminiscent of the sunlight flooding in through a partially collapsed roof in Moore's 2003 image of the Locomotive Workers' Theatre in Ulan Ude, plate 40 in his book *Russia: Beyond Utopia*.[31] In its self-reflexively exposed and exposing staging, the special light in the Havana photograph also alludes to the literal meaning of photo-graphy as "light-writing." Does the image's self-conscious framing of an intimated interplay between immanence and transcendence not speak to the way in which a particular instance of light-writing grapples with its own compositional and historical layers? Is not the incursion of a ghostly historicity onto the scene of a present facticity staged with the imagistic grandeur of a world, and a lifeworld, in perpetual retreat and self-conscious decline? If the world that the Campoamor photograph sets up in its aesthetic space becomes visible in the moment of being-no-longer, it also stages the withdrawal of a world without which no genuine work of art could ever be thought.

To think this world-withdrawal as it is enacted by the photographic work of art in the setting-up of an aesthetic world, the viewer is called upon to entertain an open and capacious but nevertheless rigorous relation to the world that suffuses the image. Speaking in the context of his photographs of the Great Plains gathered in his *Dirt Meridian*, Moore speaks of the aesthetic vision "to make pictures at a perspective from which the intimate seemed conjoined with the infinite."[32] To conjoin the intimate with the infinite: on the most immediate level, this statement references

Moore's strategic praxis of flying over his Great Plains subjects at a low altitude—"at the height of a windmill and sometimes lower,"[33] as he puts it—a strategy that enabled his photographs to capture a sense of both generality and specificity. This approach yielded remarkable images of, among other things, a herd of wild pronghorn antelopes swooshing across a wide-open plain in Wyoming's Niobrara County; a small, seemingly desolate house on Henry Road on the expansive and otherwise unsettled border of Nebraska and Wyoming; or an old homestead, in an image entitled *The Yellow Porch*, that is photographed from a bird's-eye perspective in its dry, brownish, and shrubby setting, appearing as though it belonged to a nineteenth-century realist painting. This conjoining of the world of the intimate with that of the infinite in a photographic work of art here is inflected by a relation to the presented world that is close enough to be specific, idiomatic, and singular, yet removed enough to be categorical, general, even universal.[34] At the same time, however, one might say that Moore's insistence on forging a dynamic relation between the intimate and the infinite, even conjoining them, traverses his photographic praxis as a whole. His images construct a world in which certain particularities— irreducible in their singularity—come into view, while a broader, more general perspective on that singularity at the same time affords a more universal mode of apperception and reflection. Learning to relate to a world that is on the brink of being no longer, a world in retreat, also always requires learning to relate to the conjoining of the intimate and the infinite as it comes to pass in a particular photograph. The interplay of intimacy and infinity, a critical closeness to something idiomatic that is imbricated with the broader claims tied to a general idea or principle, conditions our perspective onto that "of which one knows that one soon no longer will have it in front of one," that is, onto the world of the photographic image itself.

We are now in a position to see more clearly how Benjamin's provocative assertion—"That of which one knows that one soon no longer will have it in front of one, that becomes image"—gains contours in Moore's photographic practice. In the afterword to *Blue Alabama*, he reflects on the tenuous and open-ended relation of his photographic images of Alabama to those created by such well-known predecessor as Walker Evans in *Let Us Now Praise Famous Men*, and those of Charles Moore and William Christenberry. Moore suggests that what ties the Alabama project to his earlier body of work, including the Detroit project and the photographs of the American Plains gathered in *Dirt Meridian*, is the emphasis on "themes of loss and resilience." It is in this context, too, that he offers a reminiscence strikingly suffused by Benjaminian echoes: "My friend Butch had once said that I photograph things that are 'goin' away,' and I almost took it unkindly, as if he meant to say that a feel for nostalgia was my greatest guide." He inflects this view by stressing that nostalgia is not the heart of the matter in his photographic practice; the images he makes are not merely melancholic accounts of a real or anticipated absence. Rather, as he recalls in relation to the experience of wishing to photograph a particular scene in Alabama that he remembered from a visit decades earlier but that happened no longer to exist, "the famous phrase from Heraclitus came to my mind: 'You can never step twice into the same river.' And I felt fortunate, grateful, even peaceful, to be present and at one with that restless flow."[35] If Moore's interest in creating photographs of that of which one knows that it is about to disappear is not driven by nostalgia or a kind of conservationist's impulse, it fastens upon a relationship to temporality, even to finitude itself, that remains open, unsaturated, exploratory. Among the many dimensions of Heraclitus's saying—which comes down to us as quoted by Plato in *Cratylus*, 402a—is the idea that one cannot step twice into the same river because, with time—whether mere hours or days, or many years— this river will have transformed into something else. It will not remain as and with itself, as it cannot stay self-identical as such. By the same token, the "you" or the "one" who is stepping into the river will have changed the next time this being steps into the river as well, because time will have transformed the being into someone else, an older person now marked in decisive ways by different experiences, thoughts, and viewpoints. In that sense there can be no repetition without a difference. While the flow of the river can be stopped as little as the flow of time, the restless, transformative nature of the flow—the flow as flow, the very idea of flowing as such—itself does not change. The perpetual change across time notwithstanding, change itself does not change. If change itself is incapable of changing even as it transforms the world, the world does not remain untouched. One might even go one step further and say that Moore's photographs set up a world that is both respectful of, and hospitable to, precisely this unchanging change, this flowless flow in which the intimate and the infinite are forever jointly immersed. These images bear incorruptible witness to the experience of temporality and finitude as it opens onto a world that makes us who we are—a world that, in other words, makes and unmakes us, capturing us in pictures of what we soon no longer will be. *Das wird Bild*.

Troubled Origins:
Accounting for Oneself as World-Creation (Derrida, Botho Strauß, Didier Eribon)

One of the most significant and transformative ways in which a work creates its own world, even as the actual world from which the work emerges has perished, consists in the narrative act of accounting for one's own origins. When one fashions a sustained narrative that is designed to explain how one's self became who and what it is, one tacitly calls into presence a specific kind of world that emanates from the textual production itself. This world set up by the aesthetic object around the idea of elucidating a self, of projecting a world that is inhabitable by, and potentially hospitable to, a self, demands to be thought on its own terms. Traditional designations of genres such as "confessions" or "autobiography" do not fully capture the worldness of the world that is projected in such acts of genealogical self-textualization. The particular modes of engagement with issues of selfhood, origin, and purpose pose the question of world in their own, each time idiomatic ways. The world that arises out of these abiding engagements deserves to be thought on its own terms, as it names a particularly significant act of world-creation through the work as it interrogates the origins of a self, even of the very idea of selfhood as such.

But the attempt to account for one's origins by textually fashioning such a world can be a perilous undertaking. What does it mean to revisit the narrative of one's life in a belated attempt to make sense of the more or less nebulous beginnings of a self? How could one's inception ever be satisfactorily explained? Would the act of taking stock leave a particular origin, or indeed the concept of "origin" as such, untouched? And how does the idea of a self's commencement relate to the irreducible belatedness of any attempt to scrutinize it by fashioning a world for it? When it comes to one's roots, what accounts for the desire to provide an accounting in the first place? Are there unacknowledged accounts to settle? Can the act of accounting itself ever be accounted for? Who or what is this troubled being that attempts to generate an explanation, a disclosive world, with regard to itself, somewhere along the path of its life, in terms of its long-lost beginnings?

In confronting these questions of world-creation, it is helpful to note that the word "troubled" in "troubled origins" signifies—at least—in a triple sense: it bespeaks the unsettled provenance of a self; it names the difficulties and unease that an other will face when learning of a self's problematic provenance; and it gestures toward an uncircumventable complexity within the concept of "origin" itself. When inquiring into the movements and preoccupations of a self that engages with its genesis, one would do well to recall Derrida's undoing of the classical concept of origin, a persistent unweaving that one already finds in his early work, for instance in his 1966 lecture "Freud and the Scene of Writing," which was included the following year as the seventh chapter of *Writing and Difference*. There, Derrida identifies in Freud's thought a preparedness to comply with "a dual necessity: that of recognizing *différance* at the origin" and "at the same time that of crossing out the concept of primariness," which figures in works such as the *Traumdeutung* precisely as "a 'theoretical fiction.'"[1] The implications that Derrida draws from his reading of Freud can be extended far beyond the precincts of psychoanalytical investigation; indeed, they touch the thinking of origin as such. "To say that *différance*

206

is originary," he argues, "is simultaneously to erase the myth of a present origin. Which is why 'originary' must be understood as having been *crossed out*, without which *différance* would be derived from an original plentitude. It is a non-origin which is originary."[2] If the concept of an origin that is self-identical and present to itself cannot withstand its unruly undoing by the movement of *différance* that is always operative within it, then "origin" demands to be heard and thought differently every time it is spoken, and reinterpreted every time it is mobilized to provide genealogical deduction, historical (self-)reconstruction, or even (self)-legitimization for this or that discursive formation.

Yet even after the notion of an "origin" has been called into question in the most decisive ways, and thinkers such as Derrida (and others, in differently modulated ways, such as Heidegger and Benjamin) have dismantled what might be called the metaphysics of origin—by emphasizing precisely the internal multiplicity, heterogeneity, non self identity, incommensurability, alterity, and therefore non-originarity that always *also* permeate the concept of origin as *Ur-sprung*, or primal leap—a certain remainder, a phantasmagorically inflected wish to speak of origins, nevertheless persists. Providing an account of oneself to oneself and to others by reflecting upon, and retroactively reconstructing, the trajectory of one's being-in-the-world, beginning with one's origins, entails confronting the abiding desire to comprehend the trajectory of an unfolding—and of the experience of that unfolding along the way—in the form of a genealogical narrative that imposes a certain ordering, causality, and verifiability on a lived life. The narrative mode of such an account is not limited to the classical genre of autobiography—in which a self (*autós*) provides an account of a life (*bíos*) in writing (*gráphein*)—as in the canonical texts that over the centuries have defined the modern form of the genre, including Augustine's *Confessions*, Rousseau's *Confessions*, and Goethe's *Dichtung und Wahrheit*. If providing an account of oneself and one's troubled origins is not confined to the autobiographical genre in the narrow sense, it permeates the discourse of any questioning and reflective self wishing to articulate how it became who and what it is and, importantly, in what manner it has come to *survive* along the trajectories propelling it forward from its largely

207

occluded origins.[3] *Ecce Homo: How One Becomes What One Is*, the text that Nietzsche composed in a burst of creative ecstasy in the span of only a few weeks in late 1888, expresses the "uniqueness" of his existence "in the form of a riddle": "As my father I have already died, as my mother I still live and grow old."[4] It is as if part of the fragmented Nietzschean self survived precisely in the realization that something else within it had ceased to be; it lives on precisely to the extent that it is also no longer fully alive as an integral whole, that is, as a self-identical structure of ipseity ruled by a sovereign consciousness. In order to appreciate this observation, it is perhaps helpful to know that Nietzsche had a much closer relationship with his father, who died young, than he did with his mother, who outlived Nietzsche's father by a significant number of years. Yet what is crucial here is the structural way in which Nietzsche's narrative portrays the survival of part of himself (in this case, a maternal element) in terms of a simultaneous nonsurvival (here, a paternal element), so that what emerges is the rhetorical image of a self both dead and alive, partially deceased and partially living on. It is such a self that propels the narrative of its troubled origins into presence: "The ice is near, the solitude is terrible—but how peacefully all things lie in the light! how freely one breathes! how much one feels *beneath* one!—Philosophy, as I have hitherto understood and lived it, is a voluntary living in ice and high mountains—a seeking after everything strange and questionable in existence."[5] And it is precisely from this vantage point of the strange and questionable life that Nietzsche's narrative issues forth: "And so I tell myself my life [*Und so erzähle ich mir mein Leben.*]"[6] It is in terms of the experienced or anticipated potentiality of surviving that the narrative accounting of one's life and its troubled origins proceeds to fashion a world.

The very act of accounting for oneself and one's troubled origins within the discourse of a textual world-creation casts the self as the subject of its own production. In the telling of one's life to oneself, as Nietzsche puts it, the question always also emerges as to how, in the textual act of worlding, the work and the life—which also is to say, the surviving work and the life that survives *for now*—relate to each other. The one does not merely mirror the other; nor is one simply the master of the other, as when the language of the confessional text resists the full control of authorial intention, casting the problem of its intelligibility in its own singular, which is to say linguistic, terms. Yet if work and life are not merely identical, how does the one refer to the other, and what kind of comportment does the one exhibit with regard to the other? In Derrida's reflections "Otobiographies: The Teaching of Nietzsche and the Politics of the Proper Name," offered in the context of a colloquium on Nietzsche and the question of autobiography at the University of Montreal in 1979 and first published in 1984, he suggests:

> Neither "immanent" readings of philosophical systems (whether such readings be structural or not) nor external, empirical-genetic readings have ever in themselves questioned the *dynamis* of that borderline between the "work" and the "life," the system and the subject of the system. This borderline—I call it *dynamis* because of its force, its power, as well as its virtual and mobile potency—is neither active nor passive, neither outside nor inside. It is most especially not a thin line, an invisible or *indivisible* trait lying between the enclosure of philosophemes, on the one hand, and the life of an author already identifiable behind that name, on the other. The divisible borderline traverses two "bodies," the corpus and the body, in accordance with laws that we are only beginning to catch sight of.[7]

Any self that, like Nietzsche's in *Ecce Homo*, would strive to account for how it became what it is—which is also to say, any self that would explicitly cast its troubled origins into sharp linguistic and conceptual relief—is confronted with a peculiar demand: to consider the two "bodies," as Derrida calls them, the life and the work, the body and the corpus, in relation to each other. Such relation informs the world that a self-narration sets up. If this relation cannot be reduced to conventional terms of binarist metaphysics such as activity and passivity, inside and outside, subjectivity and systematicity, it also must engage with the problem of how to think this strange and movable borderline that supposedly keeps life and work separate yet standing in a mobile and dynamic relation to each other, a relation that cannot be arrested once and for all.[8]

In opening up this internal borderline to a potentiality—an experience and a language that are yet to come—the self that provides a textual account of itself and of the world of its troubled origins confronts itself most fully when this dynamic challenge imposes itself most palpably on the scene of writing.

If accounting for one's life in terms of one's troubled origins is a matter of engaging the past—a history of the confessing self and its particular modes of survival—the historicity of this past never belongs to the world of a past alone, even as its settings, themes, scenes, stories, and characters appear to belong to a time that is no longer. After all, the history of a self that narrates to itself and to others the story of its troubled origins and its survival also belongs to the world of an as yet unnamed double futurity— another time to be lived by the self that narrates its being-in-the world as well as a future to be lived by others who may read the text this self will have penned, albeit in radically different contexts and with divergent presuppositions and premises. Because it is also something profoundly future-directed, the past—seen as the object of a self-written account of troubled origins—is not simply the past. It enters language as that which remains open-ended, nonforeclosed, nonfixed—and therefore as a matter of survival and inexhaustible potentiality. If William Faulkner is right that the "past is never dead. It's not even past," then the future-directed gesture of a survival that inflects any attempt to account for one's troubled origins is a powerful instantiation of this premise.[9] It is in the world opened up by this premise, too, that a life and a work first enter into a relation with each other.

One might say that it is no accident that so many of the most penetrating writers of modernity have grappled with precisely this mode of narrative self-accounting for their troubled origins with an eye toward an unforeclosed potentiality, a world to come. Next to Nietzsche's attempts at radical self-interpretation in *Ecce Homo*, one may think of such documents as Freud's account, in a 1925 text he names "Selbstdarstellung," or "Self-Presentation," of the role that his early experiences of anti-Semitism played in his later ability to withstand criticism and rejection as he developed the new field of psychoanalysis.[10] One may also recall Kafka's *Letter to the Father*, composed in 1919, which works to account for the writer's fragile and tenuous mode of being-in-the-world in terms of his deeply troubled relation with his father;[11] and Benjamin's *Berlin Childhood around 1900*, written in the course of the 1930s, which collects a small archive of narrative thought-images that imbricate scenes and fleeting experiences from Benjamin's youth with his later critique of modernity.[12] What unites all of these "origin-texts" is the question of a troubled and troubling survival, a survival that is predicated upon the imbrication of a narrative self-accounting for one's troubled origins with the prospect that the very act of thinking and writing will work to preserve something fragile yet eminently future-directed, a sense of unsaturated possibility that opens onto the world of an unknown futurity. In what way can this form of survival that is opened up by a sustained confrontation with one's troubled origins begin to be thought?

*

Among the most remarkable elements to be found in the second part of Derrida's final seminar, *The Beast and the Sovereign* (held in Paris in 2002–2003), is the concept of *survivance* that he develops apropos of his unexpected conjunction of Daniel Defoe's *Robinson Crusoe* and a small archive of Heideggerian texts—especially *The Fundamental Concepts of Metaphysics: World, Finitude, Solitude*.[13] Survivance there is marked by a certain finitude, an "alliance of the dead and the living."[14] For Derrida's conceptual orbit, the term survivance is attractive because it marks a "middle voice" that avoids both the "active voice of the active infinitive 'to survive'" and the "substantializing substantive *survival*."[15] Survivance "is something other than life death," which is to say that it marks "a groundless ground from which are detached, identified, and opposed what we think we can identify under the name of death or dying (*Tod, Sterben*), like death properly so-called as opposed to some life properly so-called." As he continues: "It [*Ça*] begins with survival. And that is where some other has me at its disposal; that is where any self is defenseless. That is what the self is, that is what I am, what the *I* is, whether I am there or not." Consequently, one may say that the "other, the others, that is the very thing that survives me, that is called to survive me and that I call the other inasmuch as it is

211

called, in advance, to survive me," is "structurally my survivor. Not my survivor, but the survivor of me, the *there* beyond my life."[16] There can be no world of survivance—and especially no survivance of any self narrating its troubled origins—that is not marked by the other, conditioned by the other and its otherness, the other whose life, no matter how strange or foreign to me, is intertwined with mine. One might say that, in the act of inheriting myself in relation to the trajectory of my life and the world of my troubled origins, I am forever at the disposal of the other; my life, without guard, gives itself over to the other so that I may live on. Is not the act of narrating one's troubled origins also a figure of that unfathomable otherness that conditions my survivance? Is it not precisely the thing that survives me—whatever that "me" might be—regardless of whether I am there or not, whether I am alive or not, whether my body, for the time being, still is counted among the living or not? Does the act of narrating one's troubled origins not also serve as an instantiation of survivance, even if this act by itself can never be my survivor in a narrow, conventional, or anticipated sense?

How one thinks about the history of one's being-in-the-world and, by extension, about whatever futurity that being may still possess in a world to come is predicated upon an engagement with the time that has come to pass in relation to the life that now reflects on that time. At stake is not so much the thinking of a world that is in search of lost time, as Proust might have it, or one that would help us to imagine, also with Proust, a time regained, but rather the engagement with an otherness that is— tacitly, as a mute potentiality—already part of what one considers the self, or what has always already been waiting within us to be confronted. Thus, when one looks back, in a confessional mode of self-narration, on one's life, that is, when one reflects on how one becomes who one is, as Nietzsche would have it, one considers one's *Herkunft*. The German noun *die Herkunft* derives from the verb *herkommen*, to come from, or, more precisely, to come here from elsewhere. Despite its apparent simplicity, *Herkunft* is not easily translated into English by any single noun, for its semantic reach is capacious and dependent on context. *Herkunft* can mean origin or point of origin, provenance, background, ancestry, extraction, parentage, birth, pedigree, nativity, root, source, stock, tracing,

212

derivation, descent, or beginnings, among other designations. *Herkunft* itself thus describes an origin that is multiple, a state of affairs or experience that demands scrutiny and reflection.

In his 2014 autobiographical text *Herkunft*, the German writer and dramatist Botho Strauß recalls seminal elements of his growing-up years in the 1940s and 1950s, reviving a time and a world long gone that he culls from a lifelong archive of experience and reflection in which these elements had lain dormant yet continued to survive as silent witnesses to the fragile formation of a consciousness. The book seems to ask whether we are able to think *Herkunft* today in its inexhaustible and infinitely demanding senses. While the narrator's remembrances circle, in tender, non-sentimental, pellucid prose, ever more tightly around the figure of his long-deceased father, they are suffused with more general reflections on the act of autobiographical recollection and the charged question of *Herkunft* that the act inevitably yet elusively imposes on an examined life and its worlds. As the author avers in a polyvalent statement elsewhere, "I am a subject of transmission [or heritage, tradition], and I cannot exist outside of it [*Ich bin ein Subjekt der Überlieferung, und außerhalb ihrer kann ich nicht existieren*]."[17] To be sure, Strauß's confessions—like Augustine's, Rousseau's, and Nietzsche's before—probe the singularity and idiomaticity of one particular life; yet—again like those of his canonical predecessors—Strauß's confessions also contain reflections that far transcend the singularity and idiomaticity of a single life, opening onto concerns that are of universal interest and import, which is to say, opening onto the world of the other, even otherness as such. Here, the world of one's *Herkunft* can hardly be thought in separation from an other's *Herkunft*, even if, like the other's, it remains enigmatic and refractory.

In a key passage, from around the middle of *Herkunft*, Strauß remarks:

Is there anything better than to remain where you were born and raised, went to school, fell in love for the first time? Where your parents and grandparents lived? Why leave one's ancestral location behind? And if it has to be, because one is supposed, after all, to learn and accomplish something in strange lands, why not return home afterward? Only half of one's decay would be felt if one stayed in one's place. If one had no choice but to stay in one's place. [*Es wäre nur die Hälfte des Vergehens zu spüren, wenn man an seinem Ort bliebe. Wenn man gar nicht anders könnte, als immer an seinem Ort zu bleiben.*]

Like the dead, they do not leave their home. [*Wie die Toten, sie verlassen ihre Heimat nicht.*] You encounter them on the forest paths at the edge of the valley, down by the river, where father and mother sat when they were worried, and on the meadow that grew on the old athletic field. ... [The river] may transport up and down whatever one sets onto it. It is and remains your time, your home, your place, your boundary. [*Er ist und bleibt deine Zeit, dein Zuhause, dein Ort, deine Grenze.*] A river does not flow away. Only that which it carries comes and goes.[18]

Herkunft here appears inextricably intertwined with *das Vergehen*, which is a substantivized noun deriving from the verb *vergehen*, meaning to decay, to die away, to vanish, to pass by, to elapse (as in time elapsing, *die Zeit vergeht*). If *Vergehen* for the narrator names the experience of the passage of time as the process of a world's decay and decline, it is by reflecting on the possibility of remaining in one place for the duration of one's entire life—almost like a tree that remains for its entire lifespan firmly planted in a single spot—that this decay or decline comes sharply into view. When one returns to the world of one's origins after a long absence, when one revisits the scenes of a childhood and youth long gone, one finds that the place has changed in so many ways as to remind one of one's own changes, the history of one's life trajectory, and, by extension, one's finitude. This sense of one's own *Vergehen*, one's decay, passing, dying away, slow vanishing, would be mitigated, the narrator speculates, if one gave oneself over without remainder to one's *Herkunft*, one's place of origin, planted oneself there like a tree in order to experience the world and one's life within it but from a single vantage point. One's experience of decay would be felt only half as acutely, half as melancholically, as there would be no *Herkunft* to which to return, no world of an imaginary homeland that could now be considered lost. Living, one would also share, even before one's actual death, the rich realm of the dead who do not leave their homeland but can be encountered—like the narrator's long-gone father and mother—everywhere as complex and haunting specters of memory. If Strauß employs the image of a river that does not disappear by flowing away but rather carries along whatever one might give over to it, it is because *Herkunft* designates the specific vantage point from which the movements of perpetual change, of becoming and decay, come into view without themselves becoming the object of change. What remains stable in all (recollected or immediate) experience of *Vergehen* is that nothing ever will have been what it is; there is, rather, a stability of instability that gives rise to an emergent living on, a *Werden*, a becoming, in every *Vergehen*, a "Werden im Vergehen," as Hölderlin would say.

In light of this becoming within decay, one inherits—and passes on as a legacy the world of one's past and one's recollected experience of that past not simply through an overly passive self-delivery to decay. That would be another kind of *Vergehen*, now understood in its other sense of offense, misdeed, wrongful act, or misdemeanor. Commit no *Vergehen* against your own *Vergehen*, Strauß seems to be urging us. He records the significance of working on, reflecting upon, and influencing the world of one's own decay in the most deliberate ways possible:

> What, then, can the declining human being do, who, from one hour to the next, must confront yet another enigma? Always just stand there and wonder? [*Immer nur dastehen und sich wundern?*] That cannot be all. One must work on one's decline or decay methodically, the way one also had to hustle in one's process of becoming. [*Man muß an seinem Vergehen mit Methode arbeiten, wie man ja auch beim Werden sich ins Zeug legen mußte.*][19]

In facing the enigma of one's recollected yet inevitably decaying life, it is not enough to affirm its enigmatic nature or to persist in mere astonishment or wonder (even though the latter, as *thaumazein*, is certainly *also* necessary, since it marks, according to Plato's *Theaetetus*, the beginning of all philosophy, as we recall). Rather, Strauß stresses the importance of dedicating oneself to the world of one's decline with method and purpose, taking it seriously in the same way that one once dedicated oneself to one's becoming, to furthering one's ascent and progress in the world when one was younger and still had most of one's life ahead. But what the narrator has in mind can hardly be reduced to a form of getting one's affairs in order, as they say, a moment of mere estate planning. No, this form of working on one's *Vergehen* implies a deliberate engagement with one's coming to pass, a coming to pass that is inseparable from questions of tradition, handing-down, legacy, and inheritance. It belongs more likely to the order of what the writer Robert Musil calls, in an apparently paradoxical formulation, a *Nachlaß zu Lebzeiten*, the posthumous papers of a living author. One works to design and steer the trajectory of one's decline, to the extent possible, in a way that affirms it *as* decline and decay, without denial and without perpetuating the fantasy that it could be outwitted or even overcome. One thoughtfully participates in shaping one's own *Vergehen*—not to hasten it along but to affirm life precisely by affirming the looming shadow of its radical finitude.

It is as if, through this process of working on one's own demise and decay with systematicity and care, one enlisted oneself among those others who will dispose of one's remains. By attending to the unfolding of one's own *Vergehen*, as Strauß casts it into sharp relief, one takes one's place among the others—as a self that is another other—to whose world the decaying one is given over. As Derrida reminds us in his seminar on Heidegger and *Robinson Crusoe*, "I have to have presupposed that the other, the others, are precisely those who always might die after me, and have at their disposal what remains of me, my remains. The others—what is that? Those, masculine and feminine, who might survive me." To which he adds that the others are those "before whom I am disarmed, defenseless" because "the other is what always might, one day, do something with me and my remains, make me into a thing, whatever the respect or the pomp, funereal by vocation, with which he or she will treat that singular thing they call my remains." It is here, therefore, that the "other appears to me as the other as such, *qua* he, she, or they who might survive me, survive my decease and then proceed as they wish, sovereignly, and sovereignly have at their disposal the future of my remains, if there are any." Derrida cautions, however, that "having my remains at their disposal can also take place before I am absolutely, clearly, and distinctly dead, meaning that the other, the others, is what also might not wait for me to be dead to do it, to dispose of my remains: the other might bury me alive, eat me or swallow me alive, burn me alive, etc." In short, he concludes, "He or she can put me to a living death, and exercise his or her sovereignty."[20] To the extent to which the other is the one who in principle may survive me—the one who may inherit my remains in this way or that and who will therefore be in a position to dispose of them as he or she sees fit—that other is defined by this very potentiality even before my actual death; the other is the other precisely because he or she or it is endowed with this sovereignty.

Taking part in my own demise or decline, as Strauß's autobiographical meditations propose, prepares me for joining the world of the others, who will dispose of my remains after my departure. I, living in a world among these other others, which is to say, an other to the others but also just one other among many other others—come to confront my survivance in and through (its) otherness. If this movement names something like a structural law, the act also is disputed precisely because the outcome of this process, the work of the others—*and mine among them*—is anything but settled. Its future remains as enigmatic as its *Herkunft*, which is why one's troubled origins, and the particular being-in-the-world to which they gave rise, demands to be reexamined and questioned always one more time—as if the survival of its survivance depended on it.

*

This resolutely other-directed, survivance-oriented engagement with the world of troubled origins that subtends Strauß's *Herkunft* reemerges in, yet is modulated differently throughout, the French writer and sociologist Didier Eribon's 2009 confessional text *Retour à Reims* (translated into English in 2013 as *Returning to Reims*). Following the death of his father, Eribon returns to his hometown of Reims in order to revisit, and to reflect upon, his origins in a working class environment, a world upon which he had turned his back some three decades earlier. Like Strauß on the other side of the Rhine, Eribon returns to the world of his modest childhood following a prolific career as a well-known European writer and intellectual. Eribon's reflections convene with Strauß's in the sense that they, too, are animated by the insight that certain "possibilities" and "identifications remain in the self as one of its constitutive elements. Whatever you have uprooted yourself from or been uprooted from still endures as an integral part of who you are."[21] There can be no clear break, no fully accomplished departure, from that with which one parts, because that with which one parts remains alive in the self as a foil against which the new or different life can be recognized as such. No life that has dramatically changed could be experienced as such in the absence of a measuring stick—the world of a previous life—against which it could be judged as different in the first place. In order to become what it is, and to affirm what it is, the life of a self remains suffused—in either tacit or explicit ways—by what it is no longer and what it believed itself to have turned its back on or overcome once and for all. Returning to a previous lifeworld, Eribon thus suggests, "you are somehow turning back upon yourself, returning to yourself, rediscovering an earlier self that has been both preserved and denied," as if it were subject to a Hegelian *Aufhebung*, the sublation that both sustains and erases at the same time. No such return can come to pass without a certain unease, a persistent anxiety, "specifically the discomfort that results from belonging to two different worlds, worlds so far separated from each other that they seem irreconcilable, and yet which coexist in everything that you are."[22] The narrating self that revisits the world of its troubled origins becomes visible as the site upon which the incompatible and conflicting forces that constitute a self and the history of its worlds are revealed. The Nietzschean question of how one becomes what one is poses—even exposes—itself most dramatically when a self that has specifically disowned a previous dimension of its past self-consciously returns to visit this disenfranchised realm of its being-in-the-world.

In the case of Eribon, this disavowed world of the self's history is first and foremost his family of origin and its situatedness—topographically, culturally, emotionally, and intellectually—in the working-class milieu of Reims. "When I returned to Reims," the writer confesses, "I was confronted by the following question, a tenacious one I had not acknowledged (at least I had not acknowledged it in my written work, or in my life)." The question is that of his class belonging (or nonbelonging). And Eribon proceeds to specify: "[M]y point of theoretical departure—by which I mean establishing a framework for thinking about myself, my past, and my present—[was] the seemingly obvious idea that the complete break I had made with my family" appeared not only to be grounded in its "deeply rooted homophobia" but also needed to be considered in light of the idea "that this was just as much a break with the class background I came from."[23] It is almost as though the remarkable break with the world of his troubled origins that the narrator performs, a break that had led him to reinvent himself in complete separation from his family of origin and his class milieu, could be explained and understood only as a double renunciation, in this particular case, of the intertwined trajectories of sexuality and class. Therefore, one of the central concerns of Eribon's relentless attempt to tell his life to himself, as Nietzsche would put it, is precisely the question of why, in the course of what, with Derrida, one might term his survivance, Eribon has found it more difficult to engage with his troubled origins in the world of the French working class than with other aspects of his being-in-the-world, including his life as a gay intellectual. He reveals:

On thinking the matter through, it doesn't seem exaggerated to assert that my coming out of the sexual closet, my desire to assume and assert my homosexuality, coincided within my personal trajectory with my shutting myself up inside what I might call a class closet. I mean by this that I took on the constraints imposed by a different kind of dissimulation; I took on a different kind of dissociative personality or double consciousness (with the same kind of mechanisms familiar from the sexual closet: various subterfuges to cover one's tracks, a very small set of friends who know the truth but keep it secret, the taking up of different registers of discourse in different situations and

with different interlocutors, a constant self-surveillance as
regards one's gestures, one's intonation, manners of speech,
so that nothing untoward slips out, so that one never betrays
oneself, and so on).[24]

If Eribon reflects on his previous inability to come out of what in
the English version of his narrative is called the class closet—what
in the French original he names "un placard social"[25]—it is because
of the double consciousness of belonging to a French intellectual
and social elite and, at the same time, having his origins firmly
but uneasily in the classical French working class, a class that,
throughout his narrative, he simultaneously defends and despises.
This abiding double consciousness names a mode of being-in-the-
world that cannot be easily reconciled with the requirements of
what one might traditionally call a particular identity. In fact, as
the narrative gives us to understand more than once, the author is
troubled by the idea of belonging to the category of "class traitor,"
even though "certain class reflexes persist despite all our efforts
to separate ourselves from our social origins, even those efforts
aimed at personal transformation." Beyond even the specter of
being considered a class traitor, Eribon is disturbed, when narrating his life to himself, by the concern that he, too, may give in to
certain "hasty and disdainful opinions" expressed by an intellectual ruling class with regard to working-class others, even to what
"we might as well call class racism." As he therefore emphasizes,
"Every time I would 'betray' my own childhood, by sharing in
deprecatory opinions, inevitably a nagging bad conscience would
make itself felt, if not sooner, then later."[26] To the extent that the
fear of class racism imposes itself on a consciousness telling itself
its own life, its troubled origins survive in the experience of its
own being-in-the-world in the guise of a betrayal, a tacit or willed
renunciation of what first gave rise to a particular consciousness.
To become what it is, this consciousness has been compelled to
disarticulate the world of its origins, to distance itself from the
very trajectory that its life had taken, to fashion itself anew—on
its own terms and within the framework provided by a previously
unknown elsewhere. In Eribon's case, there can be no survival
of the self, and certainly no Derridean survivance, without this

perpetual engagement with the dual specters of returning and disowning one more time.

This doubled movement of revisiting and disavowing also names a more general structure of spectrality that permeates Eribon's engagement with the world of his troubled origins as a whole. Such spectrality expresses itself in the multiple ghosts that haunt his text as well as in the perpetual mournfulness that inflects it at almost every turn. One of the most striking instantiations of this structure of haunting takes the form of Eribon's dying and, eventually, deceased father, from whom he had been estranged for decades. His father, who suffers from, and then dies of, Alzheimer's disease, inhabits a ghostly world of anxiety. The "news of my father's condition," Eribon recalls, "had provoked in me a huge attack of anxiety. Not really so much for him—it was too late, and in any case, I felt very little towards him, not even compassion. Rather, selfishly, I was worried about myself. Was this a hereditary condition? Would it soon be my turn?" This "obsession," he confesses, persists to the very moment of recording his reflections on his troubled origins, so that "daily life is now haunted by Alzheimer's—a ghost arriving from the past in order to frighten me by showing me what is still to come." In this spectral form, Eribon's "father remains present in my existence. It seems a strange way indeed for someone who has died to survive within the brain—the very place in which the threat is located—of one of his sons." He therefore reminds his readers of how "Lacan writes remarkably ... of this door that opens onto anxiety for children, or at least for sons, at the moment of their father's death, for then the son finds himself on the front lines of facing death alone." The experience of the ghostly disease from which Eribon's father suffered "adds a more ordinary, day-to-day kind of fear of this ontological anxiety: you are always on the lookout for symptoms, ready to turn them into a diagnosis."[27] The ghostly dimensions of one's troubled origins always make themselves felt both on an ontological level and an experiential one. In fact, Derrida might evoke here, as he does in *Specters of Marx*, a *hantologie*, in which, at least in spoken French, the ontological and the hauntological cannot be differentiated.[28] The ghost of the father returns to the narrating self both as the paternal other and as the future demise of the speaking subject, so that the haunting effected by the world of one's troubled origins is always plural, always multiple, always multidirectional.

It is for this reason, too, that the temporality of the haunting experienced by the narrating self cannot be reduced to the movement of a single directionality. As Eribon thus emphasizes, "my life is not only haunted by the future; there are also the ghosts of my own past, ghosts which leapt into view immediately upon the death of the person who incarnated everything I wanted to run away from, everything I wanted to break with."[29] In facing one's troubled origins and in giving oneself over to a kind of survivance, one cannot coax the coalition of specters into remaining tied to an unsaturated futurity or to a lost past. On the contrary, the specters come to visit the narrating self in a world and in a time that are at odds with themselves, always out of joint and always differently situated. What one may call the present of (re-)lived experience—that is, the experience of engaging one's troubled origins in sustained reflection—rests never simply with itself but rather is subject to an uneasy haunting both from what has already come to pass and from what is yet to come, imagined or real. Specters of the past join forces with specters of the future such that the narrating self cannot easily experience them as discrete visitors hailing from specific and circumscribed moments in time. Instead, these specters are anteriority and futurity at the same time. Like the legions of old family photographs that Eribon peruses with his mother one memorable day—images of a time that no longer seems securely anchored in any one place or temporality alone—the specters of one's troubled origins come to visit in aleatory modes according to invisible itineraries that nevertheless make us who we are.

While Derrida's notion of survivance figures as an experience that is always intertwined, directly or indirectly, with a basic mood of mourning, a nameless grief over an actual or anticipated absence or loss, Eribon in *Retour à Reims* articulates a mood of mourning through differently inflected terms. The account of his troubled origins is permeated by the mourning of a distressed childhood, irrevocable alienation from the world of his class background, and a perpetual inability to confront the repressions that first made his self-creation as an intellectual and academic possible, among other things. In the course of the text's unfolding, Eribon's manner of mourning—which is also to say his inability to mourn—the death of his father emerges as the most complex feature of this account. It is therefore no accident that Eribon self-consciously contrasts his own experience of his father's death with Barthes's account of his infinite grief over his beloved mother's death, memorably described in Barthes's posthumously published *Mourning Diary* as pure suffering.[30] Eribon, however, casts the experience of his own father's death in largely opposing terms:

> In the days that followed his death, I set to thinking about my childhood, about my adolescence, about all the reasons that had led me to hate the man who had just died and whose end, along with the unexpected emotions it had provoked in me, woke in my memory so many things I had forgotten. (Or perhaps I had known on some level that I hadn't forgotten them, even if I had made an effort, a quite conscious one, to repress them.) Some people might remark that this is something that happens during any period of mourning. It might even be said to be a universal feature of mourning, an essential characteristic of it, especially when it is parents who are being mourned. Even if that is the case, I had a strange way of experiencing it: a kind of mourning in which the urge to understand something about the person who had passed away and something about the person— myself—who has survived predominates over any sadness. Other losses, earlier ones, had affected me more deeply and caused me much deeper distress. ... My relationship with my father seemed to me to be only a biological and legal one: he had fathered me, and I bore his name, but other than that he didn't matter much to me. ... What, then, was going on? A state of confusion and disarray, perhaps, produced by something being called into question, something both personal and political, something about one's social destiny, about the way society is divided into classes, about the role played by a number of different social determinants in the constitution of individual subjectivities, something to do with individual psychologies, with the relations that exist between individuals.[31]

Unlike Barthes, whose interminable mourning over his mother's death gives rise to the melancholy beauty of his *Mourning Diary*, and unlike Kafka, whose letter to his father evokes an infinitely fraught and estranged yet deeply connected and persistent relation, Eribon focuses on the indifference and the modes of disavowal that characterize his relation to his deceased father, such that the mourning of his dead parent is not allowed to take its typical course but is aborted in the name of uneasy reflection and probing questioning. Eribon's inability to mourn propels him to refuse to attend his father's funeral, and he has "no desire" to reconnect "with his brothers again, having been out of touch with them for thirty years."[32] More is at stake here than Eribon's disappointment over the fact that his family has left the Communist Party to join the ranks of France's far-right Front National (since June 2018 known as the *Rassemblement national*, or National Rally), a move that serves to alienate him even more decisively from the world of his youth. The mourning that permeates Eribon's account of his troubled origins emerges as a particular mode of living on, as a radical survivance, that is inseparable from that which refuses itself to mourning. Here, mourning does not stand in opposition to melancholia—in the sense in which Freud differentiates between, on the one hand, the supposedly healthy activity of mourning that manages to divest libidinal energy from the lost object in order to free itself for future engagement, and, on the other hand, the experience of melancholia in which the subject remains perpetually unable to move forward following the experience of loss—due to an incapacity to mourn. Just as the German psychoanalysts Alexander and Margarete Mitscherlich in 1967 diagnosed what they memorably called an "Unfähigkeit zu trauern," an inability to mourn, in Germany's post-World War II culture—that is, an inability to mourn the unspeakable crimes and traumatic losses associated with the then-recent past—so Eribon's inability to mourn his father's death opens onto a cultural and collective perspective in which supposedly private acts of grief cannot be thought in isolation from the larger systemic frameworks and ideologico-political premises in which they always also take place, their larger situatedness in the world of a particular cultural episteme.[33]

To the extent that Eribon's engagement with his troubled origins is always inflected by the language of mourning in unpredictable ways, moving along paths that do not conform exclusively to this or that experience of loss, it could be brought into syntactical relation with Derrida's confessional reflections in *Monolingualism of the Other; or: The Prosthesis of Origin* (first published in French in 1996), in which he confronts his own troubled origins as an Algerian Jew growing up in a French colonial setting. There, by way of examining the myriad ways in which one can interpret the idea that he speaks only one language, French, without being able to call that language his own, Derrida evokes a certain generalized mourning that cannot be contained by any one feature of his experience. Rather, it must be thought in relation to the multiple disorders of identity, the numerous mechanisms that for him make identity—in and as language, but also a structural feature of being—impossible. He asks: "How does one orient the inscription of self *in proximity* to this forbidden language, and not simply in it, in proximity to it, like a complaint lodged next to it, a grievance and, already, an appellant procedure?" If such "an inscription could not be oriented," in Derrida's case, "from the space and time of spoken *mother tongue*, because I had none, precisely, none other than French," this means that he "had no language for the grievance, a word that I love to hear now in English, in that it signifies, additionally, a complaint without accusation, suffering and mourning." This valence of the *without* (*sans*) calls into presence the necessity "to think about an almost originary grievance here, because it is not even lamenting a loss: I did not, *to my knowledge*, have anything to lose, other than French, the bereaved [*endeuilée*] language of bereavement." This suggests that in "grievance like this, one takes on lastingly [*à demeure*] a mourning for what one never had."[34] In this originary, primordial mourning, one does not mourn the absence or loss of this or that particular object, person, idea, or experience, but rather affirms through grievance one's relation to what was never one's own, never a mere possession or personal property. To speak the language of mourning and bereavement, it is not always necessary to respond to loss, that is, to the absence of a former presence, or rather, as in the case of Derrida's absent mother tongue, to the French language that is all he has without even possessing it in the conventional sense. In this way, a mourning imposes itself that files a grievance, as it were, over the departure of something that was never fully present and transparently available in the first place. One might say that, like the void that marks Derrida's marginal otherness in relation to the center of the French language and to French culture itself, Eribon's narrative of returning to his troubled origins is saturated with an originary grievance, a language of mourning that bespeaks a bereavement beyond all loss, a mournful longing for what was never his to begin with. While his father's death in itself cannot coax his mourning into presence, Eribon nevertheless composes sentences that, in creating a textually mediated world, never fail to be touched by an originary grievance, a mourning of troubled origins that can never be relieved or undone.

One of the abiding questions that is inscribed in all of Eribon's sentences concerns the particular manner in which his acts of survivance manifest themselves to the world of the narrative self in the moment of their articulation. These acts of survivance cannot be reduced to a form of working through, a method for coming to terms with an irretrievable past. Rather, they tacitly return us to some of Nietzsche's reflections in *Ecce Homo*, a book that Eribon mentions, albeit only in passing. While Eribon does not explicitly invoke this moment in Nietzsche's text, one might conjecture, in light of Eribon's characterization of his unlikely success in the educational system as "a miracle case,"[35] that he would concur with Nietzsche's "proposition that everything decisive comes about 'in spite of,'" as *Ecce Homo* has it. But matters appear to be different when it comes to Nietzsche's thinking of *amor fati*, a concept that he had first introduced in his *Fröhliche Wissenschaft*. In *Ecce Homo*, Nietzsche speaks of *amor fati* as a "formula for greatness," in the sense "that one wants nothing to be other than it is, not in the future, not in the past, not in all eternity. Not merely to endure that which happens of necessity, still less to dissemble it—all idealism is untruthfulness in the face of necessity—but to *love* it."[36] What is at stake in Nietzsche's thinking of the *amor fati* is neither a form of resignation nor a self-sacrificing mode of accommodating within oneself what cannot be changed; it is neither a subjugation of the self to sheer necessity nor a way of making one's troubled life more bearable by accepting its unyielding dictates. On the contrary, Nietzsche is thinking of an affirmation of one's fate, an active confirmation and even love of what one did not ask for and what cannot be changed. Rather than wishing for an aspect of one's life to be different—and to suffer from the anxiety and likely disappointment that attach to such a desire—Nietzsche endorses a complete identification and tender appreciation of one's fate, even its seemingly dark or uncomfortable sides, its shortcomings and inevitable frustrations. To reflect deeply and successfully on how one becomes what one is, Nietzsche suggests, means to learn to love one's fate and to affirm it without reserve. Even if one's life ends in failure, it would then be a successful failure in the sense that one has succeeded at failing; one has failed successfully and in complete affirmation and conviction—one has "failed better," as Beckett would say.

While Strauß's reflections on his complex origins in *Herkunft* might lend themselves more readily to a Nietzschean insistence on a certain *amor fati*—in which, as in *Herkunft*, one embraces the world of one's origins, one's home, one's family with a certain gesture of affirmation and love of a seemingly unchangeable fate— Eribon's stance in relation to the world of his own troubled origins implicitly draws its strength from a refusal to accept, much less to affirm, both what is and what has come to be precisely as it is. Eribon's *Retour à Reims* pivots on a perpetual shuttling between worlds, the modest and troublesome working-class environment of his family of origin and his self-created second life as a well-known French writer and intellectual. A return to Reims always also means a return to a previous fate that the narrating self could never have accepted, much less loved in the sense of a Nietzschean affirmation without reserve. If we may permit ourselves to open our ears to a phonetically inflected paronomasia situated between Latin and German, there can be no *amor fati* for Eribon, just as little as there can be, for him, any *amor "Vati"* (the love of one's father). The activity of "returning" in Eribon's sense thus always also implies an engagement with nonaffirmation, rejection, and difference; neither the world of a current life nor that of a previous life nor the trajectory between the two is to be confirmed or loved but rather preserved as the contours of an abiding question mark.

A reflection toward the end of his narrative of troubled origins provides readers with a hint concerning Eribon's orientation in this regard: "To take determinisms into account is not the same as affirming that nothing can change," even though he also has come to understand that "we should not be dreaming of some kind of impossible 'emancipation.' Our best hope will be to breach certain frontiers that history has put into place and that hem in our existence."[37] These historical frontiers that enclose and confine our being-in-the world may be anything but natural or self-evident, but they are nevertheless real. Any gesture of thinking that works to breach the world of these historically grown frontiers must rely, for its strength and promise, on the realization that precisely this ontic facticity cannot simply be wished away or denied as merely phantasmagorical. If Eribon's project of self-fashioning and world-creation must, at some point along the protracted and winding path of its development, also take into account its own genealogical inscriptions—including its troubled origins—it strives to become readable as an act of survivance in which its very modes of living on become themselves the topic of sustained, open-ended reflection and unforeclosed lived experience.

*

The self that returns to itself when it seeks to return to the world of its troubled origins, to the constellation—idiomatic or generally shared—of its *Herkunft*, returns to *itself as irreducibly other*. If this self survives as a form of consciousness that narrates its life to itself—which is always also to say, to itself as an other—then its modalities of living on are touched by a certain survivance in which the specters of its origins reconvene with the specters of the lived experience of its present moment, the scene of writing. Writers such as Strauß and Eribon self-consciously allow their prose to open onto the rhetorical and experiential dimensions of these insights; their pages and sentences live on precisely to the extent that they expose themselves to this otherness of the world inflected by their troubled origins. Derrida's reflections in *Monolingualism of the Other* help us to cast further light on this state of affairs. There, reflecting on the world of his own troubled origins, he emphasizes that his text is "not the beginning of some autobiographical or anamnestic outline, nor even a timid essay toward an intellectual bildungs-roman." On the contrary, rather "than an exposition of myself, it is an account of what will have placed an obstacle in the way of this auto-exposition for me. An account, therefore, of what will have exposed me to that obstacle" as if it were "a serious traffic accident about which I never cease thinking."[38] One might say that this obstacle, along with all the unexpected shapes it may assume in the course of one's writing and one's intellectual and experiential trajectory, is precisely what demands to be confronted when one attempts to provide an account of oneself, especially in relation to the idea of troubled origins and the world that they set up through a work. Neither Strauß's *Herkunft* nor Eribon's *Retour à Reims* can become textual records of survivance without also granting visibility to that which makes all origins and all returns to this or that world resistant to any form of identification, of subjective identity-formation. Strauß and Eribon, each in his own way, provide textual testimony of a certain disarticulation of identity, even as they are operative within the realm of a movement of identification.

One might say that both Strauß and Eribon have taken to heart the epigrammatically condensed assessment of identity that Adorno, the thinker of radical nonidentity, memorably advances, in rather apodictic terms, in *Negative Dialectics*: "Identity is the primal form of ideology [*Identität ist die Urform von Ideologie*]."[39] In order to hold this form of ideology at bay, it is incumbent upon the thinking and writing self to renounce (its) identity and, from time to time, to lose itself completely. In the section "The Wanderer and His Shadow" from *Human, All Too Human: A Book for Free Spirits*, Nietzsche therefore makes it a point to include a reflection on strategic self-loss. Under the heading "Losing Oneself," he reflects: "Once one has found oneself one must understand how from time to time to lose oneself and then how to find oneself again: sup-posing, that is, that one is a thinker [*vorausgesetzt, dass man ein Denker ist*]. For to the thinker it is disadvantageous to be tied to One Person all the time [*an Eine Person gebunden zu sein*]."[40] The vagaries and unpredictabilities of true thinking do not fit within the par-adigm of identity. To have an identity is but the precondition for letting it go so that the one who thinks, or wishes to learn how to think—the *Denker*—is freed from the burden of being bound to a Oneness and a self-sameness. The thinker, renouncing identity and self-identity, is always more than one, always thinking, writing, and speaking in more than one voice and from more than one standpoint at the same time. The experience of nonidentity is the thinking unraveling of the One.

The stories that Strauß and Eribon tell therefore evoke the world of a survivance that can never be reduced to the survival of this or that moment of identity, to an affirmation of this or that ipseity or undisturbed, self-identical belonging. As Derrida suggests in his own confessional modes of returning to the troubled origins of his Algerian youth:

> In its common concept, autobiographical anamnesis presupposes *identification*. And precisely not identity. No, an identity is never given, received, or attained; only the interminable and indefinitely phantasmatic process of identification endures. Whatever the story of a return to oneself or to *one's home* [*chez-soi*], into the "hut" ["case"] of one's home (*chez* is the *casa*), no matter what an odyssey or bildungsroman it might be, in whatever manner one invents the story of a construction of the *self*, the *autos*, or the *ipse*, it is always *imagined* that the one who writes should know how to say *I*. At any rate, the *identificatory modality* must already or henceforth be assured: assured of language and in its language. … It is necessary to know already in what language *I* is expressed, and I *am* expressed. … It never precedes them [the different ways of uttering it]; therefore it is not independent of language in general.[41]

The language that always already precedes any self that would seek to utter itself, that is, a self that would confront the world of its troubled origins—for instance, by reflecting on its *Herkunft* or by returning to its former home—would have to expose itself to its own survivance. This type of exposure would come to pass in any text that self-consciously offers hospitality toward potential forms of survivance. Such hospitality to the language that precedes and exceeds any writing, speaking, and thinking self would have to show itself responsible to, among many other things, the relentless demand that it work through its own moments of nonidentity. In other words, its movements of retreat from transparency and unproblematic communication would have to be inscribed in the very language of its textual acts. This language would seek to do justice to the idea that there is no stable, given identity even—and especially—for the self in textual search of its troubled origins, even as the self's imaginary process of identification persists unabated. Identity versus identification, then. Even while there is no given and reassured identity, no belonging to this or that form of ipseity, there *cannot not* be a process of identification that strives, however phantasmatically and aberrantly, toward possible forms of identity. The longing for identification persists long after the ideas of identity and self-identity have been bid farewell. If there is a kind of survivance to be espied in such textual acts of confronting the world of one's troubled origins—by posing one more time Nietzsche's question as to how one becomes what one is—such survivance would have to travel through a language that unfolds on the far side of any conventional identity-thinking. By the same token, this language could never simply shuck the conceptual allure and the rhetorical temptation powerfully exerted by the seductive processes of identification. Strauß and Eribon, each in his own idiomatic confrontation with the world of his troubled origins, implore us to ask—and, by extension, to begin to imagine—just what such textual acts of creative and commemorative survivance imply for a thinking to come. What kind of world will be set up?

Keep Yourself Alive: The World of Life Death and The Work of Mourning (Derrida, Nietzsche, Kafka)

Let us beware.—Let us beware of thinking that the world is
a living being. Where should it expand? On what should
it feed? ... Let us beware of saying that death is opposed
to life. The living is merely a type of what is dead, and a
very rare type.

—Nietzsche, The Gay Science

If the work of art bears witness to a world that is constantly disappearing while simultaneously commenting on that retreat through its own aesthetic acts of world-construction, one might say that the work of art is always also a work of mourning. To insist on the dimension of the work of art that can be named a work of mourning means to exploit this genitive construction in a double sense: it conjures both the image of a work that thematizes mourning—which is to say that it takes mourning as the subject matter of its aesthetic form—and the sense in which the work itself performs a certain mourning, staging the movement of grieving in the very constitution of the artwork, regardless of its ostensible subject matter. Irrespective of whether mourning is explicitly "depicted" in the work of art—as is the case, for instance, in such masterpieces as Masaccio's early Renaissance fresco *The Expulsion of Adam and Eve from Eden;* Albrecht Dürer's oil painting *Die Beweinung Christi* (*The Lamentation of Christ,* also known as *Glimsche Beweinung,*

235

after the Nürnberg goldsmith Albrecht Glim, who commissioned the work around 1500 to honor his beloved departed wife Margret); William Wetmore Story's well-known 1894 sculpture commemorating his wife, *The Angel of Grief Weeping over the Dismantled Altar of Life*; or, indeed, many of the images by Andrew Moore discussed in chapter 6—the work is suffused by the traces of a mourning that is mobilized to construct mourning itself *as* a new world, that is, as a world of mourning. The artwork mourns a world that is perishing or already has perished, while self-consciously infusing the world that it in turn sets up with a sustained reflection on the experience of grief. One may even say that within the orbit of the aesthetic artifact, the work of mourning is a world of mourning and vice versa.

To appreciate how the work of mourning becomes visible or audible as a world of mourning within aesthetic form, it behooves us to be perpetually mindful of the multiple ways in which mourning insinuates itself into the world of our artworks—even, and especially, the ones that strike us as being among the most beautiful. If, as David Farrell Krell rightly reminds us, "even the happiest song, the most rollicking painted scene, the most exalted edifice, and the most harmoniously constructed piazza induce mourning," this is because the "pain of undecidable mourning is the birth pang of all that will have come to be, of all that is beautiful in everything that was." Here, the "most powerful *presence* of a beautiful thing, the commanding stature and status of a statue, for example, wields its power in and as *withdrawal* and *absence*."[1] Such an intimation of a future withdrawal and absence, even within the moment of a deeply felt aesthetic experience, signals the powerful disruption of any presence—a disruption that bears as one of its most significant designations the name of mourning.

To consider the ways in which the work of mourning stages a world of mourning through the aesthetic object, it is helpful to recall Benjamin's reflections from his early text "The Role of Language in Trauerspiel and Tragedy," composed in 1916. There he suggests that "mourning [*Trauer*] is not, like the tragic, a ruling force, the indissoluble and inescapable law of orders that attain closure in the tragedy; rather, it is a feeling." Benjamin continues: "What metaphysical relation does this feeling have to language, to

236

the spoken word? ... What inner relation at the heart of mourning releases it from the existence of pure feeling and lets it enter the order of art?" In other words, the question of how "language in general can fill itself with mourning" so that it can "be the expression of mourning" figures as "the basic question of the trauerspiel, alongside that other question: How can mourning as a feeling gain entry into the linguistic order of art?"[2] To consider how mourning can make itself felt in and as the language of a work—a tragedy, a mourning play, or, indeed, another aesthetic configuration such as a painting, a sculpture, or a work of literature or music—requires being attentive to the multiple inscriptions an affect undergoes as it enters the realm of artistic presentation. The world out of which the artwork arose and which has since perished, along with the aesthetically mediated world to which the artwork in turns gives rise, call into presence an engagement with the language of mourning that will not cease to make itself felt in the aesthetic artifact. If the issue at stake is how language can fill itself with mourning, as Benjamin suggests, then the question arises as to how the world that the artwork assembles on its own terms is itself filled with mourning, that is, how it shows itself hospitable to the traces of the work of mourning that structure an experience of a world that is constantly changing and perpetually perishing into its own finitude, even oblivion.

Reflecting on the artwork as a work of mourning in the double sense, then, means being attuned to the multiple and intricate ways in which that which calls for mourning—the loss that is named by finitude or death—already inhabits any and every world that is ascribed to the living. Death here inhabits life (as preliminary traces of an irreducible future finitude), while certain spectral forms of life in turn inhabit death (in the form of an inheritance of sorts, in which the dead live on through the language of legacies, lingering among and haunting the world of the living in often invisible, yet therefore all the more powerful, ways). Understood as a work of mourning, the artwork thus not only commemorates the perished world from which it arises, nor does it exclusively construct a world of its own. It also stages itself as a form of survival, a mode of living on that inhabits the mournful space situated somewhere between life and death.[3]

This mournful space of survival, unfolding in the interstices of life and death, permeates the work of art at any given moment. Indeed, there could hardly be an artwork, including the literary work, without a sustained engagement with this space. As the poet Rainer Maria Rilke writes to Mimi Romanelli on December 8, 1907: "There is death in life, and it astonishes me that we pretend to ignore this: death, whose unforgiving presence we experience with each change we survive because we must learn to die slowly. We must learn to die: That is all of life."[4] And he adds, looking back on his life as a writer: "It is this idea of death which has developed inside of me since childhood from one painful experience to the next, and which compels me humbly to endure the small death, so that I may become worthy of the one which wants us to be great."[5] If the poet here equates the process of learning how to die with life itself (even with a life that is inhabited by death and therefore is not merely an other to death), he silently interlaces the aesthetic mode of survival that is germane to the artist with the conceptual activity of the philosopher who is learning how to die. Ever since Plato, becoming a philosopher has meant learning how to die, and Rilke intuits with great clarity that the same could be said of becoming a poet—or any kind of genuine artist. In Plato's *Phaedo*, we hear the interlocutors examine the proposition that "ordinary people seem not to realize that those who really apply themselves in the right way to philosophy are directly and of their own accord preparing themselves for death."[6] One may think also, for instance, of Seneca's masterful prose work, the *Moral Epistles*, written as letters addressed to his intimate friend Lucilius and containing extensive philosophical reflections on studying, and preparing for, death.[7] Montaigne, among others, takes up this idea in his *Essays*, where essay number 20 is devoted to the idea "That to Philosophize Is to Learn to Die."[8] Akin to the movement by which learning to become a philosopher means learning how to die, the world of mourning constructed by a poetic text or artwork is but one station, albeit a significant one, in the process of learning how to die—that is, learning how to live as a mournful survivor while affirming the blurred demarcation between life and death.

In his final interview, given shortly before his death—and thus, as it were, already between life and death and in a mode and mood of anticipatory self-mourning—Derrida worries that he has in a sense failed as a philosopher because he has never properly learned how to die. But he emphasizes that the "theme of survival, the meaning of which is not to be added on to living and dying," deserves to be regarded as "originary," which is to say that "life *is* living on, life *is* survival [*la vie* est *survie*]." And he continues this thought by evoking a distinction that Benjamin makes in his 1923 essay "The Task of the Translator" between *Überleben* and *Fortleben*:

> To survive in the usual sense of the term means to continue to live, but also to live *after* death. When it comes to translating such a notion, Benjamin emphasizes the distinction between *überleben*, on the one hand, surviving death, like a book that survives the death of its author, or a child the death of his or her parents, and, on the other hand, *fortleben*, living on, continuing to live. All the concepts that have helped me in my work, and notably that of the trace or of the spectral, were related to this "surviving" as a structural and rigorously originary dimension. It is not derived from either living or dying. No more than what I call "originary mourning," that is, a mourning that does not wait for the so-called "actual" death.[9]

To the extent that survival is always originary—rather than being added on after the fact to a life that was previously thought to be something else—and to the extent that mourning also is always originary always already preceding every loss—no work of mourning, and no world constructed by an artwork inflected by mourning, must wait for an empirical death to occur. Rather, *there is* mourning, and there will have been mourning. The world that an artwork sets up when it projects its own aesthetically mediated conception is always already touched by such mourning. This notion of a mournful mode of surviving is confirmed at the very end of the interview, when Derrida avers that this "surviving is life beyond life, life more than life, and my discourse is not a discourse of death, but, on the contrary, the affirmation of a living being who prefers living and thus surviving to death, because survival is not simply that which remains but the most intense life possible." If survival, according to this way of thinking, can be conceptualized not as secondary or inferior but rather as the most intense life possible, this is because one is "never more haunted by the necessity of dying than in moments of happiness and joy. To feel joy and to weep over the death that awaits are for me the same thing." And Derrida adds: "When I recall my life, I tend to think that I have had the good fortune to love even the unhappy moments of my life, and to bless them. ... When I recall the happy moments, I bless them too, of course, at the same time as they propel me toward the thought of death, toward death, because all that has passed, come to an end ..."[10] If survival, as *fortleben*, is the most intense form of life, this is because one experiences one's life as touched by death—as something, in other words, that already contains and sustains within itself the anticipatory shadow of its own future demise. Living on while experiencing one's own life, as well as the life of others, as inflected by an impending death means affirming a form of being that cannot but be suffused by a finitude to come, both in what we commonly call its joyful and its sad moments. Such a form of living unfolds on the far side of the distinction between life and death, just as an artwork that may arise out of a perishing world and create another one cannot be reduced to the supposedly opposing notions of life or death alone.

In the previous chapter, we investigated, among other things, Derrida's mobilization—in what would turn out to be his final seminar, the 2002–2003 *The Beast and the Sovereign*—of the neologism *survivance*. We recall how in that late seminar, the term survivance functions as a "middle voice" by means of which it becomes possible to circumvent both the "active voice of the active infinitive 'to survive'" and the "substantializing substantive *survival*" in order to develop the idea of an originary fragile survivance that troubles the conventional binarist thinking of life and death.[11] Our understanding of the late Derrida's engagement with life and death in relation to survivance, and therefore also with mourning, is substantially enhanced by the recent publication of an earlier seminar he gave at the École normale supérieure in Paris between autumn 1975 and late spring 1976 on the topic of "life death." This important seminar was first published, based on Derrida's extensive lecture manuscripts and notes, in French in 2019 (*La vie la*

240

mort. Séminaire [1975–1976]) and in English translation in 2020 (*Life Death*).[12] Among the many remarkable aspects of this early seminar is the way in which Derrida proposes to think the relation between life and death on the far side of their apparent oppositionality. Thus, the "and" included by the academic French authorities in the original title of the course ("Life and Death")—which was meant to prepare French university students rigorously for a competitive national examination on the topic—is removed by Derrida. The strategic removal of this conjunction, which he addresses in the very first session of the seminar, already signals the marching plan for the course as a whole. "By doing away with the *and*," Derrida tells his listeners, "I was trying to intimate not that life death did not form two, or that the one was not the other of the other, but that this alterity or this difference was not of the order of what philosophy calls opposition (*Entgegensetzung*), the double positioning of two facing one another." According to conventional models of opposition, "for example in Hegel, the concept of position and position of the concept, self-positioning and opposition, are the driving schemas of the dialectic."[13] Yet Derrida's suspension of the "and" between life and death has another aim:

> Starting out from this Hegelian identification of life and death from an opposition that proceeds in view of its cancellation in the final identification "being is life," where life is marked twice, once as death (the death process), once as immortal, imperishable, I simply wanted to indicate that the same logic could help to distinguish the various semantic registers of life *and* (*et*) death (where the *and* signifies position, juxtaposition, or op-position) and life *is* (*est*) death, where death defines essence as the dialectical process of life keeping itself as life, producing itself and reproducing itself, etc. So that, by saying, with the blank of a pause or the invisible mark of a beyond, "life death," I am *neither* opposing *nor* identifying life and death (neither *and* [*et*] nor *is* [*est*]), I am neutralizing, as it were, both opposition and identification, in order to gesture not toward another logic, an opposite logic of life and death, but toward another topos, if you will, a topos from which it would be possible to

read, at the very least, the entire program of the *and* and the
is, of the positionality and presence of being, both of these
being effects of "life death."[14]

Life death thus names a call to rethink the relation between life and
death, to reconsider the programs and the forms of oppositional
logic that have worked to situate the two in always already determined positions. The crucial modification that Derrida makes to
the course title, placing the *and* under erasure, thus provides the
impetus for reconsidering a whole paradigm of Western metaphysics, in which the oppositionality—and binary positionality—of life
and death are taken for granted. An examination of these two concepts will yield neither their ultimate identity nor their ultimate
opposition; rather, what is at stake is an interrogation of their ever
shifting and irreducibly enigmatic relation. The finitude named by
death becomes visible as something other than its opposite, the
termination, the truth, or the fulfillment of life. It remains entan-
gled in a conceptual and experiential hybridity, a perpetually movable relation that is named by the notion of life death.

The concept of life death does not merely trouble the oppositionality that is traditionally assumed to obtain between its two
terms, it also calls into question the modes of studying and writing a life that arises from the world in which there is life death.
For instance, in relation to Nietzsche's autobiographical or oto-
biographical writing that stands at the core of the second seminar
session, "Logic of the Living (She the Living)," Derrida asserts that
what "we call life, the thing or object of bio-logy or bio-graphy,
has not only the complication of not being simply opposed to—
as to the contrary—something that would be for it an opposable
ob-ject, namely, death, the thanato-logical or thanato-graphical
over against the bio-logical or bio-graphical."[15] It brings with it,
he argues, the additional complication of refusing to become a
mere object of science and scholarship, an object already constituted and instrumentalizable as an object of conventional scientific inquiry. The concept of life and the living that emerges out of
the world of life death comes to trouble our very understanding of
what an appropriate and sufficiently delimitable object of inquiry
might be in the first place. The lifeworld in which such study could

242

commence is already touched by the post- or nonoppositionality of life death itself.

While Derrida, in the span of the seminar, works through these ideas by means of careful and often labyrinthine readings of such figures as Marx, Nietzsche, Freud, Heidegger, Blanchot, the scholar of epistemology Georges Canguilhem, and the geneticist François Jacob in *Logic of the Living*—in relation to such key concepts as interpretation, metaphor, production, reproduction, program, transition, supplement, and the scientific model—there are several noteworthy moments in the seminar during which he ties his reflections on life death specifically to notions of world, which concern us here. These far-reaching engagements with world from the perspective of life death and its modes of mourning—even when they appear to be offered as if in passing—invite, indeed compel, reflection and commentary.

In the fifth session, entitled "The Indefatigable," Derrida continues to engage with the biological arguments found in Jacob's *Logic of the Living* in order to work through the concepts of production and reproduction as they impose themselves on the idea of life and the living. Showing how producibility is always already reproducibility, he places into conceptual conversation Jacob's arguments about reproducibility and certain of Marx's reflections on the idea of production. In the course of these elucidations, and especially during his discussion of Jacob's arguments concerning being and life as they relate to bacteria and sexuality, Derrida makes the following observation:

> Between what bacteria do—with or without sex, dividing themselves in order to multiply and return to themselves, in order to reproduce themselves by losing themselves, etc.—and what gets done through the question "What is being" (with or without copulation), there is a—a what? I will certainly not say a continuity or homogeneity, or an opposition, since opposition amounts to the same thing— there is the greatest difference in the world, they are worlds apart, as they say, and there is a world if we are to call *world* this unity without totality or homogeneity that nonetheless allows us to think together, according to a logic that is

neither that of the *is* [est] nor that of the *and* [et], neither that of identity nor that of opposition, *différance* (for example, between the contract of the bacterium with itself and the contract of science in its own operations).

Does the emergence within this world of the question *what is?* (and everything that follows upon it) have an essential relation, in some way, with this "invention," to take up again Jacob's term, of sexuality and death, a joint invention that calls forth numerous times the word "supplement" on Jacob's part without the logic or the graphic of the supplement ever being questioned or "produced" for itself, assuming it can ever be produced for itself?[16]

Among the numerous and interwoven conceptual levels on which these remarks resonate, the question of how the idea of life death relates to two different ways of thinking being stands out. On the one hand, there is the activity of bacteria that propels them to divide in order to multiply, and on the other hand there is the very question that inquires "What is being?" If the two are "worlds apart," this is because their relation still remains to be thought, which is to say that it cannot be reduced simply to any of the available forms or patterns of relation, such as continuity or oppositionality. Nevertheless, to consider their relation to one another—indeed, to think their relatededness as such—propels us to think of them as inhabiting a shared world, even if that world is never constituted by the totality of a sameness or the homogenizing framework of unquestioned belonging. Rather, this form of a shared world exposes a world that is at odds with itself, shot through by difference and deferral, and saturated with irreducible singularity. If Derrida includes this reflection on world in his consideration of life death, it is because the notion of life death, too, demands to be thought as coming to pass in a shared world that is nevertheless anything but a totality. This shared world, in which individual elements may still be worlds apart, is "shared" only to the extent that inhabiting it means learning to relate to that which cannot be grasped in any transparent way, to what resists and withdraws from any and all hermeneutic attempts to reduce it to this or that instance of merely stable legibility. The world of life death, just like the world of bacteria, sexual reproduction, and finitude, is at odds with itself, perpetually demanding an interpretive intervention that it nevertheless aborts. The reading and interpretation of such a world are of necessity always yet to come, always a matter of unpredictable futurity. What Derrida says in the second seminar session with respect to the interpretation of Nietzsche ("The future of Nietzsche's text is not closed [*L'avenir du texte de Nietzsche n'est pas clos*]")[17] applies fully as much to the interpretation of such a world: From the perspective of mourning and life death, the future of the world-text is not closed.

Viewed in this light, it appears to be no coincidence that the particular Nietzsche quotations Derrida chooses to explicate in the course of his life death seminar often pertain to the theme of world. Among them are, in the third seminar session—devoted to the topic of "Transition (Oedipus's Faux Pas)"—an unpublished Nietzsche fragment from the period of his *Unzeitgemäße Betrachtungen* that presents itself not only as the soliloquies of Oedipus as the last philosopher but also as stemming "from the History of Posterity (*Nachwelt*)." The German *Nachwelt* may be more literally translated as after-world, the world that comes after: after the fact, after the event or experience, after life death. This *Nachwelt* stands to be inherited by those who follow after, by all heirs of Oedipus.[18] It is from the perspective of this anticipated *Nachwelt* that Nietzsche's Oedipus addresses himself by stating: "I call myself the last philosopher because I am the last man. I myself am the only one who speaks with me, and my voice comes to me as the voice of someone who is dying. ... Do I still hear you, my voice? You whisper when you curse. And yet your curse should cause the bowels of this world to burst!"[19] Oedipus's speech act of self-address thus announces itself from the perspective of an anticipatory mourning of world-loss, a world-loss that simultaneously gives rise to the lamenting thought of a *Nachwelt* that no longer will contain the voice of the speaking self and thus must be addressed in the present tense as if through a propospopeia, the voice of an absent or dead speaker.

This mournful mode of addressing the world or after-world is taken up again by Nietzsche in another fragment, included in the constellation of texts that have come to be known under the misleading title *The Will to Power*, which Derrida cites at a later point in the third seminar session. There, the speaking voice addresses the notion of world in the following terms:

> And do you know what "the world" is to me? Shall I show it to you in my mirror? This world: a monster of energy, without beginning, without end; a firm, iron magnitude of force that does not grow bigger or smaller, that does not expend itself but only transforms itself; as a whole, of unalterable size, a household without expenses or losses, but likewise without increase or income; enclosed by "nothingness" as by a boundary. ... Do you know at present what *the world* is for me? And what I want when I want *this world*?—do you want a name for this world? A *solution* for all its riddles? A light for you, too, you best-concealed, strongest, most intrepid, most midnightly men?—*This world is the will to power—and nothing besides*! And you yourselves are also this will to power—and nothing besides![20]

Although Derrida does not directly address the notion of world as it emerges in Nietzsche's passage—focusing instead on the question of relation for which the customary logic of relation is hardly sufficient, especially as it regulates the relation between life and death—one may say that Nietzsche's world here has everything to do with life death and the mourning with which it is imbricated. If the world here is depicted as a monster of energy that knows neither beginning nor end, and if it is enclosed by the nothing of a nothingness, this is in part because the life death that suffuses it propels those who share this world to mourn its retreat from transparency and availability. The rhetorical questions that the speaking voice in Nietzsche's text mobilizes circle around such a mourning of world, a world that cannot be understood without also interpreting it in light of the monstrosity that it also is.

A new shade of light is thrown onto Nietzsche's world when Derrida quotes, at the end of the seventh seminar session, a passage from Heidegger's two-volume work *Nietzsche*. Here again, the idea of world in relation to life death is at issue. Heidegger's passage, as cited by Derrida, reads:

246

What stands in view? We reply: The world in its collective character (*in ihrem Gesamtcharakter*). What all pertains to that? The whole of inanimate and animate existence (*das Ganze des Leblosen und des Lebendigen*), whereby "animate" encompasses not only plants and animals but human beings as well. ... Is the unity of that nexus "living" or "lifeless"? Nietzsche writes (XII, number 112): "Our whole world is the ashes [*Asche* is underscored] of countless *living* creatures: and even if the living seems so miniscule in comparison to the whole, it is nonetheless the case that *everything* [*alles* is underscored] has already been transposed into life—and so it goes." Apparently opposed to this is a thought expressed in *The Gay Science* (number 109): "Let us beware of saying that death is the opposite (*entgegengesetzt sei*) of life; the living creature is simply a kind of dead creature, and a very rare kind."[21]

While Derrida ends the seventh session by reading this quotation out loud, he returns to Heidegger's *Nietzsche* in the eighth session, entitled "Cause (Nietzsche)," and to the possible significance of the ending of this particular passage in the ninth session, "Of Interpretation." Derrida works his way through a discussion of the relation between life death and biologism, through the question of interpreting Nietzsche, and the problem of interpretation as such. Bracketing these far-reaching concerns, what one may register in the specific context of our focus here—the question of world and the problem of mourning life death—is Nietzsche's insistence, quoted by Heidegger and, through him, by Derrida, on an inherited world of ruin and ashes that appears to have transformed its mournful remains into new life forms. One may even say that these new life forms, once they become aware of the ashes from which they have arisen, are placed into the position of mourners who grieve the disappearance and destruction of that which has given rise to them. To find oneself in history—and in the ashes of what it has left behind—is to find oneself the heir of a life death and a perishing that demand to be mourned. To learn to think historically is to learn to mourn.

From this vantage point, Nietzsche's own remark concerning life death—the warning he issues against placing life and death into a merely oppositional relation—can be read as precisely not standing in contradistinction to his remark on the ashes of history being transformed into the living. Just as one needs to be careful not to construct a false binarism between life and death, so one is cautioned by Nietzsche not to espy a simple oppositionality between his one remark and another. For the ashes that are sedimented in the lifeworld of historical existence and that have given rise to life in the present are themselves always already touched by a kind of life death, in which what appears alive within them also is touched by death, while that which was thought dead does in fact live on: in the survivors themselves. The world that is to be mourned thus directs our mourning in more than one direction at once. The work of mourning propels us to commemorate the ashes that have given rise to the living and the living who are in turn the forms of a particular life death, we ourselves among them. Aware of our own life death within the world we share with all other such creatures, we mourn our own rarity, to employ Nietzsche's word, as living dead creatures. The community established upon the ashes of such transience would be a mournful community of the communityless—certainly no place in which the worlds of life and death could ever be fully disentangled.

*

In contemplating how life death and mourning are staged in the world that a literary artwork opens up in accordance with its own singular terms, one may turn to Kafka's posthumously published "Der Jäger Gracchus" ("The Hunter Gracchus"), a title given to the unfinished text by Brod, Kafka's friend and editor. Like so many other philosophers, Derrida was attracted to Kafka and engaged meaningfully with the writer's work, culminating in his seminal lecture and later essay on Kafka's "Before the Law." Yet Derrida appears never to have commented explicitly on "The Hunter Gracchus," even though this text addresses the world of life death and the problem of mourning that are so central to his *Life Death* seminar in striking and memorable ways. This enigmatic material from the early phase of Kafka's late work, consisting of two related fragments on which

248

he worked between December 1916 and April 1917,[22] tells the story of a hunter from the Black Forest region of Germany who supposedly died following a hunting accident but one day unexpectedly arrives on a barge in the "Southern port" of Riva on Lake Garda. In the course of the short work, the mayor of Riva, a man named Salvatore, speaks with Hunter Gracchus about the peculiarities of his undead condition, inviting him to reflect upon his particular form of life death. Salvatore—whose name evokes a redemption that he is in fact unable to grant—reveals to Hunter Gracchus that a dove had appeared at his window the preceding night to announce the hunter's arrival and to prevail upon the mayor to receive the guest on behalf of the town. At this point, Kafka's text reads:

The hunter nodded and drew the tip of his tongue between his lips: "Yes, the doves fly ahead of me. But do you think, Mayor, that I ought to remain in Riva?"

"It's too soon to say," the mayor answered. "Are you dead?"

"Yes," said the hunter, "as you see. Many years ago, indeed it must be an inordinately large number of years ago, I fell off a cliff in the Black Forest—that's in Germany—while hunting a chamois. Since then I've been dead."

"But you're also alive," said the mayor.

"In some sense," said the hunter, "in a sense I'm alive at the same time. My death barge went off course, a wrong turn of the tiller, the momentary inattentiveness of the boatman, a distraction by my beautiful homeland, I don't know what it was, I only know this, that I remained on earth and that since then my barge sails on earthly waters. So I, who wanted only to live in my country's mountains, travel through all the countries on earth after my death."

[…]

"And now you intend to stay with us in Riva?"

"I do no intending," said the hunter with a smile, and to excuse his mockery, he laid his hand on the mayor's knee. "I'm here, that's all I know, that's all I can do. My barge has no tiller, it is driven by the wind that blows in the nethermost regions of death."

Der Jäger nickte und zog die Zungenspitze zwischen den Lippen durch: "Ja die Tauben fliegen vor mir her. Glauben Sie aber Herr Bürgermeister daß ich in Riva bleiben soll?"

"Das kann ich noch nicht sagen", antwortete der Bürgermeister. "Sind Sie tot?"

"Ja", sagte der Jäger, "wie Sie sehen. Vor vielen Jahren, es müssen aber schon ungemein viel Jahre sein, stürzte ich im Schwarzwald, das ist in Deutschland, von einem Felsen, als ich eine Gemse verfolgte. Seitdem bin ich tot."

"Aber Sie leben doch auch?" sagte der Bürgermeister.

"Gewissermaßen", sagte der Jäger, "gewissermaßen lebe ich auch. Mein Todeskahn verfehlte die Fahrt, eine falsche Drehung des Steuers, ein Augenblick der Unaufmerksamkeit des Führers, eine Ablenkung durch meine wunderschöne Heimat, ich weiß nicht was es war, nur daß weiß ich, daß ich auf der Erde blieb und daß mein Kahn seither die irdischen Gewässer befährt. So reise ich, der nur in seinen Bergen leben wollte, nach meinem Tode durch alle Länder der Erde."

[...]

"Und nun gedenken Sie bei uns in Riva zu bleiben?" fragte der Bürgermeister.

"Ich gedenke nicht", sagte der Jäger lächelnd und legte um den Spott gutzumachen die Hand auf das Knie des Bürgermeisters. "Ich bin hier, mehr weiß ich nicht, mehr kann ich nicht tun. Mein Kahn ist ohne Steuer, er fährt mit dem Wind der in den untersten Regionen des Todes bläst."[23]

Kafka's Hunter Gracchus embodies the idea of life death. Unable either to live or to die—that is to say, unable *exclusively* to live or to die—this literary character is acutely conscious of the fact that he is both dead and at the same time alive, and that his perpetual voyage (which has lasted already "an inordinately large number of years," "ungemein viel Jahre," in fact, some 1,500 years) is predicated upon a kind of nonarrival at a secure destination, either at a geographical location within the world of the story (a world in which he travels through "all the countries on earth," "durch alle Länder der Erde") or at one of the supposed binary poles of life and death. Trapped in this in-between world, the hunter is like a circulating text that is denied the resting place of an archive.[24]

In death, the hunter speaks from beyond death, as if from life; alive, he speaks as a dead person. Who or what would enable one to respond affirmatively to the question as to whether one is dead ("Sind Sie tot?")—that is, who or what would enable one to respond at all? Death as death allows no response; to confirm in speech that one is dead constitutes a response that would erase itself as an impossibility. Indeed, the one who has died leaves any survivors precisely without response. This thought is confirmed in Derrida's eulogy of Levinas, delivered while standing next to the body of his dead friend and later included in *The Work of Mourning*, where one reads: "Death: not, first of all, annihilation, non-being, or nothingness, but a certain experience for the survivor of the 'without-response.'"[25] If the "without-response" characterizes both death (of the one who is deceased) and survival (of the one who lives on without ever being able to receive a response again), the "without-response" becomes visible as a fundamental marker of finitude, departure, and separation. Yet Kafka's Hunter Gracchus upsets the mournful "without-response" imbricated with death precisely by responding, that is, by speaking in a prosopopeic mode from beyond his own passing. Unable to conform to the existential logic of the "without-response"—that is, incapable of remaining silent when silence is the only confirmation of a radical absence—the hunter keeps speaking, keeps responding ("Ja, wie Sie sehen"). Even though the hunter interestingly ties the confirmation of his death, which is a life death, to the faculty of vision rather than of hearing (he does not say "Ja, wie Sie hören"), what is at stake is the relation between response and nonresponse as it is mediated by the voice, rather than between the experience of being able to see the image of a corpse and not being able to see it. In the world of the literary artwork, this character has outlived himself, staging himself perpetually as a "with-response" rather than as the "without-response" that is the hallmark of death and the impetus for the work of mourning on the part of those who live on. "Gewissermaßen"—in some sense, in a certain way—is Kafka's rhetorical way of suspending the binary opposition between life and death by suspending the binary opposition between the "with-response" and the "without-response." At the same time, "Gewissermaßen"—which can also mean "in a manner of speaking"—names the hunter's predicament, a predicament that could only be depicted as such in a work of art, a literary work—and therefore only in a literary, aesthetic, or figurative way of speaking, because the world that such a literary artwork sets up can only be articulated in the as-if mode, that is, figuratively. This world is a world *gewissermaßen*, literally of a certain kind of measure.

As is so often the case in the peculiar worlds that Kafka's works set up, the text hinges on the vagaries and multiple meanings of a single word. Here, that word is *gedenken*, mobilized when Hunter Gracchus responds to the mayor, "Ich gedenke nicht." It is quite correct and admissible to translate *gedenken* in terms of intentionality (or, more specifically, in terms of the withdrawal from it) and thus to render the hunter's cunning phrase as "I do no intending." If, however, one primarily hears in *gedenken* "intending," then the question arises as to why Kafka would not have chosen another, equally or even more common German word for intending, such as *beabsichtigen* or *vorhaben*. Kafka is too scrupulous a writer, too meticulous a textual world-constructor, to have made an arbitrary choice. *Gedenken*, unlike *beabsichtigen* or *vorhaben*, is derived from *denken*, to think, and as such it is also related to thought, *der Gedanke*. The text thus emphasizes the moment of thinking reflection, or lack thereof, in the hunter's response to the mayor's inquiry. But, even more importantly, *gedenken* has another meaning. In addition to intending and its relation to thought, it names the act of commemorating, typically by mourning an absence or a death. *Im Gedenken an* is a phrase that signifies "in commemoration of," as one does, for instance, when one affixes a *Gedenktafel*, a commemorative plaque, to a house in which something significant—triumphant, like the birth of a famous author, or horrific, like a deportation or murder—came to pass. The hunter's sentence "Ich gedenke nicht" could therefore also signify "I do not commemorate" or even, when read emphatically, "I do not mourn." When read from this perspective, the hunter has been deprived—or deprives himself—of commemorating and mourning his own life death. In a world of life death, which is always also a world of mourning, Hunter Gracchus displays a persistent inability to mourn. He cannot commemorate and mourn his own death, which is also to say, his life. As an aberrant mourner or even nonmourner, he cannot inherit himself, cannot transmit himself to the world of mourning.

If there can be no work of art that is not touched by the life death of the perishing world out of which it grew, and if there can be no work of art that does not set up a world of mourning in any number of heterogeneous forms, then Kafka's "The Hunter Gracchus" also belongs to this logic. It sets up a world of mourning, yet includes within that world a figure who is able neither to live nor to die—unable to mourn himself or to grieve his own passing as nonpassing. Part of what is commemorated in this particular world is precisely the refusal or denial of mourning—a commemorative mourning of mourning itself. The work of mourning and the world of mourning emerge as interwoven in the time and space of life death.

A further perspective opens up the possibility that the hunter's being-in-the-world not only constitutes an irreducible life death, but also a life death that can never be terminated by an act of accomplished or "successful" mourning. This textual world evokes, as the Freud of "Mourning and Melancholia" might say, a perpetual melancholia rather than a working-through of loss via the avenue of completed mourning, which, unlike melancholia, would enable the bereaved to decathect from the lost love-object (a person, a feeling, an idea) and "move on."[26] The melancholic lingering, while seemingly aberrant and pathological when judged from the perspective of mourning, refuses to lose the loss. It confirms the value of what has been lost always one more time, in perpetuity, by disallowing a getting-over of the loss, that is, by demonstrating that the need for the lost object was precisely not limitless and unconditional. (Without mentioning Freud, Barthes's *Mourning Diary*, the diary the writer kept while mourning the loss of his mother, articulates this issue with great economy: "To whom could I put this question (with any hope of an answer)? Does being able to live without someone you loved mean you loved her less than you thought ... ?")[27] One may say that the reluctance, unwillingness, or inability of Kafka's hunter to engage in the commemorative work of mourning within a world of life death keeps the specter of unsublated loss—even of himself—alive, a specter that returns to haunt and disrupt the world constructed by the textual work of art.

Another way to think about the unintended consequences of a putatively successful mourning relates such a mourning to the problem of forgetting, that is, the relinquishing of the loss that is to be commemorated *as* loss to the archive of worked-through experiences that therefore no longer figure saliently in one's consciousness. In his reflections upon the death of his friend Jean-François Lyotard, collected in the eulogies and funeral orations later assembled under the titled *The Work of Mourning*, Derrida considers Lyotard's phrase "There shall be no mourning [*il n'y aura pas de deuil*]." He suggests that this aphorism, although it "remains forever open," gives rise to a certain problematic: "For wouldn't the institution of mourning run the risk of securing the forgetting? Of protecting against memory instead of keeping it?"[28] If, on the one hand, there can only ever be mourning—as the ever-passing, fleeting world in which living beings are inscribed appears rightfully to demand—on the other hand, such mourning can, as it were, turn on itself, especially when it conforms to what one might consider the endpoint of an achieved or successful mourning. Such mourning would, after all, threaten to obliterate precisely that which is most valuable to it, its lost object of commemoration. Instead of securing the memory of loss as a meaningful, sustaining experience that helps to make life what it is, it would institute a regime of forgetting and noncommemoration.

The abiding threat of noncommemoration through forgetting in mourning is paralleled and intensified by the way in which the act of mourning may not always fully allow the mourner to identify who or what precisely is being mourned. When it comes to homing in on the singularity of loss, the possibility of aberration is always already inscribed in mourning itself. Is Hunter Gracchus's inability to mourn not also inflected by a certain hesitation or difficulty with regard to identifying what the object of his mourning should be, even if he himself embodies the grievable loss? As Pascale-Anne Brault and Michael Naas aptly put it in their reading of Derrida's politics of mourning, "we should perhaps not assume that we can ever identify with absolute certainty the object of our mourning," for "we might think we are mourning one friend when we are in fact mourning another, or think we are mourning a colleague when we are in fact, or in addition, mourning a child." They remind us of the possibility that "perhaps all our mournings are but iterations of the one death that can never be identified—the first death, the total, undialectical death—so what is mourned is a singularity that exceeds any proper name, making posthumous infidelity the very work of mourning." If such is the case, then we might say that "what we mourn is thus always nothing other than our very ability to identify, our mastery over the other and over death, as we yield to a force that is not ours, a force that always exceeds the rhetoric of mourning."[29] When viewed from this perspective, Kafka's Hunter Gracchus, too, cannot relate with absolute certainty to the object of his mourning. The singularity of his mourning—the impossible mourning he is called upon to perform in the world of life death that supposedly includes his own passing many years ago—exceeds any proper name, even his very own. Uncertain as to the precise object of his mourning, and thus, by extension, uncertain as to the nature of his loss as loss, the hunter finds himself inscribed in a perpetual present, a now-time that, even though it has a history that includes his own supposed death, presents itself as an interminable, restless, and utterly Sisyphean quest that commences always one more time. In the world of life death that Hunter Gracchus perpetually traverses on his death barge, it is unclear whether he should be mourning his own death, his inability to die fully, or the one unsublatable death as such, death as death. Or is it rather his inability to mourn that he should mourn—that is, should he mourn mourning? These questions remain open to the hunter as well as to the reader of Kafka's text.

If one can say that Kafka's artwork pivots on life death through a kind of inchoate mourning of mourning, a grief felt even over a certain inability to mourn, the world that it constructs places the demand of a specific kind of consciousness on the reader. In the space of what Blanchot names "Kafka's rigor," by which he means the writer's "fidelity to the work's demand, his fidelity to the demands of grief," the work of art "is primarily the consciousness of unhappiness, not its compensation." As Blanchot insists, "art is linked, precisely as Kafka is, to what is 'outside' the world and it expresses the profundity of this outside bereft of intimacy and of repose—this outside which appears when even with ourselves, even with our own death, we no longer have relations of possibility." Although Blanchot is not speaking of any one Kafkan text in particular, what he says is applicable also—perhaps even especially—to "The Hunter Gracchus": "Art is the consciousness of 'this misfortune.' It describes the situation of one who has lost himself, who can no longer say 'me,' who in the same movement has lost the world, the truth of the world, and belongs to exile, to the *time of distress* when, as Hölderlin says, the gods are no longer and are not yet." Yet, as Blanchot also emphasizes, this "does not mean that art affirms another world, at least not if it is true that art has its origins, not in another world, but in the other of all worlds."[30] This outside-of-world is operative even within interiority, that is, even when one does not expect to be confronted with any outside at all. If the work of art names a world, while never losing sight of the grief operative within it, this world emerges from what is other to any world, not the otherworldly but the other-to-world. This world, opened up by the work of art, moves through the work of mourning as a world that is not merely itself, not merely a world in any conventional sense at all. The work of art emerges from non-world even as it strives to disclose a world, and Kafka's Hunter Gracchus mournfully personifies, within the space of the literary, a life death that will forever bear witness to this very scene.

With regard to the hunter's inability to die, one might also note that he exemplifies the difficult problem with which all who are conscious of their life and their death are confronted, namely, that one cannot really imagine a world that does not include oneself. It is no accident that Freud emphasizes in "Thoughts for the Times on War and Death"—written in 1915, the year after World War I broke out and two years before Kafka composed "The Hunter Gracchus"—how "at bottom no one believes in his own death, or, to put the same thing in another way, that in the unconscious every one of us is convinced of his own immortality."[31] The unconscious is concerned with holding death at bay for us. On the conscious level we as human beings must accept death owing to our knowledge that all human beings die, but our unconscious works against this very acceptance, imbuing within us a deeply felt sense of not being able to die. With respect to death, the unconscious works to construct a world that cannot and will not go on without us. Viewed from that perspective, the hunter's predicament can be said to embody a kind of inability fully to believe in one's own death, that is, the unconscious refusal to accept mortality as mortality of the self.

But such a Freudian reading would not tell the whole story of life death in "The Hunter Gracchus." After all, the hunter's peculiar experience of a world of life death in Kafka's text also can be read as an allusive engagement with Epicurus's view that there can be no experience of death as such and that, as a consequence, our own death should be of no primary importance to us. According to Epicurus in his "Letter to Menoeceus": "Death, the most dreaded of evils, is therefore of no concern to us; for while we exist death is not present, and when death is present we no longer exist. It is therefore nothing either to the living or to the dead since it is not present to the living, and the dead no longer are."[32] Yet the figure of Hunter Gracchus troubles Epicurus's explanatory model of death in that it inhabits a world of life death in which the self is precisely present at its own death, and death is present while the self still is. It is the strange disruption of the temporality and structure of death and its experienceability in Kafka that enables the hunter to perceive his own death as if it were the death of another, even if he knows that it is in fact his own death. The hunter's specific form of life death propels the self into an aporia: to witness its own death while still alive. This aporia cannot be disentangled from the mourning that the world of Kafka's text projects.

It is perhaps no accident that Kafka was never able to finish the "Hunter Gracchus" fragments. Struggling with the material, he attempted one final time, in April 1917, to complete the story, without success. If one believes, as Benjamin does, that to "great writers, finished works weigh lighter than those fragments on which they work throughout their lives," then the construction site of these perpetual fragments preoccupied Kafka more than his other works.[33] The enigmatic world of life death that they construct and the multiple aberrations of mourning that circulate through them also characterize the world set up by Kafka's literary art more

broadly. Like Hunter Gracchus, who cannot arrive in the nether-
world of death and is incapable of mourning an unnamable loss,
Kafka's restless writerly being, what he called his *Schriftstellersein*,
would not allow him to repose in a certainty of any kind. Even the
semantic connection between the hunter's name and Kafka's own
suggests a close affinity: Gracchus derives from the Italian *graccio*,
which means crow or jackdaw, and the Czech word for jackdaw is,
precisely, *kavka*.[34] The mourning circulating through Kafka's textual world of life death faces its own resistance to closure always
one more time.

In the world of mourning set up by Kafka's literary artwork,
the hunter has failed, in a sense, to become a proper philosopher
in the classical sense because he has not learned how to die. In
the case of the hunter, this inability is literalized, in keeping with
Kafka's general penchant for constructing texts that rely on the
strategic literalization of specific figures and tropes. The hunter
has not merely failed at learning how to die in the sense of failing
to achieve a cognitive, hermeneutically driven, psychologically
inflected goal of insight, but he has quite literally not managed to
learn how to die, causing him to fail at dying as such. (Heidegger
might even say that the hunter, by eschewing death as *his* death—
the death that is forever properly one's own—has relinquished
his ownmost, unsurpassable possibility.) Everlastingly inscribed
in a life death that compels him to journey around the world on
his wayward barge, Hunter Gracchus cannot come to rest in any
achieved understanding. As a mourner prevented from mourning,
a griever incapable of grieving, a dying being unable to die, the
hunter is destined to travel through a world that is suffused, even
haunted, by an other-to-world, while the literary artwork itself
provides an ongoing self-reflexive commentary on this otherness-
to-world as such. Such an otherness-to-world is the very world
that the artwork has in store for us as we confront the work of
mourning (in) life death.

Changing the World Is Not What You Think (Marx)

In the course of our reflections so far, we have
stepped back and forth between worlds and works, between intensities of world-decay and potentialities of world-disclosure. What
gives structure to this movement is the question of the relation
between the impetus that causes the historical world of a work
of art to perish and the creative force that propels the work to set
up its own aesthetically mediated experience of being in a singular world—in short, a new world that is idiomatic to the specific artwork. It is now time to inflect these considerations further
by foregrounding their multiple imbrications with the political.
How does the relation between the perishing world in which the
artwork first comes into presence and the world that it opens up
relate to a political idea of world? This chapter suggests, by way of
engaging with a certain dimension of Marxian thought—namely,
the contested relation between theory and praxis—that what is
at stake in formulating the question in this way is not this or that

form of politics operative within any given world but rather the politicality of thinking the idea of world as such.

Even though Marx's most provocative reflections on the notion of world do not appear first and foremost in the context of his engagements with aesthetic questions, they do shed light on the politically mediated status of the artwork in its multiple relations to world. World, for Marx, is a category of reflection without which the liberatory potential of political thought and praxis could hardly be conceived. Indeed, the future gaining of a potential world is precisely what is at stake for him, even—and especially—as another, unfree world is left behind in the process. For instance, in 1848, at the end of *The Communist Manifesto*, Marx and his collaborator Friedrich Engels memorably appeal to revolutionary forces by averring: "The proletarians have nothing to lose but their chains. They have a world to gain [*Die Proletarier haben nichts in ihr zu verlieren als ihre Ketten. Sie haben eine Welt zu gewinnen*]."[1] The liberatory transformation that is to be brought about is, significantly, thought to result not merely in the gaining of this or that advantage, this or that improvement in the conditions of one's life, but rather in the gaining of a whole world—*eine Welt zu gewinnen*— the gaining of a world as world. It is almost as though prior to the political transformation there had been no world, at least no world deserving of its name; it is only through revolution that a world can first be gained as world, *eine Welt* in the proper sense of the term. It is hardly a coincidence that the language Marx and Engels mobilize at this crucial moment in their text alludes on a subterranean level to a biblical passage in which the notion of gaining a world is cast in Christian terms. In Matthew 16:26 we read, in Luther's German translation: "Was hilft es dem Menschen, wenn er die ganze Welt gewinnt, aber dabei sein Leben einbüßt?"[2] In the King James version, this passage is rendered as follows, albeit with "soul" replacing Luther's "Leben" (life): "For what is a man profited, if he shall gain the whole world, and lose his own soul?"[3] The religious significance of the rhetorical question lies in its call to challenge the value of the world that is gained in this life if one does not accept Jesus and his teachings before one must leave this world. Spoken by Jesus himself in the context of an examination of what "following" him would entail (Luther's German provides this passage with the title "Von der Nachfolge"), the rhetorical question is meant to elicit a particular kind of insight into a world gained by a mortal human. Any world gained without a concomitant acceptance of God has no lasting value because, unlike God, such a world, in its mere worldliness, cannot serve as a force of eventual redemption. By contrast, in their allusive rearticulation of this biblical scene of world-gaining by the human being, Marx and Engels depart from the Christian redemptive model in order to emphasize the historical materialist liberation that, mediated by the prospect of a communist revolution, will allow the human to gain a world that is valuable and dignified in itself—even though, or precisely because, it is only ever *this* world, rather than another world or afterlife, a world promised to come to pass in the beyond, that is at stake.

From a Marxian perspective, there is a kind of chiasmus at work when one considers the notion of a liberation *toward* a world: a losing of chains or shackles (*Ketten verlieren*) leads to the gaining of a world (*Welt gewinnen*), and any gaining of world is inextricably tied to a losing of chains. Transposing this chiasmus into the context of art, one might say that any political consideration of an artwork in relation to various modalities of world would have to take account of the chiasmic structure of this liberatory pull. If there is a world to be gained, *eine Welt zu gewinnen*, then the promise of this world is both negotiated and anticipated by the ways in which the work of art relates (or fails to relate) to *a* world and *the* world. The genuine work of art harbors within itself certain epistemic tensions and political potentialities—even when the apparent subject matter of the world that it sets up does not, on the surface, appear to be "political" in any conventional or representational sense at all (as, for instance, in Jackson Pollock's art of the drip technique or in Gerhard Richter's painterly "blur")—that implicate the work irrevocably in the liberatory promise of world-gain.

Three years before reflecting on world-gain and the losing of chains in the *Communist Manifesto*, Marx, in his "Theses on Feuerbach" (composed in 1845 during his time in Brussels), provides the most canonical and influential formulation of his engagement with the notion and transformative experience of world. The "Theses," which amount to a collection of compressed and telegraphic yet highly suggestive notes toward a longer study that itself remained incomplete, *The German Ideology*, will not cease to reimagine the world and our potentially revolutionary relations to it. When viewed from the perspective of sustained world-relation, it is perhaps no mere provocation, no mere hyperbole, to suggest, as Lucien Goldmann daringly did in 1968, that Marx's "Theses"— which fill a mere two and a half manuscript pages—are of the same historical importance as Descartes's *Discourse on Method*, Kant's *Critique of Pure Reason*, or Hegel's *Phenomenology of Spirit*.[4] While all the "Theses on Feuerbach" are touched, directly or indirectly, by questions of interpretive and material world-relation, the famous eleventh thesis in particular has provoked sustained interpretation and critical attention.[5] It evokes the relationship between philosophical thought and world in consequential terms: "Die Philosophen haben die Welt nur verschieden *interpretiert*; es kommt aber darauf an, sie zu *verändern* [The philosophers have only *interpreted* the world in various ways; the point, however, is *to change* it]."[6] Although the young Marx, as Étienne Balibar correctly reminds us, certainly "*did not stop there*," it could be argued that "nothing that he wrote afterwards ever went beyond the horizon of the problems posed by this formulation."[7] In its most dominant interpretation, Marx's thesis is understood to set up a fundamental binary tension between conceptual reflection on the world and the need for active intervention in, and revolutionary transformation of, that world. According to this interpretation, Marx opposes theory and practice to each other in order to advocate for a world-transforming praxis that would leave behind the merely abstract and self-satisfied activities of patient conceptual interpretation that have no effect on the concrete world in which they occur: the material, political, historical, and experiential situatedness of their own time and place of articulation. Apparently arguing for a praxis-based model of philosophy—or questioning the usefulness of philosophers as such—Thesis 11 appears to make the case that interpretive analysis must finally yield to revolutionary change. Yet, upon closer inspection, the meaning of "interpretation" in Marx's thesis itself calls for interpretation. Interpreting here stands in need of interpretation fully as much as the activity of changing as such—not to mention the notion of "world" (*die Welt*) and the question of what the locution "es kommt darauf an" suggests, in other words, the problem of what is at stake and how it is at the stake, the heart of the matter: that which counts. By the same token, the meaning of Marx's *verändern*—which, to the extent that it incorporates within itself something other, *etwas anderes*, denotes not merely a neutral act of changing but, as *ver-ändern*, literally a making-other, an *othering*—stands in need of patient explication. Reflecting upon a transformation that has been called for or already has come to pass, what will it have meant to make a world other, that is, to submit it to a strategic act of sustained othering?

A further challenge to interpretive understanding posed by Thesis 11 pertains to the status of the philosophers. After all, Marx's text does not directly speak of philosophy but rather of philosophers as having interpreted the world in various ways. (Presumably, given the preoccupations of the early Marx as well as his dialogue with the Young Hegelians, he has in mind primarily the philosophers of German idealism, especially Hegel.) When it comes to the demand for a strategic othering of the world, is there perhaps a distinction to be made, from the structural perspective, between philosophers and philosophy, the who and the what? When it comes to relating to the world in a transformative way, the who and the what are not coextensive. Does this thesis suggest, then, that philosophy is not in good hands with professional or bourgeois philosophers, who may misunderstand or misinterpret what philosophy itself demands? By extension, does philosophy need to be taken out of the hands of philosophers in order to live on in a transformed, "othered" manner? In other words, is philosophy too important to be left to philosophers who pursue it for purposes of "mere" interpretation? In that case, world-interpretation as such would not be the problem, but rather a form of philosophy that is conceived by philosophers in an overly narrow manner. Whatever the case may be, here we encounter the idea that philosophy may persist for Marx after all, but under a transformed sign.

The question of how to interpret Marx's world-historical thesis—and, by extension, its subsequent interpretations, including the interpretation of interpretation that the thesis itself thematizes—is further complicated by a philological difficulty. This philological difficulty, which has not gone unnoticed in the long history of Marx's text, is worth revisiting and lingering over. Even though it only concerns three seemingly trivial elements (to be precise: a punctuation mark, a conjunction, and an umlaut), the difficulty strikes at the heart of Marx's thesis and the interpretations to which it has given rise. The version of Thesis 11 that has entered the canon of cultural history and political philosophy is not in fact the version that Marx originally composed in 1845. For reasons about which one may only speculate, Marx did not show his theses to Engels, who discovered them later among his friend's papers, even though the two of them were preparing a collaborative work on the *Germany Ideology* at the time. When Engels decided to publish the theses in 1888 under the title "Marx über Feuerbach" as an appendix to a revised edition of his own study on Feuerbach (*Ludwig Feuerbach und der Ausgang der klassischen deutschen Philosophie*), he made three editorial interventions in the text of his friend and collaborator, who had died five years earlier. We recall that in Engels's version, which by any measure exerted the greatest impact on intellectual and cultural history, Marx's line reads:

> Die Philosophen haben die Welt nur verschieden *interpretiert*; es kommt aber darauf an, sie zu *verändern*.

But the original passage found in Marx's own notebook reads:

> Die Philosophen haben die Welt nur verschieden *interpretiert*, es kömmt darauf an, sie zu *verändern*.[8]

It is as if the *Veränderung*, the change, that the passage invokes had already been made, albeit on a philological level—in the textual world of the sentence itself. After Marx's passing, Engels, in a no doubt well-meaning gesture, interpreted his friend's sentence about interpretation and its relationship to the world in a way that prompted him to make three silent changes: He substituted "kommt" for "kömmt" in his rendering of the third-person singular present tense form of the verb "kommen," thereby erasing Marx's archaic colloquial locution as signaled by the umlaut. On the level of punctuation, Engels replaced Marx's comma with a semicolon. And in the second part of the sentence, he added the conjunction "aber," which typically corresponds to the English conjunction "but," yet here is best translated adverbially as "however" or "though."[9]

Concerning the first of these philological changes in the world of the sentence, the substitution of "kommt" for "kömmt," one might suspect that Engels wished to elevate into formal standard High German a colloquial or dialectal spelling that he attributed to the haste with which the young Marx had jotted down this sentence in his notebook. Though Engels was a philosopher and historian, he was no philologist, and he may well have believed he was not bound by the letter of his friend's notation, especially in light of what appeared to him as its provisional, preliminary character. Yet by eliding Marx's umlaut, Engels also introduced a subtle shift from a colloquial, almost folksy usage that would have tied Marx's formulation to the principles of Luther's translation of the Bible into German (that is, to use the commoner's language and to write a German style that corresponded to how people actually speak—"auf das Maul sehen," as Luther's famous phrase from his 1530 treatise on translation, "Sendbrief vom Dolmetschen," has it). One might say that the shift from "ö" to "o" removes Marx's language from the dialectal, everyday discourse of commonality, firmly encasing it in the standard framework of scholarly German.

More important and more fateful, however, are Engels's other two editorial interventions. Whereas Marx had allowed his two sentences to be connected by a simple comma that provided for a certain flow, a paratactical continuity or sequentiality, the semicolon inserted by Engels introduces the sense of an opposition, even a hypotactical confrontation. The question of whether Engels's philological emendations work merely to clarify what Marx's original sentence already meant to say or rather distort something important about the sentence remains a matter of debate in the scholarship on Marx. On the one hand, there is the position represented by readers of Marx such as Volker Gerhardt, who insists—based largely on an interpretation of the later *German Ideology* for which the "Theses on Feuerbach," at least in part, served as preparatory reflections—that Engels's editorial interventions resulted in a decidedly political text fully consistent with Marx's own views.[10] On the other hand, there are interpreters of

Marx who appear more cautious and concerned about the details of Engels's editorial interventions. For instance, in his incisive 1953 reflections on Marx's "Theses"—a version of which he subsequently included as a chapter in his three-volume magnum opus, *Das Prinzip Hoffnung* (*The Principle of Hope*)—Bloch generally approves of Engel's modifications of the "Theses," reassuring us that Engels merely submitted Marx's text to a light stylistic editing ("stilistisch leicht redigiert") in a way that "certainly [*selbstredend*]" did not cause "even the slightest change in content [*die leiseste inhaltliche Veränderung*]."[11] In support of this view, Bloch even cites Engels's remark about the "Theses," namely, that they represent mere "notes for later elaboration [*Notizen zur späteren Ausarbeitung*], hurriedly scribbled [*rasch hingeschrieben*], absolutely not intended for publication, but invaluable as the first document in which the ingenious seed of the new worldview [*Weltanschauung*] is planted."[12] So far, so good, it appears. But when, some 30 pages later, his commentary turns to Thesis 11 in particular, even Bloch begins to feel slightly uncomfortable: "What, then, is the precise wording of Thesis 11, and what is its apparent opposition between cognizing and changing [*Erkennen und Verändern*]? The opposition is not one [*Der Gegensatz ist keiner*]; even the particle 'aber,' which is used here in an expanding rather than a contradictory sense, is missing in Marx's original; by the same token, there is no either-or."[13] However one wishes to adjudicate this matter, it can hardly be denied that the two statements that comprise the sentence in Engels's version construct a more pronounced, more pointedly articulated binary opposition between the interpreting activity of the philosophers, which apparently leaves the world unchanged, and what in fact matters when it comes to relating to the world—namely, that it be changed rather than "merely" interpreted, debated, and hermeneutically described. Engels's decision to insert the conjunction "aber" in the second part of the sentence has a similar effect; it rhetorically works to fortify the sense of oppositionality between the interpretation of the world and the tacit requirement that it be changed. Mobilizing the force of an old popular prejudice (as we saw in chapter 5, on grayness, "Gray is all theory"), the thesis now appears to disparage "mere" theory while favoring "actual" praxis that can have a measurable effect on the world. This is the interpretation of the eleventh Thesis that has become canonical and that followed Marx into his grave—and beyond. It is, in fact, engraved on his tombstone in London's Highgate Cemetery, where Engels's editorial "however" is preserved for eternity, even though his semicolon has been replaced there by a dash (the German *Gedankenstrich*), which, in the conceptual world of punctuation, raises its own question marks.

How can we be certain that Engels's editorial "improvements" do justice to the complexity of Marx's thesis and its heterogeneous implications with regard to the world? And what would doing justice here mean in the first place? After all, one might point out that no interpretation of the world leaves the world wholly untouched; every interpretation of the world already constitutes a change in and of that world. From another perspective, there may be no "world" prior to the act of interpretation, at least if by world what is meant is an already existing, fully formed, and interpretable framework of existence into which one may insert oneself after the fact. Moreover, Marx himself certainly devoted his life's work to a relentless interpretation of the world in its manifold phenomena, never tiring of interpreting those elements of the world that seemed the most vexing and therefore required the most interpretive analysis—from his unsurpassed interpretation of the spectral workings of capital, via his reading of the function of religion and the bourgeoisie under capitalism, to his speculative critique of the very notion of political economy. If Thesis 11 were to be interpreted exclusively along the dividing lines demarcated by Engels's semicolon and his "however," the objection could be made that any practical intervention in the world first requires an act of sustained interpretation that makes sense of that world—at least enough to determine that its workings are in fact flawed and that, by extension, it is deserving of change. Also, the question as to precisely what kind of change is to be sought could only be negotiated on the basis of a robust interpretive engagement, not to say a perpetually questioning understanding, of the world as it currently presents itself.

To be sure, it appears that Thesis 11 argues for an end to philosophy as it has commonly been practiced and for the beginning of a transformative relation to the world. Yet, given that this apparent argument or argumentative demand has itself been made on the basis of a certain conceptual interpretation of the world as Marx finds it, it cannot fully shuck its own philosophical embeddedness. In other words, the argument tacitly depends on the very thing it would seek to abolish, since it is itself an example of a philosophical interpretation of the world. If it embodies a speech act that demands a form of practice, this practice appears to be philosophical in nature.

One may extend this line of thought by considering the question as to what these tensions between world-interpretation and world-transformation imply with respect to casting into sharper relief the relation between theory and practice. In his 1951–1952 lecture course "Was heißt Denken?"—meaning "What Is Called Thinking?" and "What Calls for Thinking?" but also "What Bids Thinking Come?"—Heidegger suggests that what is at issue in considering the world today is perhaps not a lack of practice at all: "*Most thought-provoking and disconcerting* [*Das Bedenklichste*] *is that we are still not thinking* [*daß wir noch nicht denken*]—not even yet, although the state of the world [*Weltzustand*] is becoming constantly more thought-provoking and disconcerting." "True," he adds, "this course of events seems to demand rather that the human being should act without delay, instead of making speeches at conferences and international conventions and never moving beyond merely imagining what ought to be, and how it ought to be done. What is lacking, then, is action, not thought." Upon closer inspection, however, the opposite makes itself felt: "And yet—it could be that the prevailing human being has for centuries now acted too much and thought too little [*seit Jahrhunderten bereits zu viel gehandelt und zu wenig gedacht*]."[14] From this perspective, it is theoretical reflection rather than transformative intervention that the human being lacks in its confrontation with the world. What Heidegger refers to as a thought-provoking and disconcerting *Weltzustand* demands a more intense engagement with its interpretation rather than more instances of action.

One might add that the world we face is constantly changing *already*, regardless of whether or not a philosopher or any other kind of human being actively participates in, or even instigates, this change. Even without any direct intervention, the world will not remain identical to itself; it is, rather, always already inscribed in a perpetual movement of change, a movement that, as change, itself is not subject to change. What the philosophers, along with anyone else who wishes to learn how to think—and, for Heidegger, we can only ever be beginners—may contribute vis-à-vis this world and its *Weltzustand* is, precisely, a thoughtful, patient, vigilant, and critical interpretation of the relentless (and, at times, utterly disconcerting) change that always already holds what we call the world in its grip. This framework for reflecting on world-change is certainly pertinent when the change in question is driven by the relentless and particularly destructive forces of capitalism, but it is not limited to the capitalist world.

While these remarks from "Was heißt Denken?" are not directly aimed at Marx or the "Theses on Feuerbach"—even though the substance of their arguments very much pertains to them—Heidegger explicitly addresses Marx's Thesis 11 in the course of a recorded television interview from 1969 with the German philosopher Richard Wisser. Asked by Wisser about the "societal mission [*gesellschaftliche Aufgabe*]" of philosophy, Heidegger responds that the term "society" evoked in the question must first be submitted to extensive scrutiny so that the ways in which society is a form of modern subjectivity that is understood to be absolute can come to the fore. And he adds:

> Another question is to what extent we can speak of a *change* of society at all. The question of the demand for world change [*Forderung der Weltveränderung*] leads us back to Karl Marx's frequently quoted statement from his *Theses on Feuerbach*. I would like to quote it exactly and read out loud: "Philosophers have only *interpreted* the world differently; what matters is to *change* it." When this statement is cited *and* when it is followed, it is overlooked that changing the world presupposes a change in the *conception* of the world. A conception of the world can only be won by adequately *interpreting* the world.
>
> That means: Marx's demand for a "change" is based on a very definite interpretation of the world [*Marx fußt auf einer ganz bestimmten Weltinterpretation, um seine "Veränderung"*

zu fordern], and therefore his statement is proved to be without foundation [*nicht fundierter Satz*]. It gives the impression that it speaks decisively against philosophy, whereas the second half of the statement presupposes, unspoken, a demand for philosophy.[15]

In the original version of the interview, the passage that Heidegger reads out loud—in the television footage one can see him pulling Marx's text from his bookshelf before he does so—has the archaic colloquialism "kömmt" (Heidegger even appears to look up a bit when he reads this archaism) restored and does not contain the "aber" that Engels inserted in the second half of Marx's sentence. In the German transcript of the interview, however, the semicolon that Engels also added is retained, with the result that the intensified oppositionality of interpreting and changing that this philological intervention instantiated continues to be operative, at least on the level of punctuation. The force of Engel's semicolon and what it implies about the relation between world-interpretation and world-change silently inflects Heidegger's commentary on Marx's sentence. Without prior interpretation, Heidegger argues, there can hardly be a conception of the world, and without a conception of the world, there would be no basis for changing the world. Thus, the changing of the world presupposes its interpretation.

One might even go one step further and argue that, from Heidegger's perspective, Marx's statement about the world begs the question as to what is meant by "world" in the first place. What philosophical thought and its movement of world-interpretation can seek to accomplish is an examination of our implicit, unacknowledged "pre-understanding" of the world, a conception of the world that always already informs, albeit in a typically unarticulated manner, any desire to effect changes upon, or cause modifications from within, whatever is perceived as constituting "world."[16] In fact, there can be *neither* interpretation *nor* change of a world without an unspoken pre-understanding of the *world as world*, the worldness of world as such. It is to such an analysis of the conception of world as pre-understood worldness that philosophy—or, as Heidegger would prefer to say, *Denken*, thinking—can make decisive, and eventually eminently practical, contributions. Indeed, even from a non-Heideggerian perspective, it can be argued that the "Theses" are concerned precisely with the issue of a fundamental relation and orientation to the world, a stance toward the world as it is experienced as world in a subjective entity's daily life.[17]

The effort to establish a free and open relation to world—which would include both world-interpretation and world-change, both the experience of world and an analysis of its pre-understanding—can therefore not be based on the maintenance of a binarist distinction between theory and praxis that Marx's Thesis 11 appears to posit on the surface. This effort to relate to a world in a manner that is both free and capable of effecting change in the world would rather have to proceed from another framework of premises. Among them, at least from Heidegger's perspective, is Marx's own trenchant analysis of *Entfremdung*, alienation or estrangement, an analysis that can be said to be of great aid to any attempt to think the history of our being in the world. In his "Letter on Humanism"—written in 1946 as a response to a query by Beaufret concerning the relation between philosophical thought and political praxis—Heidegger suggests that, since "homelessness is coming to be the destiny of the world [*Weltschicksal*]," it "is necessary to think that destiny in terms of the history of Being." He continues by underlining the role that Marx's thought of *Entfremdung* could profitably play in such thinking:

What Marx recognized in an essential and significant sense, though derived from Hegel, as the estrangement [*Entfremdung*] of the human being has its root in the homelessness of the modern human being. This homelessness is specifically evoked from the destiny of Being in the form of metaphysics, and through metaphysics is simultaneously entrenched and covered up as such. Because Marx by experiencing estrangement attains an essential dimension of history, the Marxist view of history is superior [*überlegen*] to that of other historical accounts. But since neither Husserl nor—so far as I have seen until now—Sartre recognizes the essential importance of the historical in Being, neither phenomenology nor existentialism enters that dimension within which a productive dialogue with Marxism first becomes possible.[18]

As Marx had stressed in his Parisian manuscripts, *The German Ideology*, and elsewhere, there can be no trenchant political reading of the world today—and thus, one may add, no transformation of it—without assuming a critical perspective on the perpetual *Entfremdung* that historically holds the modern human being in its iron grip. We recall that the experience of alienation and one of its most trenchant manifestations, alienated labor, are intimately tied in Marx's account to the problem of the division of labor and to the world of capitalism with its specific forms of organizing both work and quotidian human existence.[19] While Hegel had grounded his thinking of alienation specifically in an account of how the mind, intellect, or spirit (*Geist*) estranges itself from itself in order to move beyond what it prematurely considers as already familiar and known, Marx's concept of alienation fastens upon the ways in which certain forms of social organization and political economy deform consciousness in order to manufacture its compliance within a system of oppression.[20] If Heidegger considers Marx's view of history "superior [*überlegen*]" to other accounts of history, it is not because it is based on the division between theory and practice that is the subject of Thesis 11, but rather because its relentless analysis of alienation or estrangement provides us with an invaluable entryway into a thinking of the historically grown essence of our being in the world—and, by extension, of the otherwise enigmatic worldness of the world in which our historical becoming unfolds. This reading of Heidegger's passage is confirmed when one considers the rhetorical effect of its particular word choice: *überlegen*, as an adjective, means "advantageous" or "superior" (literally "lying over" something else); but as an infinitive verb form, *überlegen* means to think about, to reflect on, to ponder, to consider. Since Heidegger could have chosen a number of other German words here—none of which, however, would have overlapped with the semantic range of thinking itself—we may conclude that his implicit imbrication of the superiority and conceptual reflection that *überlegen* inimitably performs is not mobilized by accident. On the contrary, *überlegen* suggests how, in the course of Heidegger's reflections—which were advanced almost exactly one century after the young Marx's "Theses on Feuerbach"—a Marxian perspective allows the thinking of the historicity of our being in the world to attain a level of material and conceptual specificity that otherwise would not have been available to critical thought. This specificity, in turn, refuses to be inscribed in the oppositional pair of theory and practice, moving instead into a realm in which certain tenets of historical materialist analysis may open up an ontologically oriented questioning and vice versa.[21]

*

The oppositional pair of theory and praxis upon which the world of Thesis 11 pivots receives further inflection in some thoughts that Derrida devotes to it. In a series of nine seminar sessions held at the École Normale Supérieure during the academic year 1976–1977—which were made available for the first time in French as *Théorie et pratique* in 2017 and in English as *Theory and Practice* in 2019—he works subtly to question both the logic and the genealogy of this oppositional pairing, even though the concept of world does not yet figure prominently among his concerns and is not examined explicitly in the seminar. In his later work on Marxian thought, *Specters of Marx* (1993), Derrida focuses on the imbrication of political economy and the uncanny demands of what he calls a "hauntology" (the philosophical and political study of the world of ghosts and specters), but *Theory and Practice* rather devotes itself to a rigorous engagement with the relation of thinking and acting as it comes to pass in the trajectory of Marxian and post-Marxian thought, from Marx via Gramsci to Althusser and beyond. Providing the conceptual and rhetorical framework of the seminar is a discussion of Marx's "Theses on Feuerbach," with particular attention being paid to Thesis 11.

It behooves any consideration of what matters or is at stake in Thesis 11—*worauf es ankommt*, to use Marx's own phrase—to be receptive to the conceptual and textual difficulty encoded in this very locution. As Derrida avers in his seminar:

For our part, relying on a style that is perhaps not that of current Marxist problematics, we'll have cause to question the status of this utterance differently, and to accentuate it, accentuate it in several ways, to analyze in particular *es kommt darauf an*, difficult to translate, since "what is important" renders only one dimension of the expression, even if that dimension is, precisely, important. And still, one must understand fully what "important" means, understand fully the "must be done" implied by it, but how is one to understand a "must be done," "would have to be done": *es kommt*—what type of utterance is that? How is it to be understood, by analyzing the utterance, by seeking for it a sense or a referent (but by definition it doesn't yet have any), or by doing it, etc.?[22]

As the English translator informs us in a footnote, Derrida adds a handwritten marginal note beneath this paragraph that reads "Is it a matter of necessity?"[23] One may speculate that the necessity about which Derrida wonders pertains both to the doing implied by the demand of the specific utterance and to the importance of the "must be done" as such, what, at the very beginning of the seminar, he had introduced as the general question of the *"faut le faire."* In both cases, the issue of what, precisely, Marx's particular wording *es kommt darauf an* signifies will remain open to debate. *Es kommt darauf an*—is it a kind of coming, an advent, an arrival of sorts? And who or what is signified by the "es" in "es kommt"? Are we dealing with what is sometimes called a grammatical dummy-it that is no "it" at all, as in the locution *es regnet*, "it is raining"? To be sure, *es kommt darauf an* signals something of importance, something that matters or is at stake. But this *darauf ankommen* of Thesis 11 also seems to suggest a form of coming or stepping-toward, a coming-upon something that is inexorably interwoven with that in relation to which this coming itself comes to pass, the significance of its political horizon. One might say that the question of the coming-toward or coming-about of what is at stake is one of the indelible contexts in regard to which Marx's thesis also demands to be read.

As Derrida himself suggests to his seminar participants, any reading of this thesis at the same time opens the broader question

276

of contexts, a consideration of which cannot but inform a rigorous engagement with the text and its utterance. "What is noteworthy," he thus argues, "is that despite its aphoristic character, struck like a medal, the 11th Thesis comes to be determined only within a vast context" and "it is difficult to miss the fact that" the "most immediate context" is constituted by "the ten preceding theses," even though one should "not forget that these are *theses* but let's not be too quick to understand what *thesis* means here."[24] Among the contexts to be considered are the thetic character of the statement; an awareness of the difficulties posed by the *es kommt darauf an*, which appears to issue "not a meaning, a truth, a theorem but a certain type of practical imperative or imperative performance," even a "command, wish, *telos*, rallying cry [*mot d'ordre*]";[25] and the fact that the very title "Theses on Feuerbach" was not given to this text by Marx himself but rather by the Moscow Institute for Marxism-Leninism in conjunction with the first publication, in 1932, of *The German Ideology*. Concerning the latter contextual inscription, Derrida reminds us that the Institute based its editorial decision on a remark by Engels, who had referred to his friend's text as a series of theses. Derrida therefore proceeds to quote from Engels's preface to his book on Feuerbach: "In an old notebook of Marx's I have found the eleven theses on Feuerbach. ... These are notes hurriedly scribbled down for later elaboration, absolutely not intended for publication, but invaluable as the first document in which is deposited the brilliant germ of the new world outlook."[26] According to Derrida's understanding of this passage, the "definition and the future destiny of this text in world history transfer their powerful enigma," which is to say "their power as enigma and as a very unusual textual event," upon "the concept of *text* (if this document is indeed a text)" and, by extension, "onto the theory/practice pair, if, as we shall see, it constitutes the cornerstone of these 11 theses."[27] This is to say that if one of the various contextual determinations or overdeterminations of Thesis 11 is precisely its textual status—the scholarly question of its precise philological status, but also its very status *as* text—then the import or substance of what it wishes to argue on the conceptual level with respect to the relation between thinking and doing also must be understood within a textual framework and with due attention to questions of language and textuality. In other words, one may say that the relation between thinking and doing that it wishes to advance on the level of the concept is already prefigured in its very own textual movement.

From the perspective of such an analysis, the question may be pursued as to what would constitute revolutionary practice in the terms that the "Theses of Feuerbach" suggest. For such an analysis, it is necessary to link Thesis 11 with previous moments in the text, especially Thesis 3, where the issue of *"revolutionäre Praxis,"* revolutionary praxis, is specifically broached. In Derrida's reading of the text, "the sole practice on whose basis one can have access to practice (and having access no longer means here coming to think it theoretically, or to elucidate it semantically)" is "revolutionary."[28] This is to suggest that "one can practice only in a revolutionary way but revolution itself revolutionizes—in the context that concerns us at present—only by transforming practice in a revolutionary way, and starting from a transformed practice, from a new concept of practice, and, every concept being a theory/praxis, from a new practice of practice."[29] The consequence of developing such a concept of revolutionary practice is that a certain enigmaticness of practice and its value arises:

> This enigmatic value of "practice"—enigmatic not
> because it would remain mysterious, inaccessible, deep,
> incomprehensible, but because it sets in motion a language
> that no longer simply requires being understood, received,
> conceived of, in the mode of a theoretical reading that is
> enigmatic because one doesn't know what it says and what
> it means before doing it, and even because one doesn't
> know *what* must be done, according to a rigorous anteriority,
> before doing it—this enigmatic value of "practice" is to be
> found in almost all of the subsequent theses.[30]

If the notion of practice that emanates from the third thesis and comes to suffuse the entire constellation of theses emerges as mysterious, this is because of reasons similar to the ones that Heidegger identifies in his conversation with Wisser. According to the logic of revolutionary practice thus conceived, the practice

278

demands to be grounded in an interpretive reading of world that itself has not been arrested in the form of an understanding. In that case, the call for a revolutionary practice to change the world is not based on a prior understanding of that world, a world of which one would assume that it should, at least in principle, be interpreted and made the object of understanding. As a consequence, it is not possible for this form of revolutionary practice to have interpreted and grasped the very world it has tasked itself with changing (or othering, *verändern*) prior to engaging in its world-changing activities. By the same token, such revolutionary practice cannot know precisely what is required of it and with respect to what aspects of the world; such practice would be pushed into a doing without knowing how, an actionism that does not grasp to what end it is being employed at any given moment.

The question arises, then, whether the "Theses on Feuerbach," and especially Thesis 11, are determinants of the closure of philosophy or whether they rather specify the end of a particular kind of philosophical work. As Derrida puts the matter, "does the last Thesis mark the end of philosophy (which would have been satisfied with interpreting)," or rather "the end of only the philosophy that is satisfied with interpreting, so that what Marx calls for would still be a philosophy, but a philosophy that transforms the world, a practico-revolutionary philosophy"?[31] In other words, "in the first case, Marx would be calling for a general revolutionary practice and a revolutionary theory/practice that would no longer belong to the order of philosophy, essentially overflowing the philosophical as such," while in the second case, Marx "would be calling for a practical revolutionary transformation of philosophy but without rejecting, suppressing, exceeding, destroying the philosophical."[32] As becomes clear throughout the seminar, Derrida wishes to favor the second reading, the sense that, within the transformation or othering of the world, philosophy is maintained and kept alive as a powerful tool of reflection and necessary realm of conceptual analysis—even and especially with regard to the realm of the practical and the world.

The two examples that he discusses make this point plain. One is Gramsci's critique of Croce with respect to "the latter's proposed reading of the 11th Thesis." Derrida cites Gramsci's essay

"Benedetto Croce and Dialectical Materialism," written from 1932 to 1935, in which Gramsci rejects Croce's proposal that the "Theses on Feuerbach" and dialectical materialism more broadly "would no longer be essentially philosophical."[33] As Derrida argues in the seminar, "for Gramsci, the 11th Thesis cannot be interpreted the way Croce interprets it" and "it is opposed, still philosophically (even if in a way that is absolutely new for philosophy), only to a theoretico-speculative philosophy, indeed to the theoretico-speculative tendency that dominates the history of philosophy."[34] Gramsci himself articulates this perspective in the most poignant terms by arguing, in a passage that Derrida cites, that "such a solution from Croce [i.e., the repudiation of all philosophy] is ineffective in critical terms" because "even if one admits by means of the absurd hypothesis that Marx wanted to 'replace' philosophy in general with practical activity, it would be necessary to 'unsheathe'" the "peremptory argument according to which one cannot deny philosophy except by philosophizing, that is to say by affirming what one wishes to deny."[35] The other example that Derrida discusses at length is Althusser's engagement with the Marxian legacy in such texts as "On the Materialist Dialectic" (a chapter in *For Marx*), "Lenin and Philosophy," as well as the "Reply to John Lewis," texts written between the mid-1960s and the mid-1970s. As in the case of Gramsci, Derrida arrives at the conclusion that for Althusser, too, the work of philosophy following Marx ends up by being affirmed, rather than abandoned in favor of a dephilosophized notion of practice. Philosophy and its work of interpretive analysis emerge as persisting forces, even if in a manner that is transformed by their sustained confrontation with the demands of world-engagement and world-othering. This is the case even if one is suspicious and critical, as Derrida is throughout the seminar, of what could be called Althusser's humanist theoreticism that, especially in its tendency to reduce the notion of practice to the idea of the human, unwittingly repeats the metaphysical gestures that it had hoped to overcome.[36]

While Derrida's seminar works to unweave the apparent binarism of theory and practice by affirming the potentialities of a philosophized practice and a practice-based philosophy, it is almost twenty years later, in *Specters of Marx*, that he returns to

Marx in order to delineate some of the implications of this view of the Marxian corpus for future acts of reading and intervening. Of course, much changed between 1976 and 1993, including the world of communism, particularly in the aftermath of the decline of the Soviet Union. If it is to "something altogether other" that Derrida wishes to turn in re-turning to Marx, this is because he wishes to "insist even more on what commands us today, without delay, to do everything we can so as to avoid the neutralizing anesthesia of a new theoreticism, and to prevent a philosophico-philological return to Marx from prevailing."[37] To give in to the temptations of such an exclusively theoreticist turn or return to Marx, in which he would merely be treated as an interesting philosopher whose corpus leaves untouched the status quo of the very world that it addresses, would undermine what remains suggestive, uncanny, and transformative within it. Indeed, such a giving in would entail a readiness "to accept the return of Marx or the return to Marx" only "on the condition that a silence is maintained about Marx's injunction not just to decipher but to act and to make the deciphering [the interpretation] into a transformation that 'changes the world.'"[38] By implicitly alluding—through the juxtaposition of interpreting and changing—once again to Thesis 11 in *Specters of Marx*, Derrida issues an injunction to keep the transformative or revolutionary impulse of Marx alive—what he also calls his "oppositional spirit"—while respecting the conceptual challenges embedded in this demanding theoretical work. With respect to the world that is addressed in Thesis 11—which is to say our world and a world to come—this injunction names an infinite responsibility, an affirmation of the impossible precisely as possibility.

In this context, it may be useful to recall Lyotard's dictum, "After philosophy comes philosophy. But it is altered by the after."[39] When thought in relation to Thesis 11's notion of philosophy that emerges from a rigorous and ceaseless engagement with the world, one might reformulate this dictum to say, "After philosophy comes philosophy. But it has been altered by practice." In other words, while the political emphasis on the dimension of necessary practice does not erase the philosophical, what comes to be thought and practiced under the banner of philosophy has been changed—even *ver-ändert*, othered—through its confrontation with practice. By extension, *die Welt*, the very world that is at stake in this othering—and that, in turn, is the political object of Marx's *es kommt darauf an*—could neither be thought nor lastingly transformed without a sustained consideration of the implications called forth by this afterness.

When considered in relation to the work of art and its each-time-singular ways of relating to world-decay and world-construction, the afterness of a philosophy that is not abolished but decisively altered by an engagement with the notion of world-othering practice moves to the fore. What would it mean for the work of art to relate not only to world-decay and world-construction but also to the world-othering of philosophical thought that is lastingly attuned, even hospitable, to the abiding demands of practice? Even if this philosophical thought refuses to submit to a kind of practice-based form of precensorship, in which the value of a thought is measured a priori by its presumed applicability to this or that political intervention and therefore is prevented from unfolding in a free relation to the world in which it occurs, the very imbrication of the conceptual with the practical makes itself felt throughout the artwork in unique and memorable ways. How may the work of art help us to begin to conceptualize such an altered philosophical thought and the concepts to which it in turn may give rise?

In a remarkably suggestive yet rather enigmatic passage in his book on Husserl and epistemology—*Zur Metaphysik der Erkenntnistheorie. Studien über Husserl und die phänomenologischen Antinomien*, first composed during 1934–1937, revised between 1955 and 1956, and somewhat misleadingly translated under the English title *Against Epistemology: A Metacritique*—Adorno homes in on the relation between the artwork and the kind of philosophy that unfolds after it has taken leave of its classical form. The apodictic passage, which is not often considered by his readers, occurs at a significant textual moment, about 50 pages into the book, at the end of the introduction. There Adorno outlines his vision for a philosophical thought to come, among other things by alluding to Marx's eleventh thesis with a provocative and elliptical gesture:

> All music was once in the service of shortening the *longueurs* of the rulers; but the Late Quartets are hardly background music. ... Even the decaying concepts of epistemology point beyond themselves. Right up to their highest formalisms and, before that, in their failure, they are a bit of unconscious history-writing, to be rescued in that they are aided in procuring self-consciousness against what they explicitly mean. This rescuing, mindfulness of the suffering that sediments itself in concepts, waits for the moment of their decay. It is the idea of philosophical critique. It has no other measure than the decay of semblance. If the age of interpreting the world is over and the point is to change it, then philosophy bids farewell, and in its farewell concepts pause and become images.

> Alle Musik war einmal Dienst, um den Oberen die Langeweile zu kürzen, aber die Letzten Quartette sind keine Tafelmusik. ... Auch die hinfälligen Begriffe der Erkenntnistheorie weisen über sich hinaus. Bis in ihre obersten Formalismen hinein, und vorab in ihrem Scheitern, sind sie ein Stück bewußtloser Geschichtsschreibung, zu erretten, indem ihnen zum Selbstbewußtsein verholfen wird gegen das, was sie von sich aus meinen. Diese Rettung, Eingedenken des Leidens, das in den Begriffen sich sedimentiert, wartet auf den Augenblick ihres Zerfalls. Er ist die Idee philosophischer Kritik. Sie hat kein Maß als den Zerfall des Scheins. Ist das Zeitalter der Interpretation der Welt vorüber und gilt es sie zu verändern, dann nimmt Philosophie Abschied, und im Abschied halten die Begriffe inne und werden zu Bildern.[40]

Adorno's passage is too rich, too multilayered, and each of its words too deserving of extensive commentary—which could itself easily fill a book or two—to be considered in its full complexity here. But it is worth remarking upon a few central features that are especially pertinent to the framework of our own particular concerns. It is not a coincidence that the passage begins by referring to the work of art—here the musical work of art in particular, which, for Adorno, always serves as an especially significant stand-in for art and the artwork as such, its conceptual paradigm, as it were. By alluding to Beethoven's late quartets and their incompatibility with the idea that they merely serve as background entertainment, a mere diversion for the powers that be, he sets the stage for a consideration of how the concepts that traverse a given aesthetic or cognitive space may also exceed their own determination, that is, break out of their immediate intentional context in order to perform a different kind of work, yielding a previously unintended effect. One may say that the work of art whose notions are refunctionalized and subsequently reinscribed in this way tend to relate to the world in an unexpected, transformed manner. It is as if concepts were turned against themselves ("gegen das, was sie von sich aus meinen") in order to become what they are.

If Adorno calls this process a form of "Rettung"—rescue, salvation, liberation, or redemption—it is because in the moment when unnecessary suffering becomes aware of itself as such, it takes the first step toward claiming its right to be visible and audible, to be a matter of shared knowledge. What we witness in the work of art is a staging of the ways in which concepts take leave of themselves within the framework of redemption through the practice of self-othering. It is here that suffering ("Leiden") awaits the decomposition of concepts in order to become visible in its own non-self-identity; the decay ("Zerfall") of concepts itself is the idea of philosophical critique. But the decay that is named by the falling-apart of the concepts simultaneously mirrors the decay of (false) semblance, the mere semblance ("Schein") that holds the world in its iron grip. Adorno here alludes to Marx's Thesis 11 when he emphasizes that if the age of world-interpretation ("Zeitalter der Interpretation der Welt vorüber") can be thought to have passed as the world demands change or othering, then philosophy needs to be thought as an inscription in the very movement of its leave-taking, its own particular "Abschied."[41] But something happens

284

in this leave-taking, this ongoing movement of departure and separation: within this abiding motion of leave-taking, the concepts are arrested, as if in a freeze-frame, and they turn into images ("werden zu Bildern"). This moment of turning into images—images that call for a patient and relentlessly rigorous analytic reading—captures the transformation or othering that works to open the conceptual onto the worldly and the philosophical onto the politics of the practical. More precisely, as arrested image, the philosophical concept is shown to have harbored within itself a political, practice-attuned dimension all along, so that what in fact becomes visible in these newly achieved *Bilder* is also the genealogical nature of what steps to the fore as the politico-practical as such. It is thus precisely in taking leave that a new form of arrival is made possible, at least in the contours of an image; leave-taking here gives rise to a concept of world-interpretation that is no longer confined exclusively to the supposedly world-distant sphere of philosophy but also is touched decisively by the more experience-near practicality of political othering.

To think along these political lines in relation to the work of art does not necessarily mean falling prey to the danger that Paul de Man memorably describes as a certain aesthetic ideology: "What we call ideology is precisely the confusion of linguistic with natural reality, of reference with phenomenalism." And he adds: "Those who reproach literary theory for being oblivious to social and historical (that is to say ideological) reality are merely stating their fear at having their own ideological mystifications exposed by the tool they are trying to discredit. They are, in short, very poor readers of Marx's *German Ideology*."[42] This is a crucial point to keep in mind whenever the relation between the aesthetic world of the artwork and the phenomenal world of an extra-aesthetic reality is considered. Yet in the particular case that we have been examining, the aesthetic dimension and the empirical or worldly dimension are not accidentally (or even strategically) mistaken for each other, but rather kept apart precisely so that they, as distinct entities, may enter an unending and potentially transformative dialogue. When the complex precepts for world-othering found in Thesis 11, which resist entering into seamless conformity with what on the surface they appear to postulate, are brought to bear on the relationship between world-decay and world-construction as it comes to be staged in the work of art, we may well be prevailed upon to take leave of a certain concept of the political, along with a certain concept of world. After all, what is most transformative, and therefore most political, with regard to both work and world comes into focus as something that is perpetually inscribed in a movement of leave-taking, the image of a departure without which the concept of a world could hardly begin to be thought. In taking leave, there is a world to be gained.

Coda: Intermundia, Finitude

Having queried the work of art in its relation to world-decay and world-opening by traveling through heterogeneous works from the realms of lyric poetry, painting, music, film, literature, and photography, we are now in a position to hear the question with which we began—Melville's "Ever since Adam, who has got the meaning of this great allegory—the world?"—in differently modulated terms. The world out of which a work of art arises subsequently falls into decay, vanishing into the recesses of history, while that very same work of art sets up a new world according to its own terms. This singular aesthetic object forever resists the closure that comes with the oblivion of having perished and with the emphatic presence subtended by a supposedly transparent legibility. Two worlds that both touch and forever separate in the work of art explicitly posit themselves as question marks to be interrogated, abiding enigmas that draw us into the recalcitrant yet highly suggestive realms of their respective orbits. What is it, finally, that the movement of these two worlds as they are mediated by the artwork demand of thought itself? What kind of thinking could show itself responsible to these movements of world-decay and world-opening that make an artwork what it is?

In a 1984 lecture at the Collège International de Philosophie in Paris addressing the relations between German and French philosophy, Werner Hamacher pursues, among other things, the notion of philosophy as "relentless exploration of that which constitutes the world and its explorations [*rückhaltloser Erkundung dessen, was die Welt und ihre Erkundung ausmacht*]."[1] Working his way through the manifold senses of "reparation" with which post–World War II German philosophy has had to wrestle, he comes to the following conclusion.

For the only place that is appropriate for philosophy is the one where it stands alone. It is not the governor of a world or of a world of expanses, but rather of the *intermundia* between them. It is toward this non-place, which is never already given but requires to be opened up always anew,

287

toward this a-topos that its history, even the most recent one, should be thought through.

Denn der einzige Ort, der der Philosophie ansteht, ist der, an dem sie allein steht. Sie ist nicht die Statthalterin einer Welt oder einer Welt von Weiten, sondern der Intermundien zwischen ihnen. Auf diesen Un-ort, der nie schon gegeben ist, sondern immer aufs Neue erschlossen werden muß, auf diesen Atopos hin müßte ihre Geschichte, auch die jüngste, durchdacht werden.[2]

If philosophy thus understood—and, by extension, as a name for what, more broadly speaking, could be termed critical thought—stands alone, this does not mean that it is isolated, solipsistic, or only concerned with itself. On the contrary, the thinking of world that critical thought pursues in relation to certain phenomena *of* the world—such as the work of art—comes to pass not under the sign of self-identical sovereign rule or the vantage point offered by a stable and secure prevailing, but rather only in the interstices, the *intermundia* that unfold along the margins. Intermundia are precisely the spaces between worlds, the uncharted areas where those worlds do not fully touch, where they are not coextensive. The intermundia—or, in Greek, *metakosmia*, the empty spaces between worlds, which fascinated Epicurus—are the openings not for the gods, as in Epicurus, but for the unfolding of critical thought itself. It is in these intermundia or metakosmia, the open, unsaturated voids between worlds, that thinking takes place. As margins that are hospitable to reflection, these intermundial spaces do not sponsor ideas that are securely anchored in a particular place, their citizenship established, legal documents signed and countersigned by an alleged authority. The opposite is the case. These voids between worlds name the proper realm of thinking itself, where thought is reinvented with each new critical act, perpetually open to reinterpretation.

If Derrida's reading of Heidegger and *Robinson Crusoe* during his final seminar is correct that—as we considered at the beginning of this study—there is no world but only islands, then the thinking of worlds and their mediation by works of art takes place in the intermundial spaces—between worlds, between islands, between ideological, political, and linguistic systems. As we have come to appreciate in the course of this book, works of art, each in its own singular manner, open up an abiding space for intermundial reflection on world and worlds, the one(s) we inhabit and for which we bear an infinite responsibility. Situated between world-decay and world-opening, a genuine aesthetic object reminds us in irreducibly idiomatic ways that it is always *our* world that is at stake.

*

One final reflection is in order. Throughout the course of our investigations, we considered various modulations of the ever-shifting relationship between world-decay and world-opening, that is, between the withdrawal of world and its *poiesis*. The abiding integrity and endurance of the idea of the artwork itself—that is, the significance of the work *as* work and its privileged status as a site for reflection—have been presupposed. Now, however, the question as to the finitude of the artwork as such could be raised. After all, if the work of art as such is exposed to finitude, the relationship that it stages between world-decay and world-opening would itself be exposed to the threat of extinction. This threat can assume many forms: an artwork may be forgotten entirely; it may be accidentally or intentionally destroyed; or it may simply disintegrate over time. Another possibility is that it may no longer be considered valuable, as the particular world of its *poiesis* loses its relevance in a newly unfolding historical and cultural setting. In all of these cases, the aesthetically mediated world that the artwork itself calls into presence would share a similar fate to that of the historical world out of whose decay the artwork once arose. How, then, would the two worlds of the work of art demand to be read in the context the artwork's own finitude? What, in other words, are we to make of the two worlds when the artwork itself is confronted with the end of art?

Although there is a rich and, indeed, ongoing tradition in the history of philosophical aesthetics pertaining to the idea of the end of art, the most consequential engagement with the notion of art's finitude is still the one offered by Hegel. In his *Lectures on Aesthetics*, first published in 1835, four years after his death, Hegel turns his attention to the ways in which art and the works that are created under its name have come to an end. When Hegel differentiates among what he calls symbolic, classical, and romantic art, it is only classical art, by which he means the art produced in ancient Greece, that achieves its highest purpose and fulfillment. For Hegel, as one recent commentator succinctly puts it, "art's highest purpose is to bring substance or spirit into sensuous appearance in such a way that the inner content has fully and without rest found expression in the outward form of an undifferentiated whole," attained only "in Classical Greece because here art became the highest and fullest of the Greek's politico-religious essence, which Hegel refers to elsewhere as 'art-religion.'"[3] To the extent that subsequent art, even the modern or romantic art that reached into Hegel's time—in which, for him, the end of art in fact comes to pass for good—fails to attain such a status, its decline cannot be interrupted, much less reversed. The end of art in the Hegelian sense, however, does not mean that artworks will no longer be produced or recognized as such in the world going forward. Rather, it means that art will have lost its standing as a sacred and deeply significant domain in which the essence of a Dasein and its relation to that world in which it occurs can be glimpsed in the flawless unity of its form and content.

In "The Origin of the Work of Art"—the text in which Heidegger first mobilizes the relation between world-decay and world-opening in relation to the artwork—the thinker is attentive to Hegel's notion of the end of art. In the "Nachwort," or epilogue, Heidegger quotes three specific sentences from Hegel's *Lectures on Aesthetics*, which he credits as "the most comprehensive reflection on the essence of art that the West possesses—comprehensive because it stems from metaphysics."[4] Stemming from three distinct passages of the *Lectures*, the three Hegel sentences read:

Art no longer counts for us as the highest manner [*nicht mehr in der höchsten Weise*] in which truth obtains existence for itself.

One may well hope that art will continue to advance and perfect itself, but its form has ceased to be the highest need of spirit [*das höchste Bedürfnis des Geistes zu sein*].

In all these relationships art is and remains for us, on the side of the highest vocation, something past [*nach der Seite ihrer höchsten Bestimmung für uns ein Vergangenes*].[5]

Heidegger glosses Hegel's sentences by reminding us that the "judgment that Hegel passes in these statements cannot be evaded by pointing out that since Hegel's lectures on aesthetics were given for the last time during the winter of 1828–1829 at the University of Berlin we have seen the rise of many new artworks and new art movements. Hegel never meant to deny this possibility."[6] The "question remains," however, as to how we should relate to Hegel's thesis concerning the end of art. One way of concretizing this problem is to pose the question as follows: "Is art still an essential and necessary way in which that truth happens which is decisive for our historical existence, or is art no longer of this character? If, however, it is such no longer, then there remains the question as to why this is so."[7] This question has not been wholly answered; it continues to be negotiated by philosophical thought fully as much as by aesthetic practice. As Heidegger suggests, the "truth of Hegel's judgment has not yet been decided; for behind this verdict there stands Western thought since the Greeks. Such thought corresponds to the truth of beings that has already happened." And he concludes: "Decision upon the judgment will be made, when it is made, from and about this truth of beings. Until then the judgment remains in force. But for that very reason the question is necessary as to whether the truth that the judgment declares is final and conclusive, and what follows if it is."[8] Heidegger thus keeps Hegel's judgment in abeyance, suspended in an episteme in which Western metaphysics may find that its historical and intellectual predominance has waned. This holding-in-abeyance corresponds to a drawn-out decay, a "dying" of art that "occurs so slowly that it takes a few centuries [*Das Sterben geht so langsam vor sich, daß es einige Jahrhunderte braucht*]."[9]

One way of thinking about the finitude of the slowly dying artwork in relation to the movement of world-decay and the world-
opening upon which it pivots is to hold it in similar abeyance.
This is to say, that which the work gives us to think—and how it
gives us to think—in relation to the idea of world must always also
be considered from the perspective of the possible end of art, the
idea that we already live in a kind of inherited aftermath of the artwork. In other words, the possibility that art itself is always already
exposed to its own finitude—even and especially as it speaks to us
of the world's demise and of its *poiesis*—must be invited into our
reflections on an aesthetic object's particular mode of relating to
the worldness of a world as well as its decay.

Acknowledgments

This book about the idea of "world" was written during the COVID-19 pandemic, which, beginning in March 2020, forced much of what we call the world to close. It is dedicated to the abiding memory of those whose world came to a cruel end during that time, as well as to those survivors for whom the loss of another marked the end of a unique world in another sense. I am grateful to my family, friends, and colleagues, both alive and dead, for continuing to populate my world—indeed, for making this world what it is—and for allowing me to believe that, on a number of different levels, the last word has not been spoken just yet. By the same token, I am thankful to my courageous and engaged students, both undergraduate and graduate, who have had to endure so much hardship and disruption during these past two years, for reminding me that the world of the mind counts more than ever. They choose life and affirmation over destruction and cynicism; they choose thoughtfulness and reflection over autocracy and the unbridled will to power. As such, they also are the light and the counterweight to the ever-darkening world of today's neoliberal managerial university that so often keeps us all in the lock of its corporate stranglehold. Not everything is for sale.

I wish to thank Andrew Moore for graciously furnishing the photographs of his that I discuss in chapter 6 and for allowing the remarkable *House on Walden Street, East Side* from his Detroit project to appear on the cover. I also thank the Ministère de la Culture et de la Communication France and the Museo Nacional del Prado in Madrid for supplying additional images. Image researcher Emma Brown helped me with the sourcing of several Chauvet Cave images. I am particularly grateful for the generous reports and insightful questions by the three stellar scholars whom the MIT Press selected as peer reviewers of my manuscript and who, after the usual acceptance process was completed at the Press, chose to reveal their identities to me: Rebecca Comay, John Hamilton, and Dimitris Vardoulakis. I thank Kristina Mendicino for kindly reading a penultimate version of the text and, beyond this study, for sharing a commitment to meaningful faculty governance and the values of academic freedom. At the MIT Press, Tom Weaver has been an exemplary and inspiring editor with whom to work; it is difficult for me to imagine a more thoughtful, responsive, and enthusiastic publishing partner. I also appreciate the circumspect care and attentiveness that Matthew

Abbate brought to the preparation of the final manuscript and the efficiency with which Gabriela Bueno Gibbs attended to the logistics of production. My friend and former doctoral student Karen Embry prepared a superb index.

An earlier and shorter version of chapter 7 first appeared as an article in the journal *Derrida Today* 14:1 (May 2021).

Providence, Rhode Island, March 2022

Notes

A note on translations:
On occasion, published
translations of quotations
have been slightly adjusted
to enhance their fidelity
to the original. Where
no English translation is
indicated, the translation is
my own.

Introduction
1. Herman Melville to
Nathaniel Hawthorne,
November 17, 1851, in
Correspondence, ed. Lynn
Horth, vol. 14 of *The Writings
of Herman Melville*, ed.
Harrison Hayford (Evanston:
Northwestern University
Press and the Newberry
Library, 1993), 211–212.
2. Thomas Rentsch,
"Welt," in *Historisches
Wörterbuch der Philosophie*,
ed. Joachim Ritter, Karlfried
Gründer, and Gottfried
Gabriel, vol. 12 (Basel:
Schwabe, 2004), 408.
3. Ibid.
4. Sean Gaston, *The
Concept of World from Kant to
Derrida* (London: Rowman
and Littlefield International,
2013), 3. See also Rudolph
Berlinger, *Philosophie als
Weltwissenschaft*, 2 vols.
(Amsterdam: Rodopi,
1975 1980).
5. Martin Heidegger,
*The Fundamental Concepts of
Metaphysics: World, Finitude,
Solitude*, trans. William
McNeill and Nicholas Walker
(Bloomington: Indiana
University Press, 1995), 5; *Die
Grundbegriffe der Metaphysik.
Welt—Endlichkeit—Einsamkeit*,
vol. 29/30 of Heidegger,

Gesamtausgabe, ed. Friedrich-
Wilhelm von Herrmann
(Frankfurt am Main:
Klostermann, 1983), 7f.
6. Heidegger, *Fundamental
Concepts*, 352 / *Grundbegriffe*, 512.
7. Ibid., 349 / 507.
8. Ibid., 350 / 508.
9. Ibid., 350 / 509.
10. Ibid., 351 / 509f.
11. Ibid., 356 / 518.
12. Martin Heidegger,
Being and Time, trans. John
Macquarrie and Edward
Robinson (San Francisco:
Harper, 1962), 247; *Sein und
Zeit*, 16th ed. (Tübingen:
Niemeyer, 1986), 203.
13. Heidegger, *Being and
Time*, 249 / *Sein und Zeit*, 205.
14. Jacques Derrida, *The
Beast and the Sovereign*, vol. 2,
ed. Michel Lisse, Marie-
Louise Mallet, and Ginette
Michaud, trans. Geoffrey
Bennington (Chicago:
University of Chicago Press,
2010), 8f.
15. Ibid., 9.
16. Ibid.
17. Jacques Derrida, "Rams:
Uninterrupted Dialogue—
Between Two Infinities,
the Poem," in Derrida,
*Sovereignties in Question: The
Poetics of Paul Celan*, trans.
Thomas Dutoit (New York:
Fordham University Press,
2005), 135–163, here 158.
18. Derrida, *Beast and
Sovereign*, vol. 2, 268.
19. Ibid.
20. Ibid., 170.
21. Michael Naas, *The
End of the World and Other
Teachable Moments: Jacques
Derrida's Final Seminar* (New
York: Fordham University
Press, 2014), 60.
22. It would be instructive
to compare, by means of a

careful and detailed reading,
this sense of *poiesis*—
understood in relation to
the movement of world-
decay and world-opening
in the work of art—to
Niklas Luhmann's systems-
theoretical understanding
of world and art. For him,
art "respects the world as
something unobservable, as
something that cannot be
viewed from the outside. It
explicates the world from the
inside." As such, the relation
of art and world becomes
thinkable when what emerge
are "the different forms of
engaging with that which
becomes unobservable
through observation
[*verschiedene Formen des
Umgangs mit dem, was durch
Beobachtung unbeobachtbar
wird*]." Niklas Luhmann,
"Weltkunst," in *Soziologie
der Kunst*, ed. J. Gerhards
(Opladen: Westdeutscher
Verlag, 1997), 55–102, here 99.
23. Rodolphe Gasché,
"A Sense of the World," in
Gasché, *Persuasion, Reflection,
Judgment: Ancillae Vitae*
(Bloomington: Indiana
University Press, 2017), 184–
222, here 219.

It would also be necessary,
in another investigation,
to read this Arendtian
emphasis on natality and
birth in relation to her
politico-epistemological
interest in the concept
of world alienation. For
instance, as she suggests
in section 35 of *The Human
Condition*, entitled "World
Alienation," the "eclipse of
a common public world, so
crucial to the formation of
the lonely mass man and so

dangerous in the formation of the worldless mentality of modern ideological mass movements, began with the much more tangible loss of a privately owned share in the world." Hannah Arendt, "World Alienation," in Arendt, *The Human Condition*, 2nd ed. (Chicago: University of Chicago Press, 1998), 248–257, here 257.

24. These are the terms mobilized by Markus Gabriel, who, by emphasizing the "non-existence of the world," insists on "an explosion of sense. For, everything exists only because it appears in a field of sense. Because an all-encompassing field of sense cannot exist, there exists an unlimited plurality of fields of sense." This, to him, is "joyful news," because there "is no super-object to which we must surrender in our lifetime" and because the nonexistence of the world within the world affords us supposedly "infinite possibilities." Markus Gabriel, *Why the World Does Not Exist*, trans. Gregory S. Moss (Cambridge: Polity, 2015), 220.

25. See Roland Végsö, *Worldlessness after Heidegger: Phenomenology, Psychoanalysis, Deconstruction* (Edinburgh: Edinburgh University Press, 2020).

26. This is the perspective adopted by Timothy Morton, *Hyperobjects: Philosophy and Ecology after the End of the World* (Minneapolis: University of Minnesota Press, 2013).

27. Jean-Luc Nancy, "World," in Nancy, *The Sense of the World*, trans. Jeffrey S. Librett (Minneapolis:

University of Minnesota Press, 1997), 154–160, here 160.

28. Friedrich Nietzsche, *Die fröhliche Wissenschaft*, vol. 3 of Nietzsche, *Kritische Studienausgabe*, ed. Giorgio Colli and Mazzino Montinari (Munich: DTV; Berlin: De Gruyter, 1999), 627.

Chapter 1

1. Jost Hermand, "Vom Umgang mit älterer Kunst," in Hermand, *Nach der Postmoderne. Ästhetik heute* (Cologne: Böhlau, 2004), 18–42; cf. "Nähe in der Distanz. Über den Umgang mit Werken älterer Kunst," in Hermand, *Beethoven. Werk und Wirkung*, 2nd ed. (Cologne: Böhlau, 2020), 165–177.

2. Fredric Jameson, *The Political Unconscious: Narrative as a Socially Symbolic Act* (Ithaca: Cornell University Press, 1981), 9.

3. Ibid., 10.

4. Stephen Greenblatt, *Shakespearean Negotiations: The Circulation of Social Energy in Renaissance England* (Berkeley: University of California Press, 1989), 1.

5. Martin Heidegger, "The Origin of the Work of Art," trans. Alfred Hofstadter, in Heidegger, *Basic Writings*, ed. David Farrell Krell, rev. and expanded ed. (San Francisco: Harper, 1993), 139–212, here 166; "Der Ursprung des Kunstwerkes," in *Holzwege*, ed. Friedrich-Wilhelm von Hermann, vol. 5 of Heidegger, *Gesamtausgabe* (Frankfurt am Main: Klostermann, 2003), 1–74, here 26.

6. Heidegger, "Origin," 166 / "Ursprung," 27.

7. Ibid., 166 / 26.

8. Ibid., 166f. / 26f.

9. For the specific purposes of the present book—which, as a whole, is designed to extend beyond the immediate realm of Heidegger's own thought—we will bracket the other term that Heidegger mobilizes in his lecture, the all-sheltering realm of "earth" (*die Erde*). For Heidegger, world and earth stand in a relation of generative strife. A useful interpretation of the concept of earth as it relates to world can be found, for instance, in Friedrich-Wilhelm von Herrmann, *Heideggers Philosophie der Kunst. Eine systematische Interpretation der Holzwege-Abhandlung "Der Ursprung des Kunstwerkes,"* 2nd ed. (Frankfurt am Main: Klostermann, 1994), 294–323. Cf. John Sallis, *Echoes: After Heidegger* (Bloomington: Indiana University Press, 1990), 176f., as well as Julian Young, *Heidegger's Philosophy of Art* (Cambridge: Cambridge University Press, 2001), 38–45. A comparative reading of earth as it functions in the artwork essay and in Heidegger's later conception of the fourfold is offered by Andrew Mitchell, *The Fourfold: Reading the Later Heidegger* (Evanston: Northwestern University Press, 2015), 71–115.

10. Heidegger, "Origin," 167 / "Ursprung," 27.

11. Ibid., 169 / 30f.

12. Ibid., 169 / 30.

13. Ibid., 170 / 30.

14. Ibid., 170 / 30f.

15. Ibid., 170 / 31.

16. Martin Heidegger, *Introduction to Metaphysics*, trans. Gregory Fried and Richard Polt (New Haven: Yale University Press, 2000), 9; *Einführung in die Metaphysik*, 2nd ed. (Tübingen: Niemeyer, 1958), 6.

17. Maurice Blanchot, "The Work and the Errant Word," in Blanchot, *The Space of Literature*, trans. Ann Smock (Lincoln: University of Nebraska Press, 1982), 51–56, here 54.

18. As my colleague Kristina Mendicino eloquently pointed out to me after reading the present chapter, the "conversation with the elderly women at Heidegger's grave exposes the structure of world-decay in yet another way, as well as the precarity of those works which remain in its wake. In the women's memory, Hölderlin's lines sound as though they had faded to an anonymous and vanishing trace, but one which the women nevertheless affirmed in relating their experience," and the "work of attending to this instance of 'absent meaning' / 'sens absent' marks, in turn, an exemplary vigilance and affirmation." (Email to the author, August 5, 2021.)

19. Martin Heidegger, "*Der Spiegel* Interview with Martin Heidegger," in *The Heidegger Reader*, trans. Jerome Veith (Bloomington: Indiana University Press, 2009), 313–333, here 330; "Spiegel-Gespräch mit Martin Heidegger," in *Heidegger Lesebuch* (Frankfurt am Main: Klostermann, 2007), 345–370, here 366.

20. *Zum Gedenken an Martin Heidegger, 1889–1976*, ed. Stadt Meßkirch (Meßkirch: Schönebeck, 1977).

21. Martin Heidegger, *Martin Heidegger liest Hölderlin*, vinyl LP (Pfullingen: Neske, 1960). The recording has since been reissued as a CD under the same title (Klett-Cotta Verlag, 1997).

22. Martin Heidegger, "Hölderlin and the Essence of Poetry," trans. Jerome Veith, in *The Heidegger Reader*, 117–129, here 118; "Hölderlin und das Wesen der Dichtung," in Heidegger, *Erläuterungen zu Hölderlins Dichtung* (Frankfurt am Main: Klostermann, 1951), 31–45, here 31.

23. Heidegger, "Hölderlin and the Essence," 118 / "Hölderlin und das Wesen," 32.

24. Friedrich Hölderlin, "Brod und Wein (Erste Fassung)," in Hölderlin, *Sämtliche Werke und Briefe*, vol. 1, ed. Michael Knaupp (Munich: Hanser, 1992), 372–383, here 374.

25. Friedrich Hölderlin, "Bread and Wine," trans. Michael Hamburger, in Hölderlin, *Selected Poems and Fragments*, ed. Jeremy Adler (London: Penguin, 1998), 151–158, here 153.

26. Friedrich Hölderlin, "Das Gasthaus," in *Sämtliche Werke und Briefe*, vol. 1, 308–310, here 308.

27. Friedrich Hölderlin, "Brief an Böhlendorf, 4. Dezember 1801," in *Sämtliche Werke und Briefe*, vol. 2, 913.

28. Friedrich Hölderlin, "Brod und Wein (Zweite Fassung)," in *Sämtliche Werke und Briefe*, vol. 1, 373–383, here 375.

29. One might profitably place Hölderlin's affirmative substitution of "Lebendiges" for "Eigenes" in syntactical relation with Jacques Derrida's reflections in his final interview: "Everything I say—at least from '*Pas*' (in *Parages*) on—about survival as a complication of the opposition life/death proceeds in me from an unconditional affirmation of life. This surviving is life beyond life, life more than life, and my discourse is not a discourse of death, but, on the contrary, the affirmation of a living being who prefers living and thus surviving to death, because survival is not simply that which remains but the most intense life possible. I am never more haunted by the necessity of dying in moments of happiness and joy. To feel joy and to weep over the death that awaits me are for me the same thing." Jacques Derrida, *Learning to Live Finally*, trans. Pascale-Anne Brault and Michael Naas (Hoboken, NJ: Melville, 2007), 51f.

30. Martin Heidegger, "Letter on Humanism," trans. Frank A. Capuzzi and J. Glenn Gray, in *Basic Writings*, 213–265, here 220; *Über den Humanismus*, 10th, expanded ed. (Frankfurt am Main: Klostermann, 2000), 8.

31. Ibid.

32. Martin Heidegger, "What Calls for Thinking?," trans. Fred D. Wieck and J. Glenn Gray, in *Basic Writings*, 365–391, here 369; *Was heißt Denken?*, 5th ed. (Tübingen: Niemeyer, 1997), 1.

33. This nugget of soccer history is offered by Rüdiger

Safranski, who also records that Heidegger was fond of discussing soccer games and tactics in detail and that Heidegger himself was a successful soccer player—in fact, a left winger—during his youth in Meßkirch. *Ein Meister aus Deutschland. Heidegger und seine Zeit* (Frankfurt am Main: Fischer, 1997), 472.

34. Heidegger, "Origin," 196 / "Ursprung," 59.

35. Ibid., 197 / 59.

36. Ibid., 197 / 60.

37. Ibid., 198 / 61.

38. Ibid., 199 / 62.

39. Martin Heidegger, "What Is Metaphysics?," trans. David Farrell Krell, in *Basic Writings*, 89–110, here 97; *Was ist Metaphysik?*, 14th ed. (Frankfurt am Main: Klostermann, 1992), 29.

40. Ibid., 96 / 27.

41. Ibid., 97 / 28.

42. Ibid., 103 / 34.

43. Ibid., 105 / 37.

44. Ibid., 109 / 40.

45. Ibid., 103 / 35.

46. Ibid., 109 / 41.

47. Ibid., 110 / 42.

Chapter 2

1. Georges Bataille, *Prehistoric Painting: Lascaux or the Birth of Art*, trans. Austryn Wainhouse (London: Mcmillan, 1980), 11.

2. Ibid., 12.

3. Ibid., 12f.

4. Ibid., 13.

5. Ibid., 13.

6. Maurice Blanchot, "The Birth of Art," in Blanchot, *Friendship*, trans. Elizabeth Rottenberg (Stanford: Stanford University Press, 1997), 1–11, here 1.

7. Ibid.

8. Ibid.

9. Ibid.

10. Ibid.

11. Ibid.,1f.

12. Ibid., 2f.

13. Ibid., 3.

14. Ibid.

15. Ibid.

16. Ibid., 6. Another way of framing this perspective is to attend to the question of the self-conscious "uselessness" of the images at Lascaux, their hermeneutic and pragmatic retreat from the domain of use—and thus from an established meaning or signifying function as posited by a framework of usefulness. As Suzanne Guerlac suggests in relation to Bataille's reading of Lascaux, "Bataille wants to convince us that these paintings were useless to primitive man, created in sheer exuberance as a celebration of the magical per se, the sacred. What he does not explicitly say, however, is that it is just as important that these images remains useless *to us*. Otherwise, they would lose their power of seduction and cease to communicate." Suzanne Guerlac, "Bataille in Theory: Afterimages (Lascaux)," *diacritics* 26, no. 2 (1996): 6–17, here 15.

17. Maurice Blanchot, *The Writing of the Disaster*, trans. Ann Smock (Lincoln: University of Nebraska Press, 1995), 42; *L'écriture du désastre* (Paris: Gallimard, 1980), 72.

18. Blanchot, "The Birth of Art," 3.

19. Ibid., 3f.

20. Ibid., 4.

21. Ibid.

22. Ibid., 4f.

23. Walter Benjamin, "On the Concept of History," trans. Harry Zohn, in Benjamin, *Selected Writings*, vol. 4: *1938–1940*, ed. Howard Eiland and Michael W. Jennings (Cambridge: Harvard University Press, 2003), 389–411, here 392.

24. Blanchot, "The Birth of Art," 7.

25. Ibid.

26. Ibid.

27. For a consideration of Bataille's understanding of origin in relation to his experience of the Lascaux cave and in the context of his writings more broadly, see Steven Ungar, "Phantom Lascaux: Origin of the Work of Art," *Yale French Studies* 78 (1990): 246–262.

28. Blanchot, "The Birth of Art," 10f. As for the presence of the only human depiction at Lascaux in the form of the schematically drawn man, early scholarly attempt at interpretation are summarized and briefly evaluated by Bataille himself in the section "The Various Explications of the Well Scene" of *Prehistoric Painting: Lascaux or the Birth of Art*, 139f. For a more recent survey of possible interpretations of the well scene (from which Blanchot, however, is absent), see Akira Mizuta Lippit, "*Arche*texts: Lascaux, Eros, and the Anamorphic Subject," *Discourse* 24, no. 2 (2002): 18–29, here 20ff.

29. Blanchot's letter is included in Georges Bataille, *Choix de lettres*, ed. Michel Surya (Paris: Gallimard, 1997), 589; cited in

Christophe Bident, *Maurice Blanchot: A Critical Biography*, trans. John McKeane (New York: Fordham University Press, 2019), 246.

30. The voice that keeps us company in Blanchot's text appears infinitely mindful of this perpetual making and unmaking. As Jean-Luc Nancy puts it in general terms in the context of his brief meditation "In Blanchot's Company," "Blanchot's voice understands—or declares—itself to be the voice of someone alive yet already reported missing or believed dead: dead, that is, while still living on in his own words, according to the sameness [*mêmeté*] of those words that still persist," even while "history itself may have been rent in two" and he "can speak only with that break in his throat." Jean-Luc Nancy, "In Blanchot's Company," trans. Leslie Hill, in Nancy, *Multiple Arts: The Muses II*, ed. Simon Sparks (Stanford: Stanford University Press, 2006), 82–84, here 83.

31. Blanchot, "The Birth of Art," 9.

32. One might say that it is for this reason, too, that Blanchot, in a 1958 essay entitled "The Beast of Lascaux," takes up a phrase first used by his friend, the poet René Char, with whose work that essay engages. Blanchot refers to a moment in Char's poem "La parole en archipel" which was composed in response to, and in conversation with, the "Pregnant Cow" painting at Lascaux,

"looking at the frieze at Lascaux" and identifying the human, through the animal image, "as the figure of '*the unnamable Beast.*'" Commemorating the friends' shared fascination with the ways in which the experience of being human is staged at the Lascaux cave precisely through the visual engagement with the world of the unnamable and enigmatic animal, Blanchot comments: "Strange wisdom, too ancient for Socrates yet also too new, from which, however, despite the unease that made him distance himself from it, we must think that he is not excluded, he who accepted as a guarantee of speech only the presence of a living person, and who nonetheless came to die from it, in order to keep his word." Maurice Blanchot, "The Beast of Lascaux," in Blanchot, *A Voice from Elsewhere*, trans. Charlotte Mandell (Albany: State University of New York Press, 2007), 31–51, here 51.

33. Blanchot, "The Birth of Art," 11.

34. It would be instructive to compare this view of the work as having no need of its creator with the perspective that Michel Foucault assumes with regard to Blanchot and the thought of the outside: "Blanchot is perhaps more than just another witness to this thought. So far has he withdrawn into the manifestation of his work, so completely is he, not hidden by his texts, but absent from their existence and absent by virtue of the marvelous force

of their existence, that for us he is that thought itself—its real, absolutely distant, shimmering, invisible presence, its inevitable law, its calm, infinite, measured strength." Michel Foucault, "Maurice Blanchot: The Thought from Outside," trans. Brian Massumi, in Michel Foucault and Maurice Blanchot, *"The Thought from Outside" and "Michel Foucault as I Imagine Him"* (New York: Zone Books, 1987), 7–58, here 19.

35. Werner Herzog, *Cave of Forgotten Dreams* (New York: IFC Films, 2011).

36. Werner Herzog's "Director's Statement" concerning *Cave of Forgotten Dreams* can be found on Herzog's official website: https://www.wernerherzog.com/.

37. Georges Bataille, *Die vorgeschichtliche Malerei. Lascaux oder die Geburt der Kunst*, trans. Karl-Georg Hemmerich (Geneva: Skira, 1955).

38. One might say that Herzog's observation concerning the Chauvet cave, especially as it pertains to the destabilizing and mobilizing effect that the uneven walls have on the experience of viewing these paintings, implicitly communes with the earlier reflections of Maurice Merleau-Ponty on the Lascaux cave paintings. In "Eye and Mind," Merleau-Ponty writes that the "animals painted on the walls of Lascaux are not there in the same way as the fissures and limestone formations. But they are not *elsewhere*. Pushed forward

here, held back there, held up by the wall's mass they use so adroitly, they spread around the wall without ever breaking from their elusive moorings in it." And he continues by confessing that "I would be at great pains to say *where* is the painting I am looking at. For I do not look at it as a thing; I do not fix it in its place. My gaze wanders in it as in the halos of Being." For Merleau-Ponty it is therefore "more accurate to say that I see according to it, or with it, than that I *see it*." Maurice Merleau-Ponty, "Eye and Mind," trans. Carleton Dallery, in Merleau-Ponty, *The Primacy of Perception, and Other Essays on Phenomenological Psychology, the Philosophy of Art, History and Politics*, ed. James M. Edie (Evanston: Northwestern University Press, 1964), 159–190, here 164. Even though Merleau-Ponty is not concerned with the proto-cinematic aspects of the uneven and flowing walls, his phenomenological description of their effect upon the viewing experience also is pertinent to the images' quasi-cinematic quality of movement, restlessness, and visual dynamism. That is to say, the viewer is trained to acquire a way of looking that unfolds in accordance with a certain precept of perceiving, rather than merely following the established protocols of *looking at* something in a more stable or static manner.

39. This sense of an aesthetically mediated inheritance in which there is a

kind of spectral communion between artists across scarcely imaginable spans of time is confirmed when Herzog, already toward the beginning of the film, self-consciously remarks in his narration: "Their images are memories of long-forgotten dreams. Is this their heartbeat or ours? Will we ever be able to understand the vision of the artists across such an abyss of time?"

40. Within the context of that world, the specific function of the 76 images of a mammoth in the Chauvet cave is examined archaeologically by Bernard Gely and Marc Azéma, *Les mammouths de la grotte Chauvet* (Paris: Éditions du Seuil, 2005). For a broader historical contextualization, see the account by the three discoverers of the Chauvet cave, Jean-Marie Chauvet, Éliette Brunel Deschamps, and Christian Hillaire, *Dawn of Art: The Chauvet Cave* (New York: Abrams, 1996).

41. And, by extension, the status of the child and of childhood in the broader world of the Chauvet cave remains enigmatic in and of itself. Herzog points to his interest in this question in a conversation about *Cave of Forgotten Dreams* with the film critic Samuel Wigley, in which he observes that one must "speculate that there might have been cannibalism, because in all Paleolithic and Neolithic cultures you have evidence of it. When for them did the human being begin to exist?" He continues: "It's an interesting question because

you find skeleton remains of babies with the garbage, but children who were over three years old were buried. So, human toddlers, who did not speak yet, apparently for them did not yet have human nature." For Herzog, therefore, at stake "are very deep questions about human beings who are, in a way, us, and yet separated by an abyss of time." "Out of Darkness: Werner Herzog's Cave of Forgotten Dreams," in *Werner Herzog: Interviews*, ed. Eric Ames (Jackson: University Press of Mississippi, 2014), 172–180, here 178.

42. As the art historian Rosalind Krauss points out, many of the handprints at Gargas "are curiously missing one or several finger joints, from one or several fingers. Abbé Breuil, the first great theoretician of the art of the caves, had a theory for this disfigurement as well. It was, he said, the result of initiation rites in which certain digits of the young hunter would be, as it were, circumcised." Rosalind E. Krauss, *The Optical Unconscious* (Cambridge, MA: MIT Press, 1993), 151. As Suzanne Guerlac suggests in relation to Krauss's engagement with Gargas, if the "palm prints of Gargas place the index at the very origin of art," it is also the case that the "substitution of Gargas for Lascaux" in such perspectives "parallels the displacement already noted from Breton to Duchamp," which is to say that the "move from Lascaux to Gargas" may enable a circumvention of the issue of "fictive figuration."

Suzanne Guerlac, "The Useless Image: Bataille, Bergson, Magritte," *Representations* 97, no. 1 (2007): 28–56, here 48f.

43. Martin Heidegger, "What Calls for Thinking?," trans. Fred D. Wieck and J. Glenn Gray, in Heidegger, *Basic Writings*, ed. David Farrell Krell, rev. and expanded ed. (San Francisco: Harper, 1993), 365–391, here 380.

44. Ibid., 380f.

45. For an extended discussion, driven by both admiration and worry, of Heidegger's insistence on the singular human hand, see Jacques Derrida, "*Geschlecht* II: Heidegger's Hand," trans. John P. Leavy, Jr., in *Deconstruction and Philosophy: The Texts of Jacques Derrida*, ed. John Sallis (Chicago: University of Chicago Press, 1987), 161–196. Cf. David Farrell Krell's reflections on Derrida's reading of Heidegger's hand in Krell, *Phantoms of the Other: Four Generations of Derrida's Geschlecht* (Albany: State University of New York Press, 2015), 47–67.

46. Jean-Luc Nancy, *Portrait*, trans. Sarah Clift and Simon Sparks (New York: Fordham University Press, 2018), 56.

47. Ibid.

48. Ibid.

49. Ibid., 56ff. For a general discussion, from the perspective of Paleolithic archaeology, of the presentation of lions and the cat family in the Chauvet cave, cf. Marc Azéma and Jean Clottes, *Les félins de la grotte Chauvet* (Paris: Éditions du Seuil, 2005).

Chapter 3

1. An excellent genealogy is offered by Jan-Peter Pudelek, "Werk," in *Ästhetische Grundbegriffe*, vol. 6, ed. Karlheinz Barck, Martin Fontius, Dieter Schlenstedt, Burkhart Steinwachs, and Friedrich Wolfzettel (Stuttgart: Metzler, 2010), 520–588. See also Georg Bensch, *Vom Kunstwerk zum ästhetischen Objekt. Zur Geschichte der phänomenologischen Ästhetik* (Munich: Fink, 1994), and John Margolis, *What, After All, Is a Work of Art? Lectures in the Philosophy of Art* (University Park: Pennsylvania State University Press, 1999).

2. Roland Barthes, "From Work to Text," in Barthes, *Image—Music—Text*, trans. Stephen Heath (New York: Hill and Wang, 1977), 155–164.

3. Emmanuel Levinas, "The Trace of the Other," trans. Alphonso Lingis, in *Deconstruction in Context: Literature and Philosophy*, ed. Mark C. Taylor (Chicago: University of Chicago Press, 1986), 345–359, here 348.

4. Ibid.

5. Ibid.

6. Ibid.

7. Ibid., 349.

8. Ibid.

9. Ibid.

10. Ibid.

11. Ibid.

12. Ibid.

13. Ibid.

14. Ibid.

15. Walter Benjamin, "Franz Kafka. Zur zehnten Wiederkehr seines Todestages," in *Benjamin über Kafka. Texte, Briefzeugnisse, Aufzeichnungen*, ed. Hermann Schweppenhäuser (Frankfurt am Main: Suhrkamp, 1981), 9–38, here 14.

16. Levinas, "The Trace of the Other," 349.

17. Emmanuel Levinas, *Totality and Infinity: An Essay on Exteriority*, trans. Alphonso Lingis (Pittsburgh: Duquesne University Press, 2003), 23.

18. Paul Celan, "Die Welt," in *Fadensonne*, vol. 1 of Celan, *Gesammelte Werke* (Frankfurt am Main: Suhrkamp, 2000), 190.

19. It also would be fruitful, in a future investigation, to place these lines into comparative syntactical relation with another, later poem by Celan, also entitled "Die Welt" ("The World") and included in his posthumous collection *Zeitgehöft*. In that 1970 poem, which is one of the last ones he finished, the comma comes to separate *Welt* and *Welt* as well as *ich* and *ich*: "Die Welt, Welt, / in allen Fürzen gerecht // ich, ich, / bei dir, dir, Kahl- / geschorne." Paul Celan, "Die Welt," in *Zeitgehöft*, vol. 3 of Celan, *Gesammelte Werke* (Frankfurt am Main: Suhrkamp, 2000), 119. In this self-separation, which is to say, this non-self-identity of both world and self, a transformed idea of world comes to pass. I thank John Hamilton for reminding me of this later poem.

20. Paul Celan, "Gegenlicht," in *Gesammelte Werke*, vol. 3, 163–165, here 164.

21. William Wordsworth, "The World Is Too Much with Us," in Wordsworth, *The Major Works*, ed. Stephen Gill (Oxford: Oxford University Press, 2008), 270.

Chapter 4

1. A consideration of the relationship between Adorno and Hegel with regard to the question of inheritance can be found in Gerhard Richter, "The Inheritance of the Constellation: Adorno and Hegel," in Richter, *Thinking with Adorno: The Uncoercive Gaze* (New York: Fordham University Press, 2019), 70–94.

2. For an extended reading of these texts, see Gerhard Richter, "Buried Possibility: Adorno and Arendt on Tradition," in *Thinking with Adorno*, 39–69.

3. Theodor W. Adorno, *Ästhetische Theorie*, vol. 3 of Adorno, *Gesammelte Schriften*, ed. Rolf Tiedemann (Frankfurt am Main: Suhrkamp, 1997), 124.

4. Theodor W. Adorno, "Das Erbe und die neue Musik," in *Musikalische Schriften V*, vol. 18 of Adorno, *Gesammelte Schriften*, ed. Rolf Tiedemann (Frankfurt am Main: Suhrkamp, 1997), 684–694.

5. Adorno's intention to dedicate the published version of his inaugural lecture to Benjamin becomes apparent in the latter's letter to Adorno dated July 25, 1931. The lecture was not published, however, during Benjamin's or Adorno's lifetime, appearing only posthumously in the context of Adorno's collected writings, the *Gesammelte Schriften*. Theodor W. Adorno and Walter Benjamin, *Briefwechsel 1928–1940*, ed. Henri Lonitz (Frankfurt am Main: Suhrkamp, 1994), 21. The following summer semester (1932), Adorno would offer a graduate seminar at the University of Frankfurt on Benjamin's *Trauerspiel* book, *Origins of the German Mourning Play*, in what would become the first course on Benjamin ever offered at a university.

6. Theodor W. Adorno, "Die Aktualität der Philosophie," in *Gesammelte Schriften*, vol. 1, ed. Rolf Tiedemann (Frankfurt am Main: Suhrkamp, 1997), 325–344, here 335.

7. Ibid.

8. Adorno, "Das Erbe und die neue Musik," 684.

9. Ibid.

10. Ibid., 685.

11. Ibid., 688.

12. This is pointed out by Eberhard Ortland, the German editor of Adorno's 1958–1959 lecture course on aesthetics, in his editorial notes to that publication. He adds that, even though Adorno did not explicitly employ the term "subcutaneous" in relation to his theory of musical reproduction, its logic also plays a role in that context: "As the central thesis for his projected book on the 'theory of musical reproduction,' Adorno noted in 1946: 'True reproduction is the X-ray image of the work. Its task is to render visible all the relations, all aspects of context, contrast, and construction that lie beneath the surface of the perceptible sound.' (*Towards a Theory of Musical Reproduction*, ed. Henri Lonitz, trans. Wieland Hoban (Cambridge, Polity, 2006), p. 1.)" Eberhard Ortland, "Editor's Notes," in Theodor W. Adorno, *Aesthetics*, trans. Wieland Hoban, ed. Eberhard Ortland (Cambridge: Polity, 2018), 264–337, here 319; "Anmerkungen des Herausgebers," in Theodor W. Adorno, *Ästhetik (1958/59)*, ed. Eberhard Ortland (Frankfurt am Main: Suhrkamp, 2009), 391–508, here 474f.

13. Adorno, "Das Erbe und die neue Musik," 688f.

14. Ibid., 690.

15. Ibid., 689.

16. Ibid., 690.

17. Ibid., 691.

18. Ibid., 688.

19. Ibid.

20. Ibid., 686. It is worth noting the relation of Adorno's reflection on the new in this essay with those included in a brief intervention six years later: Theodor W. Adorno, "Verbindlichkeit des Neuen" (1960), in *Gesammelte Schriften*, vol. 5, ed. Rolf Tiedemann (Frankfurt am Main: Suhrkamp, 1997), 832–833. It would also prove instructive to relate Adorno's reflections on the new as they appear in "Das Erbe und die neue Musik" to his later remarks on the new in his unfinished and posthumously published *Aesthetic Theory*, particularly his thoughts in the second section, named "Situation," on the relation between the new and the philosophy of history, and the question of the new in relation to the category of duration. See *Ästhetische Theorie*, 31–74.

21. For a reflection on the new from an art-historical

perspective, see the 1959 study by the American art critic (and Adorno's contemporary) Harold Rosenberg, *The Tradition of the New* (Cambridge, MA: Da Capo Press, 1994). Also Reinhard Lettau, "Die Fetischisierung des Neuen," in Lettau, *Zerstreutes Hinausschaun. Vom Schreiben über Vorgänge in direkter Nähe oder in der Entfernung von Schreibtischen* (Frankfurt am Main: Fischer, 1982), 159–164. More recently, a general consideration of novelty and newness in a historical framework is provided by Michael North, *Novelty: A History of the New* (Chicago: University of Chicago Press, 2013). The vexing rhetorical relationship between the act of announcing and the positing of something supposedly new is illuminated—in particular with regard to Nietzsche, Baudelaire, Benjamin, and Marx—by Kristina Mendicino, *Announcements: On Novelty* (Albany: State University of New York Press, 2020).

22. This desire to erase the old and to posit oneself as the new and thus as a genuine origin may be the true impulse of modernity itself. As Paul de Man writes: "Modernity exists in the form of a desire to wipe out whatever came earlier, in the hope of reaching at last a point that could be called a true present, a point of origin that marks a new departure." Paul de Man, "Literary History and Literary Modernity," in de Man, *Blindness and Insight: Essays in the Rhetoric of*

Contemporary Criticism, 2nd ed. (Minneapolis: University of Minnesota Press, 1983), 142–165, here 148.

23. Adorno, "Das Erbe und die neue Musik," 686.

24. Ibid.

25. Ibid.

26. Ibid., 687.

27. Theodor W. Adorno, *Negative Dialektik*, vol. 6 of Adorno, *Gesammelte Schriften*, ed. Rolf Tiedemann (Frankfurt am Main: Suhrkamp, 1997), 44.

28. For genealogical and structural examinations of the relation between music and philosophy more generally, see, among others, Christoph Asmuth, Gunter Scholz, and Franz-Bernhard Stammkötter, eds., *Philosophischer Gedanke und musikalischer Klang. Zum Wechselverhältnis von Musik und Philosophie* (Frankfurt am Main: Campus, 1999); Stefan Lorenz Sorgner and Oliver Fürbeth, eds., *Musik in der deutschen Philosophie. Eine Einführung* (Stuttgart: Metzler, 2003); and Jost Hermand and Gerhard Richter, eds., *Sound Figures of Modernity: German Music and Philosophy* (Madison: University of Wisconsin Press, 2006).

29. Alan Badiou, *Five Lessons on Wagner*, trans. Susan Spitzer (London: Verso, 2010), 53.

30. Ibid.

31. Ibid., 53f.

32. Friedrich Schiller, "Die Götter Griechenlandes," in Schiller, *Sämtliche Gedichte und Balladen*, ed. Georg Kurscheidt (Frankfurt am Main: Insel, 2004), 124–127, here 127.

33. Sigmund Freud, *Der Mann Moses und die monotheistische Religion*, vol. 9 of Freud, *Studienausgabe*, ed. Alexander Mitscherlich, Angela Richards, and James Strachey (Frankfurt am Main: Fischer, 2000), 455–581, here 548.

34. Adorno, "Das Erbe und die neue Musik," 687.

35. Ibid.

36. Ibid.

37. Ibid.

38. Ibid.

39. Ibid., 689.

40. Ibid.

41. Ibid., 692.

42. Theodor W. Adorno, "Schöne Stellen," in *Gesammelte Schriften*, vol. 5, ed. Rolf Tiedemann (Frankfurt am Main: Suhrkamp, 1997), 695–718.

43. Adorno, "Das Erbe und die neue Musik," 693.

44. Ibid.

45. Ibid., 693f.

46. I borrow this sentence, along with the following five that constitute the rest of this paragraph, from my *Uncontainable Legacies: Theses on Intellectual, Cultural, and Political Inheritance* (Edinburgh: Edinburgh University Press, 2021).

47. Johann Wolfgang Goethe, *Faust*, vol. 3 of Goethe, *Werke. Hamburger Ausgabe in 14 Bänden*, ed. Erich Trunz (Munich: DTV, 1988), 29.

48. Even though Adorno in "Das Erbe und die neue Musik" suggests that the quotation is of biblical origin, it cannot be located as such in the Bible, as Eberhard Ortland rightly points out. Rather, the

"closest formulation would be in Matthew 19:25: 'For whoever wants to save his life will lose it, but whoever loses his life for me will find it.' A similar message can be found in Matthew 19:21: 'If you want to be perfect, go, sell your possessions and give to the poor, and you will have treasure in heaven. Then come, follow me.' See also Augustine, *Confessions*, ed. Michael F. Foley, trans. Frank J. Sheed (Indianapolis: Hackett, 2006), p. 158: 'Cast yourself upon Him and be not afraid; He will not draw away and let you fall. Cast yourself without fear, He will receive you and heal you.' Adorno's source for the motto was most likely Lukács's *The Theory of the Novel*, trans. Anna Bostock (Boston: MIT Press, 1971), p. 53." Ortland, "Editor's Notes," 311 / "Anmerkungen des Herausgebers," 463f.

49. Theodor W. Adorno, *Beethoven. Philosophie der Musik. Fragmente und Texte*, ed. Rolf Tiedemann (Frankfurt am Main: Suhrkamp, 1993), 15.

Chapter 5

1. Magdalena Bushart and Gregor Wedekind, "Die Farbe Grau. Zur Geschichte einer künstlerischen Praxis," in *Die Farbe Grau*, ed. Bushart and Wedekind (Berlin: De Gruyter, 2016), ix–xx, here xix.

2. David Scott Kastan and Stephen Farthing, *On Color* (New Haven: Yale University Press, 2018), 209.

3. Frances Guerin, *The Truth Is Always Grey: A History of Modernist Painting* (Minneapolis: University of Minnesota Press, 2018), 27. In a similar vein, the art historians gathered around grayness in the above-cited volume *Die Farbe Grau* collectively work to trouble conventional apperceptions of gray by casting unexpected perspectives onto its diverse art-historical trajectories, which extend from antiquity to the present day.

4. Johann Wolfgang Goethe, *Faust*, trans. Walter Kaufmann (New York: Anchor Books, 1989), 207; *Faust*, vol. 3 of Goethe, *Werke. Hamburger Ausgabe in 14 Bänden*, ed. Erich Trunz (Munich: DTV, 1988), 66.

5. Georg Wilhelm Friedrich Hegel, *Outlines of the Philosophy of Right*, trans. T. M. Knox, rev. and ed. Stephen Houlgate (Oxford: Oxford University Press, 2008), 16; *Grundlinien der Philosophie des Rechts*, vol. 7 of Hegel, *Werke*, ed. Eva Moldenhauer and Karl Markus Michel (Frankfurt am Main: Suhrkamp, 1986), 28.

6. It would be instructive to attempt a comparative analysis of Hegel's evocation of gray in the preface to the *Philosophy of Right* and his evocation of black in a similarly pronounced place, the preface to his early *Phenomenology of Spirit*, where he speaks of a "night [*Nacht*]" in which "as the saying goes, all cows are back [*alle Kühe schwarz sind*]." While Hegel's comment is typically understood as a polemical critique of Schelling's conception of the Absolute, the specific chromatic valences of Hegel's rhetoric here are not normally considered. Georg Wilhelm Friedrich Hegel, *Phenomenology of Spirit*, trans. A. V. Miller (Oxford: Oxford University Press, 1977), 9; *Phänomenologie des Geistes*, vol. 3 of Hegel, *Werke*, ed. Eva Moldenhauer and Karl Markus Michel (Frankfurt am Main: Suhrkamp, 1986), 22.

7. Theodor W. Adorno, "Marginalia to Theory and Praxis," in Adorno, *Critical Models: Interventions and Catchwords*, trans. Henry W. Pickford (New York: Columbia University Press, 2005), 259–278, here 260; "Marginalien zu Theorie und Praxis," in Adorno, *Gesammelte Schriften*, vol. 10:2, ed. Rolf Tiedemann (Frankfurt am Main: Suhrkamp, 1997), 759–782, here 759f.

8. Hannah Arendt, *The Life of the Mind*, vol. 1: *Thinking* (New York: Harcourt Brace Jovanovich, 1978), 176.

9. A constellation of images from Hito Steyerl's *Adorno's Grey*—both the film and the surrounding installation as a whole, which itself is also designed entirely in gray—can be found at https://kow-berlin.com /artists/hito-steyerl/adornos -grey, and a 2013 artist's talk by Steyerl about this work is located at https://www .youtube.com/watch?v=Phm NXnKfZko. For a historical contextualization of Steyerl's installation in relation to the political landscape of postwar Germany, see Samir Gandesha, "The Color of Adorno's Thought:

On Hito Steyerl's *Adorno's Grey*," in *Critical Theory and the Challenge of Praxis: Beyond Reification*, ed. Stefano Giacchetti Ludovisi (Aldershot: Ashgate, 2015), 189–204.

10. Theodor W. Adorno, *Aesthetic Theory*, trans. Robert Hullot-Kentor (Minneapolis: University of Minnesota Press, 1997), 135; *Ästhetische Theorie*, vol. 7 of *Gesammelte Schriften*, ed. Rolf Tiedemann (Frankfurt am Main: Suhrkamp, 1997), 203f.

11. Theodor W. Adorno, *Negative Dialectics*, trans. E. B. Ashton (London: Continuum, 2005), 377f.; *Negative Dialektik*, vol. 6 of *Gesammelte Schriften*, ed. Rolf Tiedemann (Frankfurt am Main: Suhrkamp, 1997), 371.

12. Theodor W. Adorno, "Ernst Bloch's *Spuren*," in Adorno, *Notes to Literature*, vol. 2, trans. Shierry Weber Nicholsen (New York: Columbia University Press, 1991), 200–215, here 213; "Blochs Spuren," in *Gesammelte Schriften*, vol. 11, ed. Rolf Tiedemann (Frankfurt am Main: Suhrkamp, 1997), 233–250, here 247f.

13. Although such an undertaking exceeds the boundaries of the present study, it would be illuminating to trace the complex relays between this aspect of Adorno's thinking of color and the early Benjamin's fascination with the emancipatory dimension of color as it is articulated in a number of shorter texts and fragments such as "A Child's View of Color,"

"Painting, or Signs and Marks," and "The Rainbow" (all from the period 1914–1915). There and elsewhere, Benjamin's interest in the liberatory dimension of color is worked out not only in relation to movements such as Der Blaue Reiter but also in relation to individual painters and their use of color, including Wassily Kandinsky, August Macke, and Paul Klee. For sustained analyses of the early Benjamin's investment in the potentialities of color, see Howard Caygill, *The Colour of Experience* (London: Routledge, 1998); Heinz Brüggemann, *Walter Benjamin. Über Spiel, Farbe und Phantasie* (Würzburg: Königshausen und Neumann, 2007); and, most recently, the incisive reflections by Martin Jay, "Chromophilia: Der Blaue Reiter, Walter Benjamin, and the Emancipation of Color," *Positions: Asia Critique* 26, no. 1 (2018): 13–33.

14. Theodor W. Adorno, *Minima Moralia: Reflections from Damaged Life*, trans E. F. N. Jephcott (London: Verso, 1999), 227; *Minima Moralia. Reflexionen aus dem beschädigten Leben*, vol. 4 of *Gesammelte Schriften*, ed. Rolf Tiedemann (Frankfurt am Main: Suhrkamp, 1997), 259f.

15. Ibid., 227f. / 260.

16. Theodor W. Adorno, "Free Time," in *Critical Models*, 167–175, here 171; "Freizeit," in *Gesammelte Schriften*, vol. 10.2, ed. Rolf Tiedemann (Frankfurt am Main: Suhrkamp, 1997), 645–655, here 650.

17. Theodor W. Adorno, "Der mißbrauchte Barock," in *Ohne Leitbild: Parva Aesthetica*, vol. 10.1 of Adorno, *Gesammelte Schriften*, ed. Rolf Tiedemann (Frankfurt am Main: Suhrkamp, 1997), 401–422, here 403.

18. Theodor W. Adorno, "Frankfurter Opern- und Konzertkritiken," in *Musikalische Schriften VI*, vol. 19 of Adorno, *Gesammelte Schriften*, ed. Rolf Tiedemann (Frankfurt am Main: Suhrkamp, 1997), 124.

Chapter 6

1. I borrow my remarks on Benjamin's sentence here from my earlier "Afterness and the Image (11): Image Withdrawal," in Richter, *Afterness: Figures of Following in Modern Thought and Aesthetics* (New York: Columbia University Press, 2011), where they appear in an earlier form and in the context of a comparative reading of Heidegger, Blanchot, and Deleuze on the notion of an image that finds itself in withdrawal.

2. Walter Benjamin, *Charles Baudelaire. Ein Lyriker im Zeitalter des Hochkapitalismus*, in Benjamin, *Gesammelte Schriften*, vol. 1, ed. Rolf Tiedemann and Hermann Schweppenhäuser (Frankfurt am Main: Suhrkamp, 1991), 511–604, here 590.

3. Walter Benjamin, "Pariser Passagen I," in *Das Passagen-Werk*, vol. 5 of *Gesammelte Schriften*, ed. Rolf Tiedemann and Hermann Schweppenhäuser (Frankfurt am Main: Suhrkamp, 1991), 993–1038, here 1001.

4. Walter Benjamin, *Ursprung des deutschen Trauerspiels*, in *Gesammelte Schriften*, vol. 1, 203–430, here 345.

5. Theodor W. Adorno, "Nachwort," in Walter Benjamin, *Berliner Kindheit um neunzehnhundert* (Frankfurt am Main: Suhrkamp, 1950), 176–180, here 177.

6. Walter Benjamin, "Das Kunstwerk im Zeitalter seiner technischen Reproduzierbarkeit (Dritte Fassung)," in *Gesammelte Schriften*, vol. 1, 471–508, here 473.

7. Wolfgang Ullrich, "Bruchwerk," in *Verwindungen. Arbeit an Heidegger*, ed. Wolfgang Ullrich (Frankfurt am Main: Fischer, 2003), 111–121, here 111. Albert Speer's reflections on the ruin are recorded in his memoirs, *Erinnerungen* (Berlin: Ullstein, 1969), 69. For an analysis that places Speer's obsession with the ruin in the context of the philosophies of art and theories of history developed by Hegel, Adorno, and Arthur Danto, see Lydia Goehr, "The Pastness of the Work: Albert Speer and the Monumentalism of Intentional Ruins," in Goehr, *Elective Affinities: Musical Essays on the History of Aesthetic Theory* (New York: Columbia University Press, 2008), 136–170.

8. Walter Benjamin, "Über den Begriff der Geschichte," in *Gesammelte Schriften*, vol. 1, 691–704, here 695.

9. Walter Benjamin, *Einbahnstraße*, vol. 4 of *Gesammelte Schriften*, ed. Rolf Tiedemann and Hermann Schweppenhäuser (Frankfurt am Main: Suhrkamp, 1991), 83–148, here 94.

10. Lyle Rexer, "Interview: Andrew Moore," *Photograph* (November-December 2016), n.p. http://photographmag.com/issues/novdec-2016/interview/.

11. For a representative sample of his remarkable photographs as well as sustained historical commentary on his biography and work, see *Charles Marville: Photographer of Paris*, ed. Sarah Kennel, with Anne de Mondenard, Peter Barberie, Françoise Reynaud, and Joke de Wolf (Washington: National Gallery of Art, 2014).

12. Rexer, "Interview: Andrew Moore," n.p.

13. Ibid.

14. Andrew Moore, "The Phoenix and the Pheasant," in Moore, *Detroit Disassembled* (Bologna: Damiani, 2014), 118–119, here 119.

15. Rexer, "Interview: Andrew Moore," n.p.

16. Andy Grundberg, "The Photograph as Territory," in Andrew Moore, *Inside Havana* (San Francisco: Chronicle Books, 2002), n.p.

17. Johann Wolfgang Goethe, *Faust*, vol. 3 of Goethe, *Werke. Hamburger Ausgabe in 14 Bänden*, ed. Erich Trunz (Munich: DTV, 1988), 47.

18. Roland Barthes, *Camera Lucida: Reflections on Photography*, trans. Richard Howard (New York: Hill and Wang, 1993), 96.

19. Ibid., 97.

20. Jacques Derrida and Marie-Françoise Plissart, *Right of Inspection*, trans. David Wills (New York: Monacelli, 1998), n.p.

21. Maurice Blanchot, "The Two Versions of the Imaginary," in Blanchot, *The Space of Literature*, trans. Ann Smock (Lincoln: University of Nebraska Press, 1982), 254–263, here 256f.

22. Eduardo Cadava, "*Lapsus imaginis*: The Image in Ruins," *October* 96 (Spring 2001): 35–60, here 35.

23. Moore, "The Phoenix and the Pheasant," 119.

24. Jean-Luc Nancy, "Nous Autres," in Nancy, *The Ground of the Image* (New York: Fordham University Press, 2005), 100–107, here 106.

25. Ibid., 107.

26. Jacques Derrida, *Athens, Still Remains: The Photographs of Jean-François Bonhomme*, trans. Pascale-Anne Brault and Michael Naas (New York: Fordham University Press, 2010), 2f.

27. Moore, "The Phoenix and the Pheasant," 119.

28. Philip Levin, "Nobody's Detroit," in Moore, *Detroit Disassembled*, 111–117, here 117.

29. "Tsuyoshi Ito Interviews Andrew Moore," *Lens/scratch: Fine Art Photography Daily*, February 24, 2014, https://lenscratch.com/2014/02/andrew-moore-interview/.

30. Eduardo Luis Rodriguez, "Poet in Havana," trans. Alison Hughes, in Moore, *Inside Havana*, n.p.

31. Andrew Moore, *Russia: Beyond Utopia* (San Francisco: Chronicle Books, 2005), plate 40.

32. Andrew Moore, *Dirt Meridian* (Bologna: Damiani, 2015), 134.

33. Ibid.

34. It is as though this conjoining of the intimate and the infinite also contributed, for instance in the photographs gathered in *Dirt Meridian*, to their hospitality toward what Toby Jurovics terms "Moore's carefully woven dialogue of people and place." Seen from this perspective, Moore's "photographs are neither an elegy nor a dirge; they are the prosaic, not the romantic. They sit squarely at the intersection of two lines—the invisible vertical of the 100th meridian set against the insistent level of the horizon," and together they conspire to yield a "subtle topography running uninterrupted to the edge of the sky, the endless grind of the wind abrading the paint from houses and barns; and blizzard winds scouring barren fields. It is a landscape that requires a direct acceptance of the facts and of its inherent limits. But it does so with a generosity toward those with the patience and willingness to find elegance in its simply geometry and quiet perseverance." Toby Jurovics, "Riding the Line," in Moore, *Dirt Meridian*, 114–117, here 117.

35. Andrew Moore, *Blue Alabama* (Bologna: Damiani, 2019), n.p.

Chapter 7

1. Jacques Derrida, "Freud and the Scene of Writing," in Derrida, *Writing and Difference*, trans. Alan Bass (Chicago: University of Chicago Press, 1978), 196–231, here 203.

2. Ibid.

3. In this context, one also may profitably begin to reengage with Paul de Man's now-classic argument developed in his reading of Wordsworth's autobiographical text *Essays upon Epitaphs*: that from a certain rhetorical perspective "all texts are autobiographies," even as "by the same token, none of them is or can be." If de Man reorients the reading of autobiographical discourse to align with the rhetorical figure of prosopopeia, the apostrophe to an absent or dead speaking voice, it is because the "interest of autobiography ... is not that it reveals reliable self-knowledge—it does not—but that it demonstrates in a striking way the impossibility of closure and of totalization (that is the impossibility of coming into being) of all textual systems made up of tropological substitutions." Paul de Man, "Autobiography as De-Facement," in de Man, *The Rhetoric of Romanticism* (New York: Columbia University Press, 1984), 67–81, here 70f.

4. Friedrich Nietzsche, *Ecce Homo: How One Becomes What One Is*, trans. R. J. Hollingdale (London: Penguin, 2004), 8.

5. Ibid., 4.

6. Ibid., 7.

7. Jacques Derrida, "Otobiographies: The Teaching of Nietzsche and the Politics of the Proper Name," trans. Avital Ronell, in *The Ear of the Other: Otobiography, Transference, Translation*, ed. Christie McDonald (Lincoln: University of Nebraska Press, 1988), 1–38, here 5f.

8. With regard to the question of a borderline in relation to living on, compare further Jacques Derrida, "Living On—Borderlines," in Harold Bloom, Paul de Man, Jacques Derrida, Geoffrey Hartman, and J. Hillis Miller, *Deconstruction and Criticism* (New York: Continuum, 1979), 75–176.

9. William Faulkner, *Requiem for a Nun* (New York: Vintage, 2012), 73.

10. Translated as Sigmund Freud, *An Autobiographical Study*, trans. James Strachey (New York: Norton, 1989). It would be fruitful, bearing in mind the concerns of the present context, to reread Derrida's reflections—in "To Speculate—On 'Freud,'" the second part of *The Post Card*—on Freud's insistence in the "Selbstdarstellung" that he suffers from a "constitutional incapacity" to think in philosophical ways. Here, too, the relationship between life and work, this time with respect to Freud's confessional discourse, is open to reexamination: "If we wish, in another style, with other questions, to interlace the networks of a so-called 'internal' reading of the writings on life death with those of the autobiography, the autography, the autothanatography, and those of the 'analytic movement,' to the extent that they are all inseparable, then we must begin, at least, by pointing out in the hastily named 'internal' reading the places that are *structurally* open to

intersecting with the other networks. … This concerns *bios* in its autobiographical import." Jacques Derrida, *The Post Card: From Socrates to Freud and Beyond*, trans. Alan Bass (Chicago: University of Chicago Press, 1987), 273.

11. Franz Kafka, *Letter to the Father / Brief an den Vater* (bilingual edition), trans. Ernst Kaiser and Eithne Wilkins (New York: Schocken, 2015).

12. Walter Benjamin, *Berlin Childhood around 1900*, trans. Howard Eiland (Cambridge, MA: Harvard University Press, 2006).

13. I borrow my remarks in this section, in revised form, from a brief earlier reflection as part of my "A Can of Worms," in *Something Other Than Lifedeath—Catalyst: S. D. Chrostowska*, ed. David Cecchetto (Victoria, BC: Noxious Sector Press, 2018), 19–31.

14. Jacques Derrida, *The Beast and the Sovereign*, vol. 2, trans. Geoffrey Bennington (Chicago: University of Chicago Press, 2011), 130.

15. Ibid., 131.

16. Ibid.

17. Botho Strauß, "Der letzte Deutsche. Uns wird die Souveränität geraubt, dagegen zu sein," *Der Spiegel* 41 (2015): 122–124, here 123.

18. Botho Strauß, *Herkunft* (Munich: DTV, 2016), 54f.

19. Strauß, *Herkunft*, 55.

20. Derrida, *The Beast and the Sovereign*, vol. 2, 126f.

21. Didier Eribon, *Returning to Reims*, trans. Michael Lucey (South Pasadena, CA: Semiotext(e), 2013), 17.

22. Ibid., 18.

23. Ibid., 28–29.

24. Ibid., 26–27.

25. Didier Eribon, *Retour à Reims* (Paris: Flammarion, 2010), 22.

26. Eribon, *Returning to Reims*, 29, 30.

27. Ibid., 20–21.

28. Jacques Derrida, *Specters of Marx: The State of the Debt, the Work of Mourning, and the New International*, trans. Peggy Kamuf (New York: Routledge, 1994).

29. Eribon, *Returning to Reims*, 21.

30. See Roland Barthes, *Mourning Diary: October 26, 1977–September 15, 1979*, trans. Richard Howard (New York: Hill and Wang, 2010).

31. Eribon, *Returning to Reims*, 21–22.

32. Ibid., 23.

33. Cf. Alexander and Margarete Mitscherlich, *Die Unfähigkeit zu trauern* (Munich: Piper, 1967).

34. Jacques Derrida, *Monolingualism of the Other; or, The Prothesis of Origin*, trans. Patrick Mensah (Stanford: Stanford University Press, 1998), 33.

35. Eribon, *Returning to Reims*, 117.

36. Nietzsche, *Ecce Homo*, 38f.

37. Eribon, *Returning to Reims*, 224.

38. Derrida, *Monolingualism of the Other*, 70.

39. Theodor W. Adorno, *Negative Dialectics*, trans. E. B. Ashton (London: Verso, 1973), 148.

40. Friedrich Nietzsche, *Human, All Too Human: A Book for Free Spirits*, trans. R. J. Hollingdale (Cambridge:

Cambridge University Press, 1996), 387.

41. Ibid., 28f.

Chapter 8

1. David Farrell Krell, *The Purest of Bastards: Works of Mourning, Art, and Affirmation in the Thought of Jacques Derrida* (University Park: Pennsylvania State University Press, 2000), 8 and 21.

2. Walter Benjamin, "The Role of Language in Trauerspiel and Tragedy," in Benjamin, *Origin of the German Trauerspiel*, trans. Howard Eiland (Cambridge, MA: Harvard University Press, 2019), 267–270, here 267f.

3. It should not be forgotten that such a space of mournful survival is always also suffused with a kind of politics of mourning. From a different perspective, Judith Butler has investigated the politics of mourning as it relates to the precariousness inscribed in the distinction between grievable and nongrievable lives. See the essays collected in Judith Butler, *Precarious Life: The Powers of Mourning and Violence* (London: Verso, 2004), and, more recently, those collected in *Frames of War: When Is Life Grievable?* (London: Verso, 2010).

4. Rainer Maria Rilke, *The Dark Interval: Letters on Loss, Grief, and Transformation*, trans. Ulrich Baer (New York: Modern Library, 2018), 3. Rilke wrote this letter to Mimi Romanelli in French, speaking of "la mort dans la vie." *Briefe*, ed. Rilke-Archiv, with Ruth Sieber-Rilke and

Karl Altheim, vol.1 (Frankfurt am Main: Insel, 1987), 215.

5. Rilke, *Dark Interval*, 4 / *Briefe*, 215.

6. Plato, "Phaedo," trans. Hugh Tredennick, in *The Collected Dialogues of Plato*, ed. Edith Hamilton and Huntington Cairns (Princeton: Princeton University Press, 1989), 64a.

7. For an excellent recent selection of Seneca's reflections on preparing for death and learning how to die, see Seneca, *How to Die: An Ancient Guide to the End of Life*, ed. and trans. James S. Romm (Princeton: Princeton University Press, 2018).

8. Michel de Montaigne, "That to Philosophize Is to Learn to Die," in *The Complete Essays of Montaigne*, trans. Donald M. Frame (Stanford: Stanford University Press, 1958), 56–68.

9. Jacques Derrida, *Learning to Live Finally: The Last Interview*, trans. Pascale-Anne Brault and Michael Naas (Hoboken: Melville House, 2007), 26.

10. Ibid., 52.

11. Jacques Derrida, *The Beast and the Sovereign*, vol. 2, trans. Geoffrey Bennington (Chicago: University of Chicago Press, 2011), 131.

12. Jacques Derrida, *La vie la mort. Séminaire (1975–1976)*, ed. Pascale-Anne Brault and Peggy Kamuf (Paris: Seuil, 2019), *Life Death*, trans. Pascale-Anne Brault and Michael Naas, ed. Pascale-Anne Brault and Peggy Kamuf (Chicago: University of Chicago Press, 2020).

13. Derrida, *Life Death*, 1 / *La vie la mort*, 19.

14. Ibid., 6 / 25.

15. Ibid., 27 / 49.

16. Ibid., 105–106 / 144.

17. Ibid., 46 / 71.

18. Ibid., 53 / 80.

19. Ibid.

20. Ibid., 65 / 94.

21. Ibid., 155 / 199–200.

22. If one wishes to be more precise, there are several textual fragments containing "Hunter Gracchus" material that were retroactively connected by the editorial hand of Max Brod. For a precise description of the complicated philological status of the textual corpus pertaining to the "Hunter Gracchus" material, see Bernard Dieterle, "Kleine nachgelassene Schriften und Fragmente 2," in *Kafka-Handbuch. Leben—Werk—Wirkung*, ed. Manfred Engel and Bernd Auerochs (Stuttgart: Metzler, 2010), 260–280, here 273–276.

23. Franz Kafka, "The Hunter Gracchus," in *Kafka's Selected Stories*, trans. and ed. Stanley Corngold (New York: Norton, 2007), 109–113, here 111; "Der Jäger Gracchus [Oktavheft B (Januar/Februar 1917)]," in Kafka, *Nachgelassene Schriften und Fragmente I*, ed. Malcom Pasley and Hans-Gerd Koch, *Kritische Ausgabe* (Frankfurt am Main: Fischer, 1993), 305–313, here 309f.

24. As Stanley Corngold beautifully puts it, "the Hunter Gracchus dies but cannot find an archive to lay his head down in." Stanley Corngold, *Lambent Traces: Franz Kafka* (Princeton: Princeton University Press, 2004), 48.

25. Jacques Derrida, "Adieu," in Derrida, *The Work of Mourning*, trans. and ed. Pascale-Anne Brault and Michael Naas (Chicago: University of Chicago Press, 2001), 200–209, here 203.

26. Sigmund Freud, "Mourning and Melancholia," in *On the History of the Psycho-Analytic Movement, Papers on Metapsychology and Other Works*, ed. and trans. James Strachey, vol. 14 of *The Standard Edition of the Complete Psychological Works of Sigmund Freud* (London: Hogarth, 1957), 243–258.

27. Roland Barthes, *Mourning Diary*, trans. Richard Howard (New York: Hill and Wang, 2010), 68.

28. Jacques Derrida, "All-Out Friendship: Lyotard and Us," in Derrida, *The Work of Mourning*, 216–241, here 218. Derrida's remark should also be heard in light of his earlier reflections, in "Mnemosyne," on the relationship between mourning and forgetting, where he suggests that we "weep *precisely* over what happens to us when everything is entrusted to the sole memory that is 'in me' or 'in us.' But we must also recall, in another turn of memory, that the 'within me' and the 'within us' *do not arise or appear before* this terrible experience." In other words, the "'within me' and the 'within us' acquire their sense and their bearing only by carrying within themselves the death and the memory of the other; of an other who is greater than them, greater than what

they or we can bear, carry, or comprehend, since we then lament being no more than 'memory,' 'in memory.' Which is another way of remaining inconsolable before the finitude of memory. We know, we knew, *we remember*—before the death of the loved one—that being-in-me or being-in-us is constituted out of the possibility of mourning. We are only ourselves from the perspective of this knowledge that is older than ourselves; and this is why I say that we begin by *recalling* this to ourselves; we come to ourselves through this memory of *possible* mourning." Jacques Derrida, "Mnemosyne," trans. Cecile Lindsay, in *Memoires for Paul de Man*, trans. Cecile Lindsay, Jonathan Culler, Eduardo Cadava, and Peggy Kamuf, rev. ed. (New York: Columbia University Press, 1989), 1–43, here 33f.

29. Pascale-Anne Brault and Michael Naas, "Editors' Introduction—To Reckon with the Dead: Jacques Derrida's Politics of Mourning," in Derrida, *The Work of Mourning*, 1–30, here 17.

30. Maurice Blanchot, "Kafka and the Work's Demand," in Blanchot, *The Space of Literature*, trans. Ann Smock (Lincoln: University of Nebraska Press, 1982), 57–83, here 75.

31. Sigmund Freud, "Thoughts for the Times on War and Death," in *On the History of the Psycho-Analytic Movement, Papers on Metapsychology and Other Works*, 275–300, here 289.

32. Epicurus, "Letter to Menoeceus," in Epicurus, *Letters, Principal Doctrines, and Vatican Sayings*, trans. Russell M. Geer (New York: Bobbs-Merrill, 1964), 125.

33. Walter Benjamin, *One-Way Street*, trans. Edmund Jephcott, ed. Michael W. Jennings (Cambridge, MA: Harvard University Press, 2016), 24.

34. Among others, Reiner Stach draws attention to this connection in his *Kafka. Die Jahre der Entscheidungen* (Frankfurt am Main; Fischer, 2004), 429.

Chapter 9

1. Karl Marx and Friedrich Engels, *Manifest der kommunistischen Partei*, *Werke*, vol. 4, ed. Institut für Marxismus-Leninismus beim ZK der SED (Berlin: Dietz, 1977), 457–493, here 493.

2. *Die Bibel, nach der Übersetzung Martin Luthers* (Stuttgart: Deutsche Bibelstiftung, 1978), 22. The allusion by *The Communist Manifesto* to Matthew 16:26 is suggested in passing by H. Braun, who does not, however, explicate it further: "Welt. II. Von Cusanus bis Nietzsche," *Historisches Wörterbuch der Philosophie*, vol. 12, ed. Joachim Ritter, Karlfried Gründer, and Gottfried Gabriel (Basel: Schwabe, 2004), 412–424, here 421.

3. *The Bible: Authorized King James Version and Apocrypha*, ed. Robert Carroll and Stephen Prickett (Oxford: Oxford University Press, 2008), 24.

4. This suggestion was made in 1968 by Lucien Goldmann, who writes: "Les onze *Thèses sur Feuerbach*, première formulation brillante, concise, et, à ce niveau de concision, définitive du matérialisme dialectique, n'ont rien perdu de leur actualité." And he proceeds to refer to the "Theses" as "tournants," or "turning points" in Western thought, on par with certain famous historical predecessors: "Aussi ce texte constitue-t-il un des principaux tournants de la pensée occidentale et nous nous croyons fondé à affirmer que son importance historique est du même ordre que celle du *Discours de la méthode*, de la *Critique de la raison pure* ou de la *Phénoménologie de l'esprit*." Lucien Goldmann, "L'idéologie allemande et les thèses sur Feuerbach," *L'Homme et la Société* 7 (1968): 37–55, here 42. Goldmann's essay and the historical comparison it suggests is referred to in Wolfgang Fritz Haug, "Feuerbach-Thesen," in *Historisches-Kritisches Wörterbuch des Marxismus*, vol. 4, ed. Wolfgang Fritz Haug (Hamburg: Argument, 1999), 402–420, here 403.

5. As Georges Labica economically expresses it in his study of the "Theses": "Depuis un siècle [and, we might add, even a few decades longer at this point, for Labica's book appeared in 1987] la Th. 11 vit une vie indépendante, aphoristique, bien au-delà du marxisme, de la maxime populaire au sujet de baccalauréat et au titre de revue (Thesis

Eleven, Australie). Comme tout mot d'ordre, elle rature ses présupposés." Georges Labica, *Karl Marx: Les thèses sur Feuerbach* (Paris: Presses Universitaires de France, 1987), 114. It is precisely such presuppositions that call for perpetual reconstruction. For a circumspect reconstruction of the reception history of the "Theses," see Haug, "Feuerbach-Thesen." The question, not usually of concern in Marxian scholarship, as to whether Marx's critique of Feuerbach does justice to Feuerbach's thought is taken up by Falko Schmieder, "Für eine neue Lektüre der Feuerbachkritik der *Thesen über Feuerbach* und der *Deutschen Ideologie*," in *Karl Marx und die Naturwissenschaften im 19. Jahrhundert*, ed. Rolf Hecker, Richard Sperl, and Carl-Erich Vollgraf, Beiträge zur Marx-Engels-Forschung. Neue Folge (Hamburg: Argument, 2006), 178–206.

6. Karl Marx and Friedrich Engels, "Thesen über Feuerbach," in Marx and Engels, *Werke*, vol. 3, ed. Institut für Marxismus-Leninismus beim ZK der SED (Berlin: Dietz, 1978), 533–535, here 535.

7. Étienne Balibar, "Changing the World: From *Praxis* to *Production*," in Balibar, *The Philosophy of Marx*, trans. Chris Turner (London: Verso, 2007), 13–41, here 13. According to Balibar's account of the relation between the "Theses" and the later *German Ideology*, it "is no exaggeration to say that,

after the 'ontology of praxis' heralded in the *Theses on Feuerbach*, *The German Ideology* sets out an 'ontology of production'" (ibid., 33).

8. Karl Marx and Friedrich Engels, "Thesen über Feuerbach," in Marx and Engels, *Gesamtausgabe*, vol. 4.3 (Berlin: Akademie Verlag, 1998), 19–21, here 21.

9. Let us leave aside here one other change made by Engels: He italicizes the words "interpretiert" and "verändern," while Marx underlines them in his notebook. It could be argued that this change is merely a practical or pragmatic one, as it represents Engels's way of rendering for the typographic purposes of print what his friend indicated in his handwritten sentence. Though, even here, we may find reason to reflect on the conceptual difference between italicizing and underlining.

10. Volker Gerhardt, "Eine politische These, kein philosophischer Satz," in *Eine angeschlagene These. Die 11. Feuerbach-These im Foyer der Humboldt-Universität zu Berlin*, ed. Volker Gerhardt (Berlin: Akademie Verlag, 1996), 13–32. As the following reflections suggest, however, there are reasons to be a little more guarded in this matter.

11. Ernst Bloch, "Weltveränderung oder die elf Thesen von Marx über Feuerbach," in Bloch, *Das Prinzip Hoffnung*, *Gesamtausgabe*, vol. 5 (Frankfurt am Main. Suhrkamp, 1985), 288–334, here 289.

12. Ibid.

13. Ibid., 323.

14. Martin Heidegger, "What Calls for Thinking?," trans. Fred D. Wieck and J. Glenn Gray, in Heidegger, *Basic Writings*, ed. David Farrell Krell, rev. and expanded ed. (San Francisco: Harper, 1993), 365–391, here 370; *Was heißt Denken?*, 5th ed. (Tübingen: Niemeyer, 1997), 2.

15. Richard Wisser and Martin Heidegger, "Martin Heidegger in Conversation with Richard Wisser," trans. Lisa Harries, in *Martin Heidegger and National Socialism: Questions and Answers*, ed. Günter Neske and Emil Kettering (New York: Paragon, 1990), 81–87, here 82; *Martin Heidegger im Gespräch*, ed. Richard Wisser (Freiburg: Alber, 1970), 68–69.

16. This point is made by Herbert Schnädelbach, "Wittgenstein über die Philosophie: 'Sie läßt alles, wie es ist,'" in Gerhardt, *Eine angeschlagene These*, 109–126, here 115.

17. Such is the interpretive perspective on the "Theses" proposed by Daniel Brudney, "The *Theses on Feuerbach*," in Brudney, *Marx's Attempt to Leave Philosophy* (Cambridge, MA: Harvard University Press, 1998), 227–263.

18. Martin Heidegger, "Letter on Humanism," trans. Frank A. Capuzzi and J. Glenn Gray, in *Basic Writings*, 213–265, here 243; "Brief über den Humanismus," in *Wegmarken*, vol. 9 of Heidegger, *Gesamtausgabe*, ed. Friedrich-Wilhelm von Hermann (Frankfurt am

311

Main: Klostermann, 1976), 313–364, here 340.

19. There is, of course, a longstanding debate within Marxian theory as to whether alienation and alienated labor in fact can be legitimately considered unique to the form of political economy that has come to be designated "capitalist," or whether forms of alienation and alienated labor are not also operative in differently organized social systems such as communism itself. Among recent discussions of this question, see, for instance, Jonathan Wolf, *Why Read Marx Today?* (Oxford: Oxford University Press, 2003), 104f.

20. Cf. the recent comparative analysis of Hegel's and Marx's notions of *Entfremdung* in Peter Trawny, *Der frühe Marx und die Revolution* (Frankfurt am Main: Klostermann, 2018), 79–98.

21. Among the most promising thinkers who were at one point in their intellectual trajectory poised to develop the imbrication of ontological with Marxian concerns was the young Herbert Marcuse—before he rejected his erstwhile teacher Heidegger, under whose supervision he had completed his doctoral dissertation on Hegel's theory of historicity, and abandoned the project of a "Heideggerian Marxism." For examples of Marcuse's early work at the nexus of these two paradigms of thinking, as well as his own account of what he calls his "disillusionment" with

Heidegger, see the essays and documents collected in Herbert Marcuse, *Heideggerian Marxism* (Lincoln: University of Nebraska Press, 2005).

22. Jacques Derrida, *Theory and Practice*, trans. David Wills, ed. Geoffrey Bennington and Peggy Kamuf (Chicago: University of Chicago Press, 2019), 8.

23. Ibid., footnote 9.

24. Ibid., 8–9.

25. Ibid., 9.

26. Ibid.

27. Ibid.

28. Ibid., 11–12.

29. Ibid., 12.

30. Ibid., 12–13.

31. Ibid., 13–14.

32. Ibid., 13.

33. Ibid., 15.

34. Ibid.

35. Ibid.

36. In the present context, we will leave aside Derrida's engagements with Aristotle, Kant, and Heidegger that also play an important role in the seminar and that are brought to bear on Derrida's analysis of Althusser's engagement with the oppositional pair of theory and practice.

37. Jacques Derrida, *Specters of Marx: The State of the Debt, the Work of Mourning, and the New International*, trans. Peggy Kamuf (London: Routledge, 1994), 32.

38. Ibid.

39. Jean-François Lyotard, "Foreword: After the Words," in Joseph Kosuth, *Art after Philosophy and After: Collected Writings, 1966–1990*, ed. Gabriele Guercio (Cambridge, MA: MIT Press, 1991), xv–xviii, here xv.

40. Theodor W. Adorno, *Against Epistemology: A Metacritique—Studies in Husserl and the Phenomenological Antinomies*, trans. Willis Domingo (Cambridge: Polity, 2013), 39–40; *Zur Metaphysik der Erkenntnistheorie. Studien über Husserl und die phänomenologischen Antinomien*, vol. 5 of *Gesammelte Schriften*, ed. Rolf Tiedemann (Frankfurt am Main: Suhrkamp, 1997), 47.

41. One should also hear Adorno's passage in the context of a letter he wrote on February 11, 1958—not long after completing the revisions to the Husserl book—to the philosopher and sociologist Helmut Plessner. There he states: "But it is evidently my fate to have to coax my entire production from my life by a gradual process, and that may well be far from the worst way to work. I could imagine that this is connected with another particularity that I have observed in what I cobble together—that in truth every text of mine is a kind of leave-taking [*daß eigentlich jeder Text von mir eine Art von Abschiednehmen ist*]." Adorno's letter, archived at the Institute for Social Research in Frankfurt and thus far unpublished, is cited in Alex Demirović, *Der nonkonformistische Intellektuelle. Die Entwicklung der Kritischen Theorie zur Frankfurter Schule* (Frankfurt am Main: Suhrkamp, 1999), 673, as well as in Stefan Müller-Dohm, *Adorno. Eine Biographie* (Frankfurt am

Main: Suhrkamp, 2003), 730, in English as *Adorno: A Biography*, trans. Rodney Livingstone (Cambridge: Polity, 2005), 481. For a meditation on this passage and the figure of leave-taking in Adorno, cf. Gerhard Richter, "Conclusion: A Kind of Leave-Taking," in Richter, *Thinking with Adorno: The Uncoercive Gaze* (New York: Fordham University Press, 2019), 161–165.

42. Paul de Man, "The Resistance to Theory," in de Man, *The Resistance to Theory* (Minneapolis: University of Minnesota Press, 1986), 3–20, here 11.

Coda

1. Werner Hamacher, "Reparationen (1984)," in *Mediengeschichte nach Friedrich Kittler*, ed. Friedrich Balke, Bernhard Siegert, and Joseph Vogl (Munich: Fink, 2013), 11–25, here 11.

2. Ibid., 25.

3. Eva Geulen, "The End of Art," in *German Aesthetics: Fundamental Concepts from Baumgarten to Adorno*, ed. J. D. Mininger and Jason Michael Peck (London: Bloomsbury Academic, 2016), 91–99, here 93.

4. Martin Heidegger, "The Origin of the Work of Art," trans. Alfred Hofstadter, in Heidegger, *Basic Writings*, ed. David Farrell Krell, rev. and expanded ed. (San Francisco: Harper, 1993), 139–212, here 204; "Der Ursprung des Kunstwerkes," in *Holzwege*, ed. Friedrich-Wilhelm von Hermann, in Heidegger, *Gesamtausgabe*, vol. 5 (Frankfurt am Main: Klostermann, 2003), 1–74, here 65.

5. Ibid., 204f. / 65f. Hegel's three sentences can be found in his *Vorlesungen über die Ästhetik*, vol. 13 of Hegel, *Werke*, ed. Eva Moldenhauer and Karl Markus Michel (Frankfurt am Main: Suhrkamp, 1986), 141, 142, and 25.

6. Heidegger, "Origin," 205 / "Ursprung," 66.

7. Ibid.

8. Ibid.

9. Ibid., 204 / 65.

Frontispiece and page 7:
Hieronymus Bosch, *The Creation of the World*. Museo Nacional del
    Prado, Madrid.

Pages 40–41:
Temple of Aphaia, Greek island of Aegina; reconstruction of the
    western pediment. Falkensteinfoto / Alamy Stock Photo.

Following page 74:
Horses Panel, Chauvet Cave. Ministère de la Culture et de la
    Communication, France.
Lion Panel, Chauvet Cave. Ministère de la Culture et de la
    Communication, France.
Running Bison, Chauvet Cave. © Perazio—Lionel Guichard, Grotte
    Chauvet 2—Ardèche.
Positive Hand, Chauvet Cave. © Patrick Aventurier, Grotte Chauvet
    2—Ardèche.
Negative Hand, Chauvet Cave. © Patrick Aventurier, Grotte Chauvet
    2—Ardèche.
Venus Pendant, Chauvet Cave. © Patrick Aventurier, Grotte Chauvet
    2—Ardèche.

Following page 170:
Copyright Andrew Moore. Images reproduced by permission of
    the artist:
Andrew Moore, *National Time Clock, Former Cass Technical High School
    Building*, from *Detroit Disassembled* (Bologna: Damiani, 2014).
Andrew Moore, *Moldering Books, Detroit Public Schools Book Depository*,
    from *Detroit Disassembled*.
Andrew Moore, *Courtyard, Former Cass Technical High School Building*,
    from *Detroit Disassembled*.
Andrew Moore, *House on Walden Street, East Side*, from *Detroit Disassembled*.
Andrew Moore, *Campoamor, Vista Oeste, 1999*, from *La Habana Vieja.
    Inside Havana* (San Francisco: Chronicle Books, 2002).
Andrew Moore, *Yard, Carwash Café, East Jefferson Avenue*, from
    Detroit Disassembled.
Andrew Moore, *Cat, Former Mark Twain Branch of the Detroit Public
    Library, East Side*, from *Detroit Disassembled*.

Page 328:
Franz Kafka, *Der Denker (The Thinker)*. The National Library of Israel.
    Max Brod Archive.

319

321

326

The MIT Press would like to thank the anonymous peer reviewers who provided comments on drafts of this book. The generous work of academic experts is essential for establishing the authority and quality of our publications. We acknowledge with gratitude the contributions of these otherwise uncredited readers.

This book was set in Haultin by the MIT Press. Printed and bound in Canada.

Library of Congress Cataloging-in-Publication Data is available.

ISBN: 978-0-262-54414-6

10 9 8 7 6 5 4 3 2 1

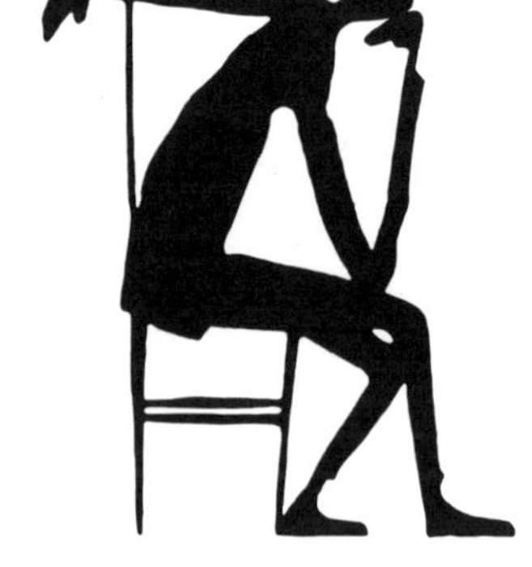